Great Documents in Black American History

GREAT DOCUMENTS IN BLACK AMERICAN HISTORY

EDITED BY GEORGE DUCAS
WITH CHARLES VAN DOREN

Introduction by C. Eric Lincoln
Editorial Consultant

PRAEGER PUBLISHERS

New York · Washington · London

The editors wish to express their gratitude for permission to reprint material from the following sources:

The Dial Press for "My Dungeon Shook," reprinted from *The Fire Next Time*, by James Baldwin, copyright © 1963, 1962 by James Baldwin.

Harcourt, Brace & World, Inc., for "The Colored World Within," from *Dusk of Dawn*, by W. E. B. Du Bois, copyright 1940 by Harcourt, Brace & World, Inc.; copyright © 1968 by Shirley Graham Du Bois.

Harper & Row, Publishers, for "How 'Bigger' Was Born," by Richard Wright, copyright 1940 by Richard Wright; renewed 1968 by Ellen Wright. Also for "Letter from Birmingham Jail"—April 16, 1963—from *Why We Can't Wait*, by Martin Luther King, Jr., copyright © 1963 by Martin Luther King, Jr.

Harvard Law School Forum for "Speech at the Harvard Law School Forum of December 16, 1964," from *The Speeches of Malcolm X at Harvard*, ed. by Archie Epps, © 1968 by Betty Shabazz.

The Macmillan Company for "Black Bourgeoisie," from *Black Bourgeoisie: The Rise of a New Middle Class in the United States*, by E. Franklin Frazier, copyright © 1962 by The Free Press, a Division of The Macmillan Company.

William Morrow and Company, Inc., for "The Legacy of Malcolm X, and the Coming of the Black Nation," from *Home: Social Essays*, by LeRoi Jones, copyright © 1965, 1966 by LeRoi Jones.

The New-York Historical Society, New York City, for "Copy of a Letter from Benjamin Banneker to the Secretary of State with His Answer."

PRAEGER PUBLISHERS
111 Fourth Avenue, New York, N.Y. 10003, U.S.A.
5, Cromwell Place, London S.W.7, England

Published in the United States of America in 1970
by Praeger Publishers, Inc.

© 1970 by Praeger Publishers, Inc.

Library of Congress Catalog Card Number: 73-96293

Printed in the United States of America

CONTENTS

Sections of illustrations follow pages 112 *and* 240.

INTRODUCTION

C. Eric Lincoln

Ten years ago, only a few Americans thought in terms of the possibility of a distinctive history of black Americans. Some Americans still reject the notion that the black experience deserves, or is capable of, sustained scholarly treatment. Americans who think this way are not a minority, even now, but their numbers are diminishing as the realities of contemporary history require a continuing reassessment of the past. Like most conquering peoples, white Americans have always assumed that *their* history is *the* history of America. History belongs to the conquerors. The right to determine the shape of the past and to use it as an instrument to determine the shape of the future is one of the sacred canons of civilized war. It is one of the means of extending the power and the privileges of conquest long after the swords have been beaten into plowshares, or found new employment in some other fray.

The Indians are a case in point. Possibly they were a great people. We shall probably never know with any assurance, unless we learn it from the Indians; for, despite the fact that they were the original Americans, they do not, in any tangible sense, belong to American history. They are not the subject of our textbooks. They were—they *are*—the conquered. As such they are dismissed from history and relegated to the realm of the white man's romanticism. We do not have to deal seriously with the romantic, because it is unreal. It is the fantasizing of reality, and in our fantasies we can be as magnanimous as the occasion demands, and we are relieved of responsibility for whatever took place on the level of reality. If we name our Boy Scout troops and our athletic teams after the noble Indian, how can we be guilty of excluding him from history that is past and, for that matter, very nearly excluding him from the possibility of any future history!

Our approach to black history has been somewhat different. We were never engaged in the military extermination of blacks, so it was never necessary to romanticize their nobility. We *were* engaged in the exploitation of black labor; so, in a democratic society, we found it was necessary to romanticize the *humanity* of blacks. First we denied them the possibility of having souls, but, when they proceeded to pray and preach and become Christians in spite of themselves, we concluded that (for political purposes at least) they were three-fifths human. We still needed their labor (and we'd rather not pay for it), so we proceeded to romanticize the black man just as we did the Indian. We did not make him noble. (We do not have any "Ashanti" or "Hausa" scout troops. No "Asantehene" football teams.) Rather, in our fantasies we made him docile, happy, contingent, and contented. And we called him "Our Negro." Obviously he had no place in *American* history. He was created, he was conquered by Americans. Indeed, as "Our Negro," he *had* no history, and so it was written, in the books of those who did, that they might always remember, and that he would not be permitted to forget.

A people who can lay claim to a history can lay claim to the full range of social and political responses that characterize human interaction. To claim a history is a way of documenting your humanity. It is no accident that white children (and blacks alike) were taught that "the Negro race has no history." * Whoever has no history has no soul and may be dealt with at the level of an incomplete or protohuman being. Or whoever has no history has no reality and can be dealt with at the level of romantic fantasy. David Walker challenged every black man's sense of history by asking the critical question: *"Are we men?"* And with the same question he indicted America, which could not say "yes" and continue the dehumanization of black people. True, it was a rhetorical question, but, more than that, it was a historical question, because it was crucial to the way America saw its blacks and to the way black people saw themselves.

By all odds, any book of this decade that addresses itself to the significant documents of black history should probably begin with David Walker, because David Walker, more than any other historical figure, wrote in the mood of today. His was a voice that the contemporary black revolution can identify with as it raises anew the question that put a price on David Walker's head: *"Are we men?"* The implications of the question are as clear now as they were in 1830: If in fact black people are men, then they are *persons*—capable of and entitled to a proper social relationship with their white counterparts, who are certainly *no more* than men! David Walker charged the white men who would deny black men their humanity ("Are they not dying worms as well as we?") with having "always been an unjust, jealous, unmerciful, avaricious and bloodthirsty set" who as Christians "are ten times more cruel, avaricious and unmerciful" than they were as heathens.

It seems clear that Walker's indictment against the Americans encompasses both their claims to racial superiority—which presupposes for themselves a unique development toward human perfection—and their alleged moral superiority, which is interpreted as a *de facto* expression of their posture as Christians. Again, the relevance of Walker to

---

* It didn't, for the simple reason that there is no Negro race, but that was hardly the point.

contemporary times is almost uncanny. It is almost as though his *Appeal* had been written with our generation in mind—or as if 147 years had passed while American history stood still.

This volume opens with an essay by John Woolman, a Quaker whose piety impelled him to lay his thoughts on the impropriety of slavery upon the consciences of other Christians. In a careful examination of the Scriptures, Woolman found no justification for slavery. Indeed, he concluded that "real Christians" are moved by their religion to a "Kindness beyond Expression" and that those "govern'd by the Spirit of Christ, and thereby made Sons of God" should, because of their favored status, "be active in the same great cause of the Eternal Happiness" of all men. Woolman was not impressed by the practical arguments of slavery. The risk involved in the procurement of slaves and the economic investment in their purchase were not sufficient reasons to continue men in servitude. "In a Practice just and reasonable, such Objections may have weight," he argued. "But if the work be wrong from the beginning, there is little or no force in them."

In the context of his times, John Woolman's was an important voice—albeit crying in the wilderness of a religious morality that had been relaxed to make slaveholding consistent with the will of God and the self-perceived destiny of the white man in America. It made no difference whether blacks were heathens or Christians. If they were black, they would labor for the white man—forever. And among the slaveholders, it made no difference whether they themselves were Christian. The confraternity of Christians was transcended by the deeper responses to the confraternity of race. The acceptance of Jesus Christ would "work no manumission" for the black heathen. The rules were suspended. And the grace of God took no adverse notice of the white Christian's requiring the alleged sons of the accursed Ham to hew wood and draw water (without pay) for perpetuity.

Once more the critical insight of David Walker compels attention. The comfortable *rapprochement* between Christianity and slavery both puzzled and enraged him: "What the American preachers can think of us, I aver this day before my God, I have never been able to define." And, "Can anything be a greater mockery of religion than the way in which it is conducted by Americans?"

Walker was himself a devout Christian, but his distrust of American religion with its strong racist overtones would doubtless have led him to accept Woolman's *Considerations on the Keeping of Negroes* with some reservations. Black people would have to raise up their own prophets and scholars. In the rhetoric of the present-day black revolution, which Walker anticipates so perfectly, the blacks would have to "take care of business" for themselves. Every black man, he urged, should "buy a copy of Mr. [Thomas] Jefferson's 'Notes on Virginia' and put it in the hands of his son. . . . The refutations written by our white friends are not enough—they are *whites;* we are *blacks*. We and the world wish to see the charges of Mr. Jefferson refuted by the blacks themselves." The editors of this volume have included Jefferson's "Notes" among their selection of "great documents." The sons of this generation of blacks will see in it some arguments they thought were new.

Walker recognized the paucity of learning among the oppressed blacks of his time, but he foresaw the inevitable development of "talents and learning" among them, and he was confident that they could speak effectively for themselves. "Every dog," he declared, "must have its day. . . . Our sufferings will come to an *end*, in spite of all the Americans this side of *eternity*." If Walker's sentiments are in any real sense reflective of the mood of blackness that structures today's black revolution, then Woolman's treatise is not, in another sense, a document of black American history at all. Nor are the selections from Thomas Jefferson and Earl Warren, for that matter, however great the influence those documents (especially that written by Justice Warren) may have had upon the *direction* of black history. Black people make their own history, a critical distinction important to these times, and critical to the disestablishment of traditional notions about "who speaks for the Negro."

Mr. Jefferson's *Notes on the State of Virginia*, which antagonized David Walker so much, had already been answered by Jefferson's distinguished black contemporary Benjamin Banneker, in a letter he wrote to Jefferson forty years before Walker addressed himself to the issue. Jefferson's *Notes* raised questions about the mental capacity of blacks—a recurring pastime that continues to exert a powerful fascination in some intellectual quarters to this day. In Jefferson's time, and since, there were always some paladins available to rush to the defense of the impugned black intelligence, that they might give the lie to the racist allegations going the rounds in the circles of American intellect. In the old days, refutation generally took the form of procuring an "outstanding Negro," who but for the fact that he was black (that is, that he *was* a "Negro") could have moved with ease and confidence among intelligent people *anywhere*, to make an answer. This was the role Benjamin Banneker—scientist, mathematician, and respected citizen—was called upon to play in a dialogue with Thomas Jefferson. Of course Banneker and most of the long line of his successors in that role lived before the current sanctification of statistical methodology as the *sine qua non* of human evaluation changed the rules. It is very doubtful that Banneker could have satisfied Christopher Jencks and David Riesman, for example, as it is very difficult these days to come up with a "composite Negro" who will look good on a computer print-out.

Despite the fact that the notion of the innate inferiority of black people lingers deep in the psychic history of white America, Mr. Jefferson's *Notes* are probably more important as a document for *white* history than it is for the understanding of the black experience. The work should be read as a historical curio, a reflection on a cultural syndrome that doesn't want to go away because it is somehow vital to the rationalization of our larger history. Benjamin Banneker was important for what he was—as a person and as a scientist. The importance of his letter to Jefferson lies in his courage to confront the then Secretary of State with the humanitarian sentiments Jefferson had expressed in the framing of the Declaration of Independence and to ask the Secretary whether or not his apprehensions of the horror of slavery and the violation of liberty were still intact.

Banneker addressed himself to what he perceived as the moral, rational understanding of Thomas Jefferson—the Virginia gentleman, the scholar, the public servant. He challenged Jefferson regarding his attitude toward blacks to "put your soul in their souls' stead," and, although Banneker accuses Jefferson of being "found guilty of the most criminal act which you professedly detested in others," the last quarter of his letter is confined to a polite discussion of the almanac that accompanies the letter. Interestingly enough, while Banneker deplores the "fraud and violence by which so numerous a part of [his] brethren are detained," he does not "presume to prescribe methods by which they may be relieved." This avoidance of presumptiveness may reflect the realities of the disparate positions Banneker, a free black, and Jefferson, a founder of the white establishment, occupied in the society, and yet presumptiveness was not a bar to Banneker's offering Jefferson "a present" of his almanac in manuscript form so that Jefferson "might view it in my own handwriting." In short, what Benjamin Banneker was searching for in Thomas Jefferson was that residual humanitarianism most black intellectuals have always been willing to look for and hope for in white folk of the better class—that is, as they imagined themselves, had they been white. Banneker could not "presume to prescribe methods" for Jefferson regarding the proper behavior toward the oppressed blacks because Banneker associated morality with intelligence, a mistake that has caused black Americans untold frustration and anguish since Banneker's time. A concomitant of the black experience has been a need to believe that the white man's behavior toward blacks was in large part a product of the white man's ignorance. If it could be explained to him that black people have souls, that they share his system of values, that they believe in law and order and the upkeep of property, how *could* he deny them? Something more than the black man's status in the society was at stake—his whole understanding of the priority of values was threatened: *If white people of superior intelligence could not express that intelligence in moral social behavior, then where did that leave the intelligent black—to say nothing of the black masses?*

Mr. Jefferson never did resolve the conflict between his intelligence and his social inclinations. And it is probable that Banneker never understood why his own industry and intelligence did not significantly enlarge his acceptance and responsibilities in a society where those values were paramount. A hundred years later, another black intellectual, W. E. B. DuBois, was to know the same frustration and was to explain it in terms of "double consciousness."

Double consciousness is a luxury in which only intellectuals can indulge. Less sophisticated minds are more unitary in their perception of the realities that surround them and press in upon them. Nat Turner is a good example. For Turner, the issues were clear, the cause was well known, the solution simple, and God was on his side.

Nat Turner's insurrection was probably inspired, at least to some degree, by David Walker's *Appeal*, although Nat had before him as a practical model the successful revolt of black Haitians under Toussaint L'Ouverture in 1803. Unfortunately, Turner's "Confessions," while attested to by six acting Justices of the Peace (all officers of the court that tried and hanged him), does not come from Nat's own pen. The "Confessions" were allegedly dictated to a white man named Thomas Gray, who published them in the hope of "removing doubts and conjectures from the public mind," and to induce all those entrusted with the execution of "our laws in restraint of this [Nat's] class of our population . . . to see that they are strictly and rigidly enforced." Gray's explanation of Turner's motivation is that his mind was "bewildered and confounded and finally corrupted" by "endeavoring to grapple with things beyond its reach." But in the same breath, narrator Gray suggests that Turner's revolt was the result of "long deliberation and a settled purpose of mind." It must be assumed that, in the nature of the circumstances, Gray's interpretation of Nat could hardly be unbiased and Gray's rendering of Nat's "Confessions" is for the same reason not above suspicion. However, as a document of black history, the importance of the deposition is that it presents a radically different profile of the free black from that of, say, Benjamin Banneker. Black history is full of surprises. That it has been so effectively reduced to stereotypes is a tribute to the remarkable effectiveness of its official suppression.

The fact is, of course, that no society can suppress history indefinitely. David Walker, Booker T. Washington, Martin Luther King, and Malcolm X are historical figures because they were notable contributors to events that took place in the context of our social interest. American history as traditionally interpreted simply defines social interest in such a way as to exclude the black experience and those who have figured significantly in its expression. But, because history is continuous with society, the repertoire of the excluded is continuously expanded. As black and white America traveled the road together, it was inevitable that they would play to each other as well as to their traditional, separate audiences. That is beginning to happen now. It is a feature of the black revolution. Frederick Douglass and Martin Delaney may eventually belong to all the people, as it is assumed that Benjamin Franklin and Franklin D. Roosevelt belong to all Americans. Why should a philosopher like Alain Locke, a poet like Langston Hughes, a novelist like Richard Wright or James Baldwin be restricted to so few when there are so many who stand to benefit by exposure to what they have had to say about life in America? And do not Marcus Garvey and Malcolm X figure prominently enough in the shaping of American social intercourse to warrant a place in American history? I do not mean the history of the white American conquerors, for that perspective on history is as obsolete as it is unrealistic and counterproductive. I am talking about the history of the American people in total context—that larger history in which red men and white men and black men have found themselves involved in a peculiar interrelationship over 350 years. That is the true American experience. It is the critical, objective documentation of that common experience that will ultimately produce the true biography of America, of which we are very greatly in need.

In the meantime, the progression of the American biography is inevitable, whether or not we write it in the texts and journals we use to socialize our young. One of the prominent features of the contemporary scene is a social construct personified as "Bigger Thomas" by Richard Wright a generation ago. Wright was clairvoyant. Most of the rest of us have still to recognize Bigger—though he is here in strength and in numbers far greater and a lot sooner than we care to think about. Wright's Bigger was, in his own words, "in a nascent state, not yet articulate." Now, Bigger has found his tongue, and he has multiplied. "Granting the emotional state, the tensity, the fear, the hate, the impatience, the sense of exclusion, the ache for violent action, the emotional and cultural hunger," said Wright, "Bigger Thomas, conditioned as his organism is will not become an ardent, or even a lukewarm supporter of the *status quo*." From a contemporary perspective, that is an understatement.

This is the era in which the American Bigger Thomas has come of age. He is not necessarily black, but the conditions of his existence are the circumstances that condition the existences of every American who is black. The process that reduces a man to the lowest level of social existence in this society is called "niggerization." Black Americans have known about it for a long time. But they have also survived it, commented on it, and projected for themselves another kind of existence, which they believe to be capable of realization. This book reflects their experience and their hope.

Great Documents in Black American History

SOME CONSIDERATIONS ON THE KEEPING OF NEGROES

John Woolman

[In retrospect, one of the arresting facts about Negro slavery in the English colonies is that it developed from a condition of Negro freedom, rather than springing up full-blown. The now-famous "twenty negars" who arrived in 1619 at Jamestown began their life in Virginia as indentured servants, just as had numerous white men who sold their time in exchange for passage to the New World. The Africans had been bound for slavery in the West Indies on a Spanish frigate, which was probably robbed of its cargo by the Dutch man-of-war that brought them to Jamestown. Very little is known about these first blacks, but the evidence indicates that they were not treated as slaves in perpetual servitude. After working out their period of indenture, many of them acquired property, and some rose to respected positions in the community. A few, like Anthony Johnson in the 1650's, acquired holdings of several hundred acres by taking advantage of the headright system that allowed fifty acres for every person brought to the colony. Black men in this period had legal rights and were able to sue, and often did, in the courts. Some, including Johnson, even owned slaves.

The question of why Negroes came to be slaves after an initial experience where this was not the case has vexed many historians. The matter still is not settled, perhaps never will be, and the usual explanation in terms of the need for labor in the wilderness actually explains very little. It is true that a need, and, therefore, a desire, for a certain kind of labor had its effect on the development of the institution; but, even if it is argued that a system of indentured labor could not have supported a plantation economy, it is not at all clear why white slavery did not develop alongside of black. One might also ask why blacks were enslaved in the Northern colonies, which lacked plantations. Not very much is added by appealing to considerations of color (although this seemed to become more important later) or even of religion. The Indians, after all, were as heathen as the blacks. Perhaps, however, it is of more than just casual significance that some of the first blacks were Christian, having been baptized by the Spaniards. It was traditional in English law that Christians were not to be enslaved. The Christianity of blacks did present an obstacle, in the minds of some whites, to enslavement, but the telling fact in this context is that it was slavery based on race, and not on religion (or the lack of it), that developed in the colonies.

Whatever answer to this question one finally accepts, the distinction between white servitude and Negro slavery began to be marked in the statutes of Maryland and Virginia as the number of Africans increased. Negroes, it seems, had always been singled out. The earliest census reports record blacks and whites separately. By 1649, there is evidence that some Negroes were in servitude for life in Virginia. In 1667, baptism was eliminated as an obstacle to slavery. There is evidence that, by 1669 (Virginia Negroes numbered 2,000 in 1670, an increase of 1,700 since 1649), all Negroes in service were bound for life. There is no evidence that perpetual and hereditary servitude ever became the lot of any white man in the colonies.

The debasement that accompanied slavery increased in the eighteenth century as Africans were brought to the New World in unprecedented numbers. As the status of slave became fixed in the community, it clearly delineated a position that whites could never occupy. Never, that is, so long as white men felt it appropriate and were able to enslave black men.

Long before slavery was brought into question by the Revolutionary ideology, the Quaker conscience had spoken out on the evils of the slave trade. As early as 1688, a protest against the slave trade "was included in the resolutions of the monthly meeting of Mennonites in Germantown (near Philadelphia), Pennsylvania. The Mennonite Germans were kindred to the Quakers and, like them, had undergone persecution in Europe for their religious beliefs. But it was not until the 1750's that any sustained antislavery sentiment became evident. It was in this decade, too, that the Quakers, led by those in Pennsylvania, mounted a drive to rid their fellowship of slaveowners. The most influential Quaker in this antislavery campaign was John Woolman. A tailor by trade and always concerned to avoid luxury, he cared little for business but devoted the better portion of his life to social and moral causes. For thirty years, he traveled, from his native New Jersey, throughout the colonies, writing and talking (mostly talking) against the slave trade, protesting unjust treatment of the Indians, and arguing against war. Woolman possessed an unfailingly generous and gentle temper and a quiet radiance of spirit. He journeyed twice to visit Friends in Virginia, in 1746 and, again, in 1757. Shortly after the first trip, he wrote *Some Considerations on the Keeping of Negroes* (which is reprinted here), although it was not published until 1754. His second and final antislavery tract appeared in 1762. Woolman, whose piety has sometimes blinded readers to his penetrating mind, was struck with what later became familiar observations. The degradation of Negroes by slavery, he argued, entails misery for the master as well. Slavery bred in the master, as well as in his children, a false pride that could not but alienate them from the Christian inheritance.

In the second tract, Woolman focused on what, through custom, had become the main obstacle to any straight thinking about slavery. "This is owing chiefly," he said, "to the idea of slavery being connected with the black colour, and liberty with the white." Both parts of this irrational principle had been stated clearly for the first time. Woolman recognized that this idea would "not suddenly leave us," failing the wisdom to choose another, simpler way of life. In effect, he saw that whiteness, rather than Christianity, had come to be the mark of moral superiority and freedom. Thereafter, Woolman's arguments became commonplace in the growing antislavery movement.]

Introduction

Customs generally approved, and *Opinions* received by youth from their Superiors, become like the natural Produce of a Soil, especially when they are suited to favourite Inclinations: But as the Judgments of God are without partiality, by which the State of the Soul must be tried, it would be the highest Wisdom to forego Customs and popular Opinions, and try the Treasures of the Soul by the infallible Standard TRUTH.

Natural Affection needs a careful Examination: Operating upon us in a soft Manner, it kindles Desires of Love and Tenderness, and there is Danger of taking it for something higher. To me it appears an Instinct like that which inferior Creatures have: each of them, we see, by the Ties of Nature, love *Self* best; that which is a Part of *Self*, they love by the same Tie or Instinct. In them, it in some Measure does the Offices of reason; by which, among other Things, they watchfully keep, and orderly feed their helpless Offspring. Thus *Natural Affection* appears to be a Branch of *Self-love*, good in the Animal Race, in us likewise, with proper Limitations; but otherwise is productive of Evil, by exciting Desires to promote *some* by Means prejudicial to *others*.

Our Blessed Lord seems to give a Check to this irregular Fondness in nature, and, at the same Time, a Precedent for us: *Who is my mother, and who are my brethren?* Thereby intimating, that the earthly Ties of Relationship, are comparatively, inconsiderable to such who thro' a steady Course of Obedience, have come to the happy Experience of the Spirit of God bearing witness with their Spirits that they are his Children: And he stretched forth his hands towards his disciples, and said, Behold my mother, and my brethren! For whosoever shall do the will of my Father which is in Heaven, (*arrives at the more noble part of true relationship*) the same is my Brother, *and Sister and Mother.* Matt. xii. 48.

This doctrine agrees well with a State truly compleat, where LOVE *necessarily operates according to the* agreeableness of Things, on principles unalterable and in themselves perfect.

If endeavouring to have my Children eminent amongst Men after my

Death, be that which no reasons grounded on these Principles can be brought to support; then, to be temperate in my Pursuit after Gain, and to keep always within the Bounds of those Principles, is an indispensable Duty; and to depart from it, a dark unfruitful Toil.

In our present Condition, to *Love* our Children is needful; but except this *Love* proceeds from the true heavenly Principle which sees beyond earthly Treasures, it will rather be injurious than of any real Advantage to them: Where the Fountain is corrupt, the Streams must necessarily be impure.

That important Injunction of our Saviour, Matt. vi. 33, with the Promise annexed, contains a short but comprehensive View of our Duty and Happiness: If then the Business of Mankind in this Life, is, to first seek another; if this cannot be done, but by attending to the Means; if a Summary of the Means is, [*not to do that to another which, in like Circumstances, we would not have done unto us;*] then these are Points of Moment, and worthy of our most serious Consideration.

[What I write on this Subject is with Reluctance, and] the Hints given are in as general Terms as my Concern would allow: [I know it is a Point about which, in all its Branches, Men that appear to aim well are not generally agreed; and for that reason, I choose to avoid being very particular:] If I may happily have let drop any Thing that may excite such as are concerned in the Practice to a close thinking on the Subject treated of, the Candid amongst them may easily do the Subject such further Justice, as, on an impartial Enquiry, it may appear to deserve; and such an Enquiry I would earnestly recommend.

SOME CONSIDERATIONS, &c.

Forasmuch as ye did it to the least of these my brethren, ye did it unto me.—*Matt.* xxv. 40.

As Many Times there are different Motives to the same Actions; and one does that from a generous Heart, which another does for selfish Ends; The like may be said in this Case.

There are various Circumstances amongst them that keep *Negroes*, and different Ways by which they fall under their Care; and, I doubt not, there are many well-disposed Persons amongst them, who desire rather to manage wisely and justly in this difficult Matter, than to make gain of it.

But the general Disadvantage which these poor *Africans*, lie under in an enlightened Christian Country, having often filled me with real sadness, and been like undigested Matter on my Mind, I now think it my Duty, through Divine Aid, to offer some Thoughts thereon to the Consideration of others.

When we remember that all Nations are of one Blood, Gen. iii. 20, that in this World we are but Sojourners, that we are subject to the like Afflictions and Infirmities of Body, the like Disorders and frailties in Mind, the like Temptations, the same Death, and the same Judgment, and that the Alwise Being is Judge and Lord over us all, it seems to raise an Idea of a general Brotherhood, and a Disposition easy to be touched with a Feeling of each others Afflictions: But when we forget these Things, and look chiefly at our outward Circumstances, in this and some Ages past, constantly retaining in our Minds the Distinction betwixt us and them, with respect to our Knowledge and Improvement in Things divine, natural and artificial, our Breasts being apt to be filled with fond Notions of Superiority, there is Danger of erring in our Conduct toward them.

We allow them to be of the same Species with ourselves, the Odds is, we are in a higher Station, and enjoy greater Favours than they: And when it is thus, that our heavenly Father endoweth some of his Children with distinguished Gifts, they are intended for good Ends: but if those thus gifted are thereby lifted up above their Brethren, not considering themselves as Debtors to the Weak, nor behaving themselves as faithful Stewards, none who judge impartially can suppose them free from Ingratitude.

When a People dwell under the liberal distribution of Favours from Heaven, it behoves them carefully to inspect their Ways, and consider the purposes for which those Favours were bestowed lest, through Forgetfulness of God, and Misusing his Gifts, they incur his heavy Displeasure whose Judgments are just and equal, who exalteth and humbleth to the Dust as he seeth meet.

It appears, by Holy Record, that Men under high Favours have been apt to err in their Opinions concerning others. Thus *Israel*, according to the Description of the Prophet Isaiah lxv. 5. when exceedingly corrupted and degenerated, yet remembered they were the chosen People of God; and could say, *Stand by thyself, come not near me, for I am holier than thou*. That this was no chance Language, but their common Opinion of other People, more fully appears, by considering the Circumstances which attended when God was beginning to fulfill his precious Promises concerning the gathering of the *Gentiles*.

The Most High, in a Vision, undeceived Peter, first prepared his Heart to believe; and, at the House of *Cornelius*, showed him of a certainty, that God was no Respecter of Persons.

The Effusion of the Holy Ghost upon a People, with whom they, the *Jewish* Christians would not so much as eat, was strange to them: All they of the Circumcision were astonished to see it: and the Apostles and Brethren of *Judea* contended with *Peter* about it, till he, having rehearsed the whole Matter, and fully shown that the Father's Love was unlimited, they were thereat struck with Admiration, and cried out, *Then hath God also to the Gentiles granted repentance unto life.*

The Opinion of peculiar Favours being confined to them, was deeply rooted, or else the above Instance had been less strange to them, for these Reasons: *First*, They were generally acquainted with the Writings of the Prophets, by whom this Time was repeatedly spoken of, and pointed at. *Secondly*, Our Blessed Lord shortly before expressly said, *I have other sheep, not of this fold, them also must I bring, &c. Lastly*, His words to them after his Resurrection, at the very Time of his Ascension, *Ye shall be witnesses to me, not only in Jerusalem, Judea, and Samaria, but to the uttermost parts of the earth.*

Those concurring Circumstances, one would think, might have raised a strong Expectation of seeing such a Time: yet, when it came, it proved Matter of Offence and Astonishment.

To consider Mankind otherwise than Brethren, to think Favours are peculiar to one Nation, and exclude others, plainly supposes a Darkness in the Understanding. For, as God's Love is universal, so where the Mind is sufficiently influenced by it, it begets a Likeness of itself, and the Heart is enlarged towards all Men. Again, to conclude a People forward, perverse, and worse by Nature than others, (who ungratefully receive Favours, and apply them to bad Ends) this will excite a Behaviour toward them, unbecoming the Excellence of true Religion.

To prevent such Error, let us calmly consider their Circumstance; and, the better to do it, make their Case ours. Suppose then, that our Ancestors and we had been exposed to constant Servitude, in the more servile and inferior Employments of Life; that we had been destitute of the Help of Reading and good Company; that amongst ourselves we had had few wise and pious Instructors; that the Religious amongst our Superiors seldom took Notice of us; that while others, in Ease, have plentifully heaped up the Fruit of our Labour, we had receiv'd barely enough to relieve Nature, and being wholly at the Command of others, had generally been treated as a contemptible, ignorant Part of Mankind: Should we, in that Case, be less abject than they now are? Again, if Oppression be so hard to bear, that a wise Man is made mad by it, Eccl. vii. 7, then a Series of those Things, altering the Behaviour and Manners of a People, is what may reasonably be expected.

When our Property is taken contrary to our Mind, by Means appearing to us unjust, it is only through Divine Influence, and the Enlargement of Heart from thence proceeding, that we can love our reputed Oppressors: If the *Negroes* fall short in this, an uneasy, if not a disconsolate Disposition will be awaken'd, and remain like Seeds in their Minds, producing Sloth and many other Habits appearing odious to us; with which, being free Men, they perhaps had not been chargeable. These and other Circumstances, rightly considered, will lessen that too great Disparity which some make between us and them.

Integrity of Heart hath appeared in some of them: so that, if we continue in the Word of Christ (previous to Discipleship, *John viii. 31*) and our Conduct toward them be seasoned with his Love, we may hope to see the good Effect of it: The which, in a good Degree, is the Case with some into whose Hands they have fallen: But that too many treat them otherwise, not seeming conscious of any Neglect, is, alas! too evident.

When *Self-love* presides in our Minds, our Opinions are bias'd in our own Favour. In this Condition, being concerned with a People so situated that they have no Voice to plead their own Cause, there's Danger of using ourselves to an undisturbed Partiality, till, by long Custom, the Mind becomes reconciled with it, and the Judgment itself infected.

To humbly apply to God for Wisdom, that we may thereby be enabled to see Things as they are, and ought to be, is very needful; hereby the hidden Things of Darkness may be brought to Light, and the Judgment made clear: We shall then consider Mankind as Brethren: though different Degrees and a variety of Qualification and Abilities, one dependent on another, be admitted, yet high Thoughts will be laid aside, and all men treated as becometh the Sons of one Father, agreeable to the Doctrine of Christ Jesus.

"He hath laid down the best Criterion, by which Mankind ought to judge of their own Conduct, and others judge for them of theirs, one towards another, viz. *Whatsoever ye would that men should do unto you, do ye even so to them.* I take it, that all Men by Nature are equally entitled to the Equity of this Rule, and under the indispensable Obliga- tions of it. One Man ought not to look upon another Man, or Society of Men, as so far beneath him, but that he should put himself in their place, in all his Actions towards them, and bring all to this Test, viz. How should I approve of this Conduct, were I in their Circumstances, and they in mine? A. Arscot's Considerations, p. III. fol. 107.

This Doctrine being of a moral, unchangeable Nature, hath been like- wise inculcated in the former dispensation; *If a Stranger sojourn with thee in your Land, ye shall not vex him: but the stranger that dwelleth with you, shall be as One born amongst you, and thou shalt love him as thyself.* Lev. xix. 33, 34. Had these People come voluntary and dwelt amongst us, to have called them Strangers would be proper; and their being brought by Force, with Regret, and a languishing Mind, may well raise Compassion in a heart rightly disposed: but there is Nothing in such Treatment, which, upon a wise and judicious Consideration, will any ways lessen their right of being treated as Strangers. If the Treatment which many of them meet with, be rightly examined, and compared with these Precepts, *Thou shalt not vex him nor oppress him; he shall be as one born amongst you, and thou shalt love him as thyself*, Lev. xix. 33. Deut. xxvii. 19, there will appear an important Difference betwixt them.

It may be objected there is Cost of Purchase, and Risque of their Lives to them who possess them, and therefore needful that they make the best use of their Time; In a Practice just and reasonable, such Objections may have Weight; but if the Work be wrong from the be- ginning, there is little or no Force in them. If I purchase a Man who hath never forfeited his Liberty, the natural Right of Freedom is in him; and shall I keep him and his Posterity in Servitude and Ignorance? *How should I approve of this conduct, were I in his Circumstances, and he in mine?* It may be thought, that to treat them as we would willingly be treated, our Gain by them would be inconsiderable: And it were, in divers Respects, better that there were none in our Country.

We may further consider that they are now amongst us, and those of our Nation the cause of their being here; that whatsoever Difficulty accrues thereon, we are justly chargeable with, and to bear all Incon- veniencies attending it, with a serious and weighty Concern of Mind to do our Duty by them, is the best we can do. To seek a Remedy by con- tinuing the Oppression, because we have Power to do it and see others do it, will, I apprehend, not be doing as we would be done by.

How deeply soever Men are involved in the most exquisite Difficulties, Sincerity of Heart and upright Walking before God, freely submitting to his Providence, is the most sure Remedy. He only is able to relieve, not only Persons, but Nations in their greatest Calamities.

David, in a great Strait, when the Sense of his past Error, and the full

Expectation of an impending Calamity as the Reward of it, were united to the aggravating his Distress, after some deliberation, saith, *Let me fall now into the Hand of the Lord, for very great are his Mercies; but let me not fall into the Hand of Man.* I Chron. xxi. 13.

To Act continually with Integrity of Heart, above all narrow or selfish Motives, is a Pure Token of our being partakers of that Salvation which *God hath appointed for Walls and Bulwarks.* Isa. v. 26; Rom. xv. 8, and is, beyond all Contradiction, a more happy Situation than can ever be promised by the utmost Reach of Art and Power united, not proceeding from heavenly Wisdom.

A supply to Nature's lawful Wants, joined with a peaceful, humble Mind, is the truest Happiness in this Life; and if here we arrive to this, and remain to walk in the Path of the Just, our case will be truly happy: And though herein we may part with, or miss of some glaring Shows of Riches, and leave our Children little else but wise Instructions, a good Example, and the Knowledge of some honest Employment, these, with the Blessing of Providence, are sufficient for their Happiness, and are more likely to prove so, than laying up Treasures for them, which are often rather a Snare, than any real Benefit; especially to them, who, instead of being exampled to Temperance, are in all Things taught to prefer the getting of Riches, and to eye the temporal Distinctions they give, as the principal business of this Life. These readily overlook the true Happiness of Man, as it results, from the enjoyment of all Things in the Fear of God, and, miserably substituting an inferior Good, dangerous in the Acquiring, and uncertain in the Fruition, they are subject to many Disappointments; and every Sweet carries its Sting.

It is the Conclusion of our blessed Lord and his Apostles, as appears by their Lives and Doctrines, that the highest Delights of Sense, or most pleasing Objects visible, ought ever to be accounted infinitely inferior to that real intellectual Happiness suited to Man in his primitive Innocence, and now to be found in true Renovation of Mind; and that the Comforts of our present Life, the Things most grateful to us, ought always to be received with Temperance, and never made the chief Objects of our Desire, Hope, or Love: But that our whole Heart and Affections be principally looking to that *city which hath foundations, whose maker and builder is God.* Did we so improve the Gifts bestowed on us, that our Children might have an Education suited to these Doctrines, and our Example to confirm it, we might rejoice in Hopes of their being Heirs of an Inheritance incorruptible.

This Inheritance, as Christians, we esteem the most valuable; and how then can we fail to desire it for our Children? Oh that we were consistent with ourselves, in pursuing Means necessary to obtain it!

It appears, by Experience, that where Children are educated in Fulness, Ease and Idleness, evil Habits are more prevalent than in common amongst such who are prudently employed in the necessary Affairs of Life. And if Children are not only educated in the Way of so great Temptation, but have also the Opportunity of lording it over their Fellow Creatures, and being Masters of Men in their Childhood, how can we hope otherwise than that their tender Minds will be possessed with Thoughts too high for them? Which, by Continuance, gaining Strength, will prove like a slow Current, gradually separating them from (or keeping from Acquaintance with) that Humility and Meekness in which alone lasting Happiness can be enjoyed.

Man is born to labour, and Experience abundantly showeth that it is for our Good: But where the Powerful lay the Burthen on the Inferior, without affording a Christian Education, and suitable Opportunity of improving the Mind, and a treatment which we, in their Ease, should approve, that themselves may live at Ease, and fare sumptuously, and lay up Riches for their posterity, this seems to contradict the Design of Providence, and, I doubt, is sometimes the Effect of a perverted Mind: For while the Life of one is made grievous by the Rigour of another, it entails Misery on both.

Amongst the manifold Works of Providence, displayed in the different Ages of the World, these which follow (with many others) may afford Instruction.

Abraham was called of God to leave his Country and Kindred, to sojourn amongst Strangers: Through Famine and danger of Death, he was forced to flee from one Kingdom to another: He, at length, not only had Assurance of being the Father of many Nations, but became a mighty Prince. Gen. xxiii. 6.

Remarkable were the Dealings of God with *Jacob* in a low Estate, the just Sense he retained of them after his Advancement, appears by his words: *I am not worthy of the least of all thy mercies.* Gen. xxxii. 10. xlviii. 15.

The numerous Afflictions of *Joseph* were very singular; the particular Providence of God therein, no less manifested. He, at length, became Governor of Egypt, and famous for Wisdom and Virtue.

The series of Troubles which *David* passed through, few amongst us are ignorant of; and yet he afterwards became as one of the great Men of the Earth.

Some Evidences of the Divine Wisdom appear in these Things, in that such who are intended for high Stations, have first been very low and dejected, that Truth might be sealed on their Hearts; and that the Characters there imprinted by Bitterness and Adversity, might in after Years remain; suggesting Compassionate ideas, and, in their Prosperity, quickening their Regard to those in the like Condition. Which yet further appears in the Case of *Israel:* They were well acquainted with grievous Sufferings, a long and rigorous Servitude, then through many notable Events, were made Chief amongst the Nations: To them we find a Repetition of Precepts to the Purpose above-said: Though, for Ends agreeable to infinite Wisdom they were chose as a peculiar People for a Time; yet the Most High acquaints them, that his Love is not confined, but extends to the Stranger; and, to excite their Compassion, reminds them of Times past; *Ye were Strangers in the Land of Egypt,* Deut. x. 19. Again, *Thou shalt not oppress a Stranger, for ye know the Heart of a Stranger, seeing ye were Strangers in the Land of Egypt.* Exod. xxiii. 9.

If we call to Mind our Beginning, some of us may find a Time, wherein our Fathers were under Afflictions, Reproaches, and manifold Sufferings.

Respecting our Progress in this Land, the Time is short since our Beginning was small and our Number few, compared with the native Inhabitants. He that sleeps not by Day nor by Night, hath watched over us, and kept us as the Apple of his Eye. His Almighty Arm hath been round about us, and saved us from Dangers.

The Wilderness and solitary Desarts in which our Fathers passed the Days of their Pilgrimage, are now turned into pleasant Fields; the Natives are gone from before us, and we established peaceably in the Possession of the Land, enjoying our civil and religious Liberties; and, while many Parts of the World have groaned under the heavy Calamities of War, our Habitation remains quiet, and our Land fruitful.

When we trace back the Steps we have trodden, and see how the Lord hath opened a Way in the Wilderness for us, to the Wise it will easily appear, that all this was not done to be buried in Oblivion; but to prepare a People for more fruitful Returns, and the Remembrance thereof ought to humble us in Prosperity, and excite in us a Christian Benevolence towards our Inferiors.

If we do not consider these Things aright, but, through a stupid Indolence, conceive Views of Interest, separate from the general Good of the great Brotherhood, and, in Pursuance thereof, treat our Inferiors with Rigour, to increase our Wealth, and gain Riches for our Children, what then shall we do when God riseth up and when he visiteth, what shall we answer him? Did not he that made us, make them? and *Did not one fashion us in the womb?* Job xxxi. 14.

To our great Master we stand or fall, to judge or condemn us as is most suitable to his Wisdom or Authority. My Inclination is to persuade, and entreat, and simply give Hints of my Way of Thinking.

If the Christian Religion be considered, both respecting its Doctrines, and the happy Influence which it hath on the Minds and Manners of all real Christians, it looks reasonable to think that the miraculous Manifestation thereof to the World, is a Kindness beyond Expression.

Are we the People thus favoured? Are we they whose Minds are opened, influenced, and govern'd by the Spirit of Christ, and thereby made Sons of God? Is it not a fair conclusion, that we, like our heavenly Father, ought in our Degree to be active in the same great Cause, of the Eternal Happiness of at least our whole Families, and more, if thereto capacitated.

If we, by the Operation of the Spirit of Christ, become Heirs with him in the Kingdom of his Father, and are redeemed from the alluring counterfeit Joys of this World, and the Joy of Christ remain in us, to suppose that One remaining in this happy Condition, can, for the sake of earthly Riches, not only deprive his Fellow Creatures of the Sweetness of Freedom, (which, rightly used, is one of the greatest temporal Blessings,) but therewith neglect using proper Means for their Acquaintance with the Holy Scriptures, and the advantage of true Religion, seems, at least, a Contradiction to Reason.

Whoever rightly advocates the Cause of some, thereby promotes the Good of all. The State of Mankind was harmonious in the Beginning, and tho' sin hath introduced Discord, yet through the wonderful Love of God in Christ Jesus our Lord, the Way is open for our Redemption, and Means are appointed to restore us to primitive Harmony. That if one suffer by the Unfaithfulness of another, the Mind, the most noble Part of him that occasions the Discord, is hereby alienated from its true and real Happiness.

Our Duty and Interest are inseparably united; and when we neglect or misuse our Talents, we necessarily depart from the heavenly Fellowship, and are in the Way to the greatest of Evils.

Therefore to examine and prove ourselves, to find what Harmony the Power presiding in us bears with the Divine Nature, is a Duty not more incumbent and necessary, than it would be beneficial.

In Holy Writ, the Divine Being saith of himself, *I am the Lord, which exercise Loving Kindness, Judgment and Righteousness in the Earth; for in these things I delight, saith the Lord.* Jer. ix. 24. Again, speaking in the Way of Man, to show his Compassion to *Israel* whose Wickedness had occasioned a Calamity, and then being humbled under it, it is said, *His Soul was grieved for their Miseries.* Judges x. 16. If we consider the Life of our Blessed Saviour when on Earth, as it is recorded by his Followers, we shall find that one uniform Desire for the eternal and temporal Good of Mankind, discovered itself in all his Actions.

If we observe Men, both Apostles and others, in many different Ages, who have really come to the Unity of the Spirit and the Fellowship of the Saints, there still appears the like Disposition, and in them the Desire of the real Happiness of Mankind, has outbalanced the Desire of Ease, Liberty, and many times Life itself.

If upon a true Search, we find that our Natures are so far renewed, that to exercise Righteousness and Loving Kindness (according to our Ability) towards all men, without Respect of Persons, is easy to us, or is our Delight; if our Love be so orderly and regular, that he who doth the Will of our Father who is in Heaven, appears in our View to be our nearest Relation, our Brother, and Sister, and Mother; if this be our Case, there is a good Foundation to Hope that the Blessing of God will sweeten our Treasures during our Stay in this Life, and our Memory be savory, when we are entered into Rest.

To conclude. 'Tis a Truth most certain, that a Life guided by the Wisdom from above, agreeable with Justice, Equity, and Mercy, is throughout consistent and amiable, and truly beneficial to Society; the Serenity and Calmness of Mind in it, affords an unparalleled Comfort in this Life, and the End of it is blessed.

And, no less true, that they who in the Midst of high Favours, remain ungrateful, and under all the Advantages that a Christian can desire, are selfish, earthly, and sensual, do miss the true Fountain of Happiness, and wander in a Maze of dark Anxiety, where all their Treasures are insufficient to quiet their Minds: Hence, from an insatiable Craving, they neglect doing Good with what they have acquired, and too often add Oppression to Vanity, that they may compass more.

O that they were Wise, that they understood this, that they would consider their latter End! Deut. xxxii. 29.

NOTES ON THE STATE OF VIRGINIA

Thomas Jefferson

[The existence of a slave system within an otherwise open and free society, and the race-thinking that accompanied and sometimes justified this condition, are periodically pointed to as the major failing of the American democratic experiment.

At the present time, historians are again re-evaluating the events that led to Appomattox and concluding that the central issue of the war was, indeed, that of slavery, and not—or not merely—political separation. The continuing second-class status of America's oldest (excepting the Indians) and now largest minority is seen by many to be more than just an embarrassment to the world's most powerful nation. It is, the critics argue, a cancer in the body politic that the patient still shows no signs of willingness to cure, if, indeed, it is curable at all. The cancer, of course, is identified as racism—the notion that America is wholly and fittingly a white man's country.

The disease began to be apparent sometime after 1660, but the tumor remained benign until the Revolutionary War with England. It began to spread after white Americans refused to extend the ideals that motivated their own war for independence to include the black-skinned people in their midst. The Civil War then can be seen as an operation that, despite the optimism generated in the period of convalescence—that is, Reconstruction—failed to cure the illness. The war and the constitutional amendments that followed, the argument continues, did abolish slavery, but the more pervasive idea that black men are naturally inferior to whites persists, threatening, in ever new ways, to undermine the Union.

Whether or not this represents a true or adequate history of a nation that has, however slowly, promoted and effected significant changes and improvements in the condition of black people is an open question. If one looks at the history of the discussion about racial issues—always conducted with a sense of urgency—it is difficult to escape the conclusion that much of what has been offered in the way of objective analysis has been motivated by a desire to defend or attack the Negro. This is especially true when the discussion centers around the Negro's supposed inferiority, an issue that has evoked controversy ever since Thomas Jefferson broached it in his *Notes on the State of Virginia.*

It is evidence of the staying power of Jefferson's book that the terms in which he formulated the issue are still widely employed. Thus, in his search for the "real distinction which nature has made" between whites and blacks, Jefferson focused not only on the obvious physical differences, but also on the Negro's mental abilities. Black men, he argued, have minds that are inferior to those of whites—a shortcoming produced by nature itself. This was not a happy conclusion for Jefferson, because, unlike most of those who argued for the Negro's inferiority, he was not presenting it as a proslavery argument. In fact, he was as much convinced of the Negro's right to freedom as he was of the folly of slavery. "Can the liberties of a nation," he remarked in the XVIIIth query of the *Notes,* "be thought secure when we have removed their only firm basis, a conviction in the minds of the people that these liberties are the gift of God? That they are not to be violated but with his wrath? Indeed I tremble for my country when I reflect that God is just; that his justice cannot sleep forever; that considering numbers, nature and natural means only, a revolution of the wheel of fortune, an exchange of situation is among possible events; that it may become probable by supernatural interference! The Almighty has no attribute which can take side with us [whites] in such a contest."

Nevertheless, Jefferson's words, as much as those of any man, helped to confirm the notion of Negro inferiority in the public mind. And, given these beliefs, it is not surprising that he approached the subject of emancipation in terms of subsequent colonization of blacks. If, as he felt, democratic government required an intelligent and educated electorate, then it was futile to suppose that the Negro could ever achieve political or social equality. It was in this context that Jefferson introduced his prejudices. "Why not retain and incorporate the blacks into the State," he asked in the XIVth query, "and thus save the expense of supplying by importation of white settlers, the vacancies they will leave?" The objections were obvious enough to him; they were political as well as physical and moral. He stated them in the XVIIIth query. "If a slave can have a country in this world, it must be any other in preference to that in which he is born to live and labor for another; in which he must lock up the faculties of his nature, contribute as far as depends upon his individual endeavors to the evanishment of the human race, or entail his own miserable condition on the endless generations proceeding from him." The slave's own previous condition thus made it mandatory that he leave the country after being freed. This, Jefferson was sure, was what an enlightened slave would want if he realized that his continued presence meant the eventual extinction of the human race! Faced with the evanishment of the human race or the possibility of race mixture (one suspects an equation of the two), whites would do better to "evanish" the Negro; and, indeed, as Jefferson's phrasing reveals, this was what he unconsciously wanted to do.

The *Notes*, which were begun in 1781 as a reply to a series of questions about Virginia asked by the Marquis de Barbé-Marbois (secretary of the French legation in Philadelphia), were not originally intended for publication. Among other reasons, Jefferson feared his antislavery sentiments would impede rather than hasten the cause of emancipation. In 1784, he reluctantly agreed to a small printing for private circulation, but, finding himself on his way to Paris, he took the manuscript with him. The first edition was a French translation published anonymously in Paris in 1785. An English edition (London, 1787), which was widely circulated, was the first to carry the author's name. A pirated edition appeared in Philadelphia in 1788. Thereafter, the career of the *Notes* paralleled the interest in Jefferson's public career, and, shortly after he became President, five new editions appeared. Query XIV, which contained the remarks on the Negro reprinted below, were a reply to the Marquis's inquiry about the administration of justice and the description of the laws in Virginia, of which, at the time Jefferson received the questionnaire, he was governor.]

Many of the laws which were in force during the monarchy being relative merely to that form of government, or inculcating principles inconsistent with republicanism, the first assembly which met after the establishment of the commonwealth appointed a committee to revise the whole code, to reduce it into proper form and volume, and report it to the assembly. This work has been executed by three gentlemen, and reported; but probably will not be taken up till a restoration of peace shall leave to the legislature leisure to go through such a work.

The plan of the revisal was this. The common law of England, by which is meant, that part of the English law which was anterior to the date of the oldest statutes extant, is made the basis of the work. It was thought dangerous to attempt to reduce it to a text; it was therefore left to be collected from the usual monuments of it. Necessary alterations in that, and so much of the whole body of the British statutes, and of acts of assembly, as were thought proper to be retained, were digested into one hundred and twenty-six new acts; in which simplicity of style was aimed at, as far as was safe. The following are the most remarkable alterations proposed:

To change the rules of descent, so as that the lands of any person dying intestate shall be divisible equally among all his children, or other representatives, in equal degree.

To make slaves distributable among the next of kin, as other movables.

To have all public expenses, whether of the general treasury, or of a parish or county, (as for the maintenance of the poor, building bridges court-houses, &c.,) supplied by assessment on the citizens, in proportion to their property.

To hire undertakers for keeping the public roads in repair, and indemnify individuals through whose lands new roads shall be opened.

To define with precision the rules whereby aliens should become citizens, and citizens make themselves aliens.

To establish religious freedom on the broadest bottom.

To emancipate all slaves born after the passing the act. The bill reported by the revisers does not itself contain this proposition; but an amendment containing it was prepared, to be offered to the legislature whenever the bill should be taken up, and farther directing, that they should continue with their parents to a certain age, then to be brought up, at the public expense, to tillage, arts, or sciences, according to their geniuses, till the females should be eighteen, and the males twenty-one years of age, when they should be colonized to such place as the circumstances of the time should render most proper, sending them out with arms, implements of household and of the handicraft arts, seeds, pairs of the useful domestic animals, &c., to declare them a free and independent people, and extend to them our alliance and protection, till they have acquired strength; and to send vessels at the same time to other parts of the world for an equal number of white inhabitants; to induce them to migrate hither, proper encouragements were to be proposed. It will probably be asked, Why not retain and incorporate the blacks into the State, and thus save the expense of supplying by importation of white settlers, the vacancies they will leave? Deep-rooted prejudices entertained by the whites; ten thousand recollections, by the blacks, of the injuries they have sustained; new provocations; the real distinctions which nature has made; and many other circumstances, will divide us into parties, and produce convulsions, which will probably never end but in the extermination of the one or the other race. To these objections, which are political, may be added others, which are physical and moral. The first difference which strikes us is that of color. Whether the black of the negro resides in the reticular membrane between the skin and scarf-skin, or in the scarf-skin itself; whether it proceeds from the color of the blood, the color of the bile, or from that of some other secretion, the difference is fixed in nature, and is as real as if its seat and cause were better known to us. And is this difference of no importance? Is it not the foundation of a greater or less share of beauty in the two races? Are not the fine mixtures of red and white, the expressions of every passion by greater or less suffusions of color in the one, preferable to that eternal monotony, which reigns in the countenances, that immovable veil of black which covers the emotions of the other race? Add to these, flowing hair, a more elegant symmetry of form, their own judgment in favor of the whites, declared by their preference of them, as uniformly as is the preference of the Oranootan for the black woman over those of his own species. The circumstance of superior beauty, is thought worthy attention in the propagation of our horses,

dogs, and other domestic animals; why not in that of man? Besides those
of color, figure, and hair, there are other physical distinctions proving a
difference of race. They have less hair on the face and body. They secrete
less by the kidneys, and more by the glands of the skin, which gives them
a very strong and disagreeable odor. This greater degree of transpiration,
renders them more tolerant of heat, and less so of cold than the whites.
Perhaps, too, a difference of structure in the pulminary apparatus, which
a late ingenious experimentalist has discovered to be the principal regu-
lator of animal heat, may have disabled them from extricating, in the
act of inspiration, so much of that fluid from the outer air, or obliged
them in expiration, to part with more of it. They seem to require less
sleep. A black after hard labor through the day, will be induced by the
slightest amusements to sit up till midnight, or later, though knowing
he must be out with the first dawn of the morning. They are at least as
brave, and more adventuresome. But this may perhaps proceed from a
want of forethought, which prevents their seeing a danger till it be
present. When present, they do not go through it with more coolness or
steadiness than the whites. They are more ardent after their female; but
love seems with them to be more an eager desire, than a tender delicate
mixture of sentiment and sensation. Their griefs are transient. Those
numberless afflictions, which render it doubtful whether heaven has
given life to us in mercy or in wrath, are less felt, and sooner forgotten
with them. In general, their existence appears to participate more of
sensation than reflection. To this must be ascribed their disposition to
sleep when abstracted from their diversions, and unemployed in labor.
An animal whose body is at rest, and who does not reflect, must be disposed to sleep of course. Comparing them by their faculties of memory,
reason, and imagination, it appears to me that in memory they are
equal to the whites; in reason much inferior, as I think one could scarcely
be found capable of tracing and comprehending the investigations of
Euclid; and that in imagination they are dull, tasteless, and anomalous.
It would be unfair to follow them to Africa for this investigation. We
will consider them here, on the same stage with the whites, and where
the facts are not apochryphal on which a judgment is to be formed. It
will be right to make great allowances for the difference of condition,
of education, of conversation, of the sphere in which they move. Many
millions of them have been brought to, and born in America. Most of
them, indeed, have been confined to tillage, to their own homes, and their
own society; yet many have been so situated, that they might have
availed themselves of the conversation of their masters; many have been
brought up to the handicraft arts, and from that circumstance have always been associated with the whites. Some have been liberally educated,
and all have lived in countries where the arts and sciences are cultivated
to a considerable degree, and all have had before their eyes samples of
the best works from abroad. The Indians, with no advantages of this
kind, will often carve figures on their pipes not destitute of design and
merit. They will crayon out an animal, a plant, or a country, so as to
prove the existence of a germ in their minds which only wants cultivation. They astonish you with strokes of the most sublime oratory; such

as prove their reason and sentiment strong, their imagination glowing and elevated. But never yet could I find that a black had uttered a thought above the level of plain narration; never saw even an elementary trait of painting or sculpture. In music they are more generally gifted than the whites with accurate ears for tune and time, and they have been found capable of imagining a small catch. Whether they will be equal to the composition of a more extensive run of melody, or of complicated harmony, is yet to be proved. Misery is often the parent of the most affecting touches in poetry. Among the blacks is misery enough, God knows, but no poetry. Love is the peculiar œstrum of the poet. Their love is ardent, but it kindles the senses only, not the imagination. Religion, indeed, has produced a Phyllis Whately; but it could not produce a poet. The compositions published under her name are below the dignity of criticism. The heroes of the Dunciad are to her, as Hercules to the author of that poem. Ignatius Sancho has approached nearer to merit in composition; yet his letters do more honor to the heart than the head. They breathe the purest effusions of friendship and general philanthropy, and show how great a degree of the latter may be compounded with strong religious zeal. He is often happy in the turn of his compliments, and his style is easy and familiar, except when he affects a Shandean fabrication of words. But his imagination is wild and extravagant, escapes incessantly from every restraint of reason and taste, and, in the course of its vagaries, leaves a tract of thought as incoherent and eccentric, as is the course of a meteor through the sky. His subjects should often have led him to a process of sober reasoning; yet we find him always substituting sentiment for demonstration. Upon the whole, though we admit him to the first place among those of his own color who have presented themselves to the public judgment, yet when we compare him with the writers of the race among whom he lived and particularly with the epistolary class in which he has taken his own stand, we are compelled to enrol him at the bottom of the column. This criticism supposes the letters published under his name to be genuine, and to have received amendment from no other hand; points which would not be of easy investigation. The improvement of the blacks in body and mind, in the first instance of their mixture with the whites, has been observed by every one, and proves that their inferiority is not the effect merely of their condition of life. We know that among the Romans, about the Augustan age especially, the condition of their slaves was much more deplorable than that of the blacks on the continent of America. The two sexes were confined in separate apartments, because to raise a child cost the master more than to buy one. Cato, for a very restricted indulgence to his slaves in this particular, took from them a certain price. But in this country the slaves multiply as fast as the free inhabitants. Their situation and manners place the commerce between the two sexes almost without restraint. The same Cato, on a principle of economy, always sold his sick and superannuated slaves. He gives it as a standing precept to a master visiting his farm, to sell his old oxen, old wagons, old tools, old and diseased servants, and everything else become useless. "Vendat boves vetulos, plaustrum vetus, feramenta vetera, servum senem, servum mor-

bosum, et si quid aliud supersit vendat." Cato de re rustica, c. 2. The
American slaves cannot enumerate this among the injuries and insults
they receive. It was the common practice to expose in the island Æscu-
lapius, in the Tyber, diseased slaves whose cure was like to become
tedious. The emperor Claudius, by an edict, gave freedom to such of
them as should recover, and first declared that if any person chose to
kill rather than to expose them, it should not be deemed homicide. The
exposing them is a crime of which no instance has existed with us; and
were it to be followed by death, it would be punished capitally. We are
told of a certain Vedius Pollio, who, in the presence of Augustus, would
have given a slave as food to his fish, for having broken a glass. With
the Romans, the regular method of taking the evidence of their slaves
was under torture. Here it has been thought better never to resort to
their evidence. When a master was murdered, all his slaves, in the same
house, or within hearing, were condemned to death. Here punishment
falls on the guilty only, and as precise proof is required against him as
against a freeman. Yet notwithstanding these and other discouraging
circumstances among the Romans, their slaves were often their rarest
artists. They excelled too in science, insomuch as to be usually employed
as tutors to their master's children. Epictetus, Terence, and Phædrus,
were slaves. But they were of the race of whites. It is not their condition
then, but nature, which has produced the distinction. Whether further
observation will or will not verify the conjecture, that nature has been
less bountiful to them in the endowments of the head, I believe that in
those of the heart she will be found to have done them justice. That
disposition to theft with which they have been branded, must be ascribed
to their situation, and not to any depravity of the moral sense. The man
in whose favor no laws of property exist, probably feels himself less
bound to respect those made in favor of others. When arguing for ourselves, we lay it down as a fundamental, that laws, to be just, must give
a reciprocation of right; that, without this, they are mere arbitrary rules
of conduct, founded in force, and not in conscience; and it is a problem
which I give to the master to solve, whether the religious precepts
against the violation of property were not framed for him as well as his
slave? And whether the slave may not as justifiably take a little from one
who has taken all from him, as he may slay one who would slay him?
That a change in the relations in which a man is placed should change
his ideas of moral right or wrong, is neither new, nor peculiar to the
color of the blacks. Homer tells us it was so two thousand six hundred
years ago.

> 'Emisu, ger t' aretes apoainutai euruopa Zeus
> Haneros, eut' an min kata doulion ema elesin.
>
> Odd. 17, 323.
>
> Jove fix'd it certain, that whatever day
> Makes man a slave, takes half his worth away.

But the slaves of which Homer speaks were whites. Notwithstanding
these considerations which must weaken their respect for the laws of
property, we find among them numerous instances of the most rigid

integrity, and as many as among their better instructed masters, of benevolence, gratitude, and unshaken fidelity. The opinion that they are inferior in the faculties of reason and imagination, must be hazarded with great diffidence. To justify a general conclusion, requires many observations, even where the subject may be submitted to the anatomical knife, to optical glasses, to analysis by fire or by solvents. How much more then where it is a faculty, not a substance, we are examining; where it eludes the research of all the senses; where the conditions of its existence are various and variously combined; where the effects of those which are present or absent bid defiance to calculation; let me add too, as a circumstance of great tenderness, where our conclusion would degrade a whole race of men from the rank in the scale of beings which their Creator may perhaps have given them. To our reproach it must be said, that though for a century and a half we have had under our eyes the races of black and of red men, they have never yet been viewed by us as subjects of natural history. I advance it, therefore, as a suspicion only, that the blacks, whether originally a distinct race, or made distinct by time and circumstances, are inferior to the whites in the endowments both of body and mind. It is not against experience to suppose that different species of the same genus, or varieties of the same species, may possess different qualifications. Will not a lover of natural history then, one who views the gradations in all the races of animals with the eye of philosophy, excuse an effort to keep those in the department of man as distinct as nature has formed them? This unfortunate difference of color, and perhaps of faculty, is a powerful obstacle to the emancipation of these people. Many of their advocates, while they wish to vindicate the liberty of human nature, are anxious also to preserve its dignity and beauty. Some of these, embarrassed by the question, "What further is to be done with them?" join themselves in opposition with those who are actuated by sordid avarice only. Among the Romans emancipation required but one effort. The slave, when made free, might mix with, without staining the blood of his master. But with us a second is necessary, unknown to history. When freed, he is to be removed beyond the reach of mixture.

COPY OF A LETTER FROM BENJAMIN BANNEKER TO THE SECRETARY OF STATE WITH HIS ANSWER

[The abrupt crystallization of opposed views often marks the appearance of forces that are becoming operative for the first time. The operation of these forces can be detected in the formation of attitudes, beliefs, and institutions, as well as in the theories of individual thinkers, all of which give form to the unconscious tendencies of a people.

The publication of the *Notes on the State of Virginia*, in 1787, marked a sudden interest in the question of Negro mental ability. There is no doubt that Jefferson stimulated others to take up the theme; but the date also suggests another preoccupation of the Americans. The *Federalist* papers, which first appeared as newspaper columns in 1787 and 1788, were justifying and promoting a new government providing for the regular election of officeholders and the regular review of policy. The Constitution embodied new ideas of political responsibility; but it almost entirely excluded the Negro from participation in the new government. (The Constitution, of course, excluded women, too; but the nation had not yet awakened to *that* problem.) Thus, it is surely not accidental that criteria by which to judge the Negro's acceptability and to justify his rejection were being eagerly sought at a time when the new nation was being formed. Once the criteria were established as intellectual— thanks largely to Jefferson's book—the defenders of Negro ability developed some form of the environmentalist argument to excuse Negro backwardness and often buttressed their claims by appealing to the achievements of individual Negroes.

The most celebrated example of Negro genius brought forward was Benjamin Banneker, whose almanacs were offered as evidence that intellectual ability was not connected with skin color. The publishers, in their preface to the first almanac (Baltimore, 1791), made this purpose explicit and, in addition, cited the approbation of David Rittenhouse, the most eminent American astronomer of the time. Banneker himself sent a copy of his first almanac to Jefferson, then Secretary of State, who had seemed to go out of his way in the *Notes* to belittle the work of Phyllis Wheatley. (Miss Wheatley—Jefferson had misspelled her name as "Whately"—was the first American Negro to publish a volume of verse, and the defenders of Negro equality had been parading her as a prize specimen.) The evasiveness of Jefferson's reply neither contradicted the *Notes* nor offended Banneker, whom Jefferson had nominated to be a member of the commission charged with surveying the new national district. The two letters were soon published together as a pamphlet (Philadelphia, 1792), together with the publishers' preface to the first almanac. The pamphlet is reprinted here in its entirety.

The difficulties of Jefferson's position on the Negro were as much philosophical as political. He apparently had no doubt (as others probably did) that the Negro was, in some sense, human and capable of moral restraint, but he was much less sure that he had enough innate intelligence to qualify as a full-fledged member of the species *homo sapiens*. Essentially, the devastating problem was whether the Negro's deficiencies were owing to nature or to nurture. If nature, then Jefferson was in trouble with his own words in the Declaration of Independence; for, if the Negro's supposed lack of intelligence reflected a difference of kind in the order of created beings, then Jefferson's position was in danger of being self-contradictory. But if the defect was merely in nurture, if it was only that blacks heretofore had received an inadequate education, then there was no theoretical reason why good black schools should not raise the race to equality with white men. This conclusion, in turn, implied that the Negro could eventually take his place in white society—a result that Jefferson simply could not face, on aesthetic grounds (as he made clear in the *Notes*) if on no other. Jefferson vacillated between the two views for a number of years. In the end, he must have realized that his position had become a muddle; in any event, he grew increasingly silent about the future of the black man in America.]

Maryland, Baltimore County, August 19, 1791

I am fully sensible of the greatness of that freedom, which I take with you on the present occasion; a liberty which seemed to me scarcely allowable, when I reflected on that distinguished and dignified station in which you stand, and the almost general prejudice and prepossession, which is so prevalent in the world against those of my complexion.

I suppose it is a truth too well attested to you, to need a proof here, that we are a race of beings, who have long labored under the abuse and censure of the world; that we have long been looked upon with an eye of contempt; and that we have long been considered rather as brutish than human, and scarcely capable of mental endowments.

Sir, I hope I may safely admit, in consequence of that report which hath reached me, that you are a man less inflexible in sentiments of this nature, than many others; that you are measurably friendly, and well disposed towards us; and that you are willing and ready to lend your aid and assistance to our relief, from those many distresses, and numerous calamities, to which we are reduced.

Now Sir, if this is founded in truth, I apprehend you will embrace every opportunity, to eradicate that train of absurd and false ideas and opinions, which so generally prevails with respect to us; and that your sentiments are concurrent with mine, which are, that one universal Father hath given being to us all; and that he hath not only made us all of one flesh, but that he hath also, without partiality, afforded us all the same sensations and endowed us all with the same faculties; and that however variable we may be in society or religion, however diversified in situation or color, we are all of the same family, and stand in the same relation to him.

Sir, if these are sentiments of which you are fully persuaded, I hope you cannot but acknowledge, that it is the indispensable duty of those, who maintain for themselves the rights of human nature, and who possess the obligations of Christianity, to extend their power and influence to the relief of every part of the human race, from whatever burden or oppression they may unjustly labor under; and this, I apprehend, a full conviction of the truth and obligation of these principles should lead all to.

Sir, I have long been convinced, that if your love for yourselves, and for those inestimable laws, which preserved to you the rights of human nature, was founded on sincerity, you could not but be solicitous, that every individual, of whatever rank or distinction, might with you equally enjoy the blessings thereof; neither could you rest satisfied short of the most active effusion of your exertions, in order to their promotion from any state of degradation, to which the unjustifiable cruelty and barbarism of men may have reduced them.

Sir, I freely and cheerfully acknowledge, that I am of the African race, and in that color which is natural to them of the deepest dye; and it is under a sense of the most profound gratitude to the Supreme Ruler of the Universe, that I now confess to you, that I am not under that state of tyrannical thraldom, and inhuman captivity, to which too many of my brethren are doomed, but that I have abundantly tasted of the fruition of those blessings, which proceed from that free and unequalled liberty with which you are favored; and which, I hope, you will willingly allow you have mercifully received, from the immediate hand of that Being, from whom proceedeth every good and perfect Gift.

Sir, suffer me to recall to your mind that time, in which the arms and tyranny of the British crown were exerted, with every powerful effort, in order to reduce you to a state of servitude: look back, I entreat you, on the variety of dangers to which you were exposed; reflect on that time, in which every human aid appeared unavailable, and in which even hope and fortitude wore the aspect of inability to the conflict, and you cannot but be led to a serious and grateful sense of your miraculous and providential preservation; you cannot but acknowledge, that the present freedom and tranquility which you enjoy you have mercifully received, and that it is the peculiar blessing of Heaven.

This, Sir, was a time when you clearly saw into the injustice of a state of slavery, and in which you had just apprehensions of the horrors of its condition. It was now that your abhorrence thereof was so excited, that you publicly held forth this true and invaluable doctrine, which is worthy to be recorded, and remembered in all succeeding ages: 'We hold these truths to be self-evident, that all men are created equal; that they are endowed by their Creator with certain unalienable rights, and that among these are, life, liberty, and the pursuit of happiness.'

Here was a time, in which your tender feelings for yourselves had engaged you thus to declare, you were then impressed with proper ideas of the great violation of liberty, and the free possession of those blessings, to which you were entitled by nature; but, Sir, how pitiable is it to reflect, that although you were so fully convinced of the benevolence of the Father of Mankind, and of his equal and impartial distribution of these rights and privileges, which he hath conferred upon them, that you should at the same time counteract his mercies, in detaining by fraud and violence so numerous a part of my brethren, under groaning captivity and cruel oppression, that you should at the same time be found guilty of that most criminal act, which you professedly detested in others, with respect to yourselves.

I suppose that your knowledge of the situation of my brethren, is too extensive to need a recital here; neither shall I presume to prescribe methods by which they may be relieved, otherwise than by recommending to you and all others, to wean yourselves from those narrow prejudices which you have imbibed with respect to them, and as Job proposed to his friends, 'put your soul in their souls' stead;' thus shall your hearts be enlarged with kindness and benevolence towards them; and thus shall you need neither the direction of myself or others, in what manner to proceed herein.

And now, Sir, although my sympathy and affection for my brethren hath caused my enlargement thus far, I ardently hope, that your candor and generosity will plead with you in my behalf, when I make known to you, that it was not originally my design; but having taken up my pen in order to direct to you, as a present, a copy of an Almanac, which I have calculated for the succeeding year, I was unexpectedly and unavoidably led thereto.

This calculation is the product of my arduous study, in this my advanced stage of life; for having long had unbounded desires to become acquainted with the secrets of nature, I have had to gratify my curiosity herein, through my own assiduous application to Astronomical Study, in which I need not recount to you the many difficulties and disadvantages, which I have had to encounter.

And although I had almost declined to make my calculation for the ensuing year, in consequence of that time which I had allotted therefor, being taken up at the Federal Territory, by the request of Mr. Andrew Ellicott, yet finding myself under several engagements to Printers of this State, to whom I had communicated my design, on my return to my place of residence, I industriously applied myself thereto, which I hope I have accomplished with correctness and accuracy; a copy of which I have taken the liberty to direct to you, and which I humbly request you will favorably receive; and although you may have the opportunity of perusing it after its publication, yet I choose to send it to you in manuscript previous thereto, that thereby you might not only have an earlier inspection, but that you might also view it in my own hand writing.

And now, Sir, I shall conclude, and subscribe myself, with the most profound respect,

Your most obedient and humble servant,

BENJAMIN BANNEKER

Philadelphia, August 30, 1791

I thank you, sincerely, for your letter of the 19th instant, and for the Almanac it contained. No body wishes more than I do, to see such proofs as you exhibit, that nature has given to our black brethren talents equal to those of the other colors of men; and that the appearance of the want of them, is owing merely to the degraded condition of their existence, both in Africa and America. I can add with truth, that no body wishes more ardently to see a good system commenced, for raising the condition, both of their body and mind, to what it ought to be, as far as the imbecility of their present existence, and other circumstances, which cannot be neglected, will admit.

I have taken the liberty of sending your Almanac to Monsieur de Condozett, Secretary of the Academy of Sciences at Paris, and Member of the Philanthropic Society, because I considered it as a document, to which your whole color had a right for their justification, against the doubts which have been entertained of them.

I am with great esteem, Sir,

Your most obedient

Humble Servant,

THOMAS JEFFERSON

The following Account, taken from BANNEKER'S Almanac, is inserted here, for the Information of the Public.

Baltimore, August 20, 1791

BENJAMIN BANNEKER, a free Black, is about 59 years of age: he was born in Baltimore county; his father an African, and his mother the offspring of African parents. His father and mother having obtained their freedom, were enabled to send him to an obscure school, where he learned, when a boy, reading, writing, and arithmetic, as far as double position; and to leave him, at their deaths, a few acres of land, upon which he has supported himself ever since, by means of economy and constant labor, and preserved a fair reputation. To struggle incessantly against want, is no ways favorable to improvement: what he had learned, however, he did not forget; for as some hours of leisure will occur, in the most toilsome life, he availed himself of these, not to read and acquire knowledge, from writings of genius and discovery, for of such he had none, but to digest and apply, as occasions presented, the few principles of the few rules of arithmetic he had been taught at school. This kind of mental exercise formed his chief amusement, and soon gave him a facility in calculation that was often serviceable to his neighbours, and at length attracted the attention of the Messrs. Ellicott, a family remarkable for their ingenuity and turn to the useful mechanics. It is about three years since Mr. George Ellicott lent him Mayer's Tables, Ferguson's Astronomy, Leadbeater's Lunar Tables, and some Astronomic Instruments, but without accompanying them with either hint or instruction, that might further his studies, or lead him to apply them to any useful result. These books and instruments, the first of the kind he had ever seen, opened a new world to Benjamin, and from thenceforward he employed his leisure in Astronomical Researches.

He now took up the idea of the calculations for an Almanac, and actually completed an entire set for the last year, upon his original stock of Arithmetic. Encouraged by this first attempt, he entered upon his calculation for 1792, which, as well as the former, he begun and finished without the least information or assistance from any person, or other books than those I have mentioned; so that whatever merit is attached to his present performance, is exclusively and peculiarly his own.

I have been the more careful to investigate those particulars, and to ascertain their reality, as they form an interesting fact in the History of Man; and as you may want them to gratify curiosity, I have no objection to your selecting them for your account of Benjamin.

ESSAY ON NEGRO SLAVERY

"Othello"

[Before Columbus opened up the New World market, the slave trade, monopolized first by Italian and Turkish traders and then by the Portuguese and Spanish, was largely confined to the Mediterranean basin. Most black slaves came from East Africa, whence they were conveyed by Arab middlemen to Cyprus, which was the center of the trade prior to the fifteenth century. Around 1440, Portuguese captains under Prince Henry the Navigator began to sail around the bulge of Africa to the Gold, Ivory, and Grain coasts (so named because of the main type of currency in which slave trading was later carried on) and to transport the first Negroes to the Iberian peninsula. The Portuguese established factories (trading posts) along the coast of Guinea and in the area between the Senegal River (Cape Verde) and the Niger River Delta. Ultimately, this coastal area, with the inland territory that it served, became the source of most of the blacks who were brought to America.

The English did not become the leading slave-trading nation until about 1700. The first English company was chartered in 1660—earlier English trader-adventurers like Sir John Hawkins had been essentially bootleggers, operating in defiance of the Portuguese and Spanish monopoly—and was the sole English company operating until 1698. After that date, other companies began to compete, and the trade boomed. Between 1680 and 1780, the annual British trade in slaves grew from 5,000 to 74,000.

Slave ships generally followed a triangular route. Setting out from English, Dutch, French, Spanish, and, later, American ports, with different cargoes (depending on their destination) and bearing gifts with which to initiate negotiations with the African chieftains, they sailed directly to the West African coast. After a slave cargo was obtained, the ships usually sailed for the West Indies. This leg of the triangle, which took from forty to sixty days, was known as the "middle passage" and usually proved to be the most brutal part of the Negroes' journey to the New World. (It was for them a "middle passage," too: between their journey from the point of capture in their homeland down to the African coast, and the subsequent journey, after a "seasoning" period in the West Indies, to a plantation either in the Caribbean or in the American colonies.) The ships sailed back to Europe on the third leg of the triangle laden with sugar and rum or, if they had touched at a colonial port, with tobacco.

As the trade, and the profits, grew, elaborate defenses of slavery were constructed. But, late in the 18th century, moral and religious disapproval of slavery also mounted, both in Europe and in the colonies. The influence of men like John Woolman, who traveled widely in the colonies and also visited England, was instrumental in persuading some owners to manumit their slaves. English Quakers, the most outspoken critics of slavery, began to campaign against the trade in 1783. In the colonies, antislavery sentiment received support, especially in the North, from the fervor for independence, with its ideal of equal rights for all men. Indeed, the Revolution presented a highly promising occasion for a legal solution of the slavery problem. Washington and Franklin spoke out against the institution. Jefferson's first draft of the Declaration of Independence listed the slave trade as one of the grievances against the British Crown. In the charged atmosphere after independence was achieved, many whites saw clearly that the new principles demanded the end of a system of bondage that could ultimately only undermine the nation's existence. And it was in this atmosphere that slavery was legally abolished in the North (between 1777 and 1804, by all the states north of Maryland), and manumission was encouraged in Virginia (which had 40 per cent of the Negro population) and North Carolina.

This was, for the time being at least, the extent of the antislavery achievement. The final draft of the Declaration had deleted the reference to the slave trade, for the sake of acceptance by the Southern colonies and Northern shippers. The "three-fifths" compromise was written into the Constitution, which also permitted the trade an extension of twenty years of life. The trade was thus abolished in 1807; but, only the year before, Virginia had amended a 1782 law and severely restricted manumissions. The demand for this change, ironically, began immediately after the discovery of the Gabriel Prosser plot (see p. 107). Evidently the revolutionary ideology was sufficient to abolish slavery in the North, where the small number of blacks helped to quell uneasiness about any future amalgamation of the races. In the South, a much larger number of Negroes and a more well-entrenched institution presented insuperable problems for white men who could not yet abide the thought of a black citizenry.

The "Essay on negro slavery" reprinted here first appeared in two issues of the *American Museum* (November and December 1788), a magazine that had begun publication shortly after the Revolution. It was signed by "Othello," ostensibly a free Negro from Maryland who is sometimes thought to have been Benjamin Banneker. The essay is typical of the antislavery writings that were produced in large numbers by aboli-

tionist circles in England and America. It shows evidence that its author
was familiar with Jefferson's *Notes on the State of Virginia*, which had
appeared the previous year. Othello's suggestion that immediate emancipation be coupled with colonization in the western territories was
fairly typical of border-state sentiment. That particular locale was
abandoned, however, after more and more Americans began to envision
the West as part of the growing nation.]

Amidst the infinite variety of moral and political subjects proper for
public commendation, it is truly surprising that one of the most important and affecting should be so very generally neglected. An encroach-
ment on the smallest civil or religious privilege shall fan the enthusiastic
flame of liberty till it shall extend over vast and distant regions, and
violently agitate a whole continent. But the cause of humanity shall be
basely violated, justice shall be wounded to the heart, and national honor
deeply and lastingly polluted, and not a breath or murmur shall arise
to disturb the prevailing quiescence or to rouse the feelings of indignation against such general, extensive, and complicated iniquity.—To
what cause are we to impute this frigid silence—this torpid indifference
—this cold inanimated conduct of the otherwise warm and generous
Americans?—Why do they remain inactive amidst the groans of injured
humanity, the shrill and distressing complaints of expiring justice and
the keen remorse of polluted integrity?—Why do they not rise up to
assert the cause of God and the world, to drive the fiend injustice into
remote and distant regions, and to exterminate oppression from the
face of the fair fields of America?

When the united colonies revolted from Great Britain, they did it upon
this principle, "that all men are by nature and of right ought to be
free."—After a long, successful, and glorious struggle for liberty, during
which they manifested the firmest attachment to the rights of mankind,
can they so soon forget the principles that then governed their determina-
tions? Can Americans, after the noble contempt they expressed for tyrants, meanly descend to take up the scourge? Blush, ye revolted colonies, for having apostatized from your own principles.

Slavery, in whatever point of light it is considered, is repugnant to
the feelings of nature, and inconsistent with the original rights of man.
It ought, therefore, to be stigmatized for being unnatural; and detested
for being unjust. 'Tis an outrage to providence and an affront offered
to divine Majesty, who has given to man his own peculiar image.—That
the Americans, after considering the subject in this light—after making

the most manly of all possible exertions in defense of liberty—after publishing to the world the principle upon which they contended, viz., "that all men are by nature and of right ought to be free," should still retain in subjection a numerous tribe of the human race merely for their own private use and emolument, is, of all things, the strongest inconsistency, the deepest reflection on our conduct, and the most abandoned apostasy that ever took place since the Almighty fiat spoke into existence this habitable world. So flagitious a violation can never escape the notice of a just Creator, whose vengeance may be now on the wing, to disseminate and hurl the arrows of destruction.

In what light can the people of Europe consider America after the strange inconsistency of her conduct? Will they not consider her as an abandoned and deceitful country? In the hour of calamity she petitioned heaven to be propitious to her cause. Her prayers were heard. Heaven pitied her distress, smiled on her virtuous exertions, and vanquished all her afflictions. The ungrateful creature forgets this timely assistance —no longer remembers her own sorrows—but basely commences oppression in her turn.—Beware, America! pause—and consider the difference between the mild effulgence of approving Providence and the angry countenance of incensed divinity!

The importation of slaves into America ought to be a subject of the deepest regret to every benevolent and thinking mind.—And one of the greatest defects in the federal system is the liberty it allows on this head. Venerable in everything else, it is injudicious here; and it is to be much deplored that a system of so much political perfection should be stained with anything that does an outrage to human nature. As a door, however, is open to amendment, for the sake of distressed humanity, of injured national reputation, and the glory of doing so benevolent a thing, I hope some wise and virtuous patriot will advocate the measure, and introduce an alteration in that pernicious part of the government.—So far from encouraging the importation of slaves, and countenancing that vile traffic in human flesh, the members of the late continental convention should have seized the happy opportunity of prohibiting forever this cruel species of reprobated villainy.—That they did not do so will forever diminish the luster of their other proceedings, so highly extolled and so justly distinguished for their intrinsic value.—Let us for a moment contrast the sentiments and actions of the Europeans on this subject with those of our own countrymen. In France the warmest and most animated exertions are making, in order to introduce the entire abolition of the slave trade; and in England many of the first characters of the country advocate the same measure with an enthusiastic philanthropy. The Prime Minister himself is at the head of that society, and nothing can equal the ardor of their endeavors but the glorious goodness of the cause.—Will the Americans allow the people of England to get the start of them in acts of humanity? Forbid it, shame!

The practice of stealing or bartering for human flesh is pregnant with the most glaring turpitude, and the blackest barbarity of disposition.— For can any one say that this is doing as he would be done by? Will such a practice stand the scrutiny of this great rule of moral government? Who can, without the complicated emotions of anger and impatience, suppose himself in the predicament of a slave? Who can bear the thoughts of his relations being torn from him by a savage enemy; carried to distant regions of the habitable globe, never more to return; and treated there as the unhappy Africans are in this country? Who can support the reflection of his father—his mother—his sister—or his wife—perhaps his children—being barbarously snatched away by a foreign invader, without the prospect of ever beholding them again? Who can reflect upon their being afterwards publicly exposed to sale—obliged to labor with unwearied assiduity—and because all things are not possible to be performed by persons so unaccustomed to robust exercise, scourged with all the rage and anger of malignity until their unhappy carcasses are covered with ghastly wounds and frightful contusions? Who can reflect on these things when applying the case to himself without being chilled with horror at circumstances so extremely shocking? —Yet hideous as this concise and imperfect description is of the sufferings sustained by many of our slaves, it is nevertheless true; and so far from being exaggerated, falls infinitely short of a thousand circumstances of distress, which have been recounted by different writers on the subject and which contribute to make their situation in this life the most absolutely wretched and completely miserable that can possibly be conceived.—In many places in America the slaves are treated with every circumstance of rigorous inhumanity, accumulated hardship, and enormous cruelty.—Yet when we take them from Africa we deprive them of a country which God hath given them for their own; as free as we are, and as capable of enjoying that blessing. Like pirates we go to commit devastation on the coast of an innocent country, and among a people who never did us wrong.

An insatiable, avaricious desire to accumulate riches, cooperating with a spirit of luxury and injustice, seems to be the leading cause of this peculiarly degrading and ignominious practice. Being once accustomed to subsist without labor, we become soft and voluptuous; and rather than afterwards forego the gratification of our habitual indolence and ease, we countenance the infamous violation, and sacrifice at the shrine of cruelty, all the finer feelings of elevated humanity.

Considering things in this view, there surely can be nothing more justly reprehensible or disgusting than the extravagant finery of many country people's daughters. It hath not been at all uncommon to observe as much gauze, lace, and other trappings on one of those country maidens as hath employed two or three of her father's slaves for twelve months afterwards to raise tobacco to pay for. It is an ungrateful reflection that all this frippery and affected finery can only be supported by the sweat of another person's brow, and consequently only by lawful rapine and injustice. If these young females could devote as much time from their amusements as would be necessary for reflection; or was there any person of humanity at hand who could inculcate the indecency of this kind of extravagance, I am persuaded that they have hearts good enough to reject with disdain the momentary pleasure of making a figure in

behalf of the rational and lasting delight of contributing by their forbearance to the happiness of many thousand individuals.

In Maryland, where slaves are treated with as much lenity as perhaps
they are anywhere, their situation is to the last degree ineligible. They
live in wretched cots that scarcely secure them from the inclemency of
the weather; sleep in the ashes or on straw; wear the coarsest clothing,
and subsist on the most ordinary food that the country produces. In
all things they are subject to their master's absolute command; and, of
course, have no will of their own. Thus circumstanced, they are subject
to great brutality, and are often treated with it. In particular instances
they may be better provided for in this state, but this suffices for a
general description. But in the Carolinas and in the island of Jamaica
the cruelties that have been wantonly exercised on those miserable
creatures are without a precedent in any other part of the world. If
those who have written on the subject may be believed, it is not uncommon there to tie a slave up and whip him to death.

On all occasions impartiality in the distribution of justice should be
observed. The little State of Rhode Island hath been reprobated by other
States for refusing to enter into measures respecting a new general
government; and so far it is admitted that she is culpable. But if she
is worthy of blame in this respect, she is entitled to the highest admiration for the philanthropy, justice, and humanity she hath displayed
respecting the subject I am treating on. She hath passed an act prohibiting the importation of slaves into that State, and forbidding her citizens
to engage in the iniquitous traffic. So striking a proof of her strong
attachment to the rights of humanity will rescue her name from oblivion
and bid her live in the good opinion of distant and unborn generations.

Slavery unquestionably should be abolished, particularly in this country; because it is inconsistent with the declared principles of the American Revolution. The sooner, therefore, we set about it the better. Either
we should set all our slaves at liberty immediately and colonize them in
the western territory, or we should immediately take measures for the
gradual abolition of it, so that it may become a known and fixed point
that ultimately universal liberty in these united states shall triumph.—
This is the least we can do in order to evince our sense of the irreparable
outrages we have committed, to wipe off the odium we have incurred,
and to give mankind a confidence again in the justice, liberality, and
honor of our national proceedings.

It would not be difficult to show, were it necessary, that America
would soon become a richer and more happy country provided this
step was adopted. That corrosive anguish of persevering in anything
improper, which now embitters the enjoyments of life, would vanish
as the mist of a foggy morn doth before the rising sun; and we should
find as great a disparity between our present situation, and that which
would succeed to it, as subsists between a cloudy winter and a radiant
spring.—Besides, our lands would not be then cut down for the support
of a numerous train of useless inhabitants—useless, I mean, to themselves, and effectually so to us by encouraging sloth and voluptuousness

among our young farmers and planters, who might otherwise know how to take care of their money as well as how to dissipate it.—In all other respects, I conceive them to be as valuable as we are—as capable of worthy purposes, and to possess the same dignity that we do, in the estimation of Providence; although the value of their work apart, for which we are dependent on them, we generally consider them as good for nothing, and accordingly treat them with the greatest neglect.

But be it remembered that their cause is the cause of heaven; and that the father of them as well as of us will not fail, at a future settlement, to adjust the account between us with a dreadful attention to justice.

Upon no better principle do we plunder the coasts of Africa and bring away its wretched inhabitants as slaves than that by which the greater fish swallows up the lesser. Superior power seems only to produce superior brutality; and that weakness and imbecility, which ought to engage our protection and interest the feelings of social benevolence in behalf of the defenseless, seems only to provoke us to acts of illiberal outrage and unmanly violence.

The practice which has been followed by the English nation since the establishment of the slave trade—I mean that of stirring up the natives of Africa against each other with a view of purchasing the prisoners mutually taken in battle—must strike the humane mind with sentiments of the deepest abhorrence, and confer on that people a reproach as lasting as time itself. It is surprising that the eastern world did not unite to discourage a custom so diabolical in its tendency, and to exterminate a species of oppression which humbles the dignity of all mankind. But this torpid inattention can only be accounted for by adverting to the savage disposition of the times which countenanced cruelties unheard of at this enlightened period. What rudeness of demeanor and brutality of manner, which had been introduced into Europe by those swarms of barbarians that overwhelmed it from the North, had hardly begun to dissipate before the enlivening sun of civilization, when this infernal practice first sprang up into existence! Before this distinguished era of refined barbarity the sons of Africa were in possession of all the mild enjoyments of peace—all the pleasing delights of uninterrupted harmony—and all the diffusive blessings of profound tranquillity. Boundless must be the punishment which an irritated Providence will inflict on those whose wanton cruelty has prompted them to destroy this fair arrangement of nature—this flowery prospect of human felicity. Engulfed in the dark abyss of never ending misery, they shall in bitterness atone for the stab thus given to human nature, and in anguish unutterable expiate crimes for which nothing less than eternal sufferings can make adequate retribution! Equally iniquitous is the practice of robbing that country of its inhabitants; and equally tremendous will be the punishment. The voice of injured thousands who have been violently torn from their native country and carried to distant and inhospitable climes—the bitter lamentations of the wretched, helpless female—the cruel, agonizing sensations of the husband, the father and the friend—will ascend to the throne of Omnipotence, and, from the elevated heights of heaven, cause him, with the whole force of Almighty vengeance, to hurl the guilty perpetrators of those inhuman deeds down the steep precipice of inevitable ruin into the bottomless gulf of final, irretrievable and endless destruction!

Ye sons of America, forbear!—Consider the dire consequences that will attend the prosecution of a practice, against which the all-powerful God of nature holds up his hands and loudly proclaims, desist!

In the insolence of self-consequence we are accustomed to esteem ourselves and the Christian powers of Europe the only civilized people on the globe; the rest, without distinction, we presumptuously denominate barbarians. But, when the practices above mentioned come to be deliberately considered—when added to these we take a view of the proceedings of the English in the East Indies, under the direction of the late Lord Clive, and remember what happened in the streets of Bengal and Calcutta—when we likewise reflect on our American mode of driving, butchering and exterminating the poor defenseless Indians, the native and lawful proprietors of the soil—we shall acknowledge, if we possess the smallest degree of candor, that the appellation of barbarian does not belong to them alone. While we continue those practices the term Christian will only be a burlesque expression signifying no more than that it ironically denominates the rudest set of barbarians that ever disgraced the hands of their Creator. We have the precepts of the gospel for the government of our moral deportment, in violation of which those outrageous wrongs are committed; but they have no such meliorating influence among them, and only adhere to the simple dictates of reason and natural religion, which they never violate.

Might not the inhabitants of Africa, with still greater justice on their side than we have on ours, cross the Atlantic, seize our citizens, carry them into Africa, and make slaves of them, provided they were able to do it? But should this be really the case, every corner of the globe would reverberate with the sound of African oppression, so loud would be our complaint and so "feeling our appeal" to the inhabitants of the world at large. We should represent them as a lawless, piratical set of unprincipled robbers, plunderers and villains, who basely prostituted the superior power and information which God had given them for worthy purposes to the vilest of all ends. We should not hesitate to say that they made use of those advantages only to infringe every dictate of justice, to trample under foot every suggestion of principle, and to spurn with contempt every right of humanity.

The Algerines are reprobated all the world over for their unlawful depredations, and stigmatized as pirates for their unreasonable exactions from foreign nations. But the Algerines are no greater pirates than the Americans; nor are they a race more destructive to the happiness of mankind. The depredations of the latter on the coast of Africa, and upon the Indian's territory, make the truth of this assertion manifest. The piratical depredations of the Algerines appear to be a judgment from heaven upon the nations to punish their perfidy and atrocious violations of justice; and never did any people more justly merit the scourge than Americans, on whom it seems to fall with peculiar and reiterated violence. When they yoke our citizens to the plow, and compel them to labor in that degraded manner, they only retaliate on us for similar barbarities. For Algiers is a part of the same country whose helpless inhabitants we are accustomed to carry away. But the English and Americans cautiously avoid engaging with a warlike people whom they fear to attack in a manner so base and unworthy; whilst the Algerines, more generous and courageous plunderers, are not afraid to make war on brave and well-disciplined enemies who are capable of making a gallant resistance.

Whoever examines into the condition of the slaves in America will find them in a state of the most uncultivated rudeness. Not instructed in any kind of learning, they are grossly ignorant of all refinement, and have little else about them belonging to the nature of civilized man than the mere form. They are strangers to almost every idea that doth not relate to their labor or their food, and though naturally possessed of strong sagacity and lively parts are, in all respects, in a state of the most deplorable brutality.—This is owing to the iron hand of oppression, which ever crushes the bud of genius and binds up in chains every expansion of the human mind.—Such is their extreme ignorance that they are utterly unacquainted with the laws of the world—the injunctions of religion—their own natural rights, and the forms, ceremonies and privileges of marriage originally established by the Divinity. Accordingly they live in open violation of the precepts of Christianity and with as little formality or restriction as the brutes of the field unite for the purpose of procreation. Yet this in a civilized country and a most enlightened period of the world! The resplendent glory of the gospel is at hand to conduct us in safety through the labyrinths of life. Science hath grown up to maturity, and is discovered to possess not only all the properties of solidity of strength, but likewise every ornament of elegance and every embellishment of fancy. Philosophy hath here attained the most exalted height of elevation, and the art of government hath received such refinements among us as hath equally astonished our friends, our enemies and ourselves. In fine, no annals are more brilliant than those of America; nor do any more luxuriantly abound with examples of exalted heroism, refined policy, and sympathetic humanity. Yet now the prospect begins to change, and all the splendor of this august assemblage will soon be overcast by sudden and impenetrable clouds, and American greatness be obliterated and swallowed up by one enormity. Slavery diffuses the gloom, and casts around us the deepest shade of approaching darkness. No longer shall the united states of America be famed for liberty. Oppression pervades their bowels; and while they exhibit a fair exterior to other parts of the world, they are nothing more than "painted sepulchers," containing within them nought but rottenness and corruption.

Ye voluptuous, ye opulent and great, who hold in subjection such numbers of your fellow creatures, and suffer these things to happen—beware! Reflect on this lamentable change that may, at a future period, take place against you. Arraigned before the Almighty Sovereign of the universe, how will you answer the charge of such complicated enormity? The presence of these slaves, who have been lost for want of your instruction and by means of your oppression, shall make you dart deeper into the flames to avoid their just reproaches, and seek out for an asylum in the hidden corners of perdition!

Many persons of opulence in Virginia, and the Carolinas, treat their unhappy slaves with every circumstance of the coolest neglect, and the most deliberate indifference. Surrounded with a numerous train of servants, to contribute to their personal care, and wallowing in all the luxurious plentitude of riches, they neglect the wretched source, whence they draw this profusion. Many of their negroes, on distant estates, are left to the entire management of inhuman overseers, where they suffer for the want of that very sustenance, which, at the proprietor's seat of residence, is wastefully given to the dogs. It frequently happens, on those large estates, that they are not clothed, 'till the winter is nearly expired; and then, the most valuable only are attended to; the young, and the labour-worn, having no other allowance, in this respect, than the tattered garments, thrown off by the more fortunate. A single peck of corn a week, or the like measure of rice, is the ordinary quantity of provision for a hard-working slave; to which a small quantity of meat is occasionally, though rarely, added. While those miserable degraded persons, thus scantily subsist, all the produce of their unwearied toil, is taken away to satiate their rapacious master. He, devoted wretch! thoughtless of the sweat and toil with which his wearied, exhausted dependents procure what he extravagantly dissipates, not contented with the ordinary luxuries of life, is, perhaps, planning, at the time, some improvement on the voluptuous art.—Thus he sets up two carriages instead of one; maintains twenty servants, when a fourth part of that number are more than sufficient to discharge the business of personal attendance; makes every animal, proper for the purpose, bleed around him, in order to supply the gluttonous profusion of his table; and generally gives away what his slaves are pining for;—those very slaves, whose labour enables him to display this liberality!—No comment is necessary, to expose the peculiar folly, ingratitude, and infamy of such execrable conduct.

But the custom of neglecting those slaves, who have been worn out in our service, is unhappily found to prevail, not only among the more opulent, but through the more extensive round of the middle and inferior ranks of life. No better reason can be given for this base inattention, than, they are no longer able to contribute to our emolument. With singular dishonor, we forget the faithful instrument of past employment, and when, by length of time, it becomes debilitated, it is, like a withered stalk, ungratefully thrown away.

Our slaves unquestionably have the strongest of all claims upon us for protection and support, we having compelled them to involuntary servitude and deprived them of every means of protecting or supporting themselves. The injustice of our conduct, and barbarity of our neglect, when this reflection is allowed to predominate, becomes so glaringly conspicuous as even to excite against ourselves the strongest emotions of detestation and abhorrence.

To whom are the wretched sons of Africa to apply for redress if their

cruel master treats them with unkindness? To whom can they resort for
protection if he is base enough to refuse it to them? The law is not their
friend—alas! too many statutes are enacted against them. The world is
not their friend—the iniquity is too general and extensive. No one who
hath slaves of his own will protect those of another, less the practice
should be retorted. Thus when their masters abandon them, their situation is destitute and forlorn, and God is their only friend!

Let us imitate the conduct of a neighboring State and immediately
take measures, at least, for the gradual abolition of slavery. Justice demands it of us, and we ought not to hesitate in obeying its inviolable
mandates.—All the feelings of pity, compassion, affection, and benevolence—all the emotions of tenderness, humanity, philanthropy, and goodness—all the sentiments of mercy, probity, honor, and integrity, unite
to solicit for their emancipation. Immortal will be the glory of accomplishing their liberation; and eternal the disgrace of keeping them in
chains.

But if the State of Pennsylvania is to be applauded for her conduct,
that of South Carolina can never be too strongly execrated. The legislature
of that State, at no very remote period, brought in a bill for prohibiting
the use of letters to their slaves and forbidding them the privilege of
being taught to read!—This was a deliberate attempt to enslave the
minds of those unfortunate objects, whose persons they already held in
arbitrary subjection—detestable deviation from the becoming rectitude
of man.

One more peculiarly distressing circumstance remains to be recounted
before I take my final leave of the subject.—In the ordinary course of
the business of the country the punishment of relatives frequently happens on the same farm, and in view of each other.—The father often sees
his beloved son—the son his venerable sire—the mother her much-loved
daughter—the daughter her affectionate parent—the husband the wife
of his bosom, and she the husband of her affection, cruelly bound up
without delicacy or mercy and punished with all extremity of incensed
rage and all the rigor of unrelenting severity, whilst these unfortunate
wretches dare not even interpose in each other's behalf. Let us reverse
the case and suppose it ours—all is silent horror!

THE LIFE
OF OLAUDAH
EQUIANO, THE
AFRICAN

Gustavus Vassa

[At age eleven, Olaudah Equiano (1745–1801?) was stolen from the African village of Benin, in present-day Nigeria, by African traders and was then sold to white slavers. After six or seven months of traveling and after serving several masters, he found himself on a ship bound for the West Indies. His fate was not to be that of the ordinary slave who came to the plantations of the West Indies or America. Olaudah was not sold in the Indies but was, instead, shipped to Virginia, where his master sold him once again to a lieutenant in the Royal Navy. Gustavus Vassa, a name acquired on shipboard, remained a seaman for several years. He was baptized and educted in England and, in 1767, was able to purchase his freedom for £40. Vassa continued to travel extensively and later explored the Arctic.

After purchasing his freedom, Vassa lent his efforts to the antislavery movement that, by the 1770's and 1780's, had attracted a host of English writers. Originally published in 1789, *The Interesting Narrative of the Life of Olaudah Equiano, or Gustavus Vassa, The African* had reached an eighth edition by 1794. It was written to acquaint Englishmen with the evils of the slave trade and to promote its abolition. Vassa's autobiography is, of course, one of the few accounts of the eighteenth-century slave trade ever written by a former slave. The *Narrative*, of which one chapter is reprinted here, reveals a number of points of interest. Despite his wanderings through various nations and among different peoples, Vassa had little difficulty in making himself understood among the Africans. Foreign tongues were easily learned, and many "new" customs corresponded with those of his childhood. The slavery that existed in Africa was relatively benign compared to the terrors of the "middle passage" and the suffering that most Africans encountered in the European colonies of the New World. Finally, the mode of Vassa's capture is instructive. Most slaves supplied by African chieftains to the traders had been captured in military expeditions. But Vassa was kidnaped. In fact, the threat of being kidnaped was a constant one in West Africa in the eighteenth century, as the demand for slaves by the European powers continued to increase.

One can detect in the *Narrative* a deliberate attempt (one sometimes even suspects coaching) to appeal to the sympathies of a white audience in terms they could understand. Here was a Negro engaged in trying to prove to whites that Africans were sensitive men and not brutes. To prefer death to slavery was to argue a nobility that was not part of the usual picture of the Negro as a barbarous animal. And the tender emotion of love exhibited by Vassa toward his family (especially his mother), the anguish suffered at the separation from his sister, could not but have been calculated to evoke pity. Vassa was reacting to his situation just as any other white Christian might have done, had he been enslaved. The whole undertaking is evidence of a good understanding, on Vassa's part, of English culture—an understanding that had no counterpart, among white men, of African culture. The literary tradition of which the *Narrative* is a part played a significant role in shaping antislavery opinion, perhaps as much as any rational antislavery arguments ever succeeded in doing.]

I hope the reader will not think I have trespassed on his patience in introducing myself to him with some account of the manners and customs of my country. They had been implanted in me with great care, and made an impression on my mind, which time could not erase, and which all the adversity and variety of fortune I have since experienced served only to rivet and record; for, whether the love of one's country be real or imaginary, or a lesson of reason, or an instinct of nature, I still look back with pleasure on the first scenes of my life, though that pleasure has been for the most part mingled with sorrow.

I have already acquainted the reader with the time and place of my birth. My father, besides many slaves, had a numerous family, of which seven lived to grow up, including myself and a sister, who was the only daughter. As I was the youngest of the sons, I became, of course, the greatest favorite with my mother, and was always with her; and she used to take particular pains to form my mind. I was trained up from my earliest years in the art of war; my daily exercise was shooting and throwing javelins; and my mother adorned me with emblems, after the manner of our greatest warriors.

In this way I grew up till I was turned the age of eleven, when an end was put to my happiness in the following manner. Generally, when the grown people in the neighborhood were gone far in the fields to labor, the children assembled together in some of the neighboring premises to play; and, commonly, some of us used to get up a tree to look out for any assailant, or kidnapper, that might come upon us—for they sometimes took those opportunities of our parents' absence to attack and carry off as many as they could seize. One day, as I was watching at the top of a tree in our yard, I saw one of those people come into the yard of our next neighbor but one to kidnap, there being many stout young people in it. Immediately on this I gave the alarm of the rogue, and he was surrounded by the stoutest of them, who entangled him with cords, so that he could not escape till some of the grown people came and secured him.

But, alas! ere long it was my fate to be thus attacked, and to be carried off, when none of the grown people were nigh. One day, when all our people were gone out to their works as usual, and only I and my dear sister were left to mind the house, two men and a woman got over our walls, and in a moment seized us both, and, without giving us time to cry out or make resistance, they stopped our mouths and ran off with us into the nearest wood. Here they tied our hands, and continued to carry us as far as they could, till night came on, when we reached a small house where the robbers halted for refreshment and spent the night. We were then unbound, but were unable to take any food; and, being quite overpowered by fatigue and grief, our only relief was some sleep, which allayed our misfortune for a short time. The next morning we left the house, and continued traveling all the day.

For a long time we had kept the woods, but at last we came into a road which I believed I knew. I had now some hopes of being delivered; for we had advanced but a little way before I discovered some people at a distance on which I began to cry out for their assistance; but my cries had no other effect than to make them tie me faster and stop my mouth, and then they put me into a large sack. They also stopped my sister's mouth and tied her hands; and in this manner we proceeded till we were out of sight of these people. When we went to rest the following night, they offered us some victuals, but we refused it; and the only comfort we had was in being in one another's arms all that night, and bathing each other with our tears. But, alas! we were soon deprived of even the small comfort of weeping together. The next day proved a day of greater sorrow than I had yet experienced; for my sister and I were then separated, while we lay clasped in each other's arms. It was in vain that we besought them not to part us; she was torn from me and immediately carried away, while I was left in a state of distraction not to be described. I cried and grieved continually; and for several days did not eat anything but what they forced into my mouth.

At length, after many days traveling, during which I had often changed masters, I got into the hands of a chieftain in a very pleasant country. This man had two wives and some children, and they all used me extremely well, and did all they could to comfort me; particularly the first wife, who was something like my mother. Although I was a great many days' journey from my father's house, yet these people spoke exactly the same language with us. This first master of mine, as I may call him, was a smith, and my principal employment was working his bellows, which were the same kind as I had seen in my vicinity. They were in some respects not unlike the stoves here in gentlemen's kitchens, and were covered over with leather; and in the middle of that leather a stick was fixed, and a person stood up and worked it in the same manner as is done to pump water out of a cask with a hand pump. I believe it was gold he worked, for it was of a lovely bright yellow color, and was worn by the women on their wrists and ankles.

I was there, I suppose, about a month, and they at last used to trust me some little distance from the house. This liberty I used in embracing every opportunity to inquire the way to my own home; and I also sometimes, for the same purpose, went with the maidens, in the cool of the evenings, to bring pitchers of water from the springs for the use of the house. I had also remarked where the sun rose in the morning and set in the evening as I had traveled along; and I had observed that my father's house was toward the rising of the sun. I therefore determined to seize the first opportunity of making my escape, and to shape my course for that quarter; for I was quite oppressed and weighed down by grief after my mother and friends; and my love of liberty, ever great, was strengthened by the mortifying circumstance of not daring to eat with the freeborn children, although I was mostly their companion.

While I was projecting my escape one day, an unlucky event happened, which quite disconcerted my plan and put an end to my hopes. I used to be sometimes employed in assisting an elderly slave to cook and take care of the poultry; and one morning, while I was feeding some chickens, I happened to toss a small pebble at one of them, which hit it on the middle and directly killed it. The old slave, having soon after missed the chicken, inquired after it; and on my relating the accident (for I told her the truth, for my mother would never suffer me to tell a lie), she flew into a violent passion and threatened that I should suffer for it; and, my master being out, she immediately went and told her mistress what I had done. This alarmed me very much, and I expected an instant flogging, which to me was uncommonly dreadful, for I had seldom been beaten at home. I therefore resolved to fly; and accordingly I ran into a thicket that was hard by, and hid myself in the bushes. Soon afterward my mistress and the slave returned, and, not seeing me, they searched all the house, but not finding me, and I not making answer when they called to me, they thought I had run away, and the whole neighborhood was raised in the pursuit of me.

In that part of the country, as in ours, the houses and villages were skirted with woods, or shrubberies, and the bushes were so thick that a man could readily conceal himself in them so as to elude the strictest search. The neighbors continued the whole day looking for me, and several times many of them came within a few yards of the place where I lay hid. I expected every moment when I heard a rustling among the trees to be found out and punished by my master; but they never discovered me, though they were often so near that I even heard their conjectures as they were looking about for me; and I now learned from them that any attempts to return home would be hopeless. Most of them supposed I had fled toward home; but the distance was so great, and the way so intricate, that they thought I could never reach it, and that I should be lost in the woods. When I heard this, I was seized with a violent panic and abandoned myself to despair. Night, too, began to approach, and aggravated all my fears. I had before entertained hopes of getting home, and had determined when it should be dark to make the attempt; but I was now convinced it was fruitless, and began to consider that, if possibly I could escape all other animals, I could not those of the human kind; and that, not knowing the way, I must perish in the woods. Thus was I like the hunted deer:

> Every leaf and every whisp'ring breath,
> Conveyed a foe, and every foe a death.

I heard frequent rustlings among the leaves, and being pretty sure they were snakes, I expected every instant to be stung by them. This increased my anguish, and the horror of my situation became now quite insupportable. I at length quitted the thicket, very faint and hungry, for I had not eaten or drank anything all the day, and crept to my master's kitchen, from whence I set out at first, which was an open shed, and laid myself down in the ashes with an anxious wish for death, to relieve me from all my pains. I was scarcely awake in the morning when the old woman slave, who was the first up, came to light the fire, and saw me in the fireplace. She was very much surprised to see me, and could scarcely believe her own eyes. She now promised to intercede for me, and went for her master, who soon after came, and, having slightly reprimanded me, ordered me to be taken care of and not ill-treated.

Soon after this, my master's only daughter, and child by his first wife, sickened and died, which affected him so much that for some time he was almost frantic, and really would have killed himself had he not been watched and prevented. However, in a short time afterward he recovered, and I was again sold.

I was now carried to the left of the sun's rising, through many dreary wastes and dismal woods, amidst the hideous roarings of wild beasts. The people I was sold to used to carry me very often, when I was tired, either on their shoulders or on their backs. I saw many convenient well-built sheds along the road at proper distances to accommodate the merchants and travelers who lay in those buildings along with their wives, who often accompany them; and they always go well armed.

From the time I left my own nation, I always found somebody that understood me till I came to the seacoast. The languages of different nations did not totally differ, nor were they so copious as those of the Europeans, particularly the English. They were therefore easily learned; and, while I was journeying thus through Africa, I acquired two or three different tongues.

In this manner I had been traveling for a considerable time, when, one evening, to my great surprise, whom should I see brought to the house where I was but my dear sister! As soon as she saw me, she gave a loud shriek and ran into my arms—I was quite overpowered; neither of us could speak, but, for a considerable time, clung to each other in mutual embraces, unable to do anything but weep. Our meeting affected all who saw us; and, indeed, I must acknowledge, in honor of those sable destroyers of human rights, that I never met with any ill-treatment, or saw any offered to their slaves, except tying them, when necessary, to keep them from running away. When these people knew we were brother and sister, they indulged us to be together; and the man to whom I supposed we belonged lay with us, he in the middle, while she and I held one another by the hands across his breast all night; and thus, for a while, we forgot our misfortunes in the joy of being together. But even this small comfort was soon to have an end; for scarcely had the fatal morning appeared when she was again torn from me forever!

I was now more miserable, if possible, than before. The small relief which her presence gave me from pain was gone, and the wretchedness of my situation was redoubled by my anxiety after her fate, and my apprehensions lest her sufferings should be greater than mine, when I could not be with her to alleviate them. Yes, thou dear partner of all my childish sports! thou sharer of my joys and sorrows! happy should I have ever esteemed myself to encounter every misery for you and to procure your freedom by the sacrifice of my own. Though you were early forced from my arms, your image has been always riveted in my heart, from which neither time nor fortune have been able to remove it; so that, while the thoughts of your sufferings have damped my prosperity, they have mingled with adversity and increased its bitterness. To that Heaven which protects the weak from the strong, I commit the care of your innocence and virtues, if they have not already received their full reward, and if your youth and delicacy have not long since fallen victims to the violence of the African trader, the pestilential stench of a Guinea ship, the seasoning in the European colonies, or the lash and lust of a brutal and unrelenting overseer.

I did not long remain after my sister. I was again sold and carried through a number of places, till after traveling a considerable time I came to a town called Tinmah, in the most beautiful country I had yet seen in Africa. It was extremely rich, and there were many rivulets which flowed through it, and supplied a large pond in the center of the town, where the people washed. Here I first saw and tasted coconuts, which I thought superior to any nuts I had ever tasted before; and the trees which were loaded were also interspersed among the houses, which had commodious shades adjoining, and were in the same manner as ours, the insides being neatly plastered and whitewashed. Here I also saw and tasted, for the first time, sugarcane.

Their money consisted of little white shells, the size of the fingernail. I was sold here for 172 of them by a merchant who lived and brought me there. I had been about two or three days at his house when a wealthy widow, a neighbor of his, came there one evening and brought with her an only son, a young gentleman about my own age and size. Here they saw me; and, having taken a fancy to me, I was bought of the merchant and went home with them. Her house and premises were situated close to one of those rivulets I have mentioned, and were the finest I ever saw in Africa; they were very extensive, and she had a number of slaves to attend her. The next day I was washed and perfumed; and when mealtime came, I was led into the presence of my mistress, and ate and drank before her with her son. This filled me with astonishment; and I could scarce help expressing my surprise that the young gentleman should suffer me, who was bound, to eat with him who was free; and not only so, but that he would not at any time either eat or drink till I had taken first, because I was the eldest, which was agreeable to our custom.

Indeed, everything here, and all their treatment of me, made me forget that I was a slave. The language of these people resembled ours so nearly that we understood each other perfectly. They had also the very same customs as we. There were likewise slaves daily to attend us, while my young master and I, with other boys, sported with our darts and bows and arrows, as I had been used to do at home. In this resemblance to my former happy state, I passed about two months; and I now began to think I was to be adopted into the family, and was beginning to be reconciled to my situation and to forget by degrees my misfortunes, when all at once the delusion vanished; for, without the least previous knowledge, one morning early, while my dear master and companion was still asleep, I was awakened out of my reverie to fresh sorrow, and hurried away even among the uncircumcised.

Thus, at the very moment I dreamed of the greatest happiness, I found myself most miserable; and it seemed as if fortune wished to give me this taste of joy only to render the reverse more poignant. The change I now experienced was as painful as it was sudden and unexpected. It was a change, indeed, from a state of bliss to a scene which is inexpressible by me, as it discovered to me an element I had never before beheld, and till then had no idea of, and wherein such instances of hardship and cruelty continually occurred as I can never reflect on but with horror.

All the nations and people I had hitherto passed through resembled our own in their manners, customs, and language; but I came at length to a country, the inhabitants of which differed from us in all those particulars. I was very much struck with this difference, especially when I came among a people who did not circumcise, and ate without washing their hands. They cooked also in iron pots, and had European cutlasses and crossbows, which were unknown to us, and fought with their fists among themselves. Their women were not so modest as ours, for they ate and drank and slept with their men. But above all, I was amazed to see no sacrifices or offerings among them. In some of those places the people ornamented themselves with scars, and likewise filed their teeth very sharp. They wanted sometimes to ornament me in the same manner, but I would not suffer them; hoping that I might some time be among a people who did not thus disfigure themselves, as I thought they did.

At last I came to the banks of a large river which was covered with canoes, in which the people appeared to live with their household utensils and provisions of all kinds. I was beyond measure astonished at this, as I had never before seen any water larger than a pond or rivulet; and

my surprise was mingled with no small fear when I was put into one of
these canoes, and we began to paddle and move along the river. We
continued going on thus till night, and when we came to land and made
fires on the banks, each family by themselves, some dragged their canoes
on shore, others stayed and cooked in theirs, and laid in them all night.
Those on the land had mats, of which they made tents, some in the shape
of little houses; in these we slept; and after the morning meal, we
embarked again and proceeded as before. I was often very much astonished to see some of the women, as well as the men, jump into the
water, dive to the bottom, come up again, and swim about.

Thus I continued to travel, sometimes by land, sometimes by water,
through different countries and various nations, till, at the end of six
or seven months after I had been kidnapped, I arrived at the seacoast.
It would be tedious and uninteresting to relate all the incidents which
befell me during this journey, and which I have not yet forgotten; of
the various hands I passed through, and the manners and customs of all
the different people among whom I lived. I shall, therefore, only observe
that in all the places where I was, the soil was exceedingly rich; the
pumpkins, eadas, plantains, yams, etc., were in great abundance and of
incredible size. There were also vast quantities of different gums, though
not used for any purpose, and everywhere a great deal of tobacco. The
cotton even grew quite wild, and there was plenty of redwood. I saw no
mechanics whatever in all the way, except such as I have mentioned. The
chief employment in all these countries was agriculture, and both the
males and females, as with us, were brought up to it, and trained in the
arts of war.

The first object which saluted my eyes when I arrived on the coast
was the sea, and a slave ship, which was then riding at anchor and
waiting for its cargo. These filled me with astonishment, which was soon
converted into terror when I was carried on board. I was immediately
handled and tossed up to see if I were sound by some of the crew; and
I was now persuaded that I had gotten into a world of bad spirits, and
that they were going to kill me. Their complexions, too, differing so
much from ours, their long hair, and the language they spoke (which
was very different from any I had ever heard) united to confirm me in
this belief. Indeed, such were the horrors of my views and fears at the
moment that, if 10,000 worlds had been my own, I would have freely
parted with them all to have exchanged my condition with that of the
meanest slave in my own country. When I looked round the ship, too,
and saw a large furnace of copper boiling, and a multitude of black
people of every description chained together, every one of their countenances expressing dejection and sorrow, I no longer doubted of my
fate; and, quite overpowered with horror and anguish, I fell motionless
on the deck and fainted.

When I recovered a little, I found some black people about me, who
I believed were some of those who had brought me on board and had
been receiving their pay; they talked to me in order to cheer me, but all
in vain. I asked them if we were not to be eaten by those white men

with horrible looks, red faces, and long hair. They told me I was not; and one of the crew brought me a small portion of spirituous liquor in a wine glass, but, being afraid of him, I would not take it out of his hand. One of the blacks, therefore, took it from him and gave it to me, and I took a little down my palate, which, instead of reviving me, as they thought it would, threw me into the greatest consternation at the strange feeling it produced, having never tasted any such liquor before. Soon after this, the blacks who brought me on board went off and left me abandoned to despair.

I now saw myself deprived of all chance of returning to my native country, or even the least glimpse of hope of gaining the shore, which I now considered as friendly; and I even wished for my former slavery in preference to my present situation, which was filled with horrors of every kind, still heightened by my ignorance of what I was to undergo. I was not long suffered to indulge my grief. I was soon put down under the decks, and there I received such a salutation in my nostrils as I had never experienced in my life; so that, with the loathsomeness of the stench and crying together, I became so sick and low that I was not able to eat, nor had I the least desire to taste anything. I now wished for the last friend, death, to relieve me; but soon, to my grief, two of the white men offered me eatables; and, on my refusing to eat, one of them held me fast by the hands and laid me across, I think, the windlass, and tied my feet, while the other flogged me severely.

I had never experienced anything of this kind before, and although not being used to the water, I naturally feared that element the first time I saw it, yet, nevertheless, could I have got over the nettings, I would have jumped over the side, but I could not; and, besides, the crew used to watch us very closely who were not chained down to the decks lest we should leap into the water. And I have seen some of these poor African prisoners most severely cut for attempting to do so, and hourly whipped for not eating. This, indeed, was often the case with myself. In a little time after, among the poor chained men, I found some of my own nation, which in a small degree gave ease to my mind. I inquired of these what was to be done with us? They gave me to understand we were to be carried to these white people's country to work for them. I then was a little revived, and thought, if it were no worse than working, my situation was not so desperate; but still I feared I should be put to death, the white people looked and acted, as I thought, in so savage a manner; for I had never seen among any people such instances of brutal cruelty; and this not only shown toward us blacks but also to some of the whites themselves. One white man in particular I saw, when we were permitted to be on deck, flogged so unmercifully with a large rope near the foremast that he died in consequence of it; and they tossed him over the side as they would have done a brute. This made me fear these people the more; and I expected nothing less than to be treated in the same manner.

I could not help expressing my fears and apprehensions to some of my countrymen; I asked them if these people had no country, but lived in this hollow place (the ship). They told me they did not, but came from a distant one. "Then," said I, "how comes it in all our country we never heard of them?" They told me because they lived so very far off. I then asked where were their women? had they any like themselves? I was told they had. "And why," said I, "do we not see them?" They answered, because they were left behind. I asked how the vessel could go? They told me they could not tell; but that there was cloth put upon the masts by the help of the ropes I saw, and then the vessel went on; and the white men had some spell or magic they put in the water when they liked in order to stop the vessel. I was exceedingly amazed at this account, and really thought they were spirits. I therefore wished much to be from among them, for I expected they would sacrifice me; but my wishes were vain, for we were so quartered that it was impossible for any of us to make our escape.

While we stayed on the coast, I was mostly on deck; and one day, to my great astonishment, I saw one of these vessels coming in with the sails up. As soon as the whites saw it, they gave a great shout, at which we were amazed; and the more so as the vessel appeared larger by approaching nearer. At last, she came to an anchor in my sight, and when the anchor was let go, I and my countrymen who saw it were lost in astonishment to observe the vessel stop—and were now convinced it was done by magic. Soon after this the other ship got her boats out, and they came on board of us, and the people of both ships seemed very glad to see each other. Several of the strangers also shook hands with us black people, and made motions with their hands, signifying, I suppose, we were to go to their country, but we did not understand them.

At last, when the ship we were in had got in all her cargo, they made ready with many fearful noises, and we were all put under deck, so that we could not see how they managed the vessel. But this disappointment was the least of my sorrow. The stench of the hold while we were on the coast was so intolerably loathsome that it was dangerous to remain there for any time, and some of us had been permitted to stay on the deck for the fresh air; but now that the whole ship's cargo were confined together, it became absolutely pestilential. The closeness of the place and the heat of the climate, added to the number in the ship, which was so crowded that each had scarcely room to turn himself, almost suffocated us. This produced copious perspirations, so that the air soon became unfit for respiration, from a variety of loathsome smells, and brought on a sickness among the slaves, of which many died—thus falling victims to the improvident avarice, as I may call it, of their purchasers. This wretched situation was again aggravated by the galling of the chains, now become insupportable; and the filth of the necessary tubs, into which the children often fell and were almost suffocated. The shrieks of the women and the groans of the dying rendered the whole a scene of horror almost inconceivable.

Happily, perhaps, for myself, I was soon reduced so low here that it was thought necessary to keep me almost always on deck; and from my extreme youth I was not put in fetters. In this situation I expected every hour to share the fate of my companions, some of whom were almost daily brought upon deck at the point of death, which I began to hope would soon put an end to my miseries. Often did I think many of the inhabitants of the deep much more happy than myself. I envied them the freedom they enjoyed, and as often wished I could change my condition for theirs. Every circumstance I met with served only to render my state more painful, and heightened my apprehensions and my opinion of the cruelty of the whites.

One day they had taken a number of fishes; and when they had killed and satisfied themselves with as many as they thought fit, to our astonishment who were on deck, rather than give any of them to us to eat, as we expected, they tossed the remaining fish into the sea again, although we begged and prayed for some as well as we could, but in vain; and some of my countrymen, being pressed by hunger, took an opportunity, when they thought no one saw them, of trying to get a little privately. But they were discovered, and the attempt procured them some very severe floggings. One day, when we had a smooth sea and moderate wind, two of my wearied countrymen who were chained together (I was near them at the time), preferring death to such a life of misery, somehow made through the nettings and jumped into the sea. Immediately, another quite dejected fellow, who, on account of his illness, was suffered to be out of irons, also followed their example; and I believe many more would very soon have done the same if they had not been prevented by the ship's crew, who were instantly alarmed. Those of us that were the most active were in a moment put down under the deck, and there was such a noise and confusion among the people of the ship, as I never heard before, to stop her and get the boat out to go after the slaves. However, two of the wretches were drowned, but they got the other, and afterward flogged him unmercifully for thus attempting to prefer death to slavery.

In this manner we continued to undergo more hardships than I can now relate, hardships which are inseparable from this accursed trade. Many a time we were near suffocation from the want of fresh air, which we were often without for whole days together. This, and the stench of the necessary tubs, carried off many.

During our passage, I first saw flying fishes, which surprised me very much; they used frequently to fly across the ship, and many of them fell on the deck. I also now first saw the use of the quadrant; I had often with astonishment seen the mariners make observations with it, and I could not think what it meant. They at last took notice of my surprise; and one of them, willing to increase it as well as to gratify my curiosity, made me one day look through it. The clouds appeared to me to be land, which disappeared as they passed along. This heightened my wonder; and I was now more persuaded than ever that I was in another world, and that everything about me was magic.

At last, we came in sight of the island of Barbados, at which the whites on board gave a great shout and made many signs of joy to us. We did not know what to think of this; but as the vessel drew nearer, we plainly saw the harbor, and other ships of different kinds and sizes, and we soon anchored among them, off Bridgetown.

Many merchants and planters now came on board, though it was in the evening. They put us in separate parcels and examined us attentively. They also made us jump, and pointed to the land, signifying we were to go there. We thought by this we should be eaten by these ugly men, as they appeared to us; and, when soon after we were all put down under the deck again, there was much dread and trembling among us, and nothing but bitter cries to be heard all the night from these apprehensions, insomuch that at last the white people got some old slaves from the land to pacify us. They told us we were not to be eaten but to work, and were soon to go on land, where we should see many of our countrypeople. This report eased us much. And sure enough, soon after we were landed, there came to us Africans of all languages.

We were conducted immediately to the merchant's yard, where we were all pent up together, like so many sheep in a fold, without regard to sex or age. As every object was new to me, everything I saw filled me with surprise. What struck me first was that the houses were built with bricks and stories, and in every other respect different from those I had seen in Africa; but I was still more astonished on seeing people on horseback. I did not know what this could mean; and, indeed, I thought these people were full of nothing but magical arts. While I was in this astonishment, one of my fellow prisoners spoke to a countryman of his about the horses, who said they were the same kind they had in their country. I understood them, though they were from a distant part of Africa; and I thought it odd I had not seen any horses there; but afterward, when I came to converse with different Africans, I found they had many horses among them, and much larger than those I then saw.

We were not many days in the merchant's custody before we were sold after their usual manner, which is this. On a signal given (as the beat of a drum), the buyers rush at once into the yard where the slaves are confined and make choice of that parcel they like best. The noise and clamor with which this is attended, and the eagerness visible in the countenances of the buyers, serve not a little to increase the apprehension of terrified Africans, who may well be supposed to consider them as the ministers of that destruction to which they think themselves devoted. In this manner, without scruple, are relations and friends separated, most of them never to see each other again. I remember, in the vessel in which I was brought over, in the men's apartment, there were several brothers, who, in the sale, were sold in different lots; and it was very moving, on this occasion, to see and hear their cries at parting.

O, ye nominal Christians! might not an African ask you—Learned you this from your God, who says unto you, "Do unto all men as you would men should do unto you"? Is it not enough that we are torn from our country and friends to toil for your luxury and lust of gain? Must every tender feeling be likewise sacrificed to your avarice? Are the dearest friends and relations, now rendered more dear by their separation from their kindred, still to be parted from each other, and thus prevented from cheering the gloom of slavery, with the small comfort of being together and mingling their sufferings and sorrows? Why are parents to lose their children, brothers their sisters, or husbands their wives? Surely, this is a new refinement in cruelty which, while it has no advantage to atone for it, thus aggravates distress and adds fresh horrors even to the wretchedness of slavery.

AN ADDRESS TO THE INHABITANTS OF PHILADELPHIA AGAINST THE COLONIZATION SOCIETY

James Forten (and Russell Perrott?)

[If it was the Negro's cultural difference that finally justified his being held a slave, this difference presented a more acute problem when white men were faced with the prospect of a Negro citizenry. The free Negro population increased substantially after the Revolutionary War. Perhaps 1,000 slaves, perhaps more, were freed fighting against the British, and individual manumission increased, despite legal restrictions against the practice. Between 1790 and 1810, the number of free men increased from 8 per cent to 13 per cent of the black population. One out of every four blacks was free in Maryland in 1810; whereas in Delaware, in the same year, over 75 per cent of the Negro population were free. On the eve of the Civil War, there were 250,000 free Negroes in the South and an equal number living in the North.

As the number of Negro freedmen grew, whites felt increasingly plagued by their presence. In a way, the free Negro had even less of a place in American society than the slave. The slave could be controlled, but the free Negro forced the issue of inclusion in or exclusion from the society. American whites recoiled from the former possibility. The early abolition schemes of the 1790's always foundered on the problem of disposing of new freedmen. Abolition, indeed, was feared because many thought it would lead to race mixture. It was for this reason, as much as any other, that these schemes were coupled with proposals for colonization, if not on some other continent, then, at least, in the Western territories. The aversion to race mixture was almost universal, even among those who thought slavery was a sin and who had strong abolitionist sentiments. This attitude was best exemplified by Jefferson. "I consider," he wrote, concerning the blacks, shortly before his death in 1826, ". . . expatriation to the governments of the W[est] I[ndies] of their own colour as entirely practicable, and greatly preferable to the mixture of colour here. To this I have great aversion."

For whites, who slowly began to realize after the Revolution that they had a race problem on their hands, colonization was a matter of expediency. Even those whites who urged emancipation included deportation of Negroes as part of the proposal. Jefferson's plan of gradual emancipation in Virginia, in 1777, was coupled with colonization, and Lincoln still had colonization in mind in 1862.

Restrictions on free Negroes (including disfranchisement) increased in the North as well as the South, even while abolitionist sentiment was mounting, in the 1820's and 1830's. These restrictions became even more pronounced as periodic fears of a slave rebellion flared. Organized efforts at Negro removal began in 1816, shortly after a group of thirty-eight Negroes voluntarily left for Sierra Leone with Paul Cuffe, a wealthy Negro shipowner from New England. The American Colonization Society was formed in December, 1816, for the purpose of transporting free Negroes to form a colony (Liberia). The society was promoted by many prominent whites, including Henry Clay and John Randolph, of Roanoke. Although designed to colonize only "free people of color," the society opened an easy and safe channel for emancipation to those masters (and there were some) who desired to free their slaves.

The following month, in January, 1817, the free black population of Philadelphia met and denounced colonization as a device to perpetuate slavery. James Forten, who, with the Reverend Richard Allen, had organized the meeting, led the attack. (The address reprinted here summarized the sentiments of the free Negroes who met again in Philadelphia in August, 1817, under the leadership of Forten.) Forten clearly saw that the basic issue was the status of free Negroes in American society. To elevate the free Negro to the status of citizen—rather than deporting him—would be the speediest path to breaking all the shackles of the slave. Colonization, he recognized, was a scheme of emancipation still tied to the idea of inequality. Throughout the 1820's, Forten organized the Northern, free Negro opposition to the colonizers.

The Colonization Society remained in existence until the Civil War, but its activities did not amount to much after 1830, when white Abolitionists turned against the scheme. The total emigration to Liberia in the nineteenth century did not exceed 12,000 blacks, most of whom were from the South.]

The free people of colour, assembled together, under circumstances of deep interest to their happiness and welfare, humbly and respectfully lay before you this expression of their feelings and apprehensions.

Relieved from the miseries of slavery, many of us by your aid, possessing the benefits which industry and integrity in this prosperous country assure to all its inhabitants, enjoying the rich blessings of religion, by opportunities of worshiping the only true God, under the light of Christianity, each of us according to his understanding; and having afforded to us and to our children the means of education and improvement; we have no wish to separate from our present homes, for any purpose whatever. Contented with our present situation and condition we are not desirous of increasing their prosperity, but by honest efforts and by the use of those opportunities for their improvement, which the constitution and laws allow to all. It is therefore with painful solicitude, and sorrowing regret, we have seen a plan for colonizing the free people of colour of the United States on the coast of Africa, brought forward under the auspices and sanction of gentlemen whose names give value to all they recommend, and who certainly are among the wisest, the best, and the most benevolent of men, in this great nation.

If the plan of colonizing is intended for our benefit and those who now promote it, will never seek our injury; we humbly and respectfully urge that it is not asked for by us; nor will it be required by any circumstances, in our present or future condition; as long as we shall be permitted to share the protection of the excellent laws, and just government which we now enjoy, in common with every individual of the community.

We therefore, a portion of those, who are objects of this plan, and among those whose happiness, with that of others of our colour, it is intended to promote, with humble and grateful acknowledgments to those who have devised it, renounce, and disclaim every connection with it, and respectfully but firmly declare our determination not to participate in any part of it.

If this plan of colonization now proposed is intended to provide a refuge and a dwelling for a portion of our brethren, who are now held in slavery in the south, we have other and stronger objections to it, and we entreat your consideration of them.

The ultimate and final abolition of slavery in the United States is, under the guidance and protection of a just God, progressing. Every year witnesses the release of numbers of the victims of oppression, and affords new and safe assurances that the freedom of all will in the end be accomplished. As they are thus, by degrees relieved from bondage, our brethren have opportunities for instruction and improvement; and thus they become in some measure fitted for their liberty.—Every year, many of us have restored to us by the gradual, but certain march of the cause of abolition—parents, from whom we have been long separated—wives and children, whom we had left in servitude—and brothers, in blood as well as in early sufferings, from whom we had been long parted.

But if the emancipations of our kindred shall, when the plan of colonization shall go into effect, be attended with transportation to a distant land, and shall be granted on no other condition; the consolation for our past sufferings and of those of our colour, who are in slavery, which have hitherto been, and under the present situation of things, would continue to be afforded to us and to them, will cease for ever. The cords, which now connect them with us will be stretched by the distance to which their ends will be carried until they break; and all the sources of happiness, which affection and connection, and blood bestow, will be ours or theirs no more.

Nor do we view the colonization of those who may become emancipated by its operation among our southern brethren, as capable of producing their happiness. Unprepared by education, and a knowledge of the truths of our blessed religion, for their new situation, those who will thus become colonists will themselves be surrounded by every suffering which can afflict the members of the human family.

Without arts, without habits of industry, and unaccustomed to provide by their own exertions and foresight for their wants, the colony will soon become the abode of every vice and the home of every misery. Soon will the light of Christianity, which now dawns among that section of our species, be shut out by the clouds of ignorance, and their day of life be closed, without the illuminations of the Gospel.

To those of our brethren who shall be left behind, there will be assured perpetual slavery and augmented sufferings.—Diminished in numbers the slave population of the southern states, which by its magnitude alarms its proprietors, will be easily secured. Those among their bondmen, who feel that they should be free, by rights which all mankind have from God and from nature, and who thus may become dangerous to the quiet of their masters, will be sent to the colony; and the tame and submissive will be retained, and subjected to increased rigour. Year after year will witness these means to assure safety and submission among their slaves; and the southern masters will colonize only those whom it may be dangerous to keep among them. The bondage of a large portion of our brethren will thus be rendered perpetual.

Should the anticipations of misery and want among the colonists, which with great deference we have submitted to your better judgment, be realized; to emancipate and transport to the colony, will be held forth by slave-holders as the worst and heaviest of punishments, and they will be threatened and successfully used to enforce increased submission to their wishes and subjection to their commands.

Nor ought the sufferings and sorrows, which must be produced by an exercise of the right to transport and colonize such only of their slaves as may be selected by the slave-holders escape the attention and consideration of those whom with all humility we now address. Parents will be torn from their children—husbands from their wives—brothers from brothers—and all the heart-rending agonies which were endured by our forefathers when they were dragged into bondage from Africa will be again renewed, and with increased anguish. The shores of America will like the sands of Africa be watered by the tears of those who will be left behind. Those who shall be carried away will roam childless, widowed, and alone, over the burning plains of Guinea.

Disclaiming, as we emphatically do, a wish or desire to interpose our opinions and feelings between all plans of colonization, and the judgment of those whose wisdom as far exceeds ours, as their situations are exalted above ours; *We humbly*, respectfully, and fervently entreat and beseech your disapprobation of the plan of colonization now offered by "the American society for colonizing the free people of colour of the United States."—Here, in the city of Philadelphia, where the voice of the suffering sons of Africa was first heard; where was first commenced the work of abolition, on which Heaven hath smiled, for it could have had success only from the Great Maker; let not a purpose be assisted which will stay the cause of the entire abolition of slavery in the United States, and which may defeat it altogether; which proffers to those who do not ask for them what it calls benefits, but which they consider injuries; and which must insure to the multitudes whose prayers can only reach you through us, *misery, and suffering, and perpetual slavery.*

APPEAL, IN FOUR ARTICLES, TOGETHER WITH A PREAMBLE TO THE COLORED CITIZENS OF THE WORLD, BUT IN PARTICULAR, AND VERY EXPRESSLY TO THOSE OF THE UNITED STATES OF AMERICA

David Walker

[David Walker was born free—his mother was a free Negro—in Wilmington, North Carolina, on September 28, 1785. He traveled extensively, especially in the South, and eventually settled in Boston in the 1820's. In 1827, he became the Boston agent for *Freedom's Journal*, which was launched that same year in New York by Samuel Cornish and John Russwurm and to which he contributed several articles. In the same year, Walker ventured into the used clothing business, opening a shop in Brattle Street, and prospered sufficiently to consider marriage, which he undertook in 1828. His wife, Eliza, bore him one son, posthumously, a coincidence that repeated his own misfortune.

Walker wrote the first edition of his *Appeal* in September, 1829, and had it printed at his own expense. The pamphlet soon began to appear in Southern cities, including Savannah, whose Mayor wrote to Harrison Gray Otis (his counterpart in Boston) demanding that the pamphlet be suppressed. A second edition of the *Appeal* and then a third (a note added to the third edition indicated that Walker did not plan a fourth) appeared in 1830. On June 28, Walker died in Boston, amid speculation that he had been poisoned. The *Appeal* was reissued again in 1848 by Henry Highland Garnet, who apended his own "Address to the Slaves of the United States of America"—a speech he had delivered to a National Convention of Negroes held in Buffalo, New York, in 1843. Garnet's speech, which advocated that Negroes stop laboring for their masters until they were given their freedom, was rejected by the Convention (the vote was 19 to 18 and Frederick Douglass spoke for the majority) as being too inflammatory. Garnet's reprint, which is reproduced below, was from the second edition of the *Appeal*. The only significant difference between the second and third was the addition of a prefatory note in which Walker characterized white men as the natural enemies of the black and emphasized that "the day of our redemption from abject wretchedness draweth near." Walker believed that a black messiah would soon arrive to lead black men from servitude, and the *Appeal* was as much designed to arouse blacks to this possibility and to encourage them to follow such a man as openly to preach armed rebellion. But the slaveholding South and moderates in the North saw the work as incendiary.

The *Appeal* was the first extended political tract to be produced by an American Negro. Yet Walker sounds familiar. If the Negroes in America were wretched, it was because the whites had made them so. If slavery bred ignorance, then it would only be fair for the white man to take upon himself the task of educating the blacks. If white men doubted that black men were destined to be free, it was only because they had come to accept a distorted view of their own religion. If, finally, it was thought expedient to deport the free black population, it was only because whites were blinded to the fact that America had become the homeland of the blacks. Only a slight reformulation of the *Appeal* would make it a contemporary tract.

If the *Appeal* was seen as incendiary, it was precisely because Walker was proposing that Africans be offered the opportunities of other Americans. Walker's aspirations for the Negroes were, indeed, very American. He had, as Americans still do, an undying faith in the blessings of education and a belief, like countless other immigrants, that a better life was possible in the New World, despite the fact that, for some, the old world had been left involuntarily.

Walker's opposition to colonization assumed more, of course, than the white population was ready to grant, even though the *Appeal* coincided with a tide of disenchantment among Northern abolitionists with the colonization movement as well as with the idea of gradual abolition. William Lloyd Garrison, who was to become the most celebrated spokesman for immediate abolition, would shortly launch the *Liberator*. (It was in late 1829 that Garrison shifted his position from gradual to immediate abolition, and it is possible that Garrison, who had read the *Appeal*, was influenced by Walker.) Both Walker and Garrison were blamed for the August, 1831, Turner revolt in Virginia. A South Carolina vigilance committee posted a $1,500 reward for the arrest of anyone distributing the *Liberator* or the *Appeal*, and the Georgia legislature offered $4,000, in October, 1831, for the arrest of Garrison. The war of words was on. The thirty years between the publication of the *Appeal* and John Brown's raid on Harpers Ferry saw the rise of a militant Abolitionist movement and the hardening of proslavery sentiment in the South.]

PREAMBLE

My dearly beloved Brethren and Fellow Citizens:

Having travelled over a considerable portion of these United States, and having, in the course of my travels taken the most accurate observations of things as they exist—the result of my observations has warranted the full and unshakened conviction, that we, (colored people of these United States) are the most degraded, wretched, and abject set of beings that ever lived since the world began, and I pray God, that none like us ever may live again until time shall be no more. They tell us of the Israelites in Egypt, the Helots in Sparta, and of the Roman Slaves, which last, were made up from almost every nation under heaven, whose sufferings under those ancient and heathen nations were, in comparison with ours, under this enlightened and christian nation, no more than a cypher—or in other words, those heathen nations of antiquity, had but little more among them than the name and form of slavery, while wretchedness and endless miseries were reserved, apparently in a phial, to be poured out upon our fathers, ourselves and our children by *christian* Americans!

These positions, I shall endeavour, by the help of the Lord, to demonstrate in the course of this *appeal*, to the satisfaction of the most incredulous mind—and may God Almighty who is the father of our Lord Jesus Christ, open your hearts to understand and believe the truth.

The *causes*, my brethren, which produce our wretchedness and miseries, are so very numerous and aggravating, that I believe the pen only of a Josephus or a Plutarch, can well enumerate and explain them. Upon subjects, then, of such incomprehensible magnitude, so impenetrable, and so notorious, I shall be obliged to omit a large class of, and content myself with giving you an exposition of a few of those, which do indeed rage to such an alarming pitch, that they cannot but be a perpetual source of terror and dismay to every reflecting mind.

I am fully aware, in making this appeal to my much afflicted and suffering brethren, that I shall not only be assailed by those whose greatest earthly desires are, to keep us in abject ignorance and wretchedness, and who are of the firm conviction that heaven has designed us and our children to be slaves and *beasts of burden* to them and their

children.—I say, I do not only expect to be held up to the public as an ignorant, impudent and restless disturber of the public peace, by such avaricious creatures, as well as a mover of insubordination—and perhaps put
in prison or to death, for giving a superficial exposition of our miseries,
and exposing tyrants. But I am persuaded, that many of my brethren,
particularly those who are ignorantly in league with slave-holders or
tyrants, who acquire their daily bread by the blood and sweat of their
more ignorant brethren—and not a few of those too, who are too ignorant to see an inch beyond their noses, will rise up and call me cursed
—Yea, the jealous ones among us will perhaps use more abject subtlety
by affirming that this work is not worth perusing; that we are well situated and there is no use in trying to better our condition, for we cannot. I will ask one question here.—Can our condition be any worse?—
Can it be more mean and abject? If there are any changes, will they
not be for the better, though they may appear for the worse at first?
Can they get us any lower? Where can they get us? They are afraid
to treat us worse, for they know well, the day they do it they are
gone. But against all accusations which may or can be preferred against
me, I appeal to heaven for my motive in writing—who knows that my
object is, if possible, to awaken in the breasts of my afflicted, degraded
and slumbering brethren, a spirit of enquiry and investigation respecting our miseries and wretchedness in this *Republican Land of
Liberty ! ! ! ! !*

The sources from which our miseries are derived and on which I
shall comment, I shall not combine in one, but shall put them under
distinct heads and expose them in their turn; in doing which, keeping
truth on my side, and not departing from the strictest rules of morality,
I shall endeavor to penetrate, search out, and lay them open for your
inspection. If you cannot or will not profit by them, I shall have done
my duty to you, my country and my God.

And as the inhuman system of *slavery*, is the *source* from which most
of our miseries proceed, I shall begin with that *curse to nations;* which
has spread terror and devastation through so many nations of antiquity,
and which is raging to such a pitch at the present day in Spain and in
Portugal. It had one tug in England, in France, and in the United States
of America; yet the inhabitants thereof, do not learn wisdom, and erase
it entirely from their dwellings and from all with whom they have to do.
The fact is, the labor of slaves comes so cheap to the avaricious usurpers, and is (as they think) of such great utility to the country where
it exists, that those who are actuated by sordid avarice only, overlook
the evils, which will as sure as the Lord lives, follow after the good.
In fact, they are so happy to keep in ignorance and degradation, and to
receive the homage and the labor of the slaves, they forget that God rules
in the armies of heaven and among the inhabitants of the earth, having
his ears continually open to the cries, tears and groans of his oppressed
people; and being a just and holy Being will at one day appear fully
in behalf of the oppressed, and arrest the progress of the avaricious
oppressors; for although the destruction of the oppressors God may
not effect by the oppressed, yet the Lord our God will bring other

destructions upon them—for not unfrequently will he cause them to rise up one against another, to be split and divided, and to oppress each other, and sometimes to open hostilities with sword in hand. Some may ask, what is the matter with this enlightened and happy people?—Some say it is the cause of political usurpers, tyrants, oppressors, &c. But has not the Lord an oppressed and suffering people among them? Does the Lord condescend to hear their cries and see their tears in consequence of oppression? Will he let the oppressors rest comfortably and happy always? Will he not cause the very children of the oppressors to rise up against them, and oftimes put them to death? "God works in many ways his "wonders to perform."

I will not here speak of the destructions which the Lord brought upon Egypt, in consequence of the oppression and consequent groans of the oppressed—of the hundreds and thousands of Egyptians whom God hurled into the Red Sea for afflicting his people in their land—of the Lord's suffering people in Sparta or Lacedemon, the land of the truly famous Lycurgus—nor have I time to comment upon the cause which produced the fierceness with which Sylla usurped the title, and absolutely acted as dictator of the Roman people—the conspiracy of Cataline—the conspiracy against, and murder of Cæsar in the Senate house—the spirit with which Marc Antony made himself master of the commonwealth—his associating Octavius and Lipidus with himself in power,—their dividing the provinces of Rome among themselves—their attack and defeat on the plains of Phillipi the last defenders of their liberty, (Brutus and Cassius)—the tyranny of Tiberius, and from him to the final overthrow of Constantinople by the Turkish Sultan, Mahomed II., A. D. 1453. I say, I shall not take up time to speak of the *causes* which produced so much wretchedness and massacre among those heathen nations, for I am aware that you know too well, that God is just, as well as merciful!—I shall call your attention a few moments to that *christian* nation, the Spaniards, while I shall leave almost unnoticed that avaricious and cruel people, the Portuguese, among whom all true hearted christians and lovers of Jesus Christ, must evidently see the judgments of God displayed. To show the judgments of God upon the Spaniards I shall occupy but little time, leaving a plenty of room for the candid and unprejudiced to reflect.

All persons who are acquainted with history, and particularly the Bible, who are not blinded by the God of this world, and are not actuated solely by avarice—who are able to lay aside prejudice long enough to view candidly and impartially, things as they were, are, and probably will be, who are willing to admit that God made man to serve him *alone*, and that man should have no other Lord or Lords but himself—that God Almighty is the *sole proprietor* or *master* of the WHOLE human family, and will not on any consideration admit of a colleague, being unwilling to divide his glory with another.—And who can dispense with prejudice long enough to admit that we are men, notwithstanding our *improminent noses* and *woolly heads*, and believe that we feel for our fathers, mothers, wives and children as well as they do for theirs.—I say, all who are permitted to see and believe these things, can easily recognize the judgments of God among the Spaniards. Though others may lay the cause of the fierceness with which they cut each other's throats, to some other circumstances, yet they who believe that God is a God of justice, will believe that SLAVERY *is the principal cause.*

While the Spaniards are running about upon the field of battle cutting each other's throats, has not the Lord an afflicted and suffering people in the midst of them whose cries and groans in consequence of oppression are continually pouring into the ears of the God of justice? Would they not cease to cut each others throats if they could? But how can they? The very support which they draw from government to aid them in perpetrating such enormities, does it not arise in a great degree from the wretched victims of oppression among them? And yet they are calling for *Peace !—Peace ! !* Will any peace be given unto them? Their destruction may indeed be procrastinated awhile, but can it continue long while they are oppressing the Lord's people? Has He not the hearts of all men in His hand? Will he suffer one part of his creatures to go on oppressing another like brutes always, with impunity? And yet those avaricious wretches are calling for *Peace ! ! ! !* I declare it does appear to me, as though some nations think God is asleep, or that he made the Africans for nothing else but to dig their mines and work their farms, or they cannot believe history, sacred or profane. I ask every man who has a heart and is blessed with the privilege of believing—Is not God a God of justice to all his creatures? Do you say he is? Then if he gives peace and tranquility to tyrants, and permits them to keep our fathers, our mothers, ourselves and our children in eternal ignorance and wretchedness to support them and their families, would he be to us a God of *justice?* I ask O ye *christians ! ! !* who hold us and our children, in the most abject ignorance and degradation, that ever a people were afflicted with since the world began—I say, if God gives you peace and tranquility, and suffers you thus to go on afflicting us and our children, who have never given you the least provocation,— Would he be to us *a God of justice?* If you will allow that we are MEN, who feel for each other, does not the blood of our fathers and of us their children, cry aloud to the Lord of Sabaoth against you, for the cruelties and murders with which you have, and do continue to afflict us. But it is time for me to close my remarks on the suburbs, just to enter more fully into the interior of this system of cruelty and oppression.

ARTICLE I

Our Wretchedness in Consequence of Slavery

My beloved brethren: The Indians of North and of South America— the Greeks—the Irish subjected under the king of Great Britain—the Jews that ancient people of the Lord—the inhabitants of the islands of the sea—in fine, all the inhabitants of the earth, (except however, the sons of Africa) are called *men*, and of course are, and ought to be free. But we, (coloured people) and our children are *brutes ! !* and of course are and ought to be SLAVES to the American people and their children forever! to dig their mines and work their farms; and thus go on enriching them, from one generation to another with our blood and our tears ! !

I promised in a preceding page to demonstrate to the satisfaction of the most incredulous, that we, (coloured people of these United States of America) are the *most wretched, degraded* and abject set of beings that ever *lived* since the world began, and that the white Americans having reduced us to the wretched state of *slavery*, treat us in that condition *more cruel* (they being an enlightened and christian people) than any heathen nation did any people whom it had reduced to our condition. These affirmations are so well confirmed in the minds of all unprejudiced men who have taken the trouble to read histories, that they need no elucidation from me. But to put them beyond all doubt, I refer you in the first place to the children of Jacob, or of Israel in Egypt, under Pharaoh and his people. Some of my brethren do not know who Pharaoh and the Egyptians were—I know it to be a fact that some of them take the Egyptians to have been a gang of *devils*, not knowing any better, and that they (Egyptians) having got possession of the Lord's people, treated them *nearly* as cruel as *christian Americans* do us, at the present day. For the information of such, I would only mention that the Egyptians, were Africans or colored people, such as we are—some of them yellow and others dark—a mixture of Ethiopians and the natives of Egypt—about the same as you see the colored people of the United States at the present day,—I say, I call your attention then, to the children of Jacob, while I point out particularly to you his son Joseph among the rest, in Egypt.

"And Pharaoh, said unto Joseph, thou shalt be over my house, and according unto thy word shall all my people be ruled; only in the throne will I be greater than thou."

"And Pharaoh said unto Joseph, see, I have set thee over all the land of Egypt."

"And Pharaoh said unto Joseph, I am Pharaoh, and without thee shall no man lift up his hand or foot in all the land of Egypt."

Now I appeal to heaven and to earth, and particularly to the American people themselves who cease not to declare that our condition is not *hard*, and that we are comparatively satisfied to rest in wretchedness and misery, under them and their children. Not; indeed, to show me a colored President, a Governor, a Legislator, a Senator, a Mayor, or an Attorney at the Bar.—But to show me a man of color, who holds the low office of a Constable, or one who sits in a Juror Box, even on a case of one of his wretched brethren, throughout this great Republic ! !— But let us pass Joseph the son of Israel a little further in review, as he existed with that heathen nation.

"And Pharaoh called Joseph's name Zaphnathpaaneah; and he gave him to wife Asenath the daughter of Potipherah priest of On. And Joseph went out over all the land of Egypt."

Compare the above, with the American institutions. Do they not institute laws to prohibit us from marrying among the whites? I would wish, candidly, however, before the Lord, to be understood, that I would not give *a pinch of snuff* to be married to any white person I ever saw in all the days of my life. And I do say it, that the black man, or man of color, who will leave his own color (provided he can get one who is good for any thing) and marry a white woman, to be a double slave to her just because she is *white,* ought to be treated by her as he surely will be, viz; as a NIGER !!! It is not indeed what I care about intermarriages with the whites, which induced me to pass this subject in review; for the Lord knows, that there is a day coming when they will be glad enough to get into the company of the blacks, notwithstanding, we are, in this generation, levelled by them almost on a level with the brute creation; and some of us they treat even worse than they do the brutes that perish. I only made this extract to show how much lower we are held, and how much more cruel we are treated by the Americans, than were the children of Jacob, by the Egyptians. We will notice the sufferings of Israel some further, under *heathen Pharaoh,* compared with ours under the *enlightened christians of America.*

"And Pharaoh spake unto Joseph, saying, thy father and thy brethren are come unto thee:"

"The land of Egypt is before thee: in the best of the land make thy father and brethren to dwell; in the land of Goshen let them dwell; and if thou knowest any men of activity among them, then make them rulers over my cattle."

I ask those people who treat us so *well,* Oh! I ask them, where is the most barren spot of land which they have given unto us? Israel had the most fertile land in all Egypt. Need I mention the very notorious fact, that I have known a poor man of color, who labored night and day, to acquire a little money, and having acquired it, he vested it in a small piece of land, and got him a house erected thereon, and having paid for the whole, he moved his family into it, where he was suffered to remain but nine months, when he was cheated out of his property by a white man, and driven out of door!—And is not this the case generally? Can a man of color buy a piece of land and keep it peaceably? Will not some white man try to get it from him even if it is in a *mud hole?* I need not comment any farther on a subject, which all, both black and white, will readily admit. But I must, really, observe that in this very city, when a man of color dies, if he owned any real estate it must generally fall into the hands of some white person. The wife and children of the deceased may weep and lament if they please, but the estate will be kept snug enough by its white posessors.

But to prove farther that the condition of the Israelites was better under the Egyptians than ours is under the whites. I call upon the professing christians, I call upon the philanthropist, I call upon the very tyrant himself, to show me a page of history, either sacred or profane, on which a verse can be found, which maintains, that the Egyptians heaped the *insupportable insult* upon the children of Israel by telling them that they were not of the *human family.* Can the whites deny this charge? Have they not, after having reduced us to the deplorable condition of slaves under their feet, held us up as descending

originally from the tribes of *Monkeys* or *Orang-Outangs?* O! my God! I
appeal to every man of feeling—is not this insupportable? Is it not
heaping the most gross insult upon our miseries, because they have got
us under their feet and we cannot help ourselves? Oh! pity us we pray
thee, Lord Jesus, Master.—Has Mr. Jefferson declared to the world, that
we are inferior to the whites, both in the endowments of our bodies
and of minds? It is indeed surprising, that a man of such great learning,
combined with such excellent natural parts, should speak so of a set of
men in chains. I do not know what to compare it to, unless, like putting
one wild deer in an iron cage, where it will be secured, and hold another
by the side of the same, then let it go, and expect the one in the cage to
run as fast as the one at liberty. So far, my brethren, were the Egyptians
from heaping these insults upon their slaves, that Pharaoh's daughter
took Moses, a son of Israel, for her own, as will appear by the following.

"And Pharaoh's daughter said unto her, [Moses' mother] take this
child away, and nurse it for me and I will pay thee thy wages. And
the woman took the child [Moses] and nursed it.

And the child grew, and she brought him unto Pharaoh's daughter and
he became her son. And she called his name Moses: and she said because I drew him out of the water."

In all probability, Moses would have become Prince Regent to the
throne, and no doubt, in process of time but he would have been seated
on the throne of Egypt. But he had rather suffer shame, with the
people of God, than to enjoy pleasures with that wicked people for
a season. O! that the colored people were long since of Moses'
excellent disposition, instead of courting favor with, and telling news
and lies to our *natural enemies*, against each other—aiding them to
keep their hellish chains of slavery upon us. Would we not long before this time, have been respectable men, instead of such wretched
victims of oppression as we are? Would they be able to drag our mothers,
our fathers, our wives, our children and ourselves, around the world in
chains and hand-cuffs as they do, to dig up gold and silver for them
and theirs? This question, my brethren, I leave for you to digest; and
may God Almighty force it home to your hearts. Remember that unless
you are united, keeping your tongues within your teeth, you will be
afraid to trust your secrets to each other, and thus perpetuate our
miseries under the *christians!!!!!* [☞ADDITION,—Remember, also to
lay humble at the feet of our Lord and Master Jesus Christ, with prayers
and fastings. Let our enemies go on with their butcheries, and at once
fill up their cup. Never make an attempt to gain our freedom or *natural
right*, from under our cruel oppressors and murderers, until you see
your way clear; when that hour arrives and you move, be not afraid or
dismayed; for be you assured that Jesus Christ the king of heaven and
of earth who is the God of justice and of armies, will surely go before
you. And those enemies who have for hundreds of years stolen our *rights*,
and kept us ignorant of Him and His divine worship, he will remove.
Millions of whom, are this day, so ignorant and avaricious, that they
cannot conceive how God can have an attribute of justice, and show
mercy to us because it pleased Him to make us black—which color,

Mr. Jefferson calls unfortunate!!!!!! As though we are not as thankful to our God for having made us as it pleased himself, as they (the whites) are for having made them white. They think because they hold us in their infernal chains of slavery that we wish to be white, or of their color—but they are dreadfully deceived—we wish to be just as it pleased our Creator to have made us, and no avaricious and unmerciful wretches, have any business to make slaves of or hold us in slavery. How would they like for us to make slaves of, or hold them in cruel slavery, and murder them as they do us? But is Mr. Jefferson's assertion true? viz. "that it is unfortunate for us that our Creator has been pleased to make us black." We will not take his say so, for the fact. The world will have an opportunity to see whether it is unfortunate for us, that our Creator *has made us* darker than the *whites*.

Fear not the number and education of our *enemies*, against whom we shall have to contend for our lawful right; guaranteed to us by our Maker; for why should we be afraid, when God is, and will continue (if we continue humble) to be on our side?

The man who would not fight under our Lord and Master Jesus Christ, in the glorious and heavenly cause of freedom and of God—to be delivered from the most wretched, abject and servile slavery, that ever a people was afflicted with since the foundation of the world, to the present day—ought to be kept with all of his children or family, in slavery, or in chains, to be butchered by his *cruel enemies.*

I saw a paragraph, a few years since, in a South Carolina paper, which, speaking of the barbarity of the Turks it said: "The Turks are the most barbarous people in the world—they treat the Greeks more like *brutes* than human beings." And in the same paper was an advertisement, which said: "Eight well built Virginia and Maryland *Negro fellows* and four *wenches* will positively be *sold* this day *to the highest bidder!*" And what astonished me still more was, to see in this same *humane* paper!! the cuts of three men, with clubs and budgets on their backs, and an advertisement offering a considerable sum of money for their apprehension and delivery. I declare it is really so *funny* to hear the Southerners and Westerners of this country talk about *barbarity*, that it is positively, enough to make a man *smile*.

The sufferings of the Helots among the Spartans, were somewhat severe, it is true, but to say that theirs were as severe as ours among the Americans I do most strenuously deny—for instance, can any man show me an article on a page of ancient history which specifies, that, the Spartans chained, and hand-cuffed the Helots, and dragged them from their wives and children, children from their parents, mothers from their sucking babes, wives from their husbands, driving them from one end of the country to the other? Notice the Spartans were heathens, who lived long before our Divine Master made his appearance in the flesh. Can Christian Americans deny these barbarous cruelties? Have you not Americans, having subjected us under you, added to these miseries, by insulting us in telling us to our face, because we are helpless that we are not of the human family? I ask you, O! Americans, I ask you, in the name of the Lord, can you deny these charges? Some perhaps may deny, by saying, that they never thought or said that we were not men. But do not actions speak louder than words?—have they not made provisions for the Greeks, and Irish? Nations who have never done the least thing for them, while *we* who have enriched their country with our blood and tears—have dug up gold and silver for them and their children, from generation to generation, and are in more miseries than any other people under heaven, are not seen, but by comparatively a handful of the American people? There are indeed, more ways to kill a dog besides choking it to death with butter. Further. The Spartans or Lacedemonians, had some frivolous pretext for enslaving the Helots, for they (Helots) while being free inhabitants of Sparta, stirred up an intestine commotion, and were by the Spartans subdued, and made prisoners of war. Consequently they and their children were condemned to perpetual slavery.

I have been for years troubling the pages of historians to find out what our fathers have done to the *white Christians of America*, to merit such condign punishment as they have inflicted on them, and do continue to inflict on us their children. But I must aver, that my researches have hitherto been to no effect. I have therefore come to the immovable conclusion, that they (Americans) have, and do continue to punish us for nothing else, but for enriching them and their country. For I cannot conceive of anything else. Nor will I ever believe otherwise until the Lord shall convince me.

The world knows, that slavery as it existed among the Romans, (which was the primary cause of their destruction) was, comparatively speaking, no more than a *cypher*, when compared with ours under the Americans. Indeed, I should not have noticed the Roman slaves, had not the very learned and penetrating Mr. Jefferson said, "When a master was murdered, all his slaves in the same house or within hearing, were condemned to death."—Here let me ask Mr. Jefferson, (but he is gone to answer at the bar of God, for the deeds done in his body while living,) I therefore ask the whole American people, had I not rather die, or be put to death than to be a slave to any tyrant, who takes not only my own, but my wife and children's lives by the inches? Yea, would I meet death with avidity far! far!! in preference to such *servile submission* to the murderous hands of tyrants. Mr. Jefferson's very severe remarks on us have been so extensively argued upon by men whose attainments in literature, I shall never be able to reach, that I would not have meddled with it, were it not to solicit each of my brethren, who has the spirit of a man, to buy a copy of Mr. Jefferson's "Notes on Virginia," and put it in the hand of his son. For let no one of us suppose that the refutations which have been written by our white friends are enough—they are *whites*—we are *blacks*. We, and the world wish to see the charges of Mr. Jefferson refuted by the blacks *themselves*, according to their chance: for we must remember that what the whites have written respecting this subject, is other men's labors and did not emanate from the blacks. I know well, that there are some talents and learning among the coloured people of this country, which we have not a chance to develope, in consequence of oppression; but our oppression ought not to hinder us from acquiring all we can.—For we will have a chance to develope them by and by. God will not suffer us, always to be oppressed. Our sufferings will come to an *end*, in spite of all the Americans this side of *eternity*. Then we will want all the learning and talents among ourselves, and pehaps more, to govern ourselves.—"Every dog must have its day," the American's is coming to an end.

But let us review Mr. Jefferson's remarks respecting us some further. Comparing our miserable fathers, with the learned philosophers of Greece, he says: "Yet notwithstanding these and other discouraging circumstances among the Romans, their slaves were often their rarest artists. They excelled too in science, insomuch as to be usually employed as tutors to their master's children; Epictetus, Terence and Phædrus, were slaves,—but they were of the race of whites. It is not their *condition* then, but *nature*, which has produced the distinction." See this, my brethren!! Do you believe that this assertion is swallowed by millions of the whites? Do you know that Mr. Jefferson was one of as great characters as ever lived among the whites? See his writings for the world, and public labors for the United States of America. Do you believe that the assertions of such a man, will pass away into oblivion unobserved by this people and the world? If you do you are much mistaken—See how the American people treat us—have we souls in our bodies? are we men who have any spirits at all? I know that there are many *swell-bellied* fellows among us whose greatest object is to fill their stomachs. Such I do not mean—I am after those who know and feel, that we are MEN as well as other people; to them, I say, that unless we try to refute Mr. Jefferson's arguments respecting us, we will only establish them.

But the slaves among the Romans. Every body who has read history, knows, that as soon as a slave among the Romans obtained his freedom, he could rise to the greatest eminence in the State, and there was no law instituted to hinder a slave from buying his freedom. Have not the Americans instituted laws to hinder us from obtaining our freedom. Do any deny this charge? Read the laws of Virginia, North Carolina, &c. Further: have not the Americans instituted laws to prohibit a man of colour from obtaining and holding any office whatever, under the government of the United States of America? Now, Mr. Jefferson tells us that our condition is not so hard, as the slaves were under the Romans! ! ! !

It is time for me to bring this article to a close. But before I close it, I must observe to my brethren that at the close of the first Revolution in this country with Great Britain, there were but thirteen States in the Union, now there are twenty-four, most of which are slave-holding States, and the whites are dragging us around in chains and handcuffs to their new States and Territories to work their mines and farms, to enrich them and their children, and millions of them believing firmly that we being a little darker than they, were made by our creator to be an inheritance to them and their children forever—the same as a parcel of *brutes ! !*

Are we MEN! !—I ask you, O my brethren! are we MEN? Did our creator make us to be slaves to dust and ashes like ourselves? Are they not dying worms as well as we? Have they not to make their appearance before the tribunal of heaven, to answer for the deeds done in the body, as well as we? Have we any other master but Jesus Christ alone? Is he not their master as well as ours?—What right then, have we to obey and call any other master, but Himself? How we could be so *submissive* to a gang of men, whom we cannot tell whether they are as *good* as ourselves or not, I never could conceive. However, this is shut up with the Lord and we cannot precisely tell—but I declare, we judge men by their works.

The whites have always been an unjust, jealous unmerciful, avaricious and blood thirsty set of beings, always seeking after power and authority.—We view them all over the confederacy of Greece, where they were first known to be any thing, (in consequence of education) we see them there, cutting each other's throats—trying to subject each other to wretchedness and misery, to effect which they used all kinds of deceitful, unfair and unmerciful means. We view them next in Rome, where the spirit of tyranny and deceit raged still higher.—We view them in Gaul, Spain and in Britain—in fine, we view them all over Europe, together with what were scattered about in Asia and Africa, as heathens, and we see them acting more like devils than accountable men. But some may ask, did not the blacks of Africa, and the mulattoes of Asia, go on in the same way as did the whites of Europe. I answer no—they never were half so avaricious, deceitful and unmerciful as the whites, according to their knowledge.

But we will leave the whites or Europeans as heathens and take a view of them as christians, in which capacity we see them as cruel, if not more so than ever. In fact, take them as a body, they are ten times more cruel avaricious and unmerciful than ever they were; for while they were heathens they were bad enough it is true, but it is positively a fact that they were not quite so audacious as to go and take vessel loads of men, women and children, and in cold blood and through devilishness, throw them into the sea, and murder them in all kind of ways. While they were heathens, they were too ignorant for such barbarity. But being christians, enlightened and sensible, they are completely prepared for such hellish cruelties. Now suppose God were to give them more sense, what would they do. If it were possible would they not *dethrone* Jehovah and seat themselves upon his throne? I therefore, in the name and fear of the Lord God of heaven and of earth, divested of prejudice either on the side of my colour or that of the whites, advance my suspicion of them, whether they are *as good by nature* as we are or not. Their actions, since they were known as a people, have been the reverse, I do indeed suspect them, but this, as I before observed, is shut up with the Lord, we cannot exactly tell, it will be proved in succeeding generations.—The whites have had the essence of the gospel as it was preached by my master and his apostles—the Ethiopians have not, who are to have it in its meridian splendor—the Lord will give it to them to their satisfaction. I hope and pray my God, that they will make good use of it, that it may be well with them.

ARTICLE II

Our Wretchedness in Consequence of Ignorance

Ignorance, my brethren, is a mist, low down into the very dark and almost impenetrable abyss of which, our fathers for many centuries have been plunged. The christians, and enlightened of Europe, and some of Asia, seeing the ignorance and consequent degradation of our fathers, instead of trying to enlighten them, by teaching them that religion and light with which God had blessed them, they have plunged them into wretchedness ten thousand times more intolerable, than if they had left them entirely to the Lord, and to add to their miseries, deep down into which they have plunged them, tell them, that they are an *inferior* and *distinct race* of beings, which they will be glad enough to recall and swallow by and by. Fortune and misfortune, two inseparable companions, lay rolled up in the wheel of events, which have from the creation of the world, and will continue to take place among men until God shall dash worlds together.

When we take a retrospective view of the arts and sciences—the wise legislators—the Pyramids, and other magnificent buildings—the turning of the channel of the river Nile, by the sons of Africa or of Ham, among whom learning originated, and was carried thence into Greece, where it was improved upon and refined. Thence among the Romans, and all over the then enlightened parts of the world, and it has been enlightening the dark and benighted minds of men from then, down to this day. I say, when I view retrospectively, the renown of that once mighty people, the children of our great progenitor, I am indeed cheered. Yea further, when I view that mighty son of Africa, HANNIBAL, one of the greatest generals of antiquity, who defeated and cut off so many thousands of the white Romans or murderers, and who carried his victorious arms, to the very gate of Rome, and I give it as my candid opinion, that had Carthage been well united and had given him good support, he would have carried that cruel and barbarous city by storm. But they were disunited, as the colored people are now, in the United States of America, the reason our natural enemies are enabled to keep their feet on our throats.

Beloved brethren—here let me tell you, and believe it, that the Lord our God, as true as he sits on his throne in heaven, and as true as our Saviour died to redeem the world, will give you a Hannibal, and when the Lord shall have raised him up, and given him to you for your possession, O my suffering brethren! remember the divisions and consequent sufferings of *Carthage* and of *Hayti*. Read the history particularly of Hayti, and see how they were butchered by the whites, and do you take warning. The person whom God shall give you, give him your support and let him go his length, and behold in him the salvation of your God. God will indeed, deliver you through him from yoor deplorable and wretched condition under the christians of America. I charge you this day before my God to lay no obstacle in his way, but let him go.

The whites want slaves, and want us for their slaves, but some of them will curse the day they ever saw us. As true as the sun ever shone in its meridian splendor, my colour will root some of them out of the very face of the earth. They shall have enough of making slaves of, and butchering, and murdering us in the manner which they have. No doubt some may say that I write with a bad spirit, and that I being a black, wish these things to occur. Whether I write with a bad or a good spirit, I say if these things do not occur in their proper time, it is because the world in which we live does not exist, and we are deceived with regard to its existence. It is immaterial however to me, who believe, or who refuse— though I should like to see the whites repent peradventure God may have mercy on them, some however, have gone so far that their cup must be filled.

But what need have I to refer to antiquity, when Hayti, the glory of the blacks and terror of tyrants, is enough to convince the most avaricious and stupid of wretches—which is at this time, and I am sorry to say it, plagued with that scourge of nations, the Catholic religion; but I hope and pray God that she may yet rid herself of it, and adopt in its stead the Protestant faith; also, I hope that she may keep peace within her borders and be united, keeping a strict look out for tyrants, for if they get the least chance to injure her, they will avail themselves of it, as true as the Lord lives in heaven. But one thing which gives me joy is, that they are men who would be cut off to a man, before they would yield to the combined forces of the whole world—in fact, if the whole world was combined against them, it could not do any thing with them, unless the Lord delivers them up.

Ignorance and treachery one against the other—a servile and abject submission to the lash of tyrants, we see plainly, my brethren, are not the natural elements of the blacks, as the Americans try to make us believe; but these are misfortunes which God has suffered our fathers to be enveloped in for many ages, no doubt in consequence of their disobedience to their Maker, and which do, indeed, reign at this time among us, almost to the destruction of all other principles: for I must truly say, that ignorance, the mother of treachery and deceit, gnaws into our very vitals. Ignorance, as it now exists among us, produces a state of things, Oh my Lord! too horrible to present to the world. Any man who is curious to see the full force of ignorance developed among the colored people of the United States of America, has only to go into the southern and western states of this confederacy, where, if he is not a tyrant, but has the feelings of a human being, who can feel for a fellow creature, he may see enough to make his very heart bleed! He may see there, a son take his mother, who bore almost the pains of death to give him birth, and by the command of a tyrant, strip her as naked as she came into the world, and apply the cow-hide to her, until she falls a victim to death in the road! He may see a husband take his dear wife, not unfrequently in a pregnant state, and perhaps far advanced, and beat her for an unmerciful wretch, until his infant falls a lifeless lump at her feet! Can the Americans escape God Almighty? If they do, can he be to us a God of Justice? God is just, and I know it—for he has convinced me to my satisfaction—I cannot doubt him. My observer may see fathers beating their sons, mothers their daughters, and children their parents, all to pacify the passions of unrelenting tyrants. He may also, see them telling news and lies, making mischief one upon another. These are some of the productions of ignorance, which he will see practised among my dear brethren, who are held in unjust slavery and wretchedness, by avaricious and unfeeling tyrants, to whom, and their hellish deeds, I would suffer my life to be taken before I would submit. And when my curious observer comes to take notice of those who are said to be free (which assertion I deny) and who are making some frivolous pretensions to common sense, he will see that branch of ignorance among the slaves assuming a more cunning and deceitful course of procedure. He may see some of my brethren in league with tyrants, selling their own brethren into *hell upon earth*, not dissimilar to the exhibitions in Africa but in a more secret, servile and abject manner. Oh Heaven! I am full!!! I can hardly move my pen! ! ! As I expect some one will try to put me to death, to strike terror into others, and to obliterate from their minds the notion of freedom, so as to keep my brethren the more secured in wretchedness where they will be permitted to stay but a short time (whether tyrants believe it or not,) I shall give the world a development of facts which are already witnessed in the courts of heaven. My observer may see some of those ignorant and treacherous creatures (colored people) sneaking about in the large cities, endeavoring to find out all strange colored people, where they work and where they reside, asking them questions and trying to ascertain whether they are runaways or not, telling them, at the same time, that they always have been, are, and always will be, friends to their brethren; and perhaps, that they themselves are absconders, and a thousand such treacherous lies to get the better information of the more ignorant!! There have been and are at this day in Boston, New York, Philadelphia, and Baltimore, coloured men, who are in league with tyrants, and receive a great portion of their daily bread, of the moneys which they acquire from the blood and tears of their more miserable brethren whom they scandalously delivered into the hands of our *natural enemies ! ! ! !*

To show the force of degraded ignorance and deceit among us some further, I will give here an extract from a paragraph, which may be found in the Columbian Centinel of this city, for September 9, 1829, on the first page of which the curious may find an article, headed

AFFRAY AND MURDER

Portsmouth, (Ohio) Aug. 22, 1829

"A most shocking outrage was committed in Kentucky, about eight miles from this place, on the 14th inst. A negro driver, by the name of Gordon, who had purchased in Maryland about sixty negroes, was taking them, assisted by an associate named Allen and the wagoner who conveyed the baggage, to the Mississippi. The men were hand-cuffed and chained together, in the usual manner for driving these poor wretches. while the women and children were suffered to proceed without incumbrance. It appears that, by means of a file the negroes unobserved had succeeded in separating the irons which bound their hands, in such a way as to be able to throw them off at any moment. About 8 o'clock in the morning, while proceeding on the state road leading from Greenup to Vanceburg, two of them dropped their shackles and commenced a fight, when the wagoner (Petit) rushed in with his whip to compel them to desist. At this moment, every negro was found to be perfectly at liberty; and one of them seizing a club, gave Petit a violent blow on the head and laid him dead at his feet; and Allen, who came to his assistance, met a similar fate from the contents of a pistol fired by another of the gang. Gordon was then attacked, seized and held by one of the negroes, whilst another fired twice at him with a pistol, the ball of which each time grazed his head, but not proving effectual, he was beaten with clubs, and left for dead. They then commenced pillaging the wagon and with an axe split open the trunk of Gordon and rifled it of the money, about $2,490. Sixteen of the negroes then took to the woods; Gordon, in the mean time, not being materially injured was enabled, by the assistance of one of the women, to mount his horse and flee; pursued, however, by one of the gang on another horse, with a drawn pistol; fortunately he escaped with his life, barely arriving at a plantation, as the negro came in sight; who then turned about and retreated.

"The neighborhood was immediately rallied, and a hot pursuit given—which, we understand, has resulted in the capture of the whole gang and the recovery of the greatest part of the money.—Seven of the negro men and one woman, it is said were engaged in the murder, and will be brought to trial at the next court in Greenupsburg."

Here my brethren, I want you to notice particularly in the above article, the ignorant and *deceitful actions* of this colored woman. I beg you to view it carefully, as for ETERNITY ! ! ! Here a *notorious wretch*, with two other confederates had SIXTY of them in a gang, driving them like *brutes*—the men all in chains and hand-cuffs, and by the help of God they got their chains and hand-cuffs thrown off and caught two of the wretches and put them to death, and beat the other until they thought he was dead, and left him for dead; however he deceived them, and rising from the ground, this *servile woman* helped him upon his horse and he made his escape. Brethren what do you think of this? Was it the natural *fine feelings* of this woman, to save such a wretch alive? I know that the blacks, take them half enlightened and ignorant, are more humane and merciful than the most enlightened and refined Europeans that can be found in all the earth. Let no one say that I assert this because I am prejudiced on the side of my color, and against the whites or Europeans. For what I write, I do it candidly, for my God and the good of both parties: Natural observations have taught me these things; there is a solemn awe in the hearts of the blacks, as it respects *murdering* men:* whereas the whites (though they are great cowards) where they have the advantage, or think that there are any prospects of getting it, they murder all before them, in order to subject men to wretchedness and degradation under them. This is the natural result of pride and

* Which is the reason the whites take the advantage of us.

avarice.—But I declare, the actions of this black woman are really insupportable. For my own part, I cannot think it was any thing but servile deceit, combined with the most gross ignorance: for we must remember that *humanity, kindness* and the *fear of the Lord*, does not consist in protecting *devils*. Here is a set of wretches, who had SIXTY of them in a gang, driving them around the country like *brutes*, to dig up gold and silver for them, (which they will get enough of yet.) Should the lives of such creatures be spared? Is GOD and Mammon in league? What has the Lord to do with a gang of desperate wretches, who go *sneaking about the country like robbers*—light upon his people wherever they can get a chance, binding them with chains and hand-cuffs, beat and murder them as they would *rattle-snakes*? Are they not the Lord's enemies? Ought they not to be destroyed? Any person who will save such wretches from destruction, is fighting against the Lord, and will receive his just recompense. The black men acted like *blockheads*. Why did they not make sure of the wretch? He would have made sure of them if he could. It is just the way with black men—eight white men can frighten fifty of them; whereas, if you can only get courage into the blacks, I do declare it, that one good black man can put to death six white men; and I give it as a fact, let twelve black men get well armed for battle, and they will kill and put to flight fifty whites. The reason is, the blacks, once you get them started, they glory in death. The whites have had us under them for more than three centuries, murdering, and treating us like brutes; and, as Mr. Jefferson wisely said, they have never *found us out*—they do not know, indeed, that there is an unconquerable disposition in the breasts of the blacks, which when it is fully awakened and put in motion, will be subdued, only with the destruction of the animal existence. Get the blacks started, and if you do not have a gang of lions and tigers to deal with, I am a deceiver of the blacks and the whites. How sixty of them could let that wretch escape unkilled, I cannot conceive—they will have to suffer as much for the two whom they secured, as if they had put one hundred to death: if you commence, make sure work—do not trifle, for they will not trifle with you—they want us for their slaves, and think nothing of murdering us in order to subject us to that wretched condition—therefore, if there is an *attempt* made by us, kill or be killed. Now, I ask you had you not rather be killed than to be a slave to a tyrant, who takes the life of your mother, wife, and dear little children? Look upon your mother, wife and children, and answer God Almighty; and believe this, that it is no more harm for you to kill a man, who is trying to kill you, than it is for you to take a drink of water when thirsty; in fact, the man who will stand still and let another murder him, is worse than an infidel, and if he has common sense, ought not to be pitied.—The actions of this deceitful and ignorant coloured woman, in saving the life of a desperate man, whose avaricious and cruel object was to drive her and her companions in miseries, through the country like cattle, to make his fortune on their carcasses, are but too much like that of thousands of our brethren in these states: if any thing is whispered by one, which has any allusion to the melioration of their dreadful condition, they run and tell tyrants, that they may be enabled to keep them the longer in wretchedness and miseries. Oh! coloured people of these United States, I ask you, in the name of that God who made us, have we, in consequence of oppression, nearly lost the spirit of man, and, in no very trifling degree, adopted that of brutes? Do you answer, No?—I ask you, then, what set of men can you point me to, in all the world, who are so abjectly employed by their oppressors as we are by our *natural enemies?* How can, Oh! how can those enemies but say that we and our children are not of the HUMAN FAMILY, but were made by our creator to be an inheritance to them and theirs forever? How can the slave-holders but say that they can bribe the best coloured person in the country, to sell his brethren for a trifling sum of money, and take that atrocity to confirm them in their avaricious opinion, that we were made to be slaves to them and their children? How could Mr. Jefferson but say, "I advance it therefore as a suspicion only, that the blacks, whether originally a distinct race, or made distinct by time and circumstances, are *inferior* to the whites in the endowments both of body and mind?" "It," says he, "is not against experience to suppose, that different species of the same genus, or varieties of the same species, may possess different qualifications." [Here, my brethren listen to him.]][☞"Will not a lover of natural history then, one who views the gradations in all the races of *animals* with the eye of philosophy, excuse an effort to keep those in the department of MAN as *distinct* as nature has formed them?" I hope you will try to find out the meaning of this verse—its widest sense and all its bearings: whether you do or not, remember the whites do. This very verse, brethren, having emanated from Mr. Jefferson, a much greater philosopher the world never afforded, has in truth injured us more, and has been as great a barrier to our emancipation as any thing that has ever been advanced against us. I hope you will not let it pass unnoticed. He goes on further, and says: "This *unfortunate* difference of colour, and *perhaps* of *faculty*, is a powerful obstacle to the emancipation of these people. Many of their advocates, while they wish to vindicate the liberty of human nature are anxious also to preserve its *dignity* and *beauty*. Some of these, embarrassed by the question, 'What further is to be done with them?' join themselves in opposition with those who are actuated by sordid avarice only." Now I ask you candidly, my suffering brethren in time, who are candidates for the eternal worlds, how could Mr. Jefferson but have given the world these remarks respecting us, when we are so submissive to them, and so much servile deceit prevails among ourselves—when we so *meanly* submit to their murderous lashes, to which neither the Indians or any other people under heaven would submit? No, they could die to a man, before they would suffer such things from men who are no better than themselves, and *perhaps not so good.* Yes, how can our friends but be embarrassed, as Mr. Jefferson says, by the question, "What further is to be done with these people?" for while they are working for our emancipation, we are, by our treachery, wickedness and deceit, working against ourselves and our children —helping ours, and the enemies of God, to keep us and our dear little children, in their infernal chains of slavery ! ! Indeed, our friends cannot but relapse and join themselves with those who are actuated by *sordid avarice* only ! ! ! ! For my part, I am glad Mr. Jefferson has advanced his position for your sake; for you will either have to contradict or confirm him by your own actions and not by what our friends have said or done for us; for those things are other men's labors and do not satisfy the Americans who are waiting for us to prove to them ourselves that we are MEN before they will be willing to admit the fact; for I pledge you my sacred word of honor that Mr. Jefferson's remarks respecting us have sunk deep into the hearts of millions of the whites and never will be removed this side of eternity. For how can they, when we are confirming him every day by our *groveling submissions* and *treachery?*

I aver that when I look upon these United States and see the ignorant deceptions and consequent wretchedness of my brethren, I am brought oft-times solemnly to a stand, and in the midst of my reflections I exclaim to my God, 'Lord didst thou make us to be slaves to our brethren, the whites?' But when I reflect that God is just, and that millions of my wretched brethren would meet death with glory—yea, more, would plunge into the very mouths of cannons and be torn into particles as minute as the atoms which compose the elements of the earth, in preference to a mean submission to the lash of tyrants, I am with streaming eyes, compelled to shrink back into nothingness before my Maker, and exclaim again, thy will be done, O Lord God Almighty.

Men of colour, who are also of sense, for you particularly is my appeal designed. Our more ignorant brethren are not able to penetrate its value. I call upon you therefore to cast your eyes upon the wretchedness of your brethren and to do your utmost to enlighten them—*go to work and enlighten your brethren!*—let the Lord see you doing what you can to rescue them and yourselves from degradation. Do any of you say that you and your family are free and happy and what have you to do with wretched slaves and other people? So can I say, for I enjoy as much freedom as any of you, if I am not quite as well off as the best of you. Look into our freedom and happiness and see of what kind they are composed !! They are of the very lowest kind—they are the very *dregs !*— they are the most servile and abject kind, that ever a people was in possession of! If any of you wish to know how FREE you are, let one of you start and go thro' the southern and western States of this country, and unless you travel as a slave to a white man (a servant is a *slave* to the man whom he serves,) or have your free papers (which if you are not careful they will get from you) if they do not take you up and put you in jail, and if you cannot give evidence of your freedom, sell you into eternal slavery, I am not a living man; or any man of color, immaterial who he is or where he came from, if he is not the 4th from the *"Negro race,"* (as we are called,) the white christians of America will serve him the same, they will sink him into wretchedness & degradation forever while he lives. And yet some of you have the hardihood to say that you are free & happy! May God have mercy on your freedom and happiness! I met a colored man in the street a short time since, with a string of boots on his shoulder; we fell into conversation, and in course of which I said to him, what a miserable set of people we are! He asked why?—

Said I, we are so subjected under the whites, that we cannot obtain the comforts of life, but by cleaning their boots and shoes, old clothes, waiting on them, shaving them, etc. Said he, (with the boots on his shoulders), "I am completely happy ! ! ! I never want to live any better or happier than when I can get a plenty of boots and shoes to clean ! ! !" Oh! how can those who are actuated by avarice only, but think that our creator made us to be an inheritance to them forever, when they see that our greatest glory is centered in such mean and low objects? Understand me, brethren, I do not mean to speak against the occupations by which we acquire enough and sometimes scarcely that, to render ourselves and families comfortable through life. I am subjected to the same inconvenience, as you all. My objections are, to our *glorying* and being *happy* in such low employments; for if we are men, we ought to be thankful to the Lord for the past, and for the future. Be looking forward with thankful hearts to higher attainments than *wielding the razor* and *cleaning boots and shoes*. The man whose aspirations are not *above*, and even *below* these, is indeed, ignorant and wretched enough. I advance it therefore to you, not as a *problematical*, but as an unshaken and forever immoveable *fact*, that your full glory and happiness, as well as all other colored people under heaven, shall never be fully consummated, but with the *entire emancipation of your enslaved brethren all over the world.* You may therefore, go to work and do what you can to rescue, or join in with tyrants to oppress them and yourselves, until the Lord shall come upon you all like a thief in the night. For I believe it is the will of the Lord that our greatest happiness shall consist in working for the salvation of our whole body. When this is accomplished a burst of glory will shine upon you, which will indeed astonish you and the world. Do any of you say this will never be done? I assure you that God will accomplish it—if nothing else will answer, he will hurl tyrants and devils into *atoms* and make way for his people. But O my brethren! I say unto you again, you must go to work and *prepare the way* of the Lord.

There is a great work for you to do, as trifling as some of you may think of it. You have to prove to the Americans and the world, that we are MEN, and not *brutes* as we have been represented, and by millions treated. Remember, to let the aim of your labours among your brethren, and particularly the youths, be the dissemination of education and religion. It is lamentable, that many of our children go to school, from four until they are eight or ten, and sometimes fifteen years of age, and leave school knowing but a little more about the grammar of their language than a horse does about handling a musket—and not a few of them are really so ignorant, that they are unable to answer a person correctly, general questions in geography, and to hear them read would only be to disgust a man who has a taste for reading; which, to do well, as trifling as it may appear to some, (to the ignorant in particular) is a great part of learning. Some few of them, may make out to scribble tolerably well, over a half sheet of paper, which I believe has hitherto been a powerful obstacle in our way, to keep us from from acquiring knowledge. An ignorant father, who knows no more than what nature has taught him, together with what little he acquires by the senses of hearing and seeing, finding his son able to write a neat hand, sets it down for granted that he has as good learning as any body; the young, ignorant gump, hearing his father or mother, who perhaps may be ten times more ignorant, in point of literature, than himself, extolling his learning, struts about in the full assurance, that his attainments in literature are sufficient to take him through the world, when, in fact, he has scarcely any learning at all! ! ! !

I promiscuously fell in a conversation once, with an elderly colored man on the topics of education, and of the great prevalency of ignorance among us: Said he, "I know that our people are very ignorant but my son has a good education: he can write as well as any white man, and I assure you that no one can fool him," etc. Said I, what else can your son do, besides writing a good hand? Can he post a set of books in a mercantile manner? Can he write a neat piece of composition in prose or in verse? To these interrogations he answered in the negative. Said I, Did your son learn, while he was at school, the width and depth of English Grammar? to which he also replied in the negative, telling me his son did not learn those things. Your son, said I, then, has hardly any learning at all—he is almost as ignorant, and more so, than many of those who never went to school one day in their lives. My friend got a little put out, and so walking off said that his son could write as well as any white man.—Most of the coloured people, when they speak of the education of one among us who can write a neat hand, and who perhaps knows nothing but to scribble and puff pretty fair on a small scrap of paper, immaterial whether his words are grammatical, or spelt correctly, or not; if it only looks beautiful, they say he has as good an education as any white man—he can write as well as any white man, etc. The poor, ignorant creature, hearing this, he is ashamed, forever after, to let any person see him humbling himself to another for knowledge but going about trying to deceive those who are more ignorant than himself, he at last falls an ignorant victim to death in wretchedness. I pray that the Lord may undeceive my ignorant brethren, and permit them to throw away pretensions, and seek after the substance of learning. I would crawl on my hands and knees through mud and mire, to the feet of a learned man, where I would sit and humbly supplicate him to instil into me, that which neither devils nor tyrants could remove, only with my life—for the Africans to acquire learning in this country, makes tyrants quake and tremble on their sandy foundation. Why what is the matter? Why, they know that their infernal deeds of cruelty will be made known to the world. Do you suppose one man of good sense and learning would submit himself, his father, mother, wife and children, to be slaves to a wretched man like himself, who, instead of compensating him for his labours, chains, handcuffs and beats him and family almost to death, leaving life enough in them, however, to work for, and call him master? No! no! he would cut his devilish throat from ear to ear, and well do slaveholders know it. The bare name of educating the coloured people, scares our cruel oppressors almost to death. But if they do not have enough to be frightened for yet, it will be, because they can always keep us ignorant, and because God approbates their cruelties, with which they have been for centuries murdering us. The whites shall have enough of the blacks, yet, as true as God sits on his throne in heaven.

Some of our brethren are so very full of learning that you cannot mention any thing to them which they do not know better than yourself!!—nothing is strange to them!!—they knew every thing years ago! —if any thing should be mentioned in company where they are, immaterial how important it is respecting us or the world, if they had not divulged it; they make light of it, and affect to have known it long before it was mentioned, and try to make all in the room, or wherever you may be, believe that your conversation is nothing—not worth hearing ! ! All this is the result of ignorance and ill-breeding; for a man of good breeding, sense, and penetration, if he had heard a subject told twenty times over and should happen to be in company where one should commence telling it again, he would wait with patience on its narrator, and see if he would tell it as it was told in his presence before—paying the most strict attention to what is said, to see if any more light will be thrown on the subject; for all men are not gifted alike in telling, or even hearing the most simple narration. These ignorant, vicious, and wretched men, contribute almost as much injury to our body as tyrants themselves, by doing so much for the promotion of ignorance amongst us; for they, making such pretensions to knowledge, such of our youth as are seeking after knowledge, and can get access to them, take them as criterions to go by, who will lead them into a channel, where, unless the Lord blesses them with the privilege of seeing their error, they will be irretrievably lost forever, while in time ! !

I must close this article by narrating the very heart-rending fact, that I have examined school-boys and young men of colour in different parts of the country, in the most simple parts of Murray's English Grammar, and not more than one in thirty was able to give a correct answer to my interrogations. If any one contradicts me, let him step out of his door into the streets of Boston, New York, Philadelphia or Baltimore, (no use to mention any other, for the Christians are too charitable further south or west!)—I say, let him who disputes me, step out of his door into the streets of either of those four cities, and promiscuously collect one hundred school boys or young men of colour, *who have been to school*, and who are considered by the coloured people to have received an excellent education, because, perhaps, some of them can write a good hand, but who notwithstanding their neat writing, may be almost as ignorant, in comparison, as horses. And, I say it, he will hardly find (in this enlightened day, and in the midst of this *charitable* people) five in one hundred, who are able to correct the false grammar of their language. The cause of this almost universal ignorance amongst us, I appeal to our school-masters to declare. Here is a fact, which I this very minute take from the mouth of a young coloured man, who has been to school in this state (Massachusetts) nearly nine years, and who knows grammar this day, *nearly* as well as he did the day he first entered the school-house, under a white master. This young man says—"My master would never allow me to study grammar."—I asked him why? "The school committee,"

said he, "forbid the colored children learning grammar—they would not
allow any but the white children to study grammar." It is a notorious
fact that the major part of the white Americans have, ever since we
have been among them, tried to keep us ignorant and make us believe
that God made us and our children to be slaves to them and theirs. *Oh!
my God, have mercy on Christian Americans ! !*

ARTICLE III

Our Wretchedness in Consequence of the Preachers of the Religion of Jesus Christ

RELIGION, my brethren, is a substance of deep consideration among all
nations of the earth. The Pagans have a kind, as well as the Mahometans, the Jews and the Christians. But pure and undefiled religion, such
as was preached by Jesus Christ and his apostles, is hard to be found in
all the earth. God, through his instrument, Moses, handed a dispensation of his divine will to the children of Israel after they had left Egypt
for the land of Canaan, or of Promise, who through hypocrisy, oppression, and unbelief, departed from the faith. He then, by his apostles
handed a dispensation of his, together with the will of Jesus Christ, to
the Europeans in Europe, who, in open violation of which, have made
merchandize of us, and it does appear as though they take this very dispensation to aid them in their infernal depredations upon us. Indeed,
the way in which religion was and is conducted by the Europeans and
their descendants, one might believe it was a plan fabricated by themselves and the *devils* to oppress us. But hark ! my master has taught me
better than to believe it—he has taught me that his gospel as it was
preached by himself and his apostles remains the same, notwithstanding
Europe has tried to mingle blood and oppression with it.

It is well known to the Christian world that Bartholomew Las Casas,
that very notoriously avaricious Catholic priest or preacher, and adventurer with Columbus in his second voyage, proposed to his countrymen, the Spaniards in Hispaniola, to import the Africans from the Portuguese settlement in Africa, to dig up gold and silver, and work their
plantations for them, to effect which, he made a voyage thence to Spain,
and opened the subject to his master, Ferdinand, then in declining
health, who listened to the plan; but who died soon after, and left it in
the hands of his successor, Charles V.—This wretch, ("Las Cassas, the
Preacher,") succeeded so well in his plans of oppression, that in 1503, the
first blacks had been imported into the new world. Elated with this
success, and stimulated by sordid avarice only, he importuned Charles
V. in 1511, to grant permission to a Flemish merchant to import 4000
blacks at one time. Thus we see, through the instrumentality of a pretended preacher of the gospel of Jesus Christ our common master, our
wretchedness first commenced in America—where it has been continued
from 1503 to this day, 1829. A period of three hundred and twenty-six
years. But two hundred and nine, from 1620—when twenty of our fathers were brought into Jamestown, Virginia, by a Dutch man-of-war,

and sold off like brutes to the highest bidders; and there is not a doubt in my mind, but that tyrants are in hopes to perpetuate our miseries under them and their children until the final consummation of all things. But if they do not get dreadfully deceived, it will be because God has forgotten them.

The Pagans, Jews and Mahometans try to make proselytes to their religions, and whatever human beings adopt their religions, they extend to them their protection. But Christian Americans not only hinder their fellow creatures, the Africans, but thousands of them will *absolutely beat a coloured person nearly to death, if they catch him on his knees, supplicating the throne of grace.* This barbarous cruelty was by all the heathen nations of antiquity, and is by the Pagans, Jews and Mahometans of the present day, left entirely to Christian Americans to inflict on the Africans and their descendants that their cup which is nearly full may be completed. I have known tyrants or usurpers of human liberty in different parts of this country take their fellow creatures, the colored people, and beat them until they would scarcely leave life in them; what for? Why they say, "The black devils had the audacity to be found *making prayers and supplications to the God who made them ! ! !"* Yes, I have known small collections of coloured people to have convened together, for no other purpose than to worship God Almighty, in spirit and in truth, to the best of their knowledge; when tyrants, calling themselves *patrols*, would also convene and wait almost in breathless silence for the poor coloured people to commence singing and praying to the Lord our God, and as soon as they had commenced the wretches would burst in upon them and drag them out and commence beating them as they would rattle-snakes—many of whom, they would beat so unmercifully, that they would hardly be able to crawl for weeks and sometimes for months.—Yet the American ministers send out missionaries to convert the heathen, while they keep us and our children sunk at their feet in the most abject ignorance and wretchedness that ever a people was afflicted with since the world began. Will the Lord suffer this people to proceed much longer? Will he not stop them in their career? Does he regard the heathens abroad, more than the heathens among the Americans? Surely the Americans must believe that God is partial, notwithstanding his Apostle Peter, declared before Cornelius and others that he has no respect to persons, but in every nation he that feareth God and worketh righteousness is accepted with him.—"The word," said he, "which God sent unto the children of Israel, preaching peace, by Jesus Christ, (he is the Lord of all.") Have not the Americans the Bible in their hands? Do they believe it? Surely they do not. See how they treat us in open violation of the Bible ! ! They no doubt will be greatly offended with me, but if God does not awaken them, it will be, because they are superior to other men, as they have represented themselves to be. Our divine Lord and Master said "all things whatsoever ye would that men should do unto you, do ye even so unto them." But an American minister, with the Bible in his hand, holds us and our children in the most abject slavery and wretchedness. Now I ask them, would they like for us to hold them and their children in abject slavery and wretchedness? No says one, that never can be done—you are too abject and ignorant to do it—you are not men—you were made to be slaves to us, to dig up gold and silver for us and our children. Know this, my dear sirs, that although you treat us and our children now, as you do your domestic beasts—yet the final result of all future events are known but to God Almighty alone, who rules in the armies of heaven and among the inhabitants of the earth, and who dethrones one earthly king and sits up another, as it seemeth good in his holy sight. We may attribute these vicissitudes to what we please, but the God of armies and of justice rules in heaven and in earth, and the whole American people shall see and know it yet, to their satisfaction. I have know pretended preachers of the gospel of my Master, who not only held us as their natural inheritance, but treated us with as much rigor as any Infidel or Deist in the world—just as though they were intent only on taking our blood and groans to glorify the Lord Jesus Christ. The wicked and ungodly, seeing their preachers treat us with so much cruelty, they say: our preachers, who must be right, if any body are, treat them like brutes, and why cannot we?—They think it is no harm to keep them in slavery and put the whip to them, and why cannot we do the same!—They being preachers of the gospel of Jesus Christ, if it were any harm, they would surely preach against their oppression and do their utmost to erase it from the country; not only in one or two cities, but one continual cry would be raised in all parts of this confederacy, and would cease only with the complete overthrow of the system of slavery, in every part of the country. But how far the American preachers are from preaching against slavery and oppression, which have carried their country to the brink of a precipice; to save them from plunging down the side of which, will hardly be effected, will appear in the sequel of this paragraph, which I shall narrate just as it transpired. I remember a Camp Meeting in South Carolina, for which I embarked in a Steam Boat at Charleston, and having been five or six hours on the water, we at last arrived at the place of hearing, where was a very great concourse of people, who were no doubt, collected together to hear the word of God, (that some had collected barely as spectators to the scene, I will not here pretend to doubt, however, that is left to themselves and their God.) Myself and boat companions, having been there a little while, we were all called up to hear; I among the rest, went up and took my seat—being seated, I fixed myself in a complete position to hear the word of my Saviour and to receive such as I thought was authenticated by the Holy Scriptures; but to my no ordinary astonishment, our Reverend gentleman got up and told us (colored people) that slaves must be obedient to their masters—must do their duty to their masters or be whipped—the whip was made for the backs of fools, &c. Here I pause for a moment, to give the world time to consider what was my surprise, to hear such preaching from a minister of my Master, whose very gospel is that of peace and not of blood and whips, as this pretended preacher tried to make us believe. What the American preachers can think of us, I aver this day before my God, I have never been able to define. They have newspapers and monthly periodicals, which they receive in continual succession, but on the pages of which, you will scarcely ever find a paragraph respecting slavery, which is ten thousand times more injurious to this country than all the other evils put together; and which will be the final overthrow of its government, unless something is very speedily done; for their cup is nearly full.—Perhaps they will laugh at, or make light of this; but I tell you Americans! that unless you speedily alter your course, *you* and your *Country are gone ! ! ! ! !* For God Almighty will tear up the very face of the earth ! ! ! ! Will not that very remarkable passage of Scripture be fulfilled on Christian Americans? Hear it Americans ! ! "He that is unjust, let him be unjust still:—and he which is filthy, let him be filthy still: and he that is righteous, let him be righteous still; and he that is holy, let him be holy still." I hope that the Americans may hear, but I am afraid that they have done us so much injury, and are so firm in the belief that our Creator made us to be an inheritance to them forever, that their hearts will be hardened, so that their destruction may be sure.—This language, perhaps is too harsh for the American's delicate ears. But Oh Americans! Americans! ! I warn you in the name of the Lord, (whether you will hear, or forbear,) to repent and reform, or you are ruined ! ! ! ! ! ! Do you think that our blood is hidden from the Lord, because you can hide it from the rest of the world by sending out missionaries, and by your charitable deeds to the Greeks, Irish, &c.? Will he not publish your secret crimes on the house top? Even here in Boston, pride and prejudice have got to such a pitch, that in the very houses erected to the Lord, they have built little places for the reception of colored people, where they must sit during meeting, or keep away from the house of God; and the preachers say nothing about it—much less, go into the hedges and highways seeking the lost sheep of the house of Israel, and try to bring them in, to their Lord and Master. There are hardly a more wretched, ignorant, miserable, and abject set of beings in all the world, than the blacks in the Southern and Western sections of this country, under tyrants and devils. The preachers of America cannot see them, but they can send out missionaries to convert the heathens, notwithstanding. Americans! unless you speedily alter your course of proceeding, if God Almighty does not stop you, I say it in his name, that you may go on and do as you please for ever, both in time and eternity—never fear any evil at all ! ! ! ! ! ! ! !

[☞ Addition.—The preachers and people of the United States form societies against Free Masonry and Intemperance, and write against Sabbath breaking, Sabbath mails, Infidelity, &c. &c. But the fountain head,* compared with which all those other evils are comparatively nothing, and from the bloody and murderous head of which, they receive no trifling support, is hardly noticed by the Americans. This is a fair illustration of the state of society in this country—it shows what a bearing *avarice* has upon a people, when they are nearly given up by the Lord to a hard heart and a reprobate mind, in consequence of afflicting their fellow creatures. God suffers some to go on until they are ruined for ever ! ! Will it be the case with our brethren the whites of the United States of America? We hope not—we would not wish to see them de-

* Slavery and oppression.

stroyed, notwithstanding they have and do now treat us more cruel than
any people have treated another, on this earth since it came from the
hands of its creator (with the exception of the French and the Dutch,
they treat us nearly as bad as the Americans of the United States.) The
will of God must however, in spite of us, *be done.*

The English are the best friends the colored people have upon earth.
Tho' they have oppressed us a little, and have colonies now in the West
Indies, which oppress us *sorely,*—Yet notwithstanding they (the English)
have done one hundred times more for the melioration of our condition,
than all the other nations of the earth put together. The blacks cannot
but respect the English as a nation, notwithstanding they have treated
us a little cruel.

There is no intelligent *black man* who knows any thing, but esteems a
real English man, let him see him in what part of the world he will—for
they are the greatest benefactors we have upon earth. We have here
and there, in other nations, good friends. But as a nation, the English
are our friends.ℭ]

How can the preachers and people of America believe the Bible? Does
it teach them any distinction on account of a man's color? Hearken,
Americans! to the injunctions of our Lord and Master, to his humble
followers.

"And Jesus came and spake unto them saying, all power is given unto
me in heaven and in earth.

Go ye, therefore, and teach all nations, baptizing them in the name of
the Father, and of the Son, and of the Holy Ghost,

Teaching them to observe all things whatsoever I have commanded
you; and lo, I am with you alway, even unto the end of the world. Amen."

I declare, that the very face of these injunctions appears to be of God
and not of man. They do not show the slightest degree of distinction.
"Go ye, therefore, (says my divine Master) and teach all nations, (or in
other words, all people) baptizing them in the name of the Father, and of
the Son, and of the Holy Ghost." Do you understand the above, Americans? We are a people, notwithstanding many of you doubt it. You have
the Bible in your hands, with this very injunction. Have you been to
Africa, teaching the inhabitants thereof the words of the Lord Jesus?
"Baptizing them in the name of the Father, and of the Son, and of the
Holy Ghost." Have you not, on the contrary, entered among us, and
learnt us the art of throat-cutting, by setting us to fight, one against
another, to take each other as prisoners of war, and sell to you for small
bits of calicoes, old swords, knives, &c. to make slaves for you and your
children? This being done, have you not brought us among you, in chains
and handcuffs, like brutes, and treated us with all the cruelties and
rigour your ingenuity could invent, consistent with the laws of your
country, which (for the blacks) are tyrannical enough? Can the American
preachers appeal unto God, the Maker and searcher of hearts, and tell
him, with the Bible in their hands, that they make no distinction on
account of men's colour? Can they say, O God! thou knowest all things—
thou knowest that we make no distinction between thy creatures to
whom we have to preach thy Word? Let them answer the Lord; and if

they cannot do it in the affirmative, have they not departed from the Lord Jesus Christ, their master? But some may say, that they never had or were in possession of a religion, which makes no distinction, and of course they could not have departed from it. I ask you then, in the name of the Lord, of what kind can your religion be? Can it be that which was preached by our Lord Jesus Christ from Heaven? I believe you cannot be so wicked as to tell him that his Gospel was that of *distinction*. What can the American preachers and people take God to be?—Do they believe his words? If they do, do they believe that he will be mocked? Or do they believe because they are whites and we blacks, that God will have respect to them? Did not God make us as it seemed best to himself? What right, then, has one of us, to despise another and to treat him cruel, on account of his colour, which none but the God who made it can alter? Can there be a greater absurdity in nature, and particularly in a free republican country? But the Americans, having introduced slavery among them, their hearts have become almost seared, as with an hot iron, and God has nearly given them up to believe a lie in preference to the truth ! ! ! and I am awfully afraid that pride, prejudice, avarice and blood, will, before long, prove the final ruin of this happy republic, or land of liberty ! ! ! Can any thing be a greater mockery of religion than the way in which it is conducted by the Americans? It appears as though they are bent only on daring God Almighty to do his best—they chain and handcuff us and our children and drive us around the country like brutes, and go into the house of the God of justice to return Him thanks for having aided him in their infernal cruelties inflicted upon us. Will the Lord suffer this people to go on much longer, taking his holy name in vain? Will he not stop them, PREACHERS and all? O Americans! Americans ! ! I call God—I call angels—I call men, to witness, that your DESTRUCTION *is at hand,* and will be speedily consummated unless you REPENT.

ARTICLE IV

Our Wretchedness in Consequence of the Colonizing Plan

My dearly beloved brethren:—This is a scheme on which so many able writers, together with that very judicious colored Baltimorean, have commented, that I feel my delicacy about touching it. But as I am compelled to do the will of my master, I declare, I will give you my sentiments upon it. Previous, however, to giving my sentiments, either for or against it, I shall give that of Mr. Henry Clay, together with that of Mr. Elias B. Caldwell, Esq. of the District of Columbia, as extracted from the National Intelligencer, by Dr. Torrey, author of a series of "Essays on Morals, and the Diffusion of Useful Knowledge."

At a meeting which was convened in the District of Columbia, for the express purpose of agitating the subject of colonizing us in some part of the world, Mr. Clay was called to the chair, and having been seated a little while, he rose and spake, in substance, as follows: Says he—"That class of the mixt population of our country [coloured people] was

peculiarly situated; they neither enjoyed the immunities of freemen, nor
were they subjected to the incapacities of slaves, but partook, in some
degree, of the qualities of both. From their condition, and the unconquerable prejudices resulting from their colour, they never could amal-
gamate with the free whites of this country. It was desirable, therefore,
as it respected them, and the residue of the population of the country, to
drain them off. Various schemes of colonization had been thought of,
and a part of our continent, it was supposed by some, might furnish a
suitable establishment for them. But, for his part, Mr. C. said, he had a
decided preference for some part of the coast of Africa. There ample
provision might be made for the colony itself, and it might be rendered
instrumental in the introduction into that extensive quarter of the globe,
of the arts, civilization, and Christianity." [Here I ask Mr. Clay, what
kind of Christianity? Did he mean such as they have among the Americans—distinction, whip, blood and oppression? I pray the Lord Jesus
Christ to forbid it.] "There," said he, "was a peculiar, a moral fitness, in
restoring them to the land of their fathers, and if instead of the evils
and sufferings which we had been the innocent cause of inflicting upon
the inhabitants of Africa, we can transmit to her the blessings of our
arts, our civilization, and our religion. May we not hope that America
will extinguish a great portion of that moral debt which she has con-
tracted to that unfortunate continent? Can there be a nobler cause than
that which, whilst it proposes, &c. * * * * * * [you know what this
means.] contemplates the spreading of the arts of civilized life, and the
possible redemption from ignorance and barbarism of a benighted quarter of the globe?"

Before I proceed any further, I solicit your notice, brethren, to the
foregoing part of Mr. Clay's speech, in which he says, (☞ look above)
"and if, instead of the evils and sufferings, which we had been the innocent cause of inflicting," &c. What this very learned statesman could have
been thinking about, when he said in his speech, "we had been the innocent cause of inflicting," etc., I have never been able to conceive. Are
Mr. Clay and the rest of the Americans, innocent of the blood and groans
of our fathers and us, their children? Every individual may plead innocence, if he pleases, but God will, before long, separate the innocent from
the guilty, unless something is speedily done—which I suppose will
hardly be, so that their destruction may be sure. Oh Americans! let me
tell you, in the name of the Lord, it will be good for you, if you listen to
the voice of the Holy Ghost, but if you do not you are ruined ! ! ! ! Some
of you are good men; but the will of my God must be done. Those
avaricious and ungodly tyrants among you, I am awfully afraid will drag
down the vengeance of God upon you.—When God Almighty commences
his battle on the continent of America, for the oppression of his people,
tyrants will wish they never were born.

But to return to Mr. Clay, whence I digressed. He says, "It was proper
and necessary distinctly to state, that he understood it constituted no
part of the object of this meeting, to touch or agitate in the slightest
degree, a delicate question, connected with another portion of the col-

oured population of our country. It was not proposed to deliberate upon or consider at all, any question of emancipation, or that which was connected with the abolition of slavery. It was upon that condition alone, he was sure, that many gentlemen from the South and the West, whom he saw present, had attended, or could be expected to co-operate. It was on that condition only, that he himself had attended."—That is to say, to fix a plan to get those of the coloured people, who are said to be free, away from among those of our brethren whom they unjustly hold in bondage, so that they may be enabled to keep them the more secure in ignorance and wretchedness, to support them and their children, and consequently they would have the more obedient slaves. For if the free are allowed to stay among the slaves, they will have intercourse together, and, of course, the free will learn the slaves *bad habits,* by teaching them that they are MEN, as well as other people, and certainly *ought,* and *must* be FREE.

I presume, that every intelligent man of colour must have some idea of Mr. Henry Clay, originally of Virginia, but now of Kentucky; they know too, perhaps, whether he is a friend, or a foe, to the coloured citizens of this country, and of the world. This gentleman, according to his own words, had been highly favoured and blessed of the Lord, though he did not acknowledge it; but to the contrary, he acknowledged men, for all the blessings which God had favoured him. At a public dinner given him at Fowler's Garden, Lexington, Kentucky, he delivered a public speech to a very large concourse of people—in the concluding clause of which, he says, "And now, my friends and fellow citizens, I cannot part from you, on possibly the last occasion of my ever publicly addressing you, without reiterating the expression of my thanks, from a heart over-flowing with gratitude. I came among you, now more than thirty years ago, an orphan boy pennyless, a stranger to you all, without friends without the favour of the great, you took me up, cherished me, protected me, honoured me, you have constantly poured upon me a bold and un-abated stream of innumerable favors, time which wears out every thing has increased and strengthened your affection for me. When I seemed deserted by almost the whole world, and assailed by almost every tongue, and pen, and press, you have fearlessly and manfully stood by me, with unsurpassed zeal and undiminished friendship. When I felt as if I should sink beneath the storm of abuse and detraction, which was violently raging around me, I have found myself upheld and sustained by your encouraging voices and approving smiles. I have doubtless, committed many faults and indiscretions, over which you have thrown the broad mantle of your charity. But I can say, and in the presence of God and this assembled multitude, I will say, that I have honestly and faithfully served my country—that I have never wronged it—and that, however unprepared, I lament that I am to appear in the Divine presence on other accounts, I invoke the stern justice of his judgment on my public con-duct without the slightest apprehension of his displeasure."

Hearken to this statesman indeed, but no philanthropist, whom God sent into Kentucky, an orphan boy, pennyless and friendless, where he

not only gave him a plenty of friends and the comforts of life, but
raised him almost to the very highest honour in the nation, where his
great talents, with which the Lord has been pleased to bless him, has
gained for him the affection of a great portion of the people with whom
he had to do. But what has this gentleman done for the Lord, after
having done so much for him? The Lord has a suffering people, whose
moans and groans at his feet for deliverance from oppression and
wretchedness, pierce the very throne of Heaven, and call loudly on the
GOD of Justice, to be revenged. Now what this gentleman who is so
highly favored of the Lord, has done to liberate those miserable victims
of oppression, shall appear before the world, by his letters to Mr. Gallatin, Envoy Extraordinary and Minister Plenipotentiary to Great
Britain, dated June 19, 1826. Though Mr. Clay was writing for the states,
yet nevertheless, it appears from the very face of his letters to that
gentleman, that he was as anxious, if not more so, to get those free
people and sink them into wretchedness, as his constituents for whom
he wrote.

The Americans of North and of South America, including the West
India Islands—no trifling portion of whom were, for stealing, murdering,
&c. compelled to flee from Europe, to save their necks or banishment,
have effected their escape to this continent, where God blessed them with
all the comforts of life—He gave them a plenty of every thing calculated
to do them good—not satisfied with this, however, they wanted slaves,
and wanted us for their slaves, who belong to the Holy Ghost, and no
other, who we shall have to serve instead of tyrants. I say, the Americans
want us, the property of the Holy Ghost, to serve them. But there is a
day fast approaching when (unless there is a universal repentance on
the part of the whites, which will scarcely take place—they have got to
be so hardened in consequence of our blood, and so wise in their own
conceit.) To be plain and candid with you, Americans! I say that the
day is fast approaching when there will be a greater time on the continent of America than ever was witnessed upon this earth since it came
from the hands of its Creator. Some of you have done us so much injury
that you will never be able to repent. Your cup must be filled. You want
us for your slaves and shall have enough of us—God is just, *who will
give you your fill of us*. But Mr. Henry Clay, speaking to Mr. Gallatin
respecting coloured people who had effected their escape from the U.
States (or to them *hell upon earth ! !*) to the hospitable shores of
Canada * from whence it would cause more than the lives of the Americans to get them, to plunge into wretchedness—he says: "The General
Assembly of Kentucky, one of the states which is most affected by the
escape of slaves into Upper Canada, has again, at their session which has
just terminated, invoked the interposition of the General Government.
In the treaty which has been recently concluded with the United Mexican
States, and which is now under the consideration of the Senate, provision
is made for the restoration of fugitive slaves. As it appears from your
statements of what passed on that subject with the British Plenipoten-
tiaries, that they admitted the correctness of the principle of restoration,

* Among the English, our real friends and benefactors.

it is hoped that you will be able to succeed in making satisfactory arrangements."

There are a series of these letters, all of which are to the same amount; some however presenting a face more of his own responsibility. I wonder what would this gentleman think if the Lord should give him among the rest of his blessings enough of slaves? Could he blame any other being but himself? Do we not belong to the Holy Ghost? What business has he or any body else, to be sending letters about the world respecting us? Can we not go where we want to, as well as other people, only if we obey the voice of the Holy Ghost? This gentleman, (Henry Clay) not only took an active part in this colonizing plan, but was absolutely chairman of a meeting held at Washington the 21st day of December, 1816 to agitate the subject of colonizing us in Africa.—Now I appeal and ask every citizen of these United States and of the world, both *white* and *black*, who has any knowledge of Mr. Clay's public labors for these States—I want you candidly to answer the Lord, who sees the secrets of your hearts, Do you believe that Mr. Henry Clay, late Secretary of State, and now in Kentucky, is a friend to the blacks, further than his personal interest extends? Is it not his greatest object and glory upon earth to sink us into miseries and wretchedness by making slaves of us, to work his plantation to enrich him and his family? Does he care a pinch of snuff about Africa—whether it remains a land of Pagans and of blood, or of Christians, so long as he gets enough of her sons and daughters to dig up gold and silver for him? If he had no slave, and could obtain them in no other way if it were not repugnant to the laws of his country, which prohibit the importation of slaves, (which act was indeed more through apprehension than humanity) would he not try to import a few from Africa to work his farm? Would he work in the hot sun to earn his bread if he could make an African work for nothing, particularly if he could keep him in ignorance and make him believe that God made him for nothing else but to work for him? Is not Mr. Clay a white man, and too delicate to work in the hot sun? Was he not made by his Creator to sit in the shade, and make the blacks work without remuneration for their services, to support him and his family? I have been for some time taking notice of this man's speeches and public writings, but never to my knowledge have I seen any thing in his writings which insisted on the emancipation of slavery, which has almost ruined his country. Thus we see the depravity of men's hearts, when in pursuit only of gain—particularly when they oppress their fellow creatures to obtain that gain— God suffers some to go on until they are lost for ever. This same Mr. Clay wants to know what he has done to merit the disapprobation of the American people. In a public speech delivered by him, he asked: "Did I involve my country in an unnecessary war?" to merit the censure of the Americans—"Did I bring obloquy upon the nation, or the people whom I represented—did I ever lose an opportunity to advance the fame, honor and prosperity of this State and the Union?" How astonishing it is, for a man who knows so much about God and his ways, as Mr. Clay, to ask such frivolous questions. Does he believe that a man of his talents and standing in the midst of a people, will get along unnoticed by the penetrating and all-seeing eye of God who is continually taking cognizance of the hearts of men? Is not God against him, for advocating the murderous cause of slavery? If God is against him, what can the Americans, together with the whole world do for him? Can they save him from the hand of the Lord Jesus Christ?

I shall now pass in review the speech of Mr. Elias B. Caldwell, Esq. of the District of Columbia, extracted from the same page on which Mr. Clay's will be found. Mr. Caldwell, giving his opinion respecting us, at that ever memorable meeting, he says: "The more you improve the condition of these people, the more you cultivate their minds, the more miserable you make them in their present state. You give them a higher relish for those privileges which they can never attain, and turn what we intend for a blessing into a curse." Let me ask this benevolent man, what he means by a blessing intended for us? Did he mean sinking us and our children into ignorance and wretchedness, to support him and his family? What he meant will appear evident and obvious to the most ignorant in the world. ☞ See Mr. Caldwell's intended blessings for us, O! my Lord ! ! ! "No," said he, "if they must remain in their present situation, keep them in the *lowest state of degradation and ignorance.* The nearer you bring them to the condition of brutes, the better chance do you give them of possessing their *apathy.*" Here, I pause to get breath, having labored to extract the above clause of this gentleman's speech, at that colonizing meeting. I presume that every body knows the meaning of the word *"apathy"*—if they do not, let him get Sheridan's Dictionary, where he will find it explained in full. I solicit the attention of the world to the foregoing part of Mr. Caldwell's speech, that they may see what man will do with his fellow men, when he has them under his feet. To what length will not man go in iniquity, when given up to a hard heart and reprobate mind, in consequence of blood and oppression? The last clause of this speech, which was written in a very artful manner and which will be taken for the speech of a friend, without close examination and deep penetration, I shall now present. He says, "Surely Americans ought to be the last people on earth to advocate such slavish doctrines, to cry peace and contentment to those who are deprived of the privileges of civil liberty, they who have so largely partaken of its blessings, who know so well how to estimate its value, ought to be among the foremost to extend it to others." The real sense and meaning of the last part of Mr. Caldwell's speech is, get the free people of colour away to Africa, from among the slaves, where they may at once be blessed and happy, and our slaves will be contented to rest in ignorance and wretchedness, to dig up gold and silver for us and our children. Men have indeed, got to be so cunning, these days, that it would take the eye of a Solomon to penetrate and find them out.

Extract from the speech of Mr. John Randolph, of Roanoke.

Said he:—"It had been properly observed by the Chairman, as well as by the gentlemen from this District (meaning Messrs. Clay and Caldwell) that there was nothing in the proposition submitted to consideration which in the smallest degree touches another very important and delicate question, which ought to be left as much out of view as possible, (Negro Slavery.) *

There was no fear, Mr. R. said, that this proposition would alarm the slave-holders; they had been accustomed to think seriously of the subject. There was a popular work on agriculture, by John Taylor of Carolina, which was widely circulated, and much confided in, in Virginia. In that book, much read because coming from a practical man, this description of people, [referring to us half free ones,] were pointed out as a great evil. They had indeed been held up as the greater bug-bear to every man who feels an inclination to emancipate his slaves, not to create in the bosom of his country so great a nuisance. If a place could be provided for their reception, and a mode of sending them hence, there were hundreds, nay thousands of citizens, who would, by manumitting their slaves, relieve themselves from the cares attendant on their possession. The great slave-holder, Mr. R. said, was frequently a mere sentry at his own door—bound to stay on his plantation to see that his slaves were properly treated, &c. Mr. R. concluded by saying that he had thought it necessary to make these remarks, being a slave-holder himself, to show that, so far from being connected with abolition of slavery, the measure proposed would prove one of greatest securities to enable the master to keep in possession his own property."

Here is a demonstrative proof, of a plan got up by a gang of slave-holders to select the free people of colour from among the slaves, that our more miserable brethren may be the better secured in ignorance and wretchedness, to work their farms and dig their mines, and thus go on enriching the christians with their blood and groans. What our brethren could have been thinking about, who have left their native land and home and gone away to Africa I am unable to say. This country is as much ours at it is the whites, whether they will admit it now or not, they will see and believe it by and by. They tell us about prejudice—what have we to do with it? Their prejudices will be obliged to fall like lightning to the ground, in succeeding generations; not, however with the will and consent of all the whites, for some will be obliged to hold on to the old adage, viz.: the blacks are not men, but were made to be an inheritance to us and our children forever ! ! ! ! ! ! I hope the residue of the coloured people will stand still and see the salvation of God, and the miracle which he will work for our delivery from wretchedness under the christians ! ! ! ! ! !

[☞ ADDITION.—If any of us see fit to go away, go to those who have been for many years, and are now our greatest earthly friends and benefactors—the English. If not so, go to our brethren, the Haytians, who, according to their word, is bound to protect and comfort us. The Americans say that we are ungrateful—but I ask them for heaven's sake, what

---

* "Niger" is a word derived from the Latin, which was used by the old Romans to designate inanimate beings which were black, such as soot, pot, wood, house, &c. Also, of animals which they considered inferior to the human species, as a black horse, cow, hog, bird, dog, &c. The white Americans have applied this term to Africans, by way of reproach for our color, to aggravate and heighten our miseries, because they have their feet on our throats, and we cannot help ourselves.

we should be grateful to them for—for murdering our fathers and mothers?—Or do they wish us to return thanks to them for chaining and handcuffing us, branding us, cramming fire down our throats, or for keeping us in slavery, and beating us nearly or quite to death to make us work in ignorance and miseries, to support them and their families. They certainly think that we are a gang of fools. Those among them, who have volunteered their services for our redemption, though we are unable to compensate them for their labors, we nevertheless thank them from the bottom of our hearts, and have our eyes steadfastly fixed upon them, and their labors of love for God and man. But do slaveholders think that we thank them for keeping us in miseries, and taking our lives by the inches?

Before I proceed further with this scheme, I shall give an extract from the letter of the truly Reverend Divine, (Bishop Allen,) of Philadelphia, respecting this trick. At the instance of the Editor of the Freedom's Journal, he says, "Dear Sir, I have been for several years trying to reconcile my mind to the Colonizing of Africans in Liberia, but there have always been, and there still remain great and insurmountable objections against the scheme. We are an unlettered people, brought up in ignorance, not one in a hundred can read or write, not one in a thousand has a liberal education; is there any fitness for such to be sent into a far country, among heathens, to convert or civilize them, when they themselves are neither civilized or christianized? See the great bulk of the poor, ignorant Africans in this country, exposed to every temptation before them: all for the want of their morals being refined by education and proper attendance paid unto them by their owners, or those who had the charge of them. It is said by the Southern slave-holders, that the more ignorant they can bring up the Africans, the better slaves they make, 'go and come.' Is there any fitness for such people to be colonized in a far country, to be their own rulers? Can we not discern the project of sending the free people of colour away from their country? Is it not for the interest of the slave-holders to select the free people of colour out of the different states, and send them to Liberia? Will it not make their slaves uneasy to see free men of colour enjoying liberty? It is against the law, in some of the southern states, that a person of colour should receive an education, under a severe penalty. Colonizationists speak of America being first colonized, but is there any comparison between the two? America was colonized by as *wise, judicious* and *educated* men as the world afforded. WILLIAM PENN did not want for *learning, wisdom, or intelligence.* If all the people in Europe and America were as ignorant, and in the same situation as our brethren, what would become of the world? where would be the principle or piety that would govern the people? We were *stolen* from our mother country, and brought *here.* We have *tilled* the ground and made fortunes for thousands, and still they are not weary of our services. *But they who stay to till the ground must be slaves.* Is there not land enough in America, or 'corn enough in Egypt?' Why should they send us into a far country to die? See the thousands of foreigners emigrating to America every year: and if there be ground sufficient for them to cultivate, and bread for them to eat;

why would they wish to send the *first tillers* of the land away? Africans have made fortunes for thousands, who are yet unwilling to part with their services; but the free must be sent away, and those who remain must be *slaves*. I have no doubt that there are many good men who do not see as I do, and who are for sending us to Liberia; but they have not duly considered the subject—they are not men of colour. This land which we have watered with our *tears* and *our blood*, is now our *mother country*, and we are well satisfied to stay where wisdom abounds and the gospel is free."

RICHARD ALLEN,
*Bishop of the African Methodist Episcopal
Church in the United States.*

I have given you, my brethren, an extract verbatim from the letter of that godly man as you may find it on the aforementioned page of Freedom's Journal. I know that thousands and perhaps millions of my brethren in these States, have never heard of such a man as Bishop Allen—a man whom God many years ago raised up among his ignorant and degraded brethren, to preach Jesus Christ and him crucified to them—who notwithstanding, had to wrestle against principalities and the powers of darkness to diffuse that gospel with which he was endowed, among his brethren—but who having overcome the combined powers of devils and wicked men has under God planted a church among us which will be as durable as the foundation of the earth on which it stands. Richard Allen! O my God! ! the bare recollection of the labours of this man, and his ministers among his deplorably wretched brethren (rendered so by the whites,) to bring them to a knowledge of the God of heaven, fills my soul with all those very high emotions which would take the pen of an Addison to portray. It is impossible, my brethren, for me to say much in this work respecting that man of God. When the Lord shall raise up coloured historians in succeeding generations, to present the crimes of this nation to the then gazing world, the Holy Ghost will make them do justice to the name of Bishop Allen, of Philadelphia. Suffice it for me to say, that the name of this very man (Richard Allen,) though now in obscurity and degradation, will notwithstanding stand on the pages of history among the greatest divines who have lived since the apostolic age, and among the African's, Bishop Allen's will be entirely pre-eminent. My brethren, search after the character and exploits of this godly man among his ignorant and miserable brethren, to bring them to a knowledge of the truth as it is in our Master. Consider upon the tyrants and false christians against whom he had to contend in order to get access to his brethren. See him and his ministers in the states of New York, New Jersey, Penn. Delaware and Maryland, carrying the gladsome tidings of free and full salvation to the colored people. Tyrants and false christians however, would not allow him to penetrate far into the South for fear that he would awaken some of his ignorant brethren, whom they held in wretchedness and miseries—for fear, I say it, that he would awaken and bring them to a knowledge of their Maker. O my Master! my Master! I cannot but think upon Christian Americans! !

What kind of people can they be? Will not those who were burnt up in Sodom and Gomorrah rise up in judgment against Christian Americans with the Bible in their hands, and condemn them? Will not the Scribes and Pharisees of Jerusalem, who had nothing but the laws of Moses and the Prophets to go by, rise up in judgment against Christian Americans, and condemn them * who in addition to these have a revelation from Jesus Christ the son of the living God? In fine, will not the Antediluvians, together with the whole heathen world of antiquity, rise up in judgment against Christian Americans and condemn them? The Christians of Europe and America go to Africa, bring us away, and throw us into the seas, and in other ways murder us, as they would wild beasts. The Antediluvians and heathens never dreamed of such barbarities. Now the Christians believe because they have a name to live, while they are dead, that God will overlook such things. But if he does not deceive them, it will be because he has overlooked it sure enough. But to return to this godly man, Bishop Allen. I do hereby openly affirm it to the world, that he has done more in a spiritual sense for his ignorant and wretched brethren than any other man of colour has, since the world began. And as for the greater part of the whites, it has hitherto been their greatest object and glory to keep us ignorant of our Maker, so as to make us believe that we were made to be slaves to them and their children to dig up gold and silver for them. It is notorious that not a few professing christians among the whites who profess to love our Lord and Saviour Jesus Christ, have assailed this man and laid all the obstacles in his way they possibly could, consistent with their profession—and what for? Why, their course of proceeding and his, clashed exactly together—they trying their best to keep us ignorant that we might be the better and more obedient slaves—while he on the other hand, doing his very best to enlighten us and teach us a knowledge of the Lord. And I am sorry that I have it to say, that many of our brethren have joined in with our oppressors, whose dearest objects are only to keep us ignorant and miserable, against this man to stay his hand. However, they have kept us in so much ignorance that many of us know no better than to fight against ourselves, and by that means strengthen the hands of our natural enemies, to rivet their infernal chains of slavery upon us and our children. I have several times called the white Americans our *natural enemies*—I shall here define my meaning of the phrase. Shem, Ham, and Japheth, together with their father Noah and wives, I believe were not natural enemies to each other. When the ark rested after the flood upon Mount Arrarat in Asia, they (eight) were all the people which could be found alive in all the earth—in fact if scriptures be true (which I believe are) there were no other living men in all the earth, notwithstanding some ignorant creatures hesitate not to tell us, that we, (the blacks) are the seed of Cain, the murderer of his brother Abel. But where these ignorant and avaricious wretches could have got their information, I am unable to declare. Did they receive it from the Bible? I have searched the

---

* I mean those whose labors for the good, or rather destruction of Jerusalem, and the Jews. Ceased before our Lord entered the Temple, and over turned the tables of the Money Changers.

Bible as well as they, if I am not as well learned as they are, and have never seen a verse which testifies whether we are the seed of Cain or of Abel.—Yet those men tell us that we are of the seed of Cain and that God put a dark stain upon us, that we might be known as their slaves! ! ! Now I ask those avaricious and ignorant wretches, who act more like the seed of Cain, by murdering, the whites or the blacks? How many vessel loads of human beings have the blacks thrown into the seas? How many thousand souls have the blacks murdered in cold blood to make them work in wretchedness and ignorance, to support them and their families? *—However, let us be the seed of Cain, Harry, Dick or Tom! ! ! God will show the whites what we are yet. I say, from the beginning, I do not think that we were natural enemies to each other. But the whites having made us so wretched, by subjecting us to slavery, and having murdered so many millions of us in order to make us work for them, and out of devilishness—and they taking our wives, whom we love as we do ourselves—our mothers who bore the pains of death to give us birth— our fathers & dear little children, and ourselves, and strip and beat us one before the other—chain, handcuff and drag us about like rattle- snakes—shoot us down like wild bears, before each other's faces, to make us submissive to and work to support them and their families. They (the whites) know well if we are *men*—and there is a secret monitor in their hearts which tells them we are—they know, I say, if we *are* men, and see them treating us in the manner they do, that there can be nothing in our hearts but death alone, for them; notwithstanding we may appear cheerful, when we see them murdering our dear mothers and wives, because we cannot help ourselves. Man, in all ages and all nations of the earth, is the same. Man is a peculiar creature—he is the image of his God, though he may be subjected to the most wretched condition upon earth, yet that spirit and feeling which constitute the creature man, can never be entirely erased from his breast, because the God who made him after his own image, planted it in his heart; he cannot get rid of it. The whites knowing this, they do not know what to do; they are afraid that we, being men, and not brutes, will retaliate, and woe will be to them; therefore, that dreadful fear, together with an avaricious spirit, and the natural love in them to be called masters, (which term we will yet honour them with to their sorrow) bring them to the resolve that they will keep us in ignorance and wretchedness, as long as they possibly can † and make the best of their time while it lasts. Consequently they,

* How many millions souls of the human family have the blacks, beat nearly to death, to keep them from learning to read the Word of God and from writing. And telling lies about them, by holding them up to the world as a tribe of TALKING APES, void of *intellect!!! incapable* of LEARNING, &c.

† And still hold us up with indignity as being incapable of acquiring knowledge!!! See the inconsistency of the assertions of those wretches—they beat us inhumanly, sometimes almost to death, for attempting to inform ourselves, by reading the *Word* of our Maker, and at the same time tell us, that we are beings *void of intellect!!!!* How admirably their practices agree with their professions in this case. Let me cry shame upon you Americans, for such outrages upon human nature!!!! If it were possible for the whites always to keep us ignorant and miserable, and make us work to enrich them and their children, and insult our feelings by representing us as *talking Apes*, what would they do? But glory honour and praise to Heaven's King, that the sons and daughters of Africa, will, in spite of all the opposition of their enemies, stand forth in all the dignity and glory that is granted by the Lord to his creature man.

themselves, (and not us) render themselves our natural enemies, by treating us so cruel. They keep us miserable now, and call us their property, but some of them will have enough of us by and by—their stomachs shall run over with us; they want us for their slaves, and shall have us to their fill. (We are all in the world together!!) I said above, because we cannot help ourselves, (viz. we cannot help the whites murdering our mothers and our wives) but this statement is incorrect—for we can help ourselves; for, if we lay aside abject servility, and be determined to act like men, and not brutes—the murderers among the whites would be afraid to show their cruel heads. But O, my God!—in sorrow I must say it, that my colour, all over the world, have a mean, servile spirit. They yield in a moment to the whites, let them be right or wrong—the reason the whites are able to keep their feet on our throats. Oh! my coloured brethren, all over the world, when shall we arise from this death-like apathy?—And be men!! You will notice, if ever we become men (I mean *respectable* men, such as other people are,) we must exert ourselves to the full. For remember, that it is the greatest desire and object of the greater part of the whites, to keep us ignorant, and make us work to support them and their families.—Here now, in the Southern and Western Sections of this country. there are at least three coloured persons for one white, why is it, that those few weak, good-for-nothing whites, are able to keep so many able men, one of whom, can put to flight a dozen whites, in wretchedness and misery? It shows at once, what the blacks are, we are ignorant, abject, servile, and mean—and the whites know it— they know that we are too servile to assert our rights as men—or they would not fool with us as they do. Would they fool with any other people as they do with us? No, they know too well that they would get themselves ruined. Why do they not bring the inhabitants of Asia to be body servants to them? They know they would get their bodies rent and torn from head to foot. Why do they not get the Aboriginies of this country to be slaves to them and their children, to work their farms and dig their mines? They know well that the Aboriginies of this country, (or Indians) would tear them from the earth. The Indians would not rest day or night, they would be up all times of night, cutting their cruel throats. But my colour, (some, not all,) are willing to stand still and be murdered by the cruel whites. In some of the West-India Islands, and over a large part of South America, there are six or eight coloured persons for one white. Why do they not take possession of those places? Who hinders them? it is not the avaricious whites—for they are too busily engaged in laying up money—derived from the blood and tears of the blacks. The fact is they are too servile, they love to have Masters too well!!!!!! Some of our brethren, too, who seeking more after self aggrandizement, than the glory of God, and the welfare of their brethren, join in with our oppressors, to ridicule and say all manner of evils falsely against our Bishop. They think that they are doing great things, when they get in company with the whites, to ridicule and make sport of those who are labouring for their good. Poor ignorant creatures, they do not know that the sole aim and object of the whites, are only to make fools and slaves of them and put the whip to them, and make them work to support them

and their families. But I do say, that no man can well be a despiser of
Bishop Allen, for his public labors among us, unless he is a despiser of
God and Righteousness. Thus, we see, my brethren, the two very opposite
positions of those great men, who have written respecting this "Colonizing Plan," (Mr. Clay and his slave holding party,) men who are resolved
to keep us in eternal wretchedness, are also bent upon sending us to
Liberia. While the Reverend Bishop Allen, and his party, men who have
the fear of God, and the welfare of their brethren at heart. The Bishop
in particular, whose labors for the salvation of his brethren, are well
known to a large part of those, who dwell in the United States, are completely opposed to the plan—and advise us to stay where we are. Now
we have to determine whose advice we will take respecting this all important matter, whether we will adhere to Mr. Clay and his slave-holding
party, who have always been our oppressors and murderers, and who
are for colonizing us, more through apprehension than humanity, or to
this godly man who has done so much for our benefit, together with the
advice of all the good and wise among us and the whites. Will any of
us leave our homes and go to Africa? I hope not.* Let them commence
their attack upon us as they did on our brethren in Ohio, driving and
beating us from our country, and my soul for theirs, they will have
enough of it. Let no man of us budge one step, and let slave-holders come
to beat us from our country. America is more our country, than it is the
whites—we have enriched it with our *blood and tears*. The greatest
riches in all America have arisen from our blood and tears:—and will
they drive us from our property and homes, which we have earned with
our *blood?* They must look sharp or this very thing will bring swift
destruction upon them. The Americans have got so fat upon our blood
and groans, that they have almost forgotten the God of armies. But let
them go on.

How cunning slave-holders think they are!!!!—How much like the king
of Egypt, who after he saw plainly that God was determined to bring
out his people, in spite of him and his, as powerful as they were. He
was willing that Moses, Aaron and the Elders of Israel, but not all the
people should go and serve the Lord. But God deceived him as he will
christian Americans, unles they are very cautious how they move.
What would have become of the United States of America, was it not for
those among the whites, who not in words barely, but in truth and in
deed, love and fear the Lord? Our Lord and Master said:—"Whoso shall
offend one of these little ones which believe in me, it were better for
him that a millstone were hanged about his neck, and that he were
drowned in the depths of the sea." But the Americans with this very
threatening of the Lord's, not only beat his little ones among the Africans, but many of them they put to death or murder. Now the avaricious
Americans think that the Lord Jesus Christ will let them off, because his
words are no more than the words of a man! In fact, many of them
are so avaricious and ignorant that they do not believe in our Lord

---

* Those who are ignorant enough to go to Africa, the coloured people ought to be glad
to have them go, for if they are ignorant enough to let the whites *fool* them off to Africa,
they would be no small injury to us if they reside in this country.

and Saviour Jesus Christ. Tyrants may think they are so skilful in State affairs is the reason that the government is preserved. But I tell you, that this country would have been given up long ago, was it not for the lovers of the Lord. They are indeed, the salt of the earth. Remove the people of God among the whites, from this land of blood, and it will stand until they cleverly get out of the way. I adopt the language of the Rev. S. E. Cornish, of N. York, editor of the Rights of All, and say: "Any colored man of common intelligence who gives his countenance and influence to that colony further than its missionary object and interest extend, should be considered as a traitor to his brethren, and discarded by every respectable man of colour; and every member of that society, however pure his motive, whatever may be his religious character and moral worth, should in his efforts to remove the coloured population from their rightful soil, the land of their birth and nativity, be considered as acting gratuitously unrighteous and cruel."

Let me make an appeal brethren, to your hearts, for your cordial co-operation in the circulation of "The Rights of All," among us. The utility of such a vehicle, if rightly conducted, cannot be estimated. I hope that the well informed among us, may see the absolute necessity of their co-operation in its universal spread among us. If we should let it go down, never let us undertake any thing of the kind again, but give up at once and say that we are really so ignorant and wretched that we cannot do any thing at all! As far as I have seen the writings of its editor, I believe he is not seeking to fill his pockets with money, but has the welfare of his brethren truly at heart. Such men, brethren, ought to be supported by us.

But to return to the colonizing trick. It will be well for me to notice here at once, that I do not mean indiscriminately to condemn all the members and advocates of this scheme, for I believe that there are some friends to the sons of Africa, who are laboring for our salvation, not in words only but in truth and in deed, who have been drawn into this plan. Some, more by persuasion than any thing else; while others, with humane feelings and lively zeal for our good, seeing how much we suffer from the afflictions poured upon us by unmerciful tyrants, are willing to enroll their names in any thing which they think has for its ultimate end our redemption from wretchedness and miseries; such men, with a heart truly overflowing with gratitude for their past services and zeal in our cause, I humbly beg to examine this plot minutely, and see if the end which they have in view will be completely consummated by such a course of procedure. Our friends who have been imperceptibly drawn into this plot I view with tenderness, and would not for the world injure their feelings, and I have only to hope for the future, that they will withdraw themselves from it; for I declare to them, that the plot is not for the glory of God, but on the contrary the perpetuation of slavery in this country, which will ruin them and the country forever, unless something is immediately done.

Do the colonizationists think to send us off without first being reconciled to us? Do they think to bundle us up like brutes and send us off, as they did our brethren of the State of Ohio? Have they not to be reconciled to us, or reconcile us to them, for the cruelties with which they have afflicted our fathers and us? Methinks colonizationists think they have a set of brutes to deal with, sure enough. Do they think to drive us from our country and homes, after having enriched it with our blood and tears, and keep back millions of our dear brethren, sunk in the most barbarous wretchedness, to dig up gold and silver for them and their children? Surely, the Americans must think that we are brutes, as some of them have represented us to be. They think that we do not feel for our brethren, whom they are murdering by the inches, but they are dreadfully deceived. I acknowledge that there are some deceitful and hypocritical wretches among us, who will tell us one thing while they mean another, and thus they go on aiding our enemies to oppress themselves and us. But I declare this day before my Lord and Master, that I believe there are some true-hearted sons of Africa, in this land of oppression, but pretended *liberty ! ! ! !*—who do in reality feel for their suffering brethren, who are held in bondage by tyrants. Some of the advocates of this cunningly devised plot of Satan represent us to be the greatest set of cut throats in the world, as though God, wants us to take his work out of his hand before he is ready. Does not vengeance belong to the Lord? Is he not able to repay the Americans for their cruelties, with which they have afflicted Africa's sons and daughters, without our interference, unless we are ordered? Is it surprising to think that the Americans, having the bible in their hands, do not believe it. Are not the hearts of all men in the hands of the God of battles? And does he not suffer some, in consequence of cruelties, to go on until they are irrecoverably lost? Now, what can be more aggravating, than for the Americans, after having treated us so bad, to hold us up to the world as such great throat cutters? It appears to me as though they are resolved to assail us with every species of affliction that their ingenuity can invent. (☞ See the African Repository and Colonial Journal, from its commencement to the present day—see how we are, through the medium of that periodical, abused and held up by the Americans, as the greatest nuisance to society, and throat-cutters in the world.) But the Lord sees their actions. Americans! notwithstanding you have and do continue to treat us more cruel than any heathen nation ever did a people it had subjected to the same condition that you have us. Now let us reason—I mean you of the United States, whom I believe God designs to save from destruction, if you will hear. For I declare to you, whether you believe it or not, that there are some on the continent of America, who will never be able to repent. God will surely destroy them, to show you his disapprobation of the murders they and you have inflicted on us. I say, let us reason; had you not better take our body, while you have it in your power, and while we are yet ignorant and wretched, not knowing but a little, give us education, and teach us the pure religion of our Lord and Master, which is calculated to make the lion lay down in peace with the lamb, and which millions of you have beaten us nearly to death for trying to obtain since we have been among you, and thus, at once, gain our affection, while we are ignorant? Remember Americans, that we must and shall be free, and enlightened as you are, will you wait until we shall, under God, obtain our liberty by the crushing arm of power? Will it not be dreadful for you? I speak Americans for your good. We must and shall be free I say, in spite of you. You may do your best to keep us in wretchedness and misery, to enrich you and your children but God will deliver us from under you. And wo, wo, will be to you if we have to obtain our freedom by fighting. Throw away your fears and prejudices then, and enlighten us and treat us like men, and we will like you more than we do now hate you,* and tell us now no more about colonization, for America is as much our country, as it is yours.—Treat us like men, and there is no danger but we will all live in peace and happiness together. For we are not like you, hard hearted, unmerciful, and unforgiving. What a happy country this will be, if the whites will listen. What nation under heaven, will be able to do any thing with us, unless God gives us up into his hand? But Americans, I declare to you, while you keep us and our children in bondage, and treat us like brutes, to make us support you and your families, we cannot be your friends. You do not look for it, do you? Treat us then like men, and we will be your friends. And there is not a doubt in my mind, but that the whole of the past will be sunk into oblivion, and we yet, under God, will become a united and happy people. The whites may say it is impossible, but remember that nothing is impossible with God.

The Americans may say or do as they please, but they have to raise us from the condition of brutes to that of respectable men, and to make a national acknowledgement to us for the wrongs they have inflicted on us. As unexpected, strange, and wild as these propositions may to some appear, it is no less a fact, that unless they are complied with, the Americans of the United States, though they may for a little while escape, God will yet weigh them in a balance, and if they are not superior to other men, as they have represented themselves to be, he will give them wretchedness to their very heart's content.

And now brethren, having concluded these four Articles, I submit them, together with my Preamble, dedicated to the Lord for your inspection, in language so very simple, that the most ignorant, who can read at all, may easily understand—of which you may make the best you possibly can.† Should tyrants take it into their heads to emancipate any of you, remember that your freedom is your natural right. You are men, as well as they, and instead of returning thanks to them for your freedom, return it to the Holy Ghost, who is your rightful owner. If they do not

---

* You are not astonished at my saying we hate you, for if we are men, we cannot but hate you, while you are treating us like dogs.

† Some of my brethren, who are sensible, do not take an interest in enlightening the minds of our more ignorant brethren respecting this *Book*, and in reading it to them, just as though they will not have either to rise or fall by what is written in this book. Do they believe that I would be so foolish as to put out a book of this kind, without strict—ah! very strict commandments of the Lord?—Surely the blacks and whites must think that I am ignorant enough. Do they think that I would have the audacious wickedness to take the name of my God in vain?

Notice, I said in the concluding clause of Article 3—I call God, I call Angels, I call men to witness, that the destruction of the Americans is at hand, and will be speedily consumated unless they repent. Now I wonder if the world think that I would take the name of God in this way in vain? What do they think I take God to be? Do they suppose that I would trifle with that God who will not have his holy name taken in vain?—He will show you and the world, in due time, whether this book is for his glory, or written by me through envy to the whites, as some have represented.

want to part with your labours, which have enriched them, let them keep you, and my word for it, that God Almighty, will break their strong band. Do you believe this my brethren?—See my Address delivered before the General Coloured Association of Massachusets, which may be found in Freedom's Journal, for Dec. 20, 1828.—See the last clause of that Address. Whether you believe it or not, I tell you that God will dash tyrants, in combination with devils, into atoms, and will bring you out from your wretchedness and miseries, under these *Christian People! ! ! ! !*

Those philanthropists and lovers of the human family, who have volunteered their services for our redemption from wretchedness, have a high claim on our gratitude, and we should always view them as our greatest earthly benefactors.

If any are anxious to ascertain who I am, know the world, that I am one of the oppressed, degraded and wretched sons of Africa, rendered so by the avaricious and unmerciful among the whites.—If any wish to plunge me into the wretched incapacity of a slave, or murder me for the truth, know ye, that I am in the hand of God, and at your disposal. I count my life not dear unto me, but I am ready to be offered at any moment. For what is the use of living when in fact I am dead. But remember, Americans, that as miserable, wretched, degraded and abject as you have made us in preceding, and in this generation, to support you and your families, that some of you (whites) on the continent of America, will yet curse the day that you ever were born. You want slaves, and want us for your slaves ! ! ! My colour will yet, root some of you out of the very face of the earth ! ! ! ! ! ! You may doubt it if you please. I know that thousands will doubt—they think they have us so well secured in wretchedness, to them and their children, that it is impossible for such things to occur. So did the antideluvians doubt Noah, until the day in which the flood came and swept them away. So did the Sodomites doubt, until Lot had got out of the City, and God rained down fire and brimstone from heaven, upon them and burnt them up. So did the king of Egypt doubt the very existence of a God, he said, "who is the Lord, that I should let Israel go?" Did he not find to his sorrow, who the Lord was, when he and all his mighty men of war, were smothered to death in the Red Sea?—So did the Romans doubt, many of them were really so ignorant, that they thought the world of mankind were made to be slaves to them; just as many of the Americans think now, of my colour.— But they got dreadfully deceived. When men got their eyes opened, they made the murderers scamper. The way in which they cut their tyrannical throats, was not much inferior to the way the Romans or murderers, served them, when they held them in wretchedness and degradation under their feet. So would Christian Americans doubt, if God should send an Angel from heaven to preach their funeral sermon. The fact is, the christians having a name to live, while they are dead, think that God will screen them on that ground.

See the hundreds and thousands of us that are thrown into the seas by Christians, and murdered by them in other ways. They cram us into their vessel holds in chains and in hand-cuffs—men, women and children, all together ! ! O! save us, we pray thee, thou God of heaven and of earth, from the devouring hands of the white Christians ! ! ! ! !

Oh! thou Alpha and Omega!
The beginning and the end,
Enthron'd thou art, in Heaven above,
Surrounded by angels there:

From whence thou seest the miseries
To which we are subject;
The whites have murder'd us, O God!
And kept us ignorant of thee.

Not satisfied with this, my Lord!
They throw us in the seas:
Be pleas'd, we pray, for Jesus' sake,
To save us from their grasp.

We believe that, for thy glory's sake,
Thou wilt deliver us;
But that thou may'st effect these things,
Thy glory must be sought.

In conclusion, I ask the candid and unprejudiced of the whole world, to search the pages of historians diligently, and see if the Antediluvians— the Sodomites—the Egyptians—the Babylonians—the Ninevites—the Carthagenians—the Persians—the Macedonians—the Greeks—the Romans— the Mahometans—the Jews—or devils, ever treated a set of human beings, as the white Christians of America do us, the blacks, or Africans.— I also ask the attention of the world of mankind to the declaration of these very American people, of the United States.

A Declaration Made July 4, 1776

It says, "When in the course of human events, it becomes necessary for one people to dissolve the political bands which have connected them with another, and to assume among the Powers of the earth, the separate and equal station to which the laws of nature and of nature's God entitle them, a decent respect for the opinions of mankind requires that they should declare the causes which impel them to the separation. We hold these truths to be self evident, that all men are created equal, that they are endowed by their Creator with certain unalienable rights; that among these are life, liberty, and the pursuit of happiness; that to secure these rights, governments are instituted among men, deriving their just powers from the consent of the governed; that whenever any form of government becomes destructive of these ends it is the right of the people to alter or to abolish it, and to institute a new government laying its foundation on such principles, and organizing its powers in such form as to them shall seem most likely to effect their safety and happiness. Prudence, indeed, will dictate that governments long established should not be changed for light and transient causes; and accordingly all experience hath shewn, that mankind are more disposed to suffer, while evils are sufferable, than to right themselves by abolishing the forms to

which they are accustomed. But when a long train of abuses and usurpations, pursuing invariably the same object, evinces a design to reduce
them under absolute despotism, it is their right, it is their duty to throw
off such government, and to provide new guards for their future security." See your declaration, Americans! ! Do you understand your own
language? Hear your language, proclaimed to the world, July 4, 1776—☞
"We hold these truths to be self evident—that *ALL* MEN ARE CREATED
EQUAL! *that they are endowed by their Creator with certain unalienable
rights; that among these are life, liberty, and the pursuit of happiness! !*"
Compare your own language above, extracted from your Declaration of
Independence, with your cruelties and murders inflicted by your cruel
and unmerciful fathers on ourselves on our fathers and on us, men who
have never given your fathers or you the least provocation ! ! !

Hear your language further!   ☞"But when a long train of abuses
and usurpations, pursuing invariably the same object, evinces a design
to reduce them under absolute despotism, it is their *right*, it is their
duty, to throw off such government, and to provide new guards for their
future security."

Now, Americans! I ask you candidly, was your sufferings under Great
Britain one hundredth part as cruel and tyrannical as you have rendered
ours under you? Some of you, no doubt, believe that we will never throw
off your murderous government, and "provide new guards for our future
security." If Satan has made you believe it, will he not deceive you? * Do
the whites say, I being a black man, ought to be humble, which I readily
admit? I ask them, ought they not to be as humble as I? or do they
think they can measure arms with Jehovah? Will not the Lord yet humble
them? or will not these very coloured people, whom they now treat
worse than brutes, yet under God, humble them low down enough? Some
of the whites are ignorant enough to tell us, that we ought to be submissive to them, that they may keep their feet on our throats. And if we
do not submit to be beaten to death by them, we are bad creatures and
of course must be damned, &c. If any man wishes to hear this doctrine
openly preached to us by the American preachers, let him go into the
Southern and Western sections of this country—I do not speak from
hearsay—what I have written, is what I have seen and heard myself.
No man may think that my book is made up of conjecture—I have
travelled and observed nearly the whole of those things myself, and what
little I did not get by my own observation, I received from those among
the whites and blacks, in whom the greatest confidence may be placed.

The Americans may be as vigilant as they please, but they cannot be
vigilant enough for the Lord, neither can they hide themselves, where he
will not find and bring them out.

> 1 Thy presence why withdraw'st thou, Lord?
>   Why hid'st thou now·thy face,
>   When dismal times of deep distress
>   Call for thy wonted grace?

* The Lord has not taught the Americans that we will not some day or other throw off
their chains and hand-cuffs, from our hands and feet, and their devilish lashes (which
some of them shall have enough of yet) from off our backs.

2 The wicked, swell'd with lawless pride,
    Have made the poor their prey;
  O let them fall by those designs
    Which they for others lay.

3 For straight they triumph, if success
    Their thriving crimes attend;
  And sordid wretches, whom God hates,
    Perversely they commend.

4 To own a pow'r above themselves
    Their haughty pride disdains;
  And, therefore, in their stubborn mind
    No thought of God remains.

5 Oppressive methods they pursue,
    And all their foes they slight;
  Because thy judgments, unobserv'd,
    Are far above their sight.

6 They fondly think their prosp'rous state
    Shall unmolested be;
  They think their vain designs shall thrive,
    From all misfortune free.

7 Vain and deceitful is their speech,
    With curses fill'd, and lies;
  By which the mischief of their heart
    They study to disguise.

8 Near public roads they lie conceal'd,
    And all their art employ,
  The innocent and poor at once
    To rifle and destroy.

9 Not lions crouching in their dens,
    Surprise their heedless prey
  With greater cunning, or express
    More savage rage than they.

10 Sometimes they act the harmless man,
    And modest looks they wear;
  That so, deceiv'd, the poor may less
    Their sudden onset fear

PART II

11 For God, they think, no notice takes
    Of their unrighteous deeds;
  He never minds the suff'ring poor,
    Nor their oppression heeds.

12 But thou, O Lord, at length arise,
    Stretch forth thy mighty arm,
  And by the greatness of thy pow'r,
    Defend the poor from harm.

13 No longer let the wicked vaunt,
    And, proudly boasting, say,

"Tush, God regards not what we do;
 He never will repay."—*Common Prayer Book.*

1 Shall I for fear of feeble man,
   The Spirit's course in me restrain?
   Or, undismay'd in deed and word.
   Be a true witness of my Lord.

2 Aw'd by mortal's frown shall I
   Conceal the word of God Most High!
   How then before thee shall I dare
   To stand, or how thine anger bear?

3 Shall I, to sooth th' unholy throng,
   Soften the truth, or smooth my tongue.
   To gain earth's gilded toys, or flee
   The cross endur'd, my Lord, by thee?

4 What then is he whose scorn I dread?
   Whose wrath or hate makes me afraid
   A man! an heir of death! a slave
   To sin! a bubble on the wave!

5 Yea, let men rage: since thou wilt spread
   Thy shadowing wings around my head:
   Since in all pain thy tender love
   Will still my sure refreshment prove.
                         Wesley's Collection.

THE CONFESSIONS OF NAT TURNER, THE LEADER OF THE LATE INSURRECTION IN SOUTHAMPTON, VA., AS FULLY AND VOLUNTARILY MADE TO THOMAS R. GRAY

[The picture of the Negro as a contented slave did not become central to the defense of slavery until after the rise of militant abolitionism in the 1830's. Ironically, this defense became current after a period in which the South witnessed two major attempts at rebellion and one armed revolt.

Ever since the 1790's, there had been growing concern, sometimes mounting to panic, that slaves would turn on their masters. Certainly, Americans knew that slaves were capable of resistance. In 1803, black revolutionaries had concluded a bloody war that established an independent Haiti. Thousands of lives had been lost in the fighting that began with the mulatto revolt in 1791. Within ten years, control of the island was in the hands of Toussaint L'Ouverture, whose self-styled epithet "first of the blacks" emphasized his unmixed Negro blood. The news of a massacre of the remaining whites by Dessalines, following the seizure of Toussaint in 1802, was received with dismay by Americans. The events in the Caribbean, coupled with the American rebellions and conspiracies of Gabriel Prosser in 1800, Denmark Vesey in 1822, and Nat Turner in 1831, were sufficient proof that slave discontent was a reality.

The Prosser uprising had been planned for August in Virginia, in 1800—the year Thomas Jefferson waged a successful contest for the presidency and nine years after the by-now-successful revolution had begun in Haiti. The plot was extensive, and Gabriel apparently had hopes that news of his success would trigger a general revolt in other areas as well. Gabriel knew about events in Haiti. The revolution in the Caribbean was general knowledge in the United States, and Gabriel, who was a blacksmith living near Richmond, could have followed its progress easily. No one was killed in this abortive uprising—the plot was frustrated by two informers and a heavy rain that knocked out a key bridge—but Virginians promptly hanged over thirty blacks, including Gabriel, on October 7.

Many Southerners doubtless had their worst fears confirmed by these developments. Rumors of other plots flourished in this charged atmosphere, and the succeeding two years did, in fact, reveal other plots in Virginia and North Carolina, whose slave systems were generally thought to be more lenient than that of, say, Georgia. Virginians often took pride publicly in their relative enlightenment in this matter even though this did not alleviate their fears about possible uprisings.

But rumors of plots were far more frequent than actual uprisings.

Aside from the fact that an uncovered plot was rarely publicized, one of the difficulties that surrounds the task of discovering the magnitude or even the existence of a conspiracy (the count by various observers varies from as few as 12 to over 200) turns on the extent to which the fears of slaveholders about a possible uprising were reflected in the reports and even the confessions of slaves. Blacks were sometimes forced to reveal what white men wanted to hear, and, once there was any evidence to support rumors of revolt, whites wanted verification from whoever might be implicated. A confession at such a point would confirm the white man's belief that he had the ability to thwart any and all rebellions. If he did not fully believe that his slaves were content, he did not doubt his power to suppress revolution.

Whatever complacency existed among the inhabitants of Charleston, South Carolina, a city where blacks outnumbered whites about seven to five, was severely shaken by developments there in the summer of 1822. A rumor of a conspiracy was reported by a slave to his master. The Mayor was alerted, and inquiries were begun, but suspicion did not become rampant until the original story was corroborated by another slave. Ten slaves were arrested on June 16, the presumed day of the uprising, and the secret hearings that followed led to the arrest of Denmark Vesey five days later. He and five other blacks were hanged on July 2. Vesey, to whom all evidence pointed as the leader of the plot, was a carpenter living in Charleston who had purchased his freedom in 1800. Although several blacks later turned state's evidence, Vesey himself confessed to nothing other than knowing a white barber who supposedly had made a wig for Vesey's disguise. During his trial, Vesey questioned witnesses who had made charges against him but was unable to confound them or elicit a change in their story. In his closing speech, Vesey tried to convince the court that, being free, he would have had nothing to gain from such an attempt and attributed the charges against him to the great hatred that he alleged the other blacks—Vesey was the only

Negro freedman among the leaders of the plot—had for him. The hangings, which presumably squelched the plot, only served to increase the hysteria in Charleston. Panic spread in both the white and Negro communities. More suspects were interrogated throughout July, and three men, after they were slated for execution, came forth with confessions that implicated several dozen others. By this time, it was thought that the plot involved thousands of blacks, but none of the supposed lists of actual conspirators were ever produced. These lists, and other papers in Vesey's possession, were presumed burned. One hundred thirty-six were finally arrested; of these, sixty-seven were convicted and thirty-five executed. The actual extent of the conspiracy is still something of a mystery, but few observers doubt that some plot was afoot.

The most effective of all Southern slave revolts, which occurred on August 21, 1831, was led by Nat Turner, in Southampton County, Virginia. Like Denmark Vesey—the name Denmark had come from "Telmak" which was short for Télémaque—Turner commanded a great deal of respect from the blacks in his community and, also like Vesey, was a student of the Bible. After ruminating about his life's mission, Turner was successful in convincing his followers that he was divinely appointed to lead them from bondage. He apparently had no general plan other than to begin in earnest by slaying his master and to continue, sparing no man, woman, or child. He stuck to this plan resolutely and doubtless had hopes, like his predecessors, that news of his success would spark a general revolt. The statistics of the revolt were themselves sufficient to alarm the whole South: sixty whites killed by Turner's men and at least one hundred blacks killed in suppressing the revolt. Of the sixty or seventy men and one woman involved in the revolt, twenty-eight were convicted, thirteen—including Turner and the woman—were hanged, and the rest deported. The details of the episode as Turner described it in his confession struck the slaveholding South with even greater fear and put an end to the work of emancipation societies there. Whatever abolitionist sentiment there was in the South began to wane, and the Abolitionists themselves were accused of fomenting revolution. The slaves, many Southerners began to protest more loudly, were content to remain in bondage, but, after Turner, the possibility of a slave uprising was a constant worry among white Southerners up through the Civil War.

The confession reprinted here was given to one Thomas R. Gray, sometimes mistakenly identified as the defense attorney in the case, while Nat Turner was in confinement in Southampton County jail from October 31 to November 5. The occasional questions and parenthetical remarks in the text, and possibly more, are by Gray, whose pamphlet appeared on November 21, ten days after Turner was executed. Whatever its shortcomings as an authentic account, it remains the central document in the Turner affair, and there is not much doubt that Gray spoke with Turner and obtained a confession.]

The late insurrection in Southampton has greatly excited the public mind, and led to a thousand idle, exaggerated and mischievous reports. It is the first instance in our history of an open rebellion of the slaves, and attended with such atrocious circumstances of cruelty and destruction, as could not fail to leave a deep impression, not only upon the minds of the community where this fearful tragedy was wrought, but throughout every portion of our country in which this population is to be found. Public curiosity has been on the stretch to understand the origin and progress of this dreadful conspiracy, and the motives which influenced its diabolical actors. The insurgent slaves had all been destroyed, or apprehended, tried and executed, (with the exception of the leader) without revealing anything at all satisfactory as to the motives which governed them, or the means by which they expected to accomplish their object. Everything connected with this sad affair was wrapt in mystery until Nat Turner, the leader of this ferocious band whose name has resounded throughout our widely extended empire, was captured. This "great Bandit" was taken by a single individual, in a cave near the residence of his late owner, on Sunday the thirtieth of October, without attempting to make the slightest resistance, and on the following day safely lodged in the jail of the County. His captor was Benjamin Phipps, armed with a shot gun well charged. Nat's only weapon was a small light sword, which he immediately surrendered, and begged that his life might be spared. Since his confinement, by permission of the jailer, I have had ready access to him, and finding that he was willing to make a full and free confession of the origin, progress and consummation of the insurrectionary movements of the slaves, of which he was the contriver and head; I determined, for the gratification of public curiosity, to commit his statements to writing, and publish them, with little or no variation from his own words. That this is a faithful record of his confessions, the annexed certificate of the County Court of Southampton will attest. They certainly bear the stamp of truth and sincerity. He makes no attempt (as all the other insurgents who were arrested and examined did) to exculpate himself, but frankly acknowledged his full participation in all the guilt of the transaction. He was not only the contriver of the conspiracy, but gave the first blow towards its execution. It will thus appear, that whilst everything upon the surface of society wore a calm and peaceful aspect, that whilst not one preparation was heard to warn the devoted inhabitants of woe and death, a gloomy fanatic was revolving in the recesses of his own dark, bewildered, and overwrought mind, schemes of indiscriminate massacre to the whites. Schemes too fearfully executed, as far as this fiendish band proceeded in their desolating march. No cry for mercy penetrated their flinty bosoms. No acts of remembered kindness made the least impression on these remorseless murderers. Men, women, and children, from hoary age to helpless infancy, were involved in the same cruel fate. Never did a band of savages do their work of death more unsparingly. Apprehension for their own personal safety seems to have been the only principle of restraint in the whole course of their bloody proceedings. And it is not the least remarkable feature in this horrid transaction, that a band actuated by such hellish purposes, should have resisted so feebly, when met by the whites in arms. Desperation alone, one would think, might have led to greater efforts. More than 20 of them attacked Dr. Blunt's house on Tuesday morning, a little before daybreak, defended by two men and three boys. They fled precipitately at the first fire; and their future plans of mischief were entirely disconcerted and broken up. Escaping hence, each individual sought his own safety either in concealment, or by returning home, with the hope that his participation might escape detection, and all were shot down in the course of a few days or captured and brought to trial and punishment. Nat has survived all his followers, and the gallows will speedily close his career. His own account of the conspiracy is submitted to the public, without comment. It reads an awful, and it is hoped, a useful lesson, as to the operation of a mind like his, endeavoring to grapple with things beyond its reach, how it first became bewildered and confounded, and finally corrupted, and led to the conception and perpetration of the most atrocious and heartrending deeds.

It is also calculated to demonstrate the policy of our laws in restraint of this class of our population, and to induce all those entrusted with their execution, as well as our citizens generally, to see that they are strictly and rigidly enforced. Each particular community should look to its own safety, whilst the general guardians of the laws keep a watchful eye over all. If Nat's statement can be relied on, the insurrection in this county was entirely local, and his designs confided but to a few, and these in his immediate vicinity. It was not instigated by motives of revenge or sudden anger, but the results of long deliberation, and a settled purpose of mind. The offspring of gloomy fanaticism, acting upon materials but too well prepared for such impressions. It will be long remembered in the annals of our country, and many a mother, as she presses her infant darling to her bosom, will shudder at the recollection of Nat Turner and his band of ferocious miscreants.

Believing the following narrative, by removing doubts and conjectures from the public mind which otherwise must have remained would give general satisfaction, it is respectfully submitted to the public by their obedient servant,

T. R. GRAY
Jerusalem, Southampton Co., Va.
Nov. 5, 1831.

We, the undersigned, members of the Court convened at Jerusalem, on Saturday the 5th day of November, 1831, for the trial of Nat, *alias* Nat Turner, a negro slave, late the property of Putnam Moore, deceased, do hereby certify, that the confession of Nat to Thomas R. Gray, was read to him in our presence, and that Nat acknowledged the same to be full, free and voluntary; and that furthermore, when called upon by the presiding magistrate of the Court to state if he had anything to say, why a sentence of death should not be passed upon him, replied that he had nothing further than he had communicated to Mr. Gray.

Given under our hands and seals at Jerusalem, 5th day of November, 1831.

JEREMIAH COBB,   (*Seal*)
THOMAS PRETLOW,   (*Seal*)
JAMES W. PARKER,   (*Seal*)
CARR BOWERS,   (*Seal*)
SAMUEL B. HINES,   (*Seal*)
ORRIS A. BROWNE.   (*Seal*)

State of Virginia,
Southampton County, to wit:

I, James Rochelle, Clerk of the County Court of Southampton, in the State of Virginia, do hereby certify, that Jeremiah Cobb, Thomas Pretlow, James W. Parker, Carr Bowers, Samuel B. Hines, and Orris A. Browne, Esquires, are acting Justices of the Peace, in and for the County aforesaid, and were members of the court which convened at Jerusalem, on Saturday the 5th day of November, 1831, for the trial of Nat *alias* Nat Turner, a negro slave, late the property of Putnam Moore, deceased, who was tried and convicted, as an insurgent in the late insurrection in the County of Southampton, aforesaid, and that full faith and credit are due, and ought to be given to their acts as Justices of the Peace aforesaid.

In testimony whereof, I have hereunto set my hand and caused the seal of the Court aforesaid to be affixed this 5th day of November, 1831.

(*Seal*)

JAMES ROCHELLE, C.S.C.C.

CONFESSION

Agreeable to his own appointment, on the evening he was committed to prison, with permission of the jailer, I visited Nat on Tuesday the 1st of November, when, without being questioned at all, he commenced his narrative in the following words:

Sir, you have asked me to give a history of the motives which induced me to undertake the late insurrection, as you call it. To do so I must go back to the days of my infancy, and even before I was born. I was thirty-one years of age the 2nd of October last and born the property of Benj. Turner, of this county. In my childhood a circumstance occurred which made an indelible impression on my mind and laid the groundwork of that enthusiasm which has terminated so fatally to many both white and black, and for which I am about to atone at the gallows. It is here necessary to relate this circumstance, trifling as it may seem; it was the commencement of that belief which has grown with time, and even now, sir, in this dungeon, helpless and forsaken as I am, I cannot divest myself of. Being at play with other children, when three or four years old, I was telling them something, which my mother overhearing, said it had happened before I was born; I stuck to my story, however, and related some things which went in the opinion to confirm it; others being called on were greatly astonished, knowing that these things had happened, and caused them to say in my hearing, I surely would be a prophet, as the Lord had shown me things that had happened before my birth. And my father and mother strengthened me in this my first impression, saying in my presence, I was intended for some great purpose, which they had always thought from certain marks on my head and breast [a parcel of excrescences which I believe are not at all uncommon, particularly among Negroes, as I have seen several with the same. In this case he has either cut them off, or they have nearly disappeared].

My grandmother, who was very religious and to whom I was much attached, my master, who belonged to the church, and other religious persons who visited the house, and whom I often saw at prayers, noticing the singularity of my manners, I suppose, and my uncommon intelligence for a child, remarked I had too much sense to be raised and if I was, I would never be of any service to anyone as a slave. To a mind like mine, restless, inquisitive and observant of everything that was passing, it was easy to suppose that religion was the subject to which it would be directed, and although this subject principally occupied my thoughts, there was nothing that I saw or heard of to which my attention was not directed. The manner in which I learned to read and write not only had great influence on my own mind—as I acquired it with the most perfect ease; so much so, that I have no recollection whatever of learning the alphabet—but to the astonishment of the family, one day, when a book was shown to me to keep me from crying, I began spelling the names of different objects. This was a source of wonder to all in the neighborhood, particularly the blacks; and this learning was constantly improved at all opportunities. When I got large enough to go to work, while employed, I was reflecting on many things that would present themselves to my imagination, and, whenever an opportunity occurred of looking at a book, when the school children were getting their lessons, I would find many things that the fertility of my own imagination had depicted to me before; all my time not devoted to my master's service was spent either in prayer, or in making experiments in casting different things in molds made of earth, in attempting to make paper, gunpowder, and many other experiments that, although I could not perfect, yet convinced me of its practicability if I had the means.

I was not addicted to stealing in my youth, nor have ever been. Yet such was the confidence of the Negroes in the neighborhood, even at this early period of my life, in my superior judgment, that they would often carry me with them when they were going on any roguery, to plan for them. Growing up among them, with this confidence in my superior judgment, and when this, in their opinions, was perfected by Divine inspiration, from the circumstances already alluded to in my infancy, and which belief was ever afterwards zealously inculcated by the austerity of my life and manners, which became the subject of remark with white and black.

Having soon discovered to be great, I must appear so and, therefore, studiously avoided mixing in society and wrapped myself in mystery, devoting my time to fasting and prayer. By this time, having arrived to

Blacks have been an important part of the American experience from the very beginning. The first blacks in the English colonies were, like many whites, indentured servants, not slaves. After their period of service, many acquired property and rose to positions of prominence in their communities. Before long, however, it became common to extend black indenture for life, and, twenty-five years after the first blacks had arrived in Jamestown, slavery had gained a foothold. But, as tension between England and the colonies grew, many blacks, whether slave or free, were moved by the ideas of freedom expressed by the colonists. One such was Crispus Attucks, a runaway slave, who was the first American patriot to fall in the Boston Massacre of 1770.

*New York Public Library
Picture Collection*

An estimated 5,000 blacks, free and slave, served in the Continental Army. James (Armistead) Lafayette was a spy and courier who served under Lafayette.

Valentine Museum

THOMAS JEFFERSON

As early as 1688, a Quaker group had published a denunciation of slavery. But, until the Revolutionary War, antislavery sentiment was found almost exclusively among Quaker reformers, the greatest of whom was John Woolman. In the years immediately preceding the war with England, many colonists began to see that the belief in basic freedom expressed in revolutionary rhetoric would have to include freedom for blacks. Thomas Jefferson submitted a vehement "philippic" against slavery to the Continental Congress, but it was deleted from the final draft of the Declaration of Independence. Despite his stanch antislavery sentiments, Jefferson could not envision full social and political equality for blacks. The conflict in Jefferson between humanitarian ideals and social inclinations was symptomatic of what was to come.

New York Public Library Picture Collection

Benjamin Banneker, a free-born black scientist and mathematician, was a living refutation of Jefferson's assertion that blacks are inferior to whites. He sent a copy of his first almanac to Jefferson. Shortly afterward, on Jefferson's recommendation, George Washington appointed Banneker to the commission that drew up plans for what is now the District of Columbia.

Though the status of free blacks declined considerably after the Revolutionary era, many blacks continued to make significant contributions to America. In the War of 1812, black soldiers and seamen fought with courage and loyalty for the American cause.

Despite severe restrictions, some free blacks, especially in the North, became prosperous and respected members of society. This "Portrait of a Gentleman" by an unknown artist dates from around 1830.

Bowdoin College
Museum of Art

Blacks did not accept their enslavement without protest. Between 1663 and 1845, there were numerous revolts on land and on slave ships at sea. On land, the major slave revolt of the nineteenth century was that led by Nat Turner; on sea, the most important was the one that occurred on the *Amistad*. In 1839, a group of slaves led by Cinqué mutinied and brought the slaveship into Montauk, Long Island. John Quincy Adams defended the rebel slaves before the Supreme Court and won their freedom.

New York State Historical Association

The first federal Fugitive Slave Law was enacted in 1793 in an attempt to stem the tide of runaway slaves. The second, passed in 1850, made life especially hazardous for blacks living as free men, either legally or illegally. An accused runaway was assumed to be guilty and could be returned to slavery even if he had been living undisturbed for many years. Outraged abolitionists called this the "Man-Stealing Law."

One result of the Fugitive Slave Law was renewed interest among free blacks in emigration. Such a course had been discussed by blacks since 1787 but did not receive much support until passage of the 1850 law. Martin R. Delany, a free-born black who studied medicine at Harvard, was one of the chief spokesmen for emigration and largely responsible for the National Emigration Convention in 1854. During the Civil War, Delany accepted a major's commission in the Union Army and served as an army physician.

Though the central issue of the Civil War was slavery, the Emancipation Proclamation was not issued until January 1, 1863. The Proclamation, which declared that all slaves should be free, was greeted with an explosion of joy and gratitude by blacks and abolitionists.

New York Public Library Picture Collection

From the beginning of the Civil War, blacks fought alongside Union troops. But runaway slaves, such as the one depicted here, did not participate in large numbers until the Emancipation Proclamation authorized their enrollment in the Union Army and Navy.

Harper's Weekly

After the Civil War, a new sense of freedom and personal responsibility spurred many former slaves to take to the open road in search of relatives and employment.

During Reconstruction, the enfranchisement of former slaves enabled several Southern blacks to win seats in the U.S. Senate and the House of Representatives.

Entered according to act of Congress in the year 1872 by Currier & Ives, in the Office of the Librarian of Congress at Washington.
ROBERT C. DE LARGE, M.C. of S. Carolina.   JEFFERSON H. LONG, M.C. of Georgia.

U.S. Senator H.R. REVELS, of Mississippi   BENJ. S. TURNER, M.C. of Alabama.   JOSIAH T. WALLS, M.C. of Florida.   JOSEPH H. RAINY, M.C. of S. Carolina.   R. BROWN ELLIOT, M.C. of S. Carolina.

THE FIRST COLORED SENATOR AND REPRESENTATIVES.

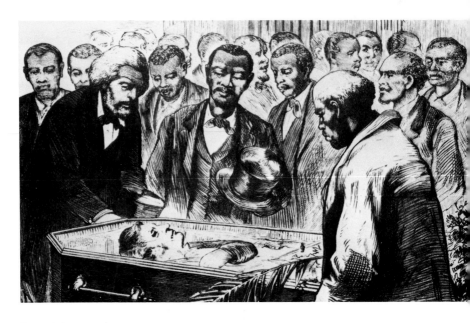

One of the greatest champions of the black cause in the U.S. Senate was Charles Sumner, who was a leader in the fight to force Southern states to grant blacks equal voting rights as a condition for reconstruction. Sumner's death in 1874 was greatly mourned by the black population.

Frederick Douglass was a symbol of his time. Born a slave in Tuckahoe, Maryland, in 1817, he escaped and settled in Massachusetts, where he became interested in the abolition movement. He organized black troops during the Civil War, and, in 1877, was appointed Marshal of the District of Columbia. He was appointed Recorder of Deeds for the District of Columbia in 1881, and Minister to Haiti in 1889. During the last years of his life, he continued to speak out on matters concerning the black citizen's civil rights. In 1895, the year of Douglass's death, Booker T. Washington delivered an address to the Atlanta Cotton States and International Exposition that inaugurated a new phase in the black-American experience.

man's estate and hearing the Scriptures commented on at meetings, I was struck with that particular passage which says: "Seek ye the kingdom of Heaven and all things shall be added unto you." I reflected much on this passage and prayed daily for light on this subject: As I was praying one day at my plow, the Spirit spoke to me, saying "Seek ye the kingdom of Heaven and all things shall be added unto you."

Question: What do you mean by the Spirit?

Answer: The Spirit that spoke to the prophets in former days.

And I was greatly astonished and for two years prayed continually, whenever my duty would permit. And then again I had the same revelation, which fully confirmed me in the impression that I was ordained for some great purpose in the hands of the Almighty.

Several years rolled round, in which many events occurred to strengthen me in this belief. At this time I reverted in my mind to the remarks made of me in my childhood, and the things that had been shown me, and as it had been said of me in my childhood by those by whom I had been taught to pray, both white and black, and in whom I had the greatest confidence, that I had too much sense to be raised, and if I was I would never be of any use to anyone as a slave. Now finding I had arrived to man's estate and was a slave, and these revelations being made known to me, I began to direct my attention to this great object, to fulfill the purpose for which, by this time, I felt assured I was intended. Knowing the influence I had obtained over the minds of my fellow servants, (not by the means of conjuring and such like tricks, for to them I always spoke of such things with contempt) but by the communion of the Spirit whose revelations I often communicated to them, and they believed and said my wisdom came from God. I now began to prepare them for my purpose, by telling them something was about to happen that would terminate in fulfilling the great promise that had been made to me.

About this time I was placed under an overseer, from whom I ran away; and after remaining in the woods thirty days, I returned, to the astonishment of the Negroes on the plantation, who thought I had made my escape to some other part of the country, as my father had done before. But the reason of my return was, that the Spirit appeared to me and said I had my wishes directed to the things of this world, and not to the kingdom of Heaven, and that I should return to the service of my earthly master, "For he who knoweth his Master's will, and doeth it not, shall be beaten with many stripes, and thus have I chastened you." And the Negroes found fault, and murmured against me, saying that if they had my sense they would not serve any master in the world. And about this time I had a vision, and I saw white spirits and black spirits engaged in battle, and the sun was darkened, the thunder rolled in the heavens, and blood flowed in streams, and I heard a voice saying, "Such is your luck, such you are called to see, and let it come rough or smooth, you must surely bear it."

I now withdrew myself as much as my situation would permit from the intercourse of my fellow servants, for the avowed purpose of serving the Spirit more fully, and it appeared to me, and reminded me of

the things it had already shown me, and that it would then reveal to me
the knowledge of the elements, the revolution of the planets, the operation of tides, and changes of the seasons. After this revelation in the
year 1825 and the knowledge of the elements being made known to me,
I sought more than ever to obtain true holiness before the great day
of judgment should appear, and then I began to receive the true knowledge of faith. And from the first steps of righteousness until the last,
was I made perfect; and the Holy Ghost was with me, and said "Behold
me as I stand in the Heavens," and I looked and saw the forms of men
in different attitudes, and there were lights in the sky to which the
children of darkness gave other names than what they really were, for
they were the lights of the Savior's hands, stretched forth from east to
west, even as they were extended on the cross on Calvary for the redemption of sinners. And I wondered greatly at these miracles, and
prayed to be informed of a certainty of the meaning thereof, and shortly
afterwards, while laboring in the field, I discovered drops of blood on
the corn, as though it were dew from heaven, and I communicated it to
many, both white and black in the neighborhood; and I then found on
the leaves in the woods hieroglyphic characters and numbers, with the
forms of men in different attitudes, portrayed in blood, and representing
the figures I had seen before in the heavens. And now the Holy Ghost
had revealed itself to me and made plain the miracles it had shown
me. For as the blood of Christ had been shed on this earth, and had
ascended to heaven for the salvation of sinners, and was now returning
to earth again in the form of dew, and as the leaves on the trees bore
the impression of the figures I had seen in the heavens, it was plain to
me that the Savior was about to lay down the yoke He had borne for
the sins of men, and the great day of judgment was at hand.

About this time, I told these things to a white man (Etheldred T.
Brantley) on whom it had a wonderful effect, and he ceased from his
wickedness and was attacked immediately with a cutaneous eruption,
and blood oozed from the pores of his skin, and after praying and fasting
nine days, he was healed, and the Spirit appeared to me again and
said, as the Savior had been baptized, so should we be also; and when
the white people would not let us be baptized by the church, we went
down into the water together, in the sight of many who reviled us, and
were baptized by the Spirit. After this I rejoiced greatly, and gave
thanks to God. And on May 12, 1828, I heard a loud noise in the heavens,
and the Spirit instantly appeared to me and said the Serpent was loos-
ened, and Christ had laid down the yoke He had borne for the sins of
men, and that I should take it on and fight against the Serpent, for
the time was fast approaching, when the first should be last and the
last should be first.

Question: Do you not find yourself mistaken now?

Answer: Was not Christ crucified?

And by signs in the heavens that it would make known to me when I
should commence the great work, and until the first sign appeared, I
should conceal it from the knowledge of men. And on the appearance
of the sign, (the eclipse of the sun last February) I should arise and

prepare myself and slay my enemies with their own weapons. And immediately on the sign appearing in the heavens, the seal was removed from my lips, and I communicated the great work laid out for me to do, to four in whom I had the greatest confidence (Henry, Hark, Nelson, and Sam). It was intended by us to have begun the work of death on the 4th of July last. Many were the plans formed and rejected by us, and it affected my mind to such a degree that I fell sick, and the time passed without our coming to any determination how to commence; still forming new schemes and rejecting them, when the sign appeared again, which determined me not to wait longer.

Since the commencement of 1830, I had been living with Mr. Joseph Travis, who was to me a kind master and placed the greatest confidence in me; in fact, I had no cause to complain of his treatment to me. On Saturday evening, the 20th of August, it was agreed between Henry, Hark and myself, to prepare a dinner the next day for the men we expected, and then to concert a plan, as we had not yet determined on any. Hark on the following morning brought a pig, and Henry brandy, and being joined by Sam, Nelson, Will, and Jack, they prepared in the woods a dinner, where, about three o'clock, I joined them.

Question: Why were you so backward in joining them?

Answer: The same reason that had caused me not to mix with them for years before.

I saluted them on coming up and asked Will how came he there; he answered, his life was worth no more than others, and his liberty as dear to him. I asked him if he thought to obtain it? He said he would, or lose his life. This was enough to put him in full confidence. Jack, I knew, was only a tool in the hands of Hark, it was quickly agreed we should commence at home (Mr. J. Travis') on that night, and until we had armed and equipped ourselves and gathered sufficient force, neither age nor sex was to be spared (which was invariably adhered to).

We remained at the feast until about two hours in the night, when we went to the house and found Austin; they all went to the cider press and drank, except myself. On returning to the house, Hark went to the door with an axe, for the purpose of breaking it open, as we knew we were strong enough to murder the family, if they were awaked by the noise; but, reflecting that it might create an alarm in the neighborhood, we determined to enter the house secretly and murder them while sleeping. Hark got a ladder and set it against the chimney on which I ascended and, hoisting a window, entered and came down stairs, unbarred the door, and removed the guns from their places. It was then observed that I must spill the first blood. On which, armed with a hatchet and accompanied by Will, I entered my master's chamber. It being dark, I could not give a death blow; the hatchet glanced from his head; he sprang from the bed and called his wife. It was his last word. Will laid him dead with a blow of his axe, and Mrs. Travis shared the same fate, as she lay in bed.

The murder of this family, five in number, was the work of a moment, not one of them awoke; there was a little infant, sleeping in a cradle, that was forgotten until we had left the house and gone some distance, when Henry and Will returned and killed it; we got here four guns that would shoot and several old muskets, with a pound or two of powder. We remained some time at the barn, where we paraded; I formed them in a line as soldiers and, after carrying them through all the maneuvers I was master of, marched them off to Mr. Salathul Francis', about 600 yards distant. Sam and Will went to the door and knocked. Mr. Francis asked who was there; Sam replied it was him and he had a letter for him, on which he got up and came to the door; they immediately seized him, and dragging him out a little from the door, he was dispatched by repeated blows on the head; there was no other white person in the family.

We started from there for Mrs. Reese's, maintaining the most perfect silence on our march, where finding the door unlocked, we entered and murdered Mrs. Reese in her bed, while sleeping; her son awoke, but it was only to sleep the sleep of death. He had only time to say who is that, and he was no more. From Mrs. Reese's we went to Mrs. Turner's, a mile distant, which we reached about sunrise on Monday morning. Henry, Austin, and Sam went to the still, where, finding Mr. Peebles, Austin shot him, and the rest of us went to the house; as we approached, the family discovered us and shut the door. Vain hope! Will, with one stroke of his axe, opened it, and we entered and found Mrs. Turner and Mrs. Newsome in the middle of a room almost frightened to death. Will immediately killed Mrs. Turner with one blow of his axe. I took Mrs. Newsome by the hand, and with the sword I had when I was apprehended, I struck her several blows over the head, but not being able to kill her, as the sword was dull. Will turning around and discovering it, dispatched her also.

A general destruction of property and search for money and ammunition always succeeded the murders. By this time my company amounted to fifteen, and nine men mounted, who started for Mrs. Whitehead's (the other six were to go through a by way to Mr. Bryant's and rejoin us at Mrs. Whitehead's). As we approached the house we discovered Mr. Richard Whitehead standing in the cotton patch, near the lane fence; we called him over into the lane, and Will, the executioner, was near at hand, with his fatal axe, to send him to an untimely grave. As we pushed on to the house, I discovered some one run round the garden, and, thinking it was some of the white family, I pursued them, but finding it was a servant girl belonging to the house, I returned to commence the work of death, but they whom I left had not been idle; all the family were already murdered but Mrs. Whitehead and her daughter Margaret. As I came round to the door I saw Will pulling Mrs. Whitehead out of the house, and at the step he nearly severed her head from her body with his broad axe. Miss Margaret, when I discovered her, had concealed herself in the corner formed by the projection of the cellar cap from the house; on my approach she fled, but was soon overtaken, and after repeated blows with a sword, I killed her by a blow on the head with a fence rail. By this time, the six who had gone by Mr. Bryant's rejoined us and informed me they had done the work of death assigned them.

We again divided, part going to Mr. Porter's, and from thence to Nathaniel Francis', the others to Mr. Howell Harris' and Mr. T. Doyle's. On my reaching Mr. Porter's, he had escaped with his family. I understood there, that the alarm had already spread, and I immediately returned to bring up those sent to Mr. Doyle's and Mr. Howell Harris'; the party I left going on to Mr. Francis', having told them I would join them in that neighborhood. I met these sent to Mr. Doyle's and Mr. Harris' returning, having met Mr. Doyle on the road and killed him; and learning from some who joined them that Mr. Harris was from home, I immediately pursued the course taken by the party gone on before; but knowing they would complete the work of death and pillage at Mr. Francis' before I could get there, I went to Mr. Peter Edwards', expecting to find them there, but they had been here also. I then went to Mr. John T. Barrow's; they had been here and murdered him. I pursued on their track to Capt. Newit Harris', where I found the greater part mounted and ready to start; the men, now amounting to about forty, shouted and hurrahed as I rode up; some were in the yard, loading their guns, others drinking. They said Captain Harris and his family had escaped, the property in the house they destroyed, robbing him of money and other valuables. I ordered them to mount and march instantly, this was about nine or ten o'clock Monday morning.

I proceeded to Mr. Levi Waller's, two or three miles distant. I took my station in the rear, and as it was my object to carry terror and devastation wherever we went, I placed fifteen or twenty of the best mounted and most to be relied on in front, who generally approached the houses as fast as their horses could run; this was for two purposes, to prevent their escape and strike terror to the inhabitants; on this account I never got to the houses, after leaving Mrs. Whitehead's until the murders were committed, except in one case. I sometimes got in sight in time to see the work of death completed, viewed the mangled bodies as they lay, in silent satisfaction, and immediately started in quest of other victims.

Having murdered Mrs. Waller and ten children, we started for Mr. William Williams'; having killed him and two little boys that were there; while engaged in this, Mrs. Williams fled and got some distance from the house, but she was pursued, overtaken, and compelled to get up behind one of the company, who brought her back, and after showing her the mangled body of her lifeless husband, she was told to get down and lay by his side, where she was shot dead. I then started for Mr. Jacob Williams', where the family were murdered. Here we found a young man named Drury, who had come on business with Mr. Williams; he was pursued, overtaken and shot. Mrs. Vaughan's was the next place we visited, and, after murdering the family here, I determined on starting for Jerusalem. Our number amounted now to fifty or sixty, all mounted and armed with guns, axes, swords, and clubs.

On reaching Mr. James W. Parker's gate, immediately on the road leading to Jerusalem and about three miles distant, it was proposed to me to call there, but I objected, as I knew he was gone to Jerusalem, and my object was to reach there as soon as possible; but some of the men having relations at Mr. Parker's, it was agreed that they might call and get his people. I remained at the gate on the road with seven or eight; the others going across the field to the house about half a mile off. After waiting some time for them, I became impatient and started to the house for them, and on our return we were met by a party of white men, who had pursued our blood-stained track, and who had fired on those at the gate and dispersed them, which I knew nothing of, not having been at that time rejoined by any of them.

Immediately on discovering the whites, I ordered my men to halt and form, as they appeared to be alarmed. The white men, eighteen in number, approached us in about one hundred yards, when one of them fired (this was against the positive orders of Captain Alexander P. Peete, who commanded, and who had directed the men to reserve their fire until within thirty paces). And I discovered about half of them retreating. I then ordered my men to fire and rush on them; the few remaining stood their ground until we approached within fifty yards, when they fired and retreated. We pursued and overtook some of them who we thought we left dead (they were not killed); after pursuing them about two hundred yards and rising a little hill, I discovered they were met by another party, and had halted and were reloading their guns. (This was a small party from Jerusalem who knew the Negroes were in the field and had just tied their horses to await their return to the road knowing that Mr. Parker and family were in Jerusalem, but knew nothing of the party that had gone in with Captain Peete. On hearing the firing they immediately rushed to the spot and arrived just in time to arrest the progress of these barbarous villians and save the lives of their friends and fellow citizens.)

Thinking that those who retreated first, and the party who fired on us at fifty or sixty yards distant, had all only fallen back to meet others with ammunition. As I saw them reloading their guns, and more coming up than I saw at first, and several of my bravest men being wounded, the others became panic struck and scattered over the field; the white men pursued and fired on us several times. Hark had his horse shot under him, and I caught another for him as it was running by me; five or six of my men were wounded, but none left on the field; finding myself defeated here I instantly determined to go through a private way and cross the Nottoway River at the Cypress Bridge, three miles below Jerusalem, and attack that place in the rear, as I expected they would look for me on the other road, and I had a great desire to get there to procure arms and ammunition. After going a short distance in this private way, accompanied by about twenty men, I overtook two or three who told me the others were dispersed in every direction. After trying in vain to collect a sufficient force to proceed to Jerusalem, I determined to return, as I was sure they would make back to their old neighborhood, where they would rejoin me, make new recruits, and come down again. On my way back, I called at Mrs. Thomas', Mrs. Spencer's, and several other places, the white families having fled; we found no more victims to gratify our thirst for blood. We stopped at Maj. Ridley's quarter for the night, and being joined by four of his men, with the recruits made since my defeat, we mustered now about forty strong.

After placing out sentinels, I laid down to sleep, but was quickly roused by a great racket; starting up, I found some mounted and others in great confusion; one of the sentinels having given the alarm that we were about to be attacked, I ordered some to ride around and reconnoiter, and on their return the others being more alarmed, not knowing who they were, fled in different ways, so that I was reduced to about twenty again, with this I determined to attempt to recruit, and proceed on to rally in the neighborhood I had left. Dr. Blunt's was the nearest house, which we reached just before day; on riding up the yard, Hark fired a gun. We expected Dr. Blunt and his family were at Maj. Ridley's, as I knew there was a company of men there; the gun was fired to ascertain if any of the family were at home; we were immediately fired upon and retreated leaving several of my men. I do not know what became of them, as I never saw them afterwards.

Pursuing our course back and coming in sight of Captain Harris', where we had been the day before, we discovered a party of white men at the house, on which all deserted me but two (Jacob and Nat). We concealed ourselves in the woods until near night, when I sent them in search of Henry, Sam, Nelson, and Hark, and directed them to rally all they could at the place we had had our dinner the Sunday before, where they would find me, and I accordingly returned there as soon as it was dark and remained until Wednesday evening, when discovering white men riding around the place as though they were looking for some one, and none of my men joining me, I concluded Jacob and Nat had been taken and compelled to betray me.

On this I gave up all hope for the present; and on Thursday night, after having supplied myself with provisions from Mr. Travis', I scratched a hole under a pile of fence rails in a field, where I concealed myself for six weeks, never leaving my hiding place but for a few minutes in the dead of night to get water, which was very near. Thinking by this time I could venture out, I began to go about in the night and eavesdrop the houses in the neighborhood; pursuing this course for about a fortnight and gathering little or no intelligence, afraid of speaking to any human being, and returning every morning to my cave before the dawn of day. I know not how long I might have led this life, if accident had not betrayed me. A dog in the neighborhood, passing by my hiding place one night while I was out, was attracted by some meat I had in my cave, and crawled in and stole it, and was coming out just as I returned. A few nights after, two Negroes having started to go hunting with the same dog, and passed that way, the dog came again to the place, and having just gone out to walk about, discovered me and barked, on which thinking myself discovered, I spoke to them to beg concealment. On making myself known, they fled from me. Knowing then they would betray me, I immediately left my hiding place and was pursued almost incessantly until I was taken a fortnight afterwards by Mr. Benjamin Phipps, in a little hole I had dug out with my sword, for the purpose of concealment, under the top of a fallen tree. On Mr. Phipps discovering the place of my concealment, he cocked his gun and aimed at me. I requested him not to shoot, and I would give up, upon which he demanded my sword. I delivered it to him, and he brought me to prison. During the time I was pursued, I had many hairbreadth escapes, which your time will not permit you to relate. I am here loaded with chains, and willing to suffer the fate that awaits me.

I here proceeded to make some inquiries of him, after assuring him of the certain death that awaited him, and that concealment would only bring destruction on the innocent as well as guilty, of his own color, if he knew of any extensive or concerted plan. His answer was, I do not. When I questioned him as to the insurrection in North Carolina happening about the same time, he denied any knowledge of it; and when I looked him in the face as though I would search his inmost thoughts, he replied, "I see sir, you doubt my word; but can you not think the same ideas and strange appearances about this time in the heavens might prompt others, as well as myself, to this undertaking." I now had much conversation with and asked him many questions, having forborne to do so previously, except in the cases noted in parentheses; but during his statement, I had, unnoticed by him, taken notes as to some particular circumstances, and, having the advantage of his statement before me in writing, on the evening of the third day that I had been with him, I began a cross examination and found his statement corroborated by every circumstance coming within my own knowledge or the confessions of others who had been either killed or executed and whom he had not seen or had any knowledge since 22nd of August last. He expressed himself fully satisfied as to the impracticability of his attempt.

It has been said he was ignorant and cowardly, and that his object was to murder and rob for the purpose of obtaining money to make his escape. It is notorious, that he was never known to have a dollar in his life, to swear an oath, or drink a drop of spirits. As to his ignorance, he certainly never had the advantages of education, but he can read and write (it was taught him by his parents) and for natural intelligence and quickness of apprehension is surpassed by few men I have ever seen. As to his being a coward, his reason as given for not resisting Mr. Phipps shows the decision of his character. When he saw Mr. Phipps present his gun, he said he knew it was impossible for him to escape, as the woods were full of men; he therefore thought it was better to surrender and trust to fortune for his escape. He is a complete fanatic, or plays his part most admirably.

On other subjects he possesses an uncommon share of intelligence, with a mind capable of attaining anything; but warped and perverted by the influence of early impressions. He is below the ordinary stature, though strong and active, having the true Negro face, every feature of which is strongly marked. I shall not attempt to describe the effect of his narrative, as told and commented on by himself, in the condemned hole of the prison. The calm, deliberate composure with which he spoke of his late deeds and intentions, the expression of his fiendlike face when excited by enthusiasm, still bearing the stains of the blood of helpless innocence about him; clothed with rags and covered with chains; yet daring to raise his manacled hands to heaven, with a spirit soaring above the attributes of man; I looked on him and my blood curdled in my veins.

I will not shock the feelings of humanity, nor wound afresh the bosoms of the disconsolate sufferers in this unparalleled and inhuman massacre, by detailing the deeds of their fiendlike barbarity. There were two or three who were in the power of these wretches, had they known it, and who escaped in the most providential manner. There were two whom they thought they had left dead on the field at Mr. Parker's but who were only stunned by the blows of their guns, as they did not take time to reload when they charged on them.

The escape of a little girl who went to school at Mr. Waller's, and where the children were collecting for that purpose, excited general sympathy. As their teacher had not arrived, they were at play in the yard, and, seeing the Negroes approach, she ran up on a dirt chimney (such as are common to log houses) and remained there unnoticed during the massacre of the eleven that were killed at this place. She remained on her hiding place till just before the arrival of a party, who were in pursuit of the murderers, when she came down and fled to a swamp, where, a mere child as she was, with the horrors of the late scene before her, she lay concealed until the next day, when seeing a party go up to the house, she came up and, on being asked how she escaped, replied with the utmost simplicity: The Lord helped her. She was taken up behind a gentleman of the party and returned to the arms of her weeping mother.

Miss Whitehead concealed herself between the bed and the mat that supported it, while they murdered her sister in the same room, without discovering her. She was afterwards carried off and concealed for protection by a slave of the family, who gave evidence against several of them on their trial. Mrs. Nathaniel Francis, while concealed in a closet heard their blows and the shrieks of the victims of these ruthless savages; they then entered the closet where she was concealed, and went out without discovering her. While in this hiding place she heard two of her women in a quarrel about the division of her clothes. Mr. John T. Baron, discovering them approaching his house, told his wife to make her escape and, scorning to fly, fell fighting on his own threshold. After firing his rifle, he discharged his gun at them and then broke it over the villain who first approached him, but he was overpowered and slain. His bravery, however, saved from the hands of these monsters his lovely and amiable wife, who will long lament a husband as deserving of her love. As directed by him, she attempted to escape through the garden, when she was caught and held by one of her servant girls, but another coming to her rescue, she fled to the woods and concealed herself. Few indeed, were those who escaped their work of death. But fortunate for society, the hand of retributive justice has overtaken them; and not one that was known to be concerned has escaped.

THE COMMONWEALTH V. NAT TURNER:

Charged with making insurrection, and plotting to take away the lives of divers free white persons, etc., on the 22nd of August, 1831. The court composed of———, having met for the trial of Nat Turner, the prisoner was brought in and arraigned, and upon his arraignment pleaded *not guilty;* saying to his counsel, that he did not feel so.

On the part of the Commonwealth, Levi Waller was introduced, who being sworn, deposed as follows: (*agreeably to Nat's own Confession*). Col Trezvant [the committing magistrate] was then introduced, who being sworn, numerated Nat's Confession to him, as follows: (*his Confession as given to Mr. Gray*). The prisoner introduced no evidence, and the case was submitted without argument to the court, who having found him guilty, Jeremiah Cobb, Esq., chairman, pronounced the sentence of the court, in the following words: "Nat Turner! Stand up. Have you anything to say why sentence of death should not be pronounced against you?"

Answer: I have not. I have made a full confession to Mr. Gray, and I have nothing more to say.

"Attend then to the sentence of the court. You have been arraigned and tried before this court, and convicted of one of the highest crimes in our criminal code. You have been convicted of plotting in cold blood the indiscriminate destruction of men, of helpless women, and of infant children. The evidence before us leaves not a shadow of doubt, but that your hands were often imbrued in the blood of the innocent; and your own confession tells us that they were stained with the blood of a master, in your own language, too indulgent. Could I stop here, your crime would be sufficiently aggravated. But the original contriver of a plan, deep and deadly, one that never can be effected, you managed so far to put it into execution, as to deprive us of many of our most valuable citizens; and this was done when they were asleep, and defenseless, under circumstances shocking to humanity. And while upon this part of the subject, I cannot but call your attention to the poor misguided wretches who have gone before you. They are not few in number; they were your bosom associates; and the blood of all cries aloud, and calls upon you, as the author of their misfortune. Yes! You forced them unprepared, from Time to Eternity. Borne down by this load of guilt, your only justification is, that you were led away by fanaticism. If this be true, from my soul I pity you; and while you have my sympathies, I am, nevertheless, called upon to pass the sentence of the court. The time between this and your execution will necessarily be very short; and your only hope but must be in another world. The judgment of the court is, that you be taken hence to the jail from whence you came, thence to the place of execution, and on Friday next, between the hours of 10 A.M. and 2 P.M., be hung by the neck until you are dead! dead! dead! and may the Lord have mercy upon your soul."

THE EXECUTION

Nat Turner was executed according to sentence, on Friday, the 11th November, 1831, at Jerusalem, between the hours of 10 A.M. and 2 P.M. He exhibited the utmost composure throughout the whole ceremony, and, although assured that he might, if he thought proper, address the immense crowd assembled on the occasion, declined availing himself of the privilege, and, being asked if he had any further confession to make, replied that he had nothing more than he had communicated, and told the Sheriff in a firm voice, that he was ready. Not a limb or a muscle was observed to move. His body, after death, was given over to the surgeons for dissection.

*A list of persons murdered in the Insurrection, on the
21st and 22nd of August, 1831*

Joseph Travers and wife and three children, Mrs. Elizabeth Turner, Hartwell Prebles, Sarah Newsome, Mrs. P. Reese and son William, Trajan Doyle, Henry Bryant and wife and child and wife's mother, Mrs. Catherine Whitehead and son Richard and four daughters and grandchild, Salathiel Francis, Nathaniel Francis' overseer and two children, John T. Barrow, George Vaughan, Mrs. Levi Waller and ten children, William Williams, wife and two boys, Mrs. Caswell Worell and child, Mrs. Rebecca Vaughan, Ann Eliza Vaughan and son Arthur, Mrs. John K. Williams and child, Mrs. Jacob Williams and three children, and Edwin Drury—amounting to fifty five.

NARRATIVE OF THE LIFE OF FREDERICK DOUGLASS, AN AMERICAN SLAVE, WRITTEN BY HIMSELF

[The struggles and experiences of American Negroes have found expression not only in their music but also in a form of writing that is evidence of the abiding interest inherent in the life histories of exceptional black men. These "narratives," which go back to the eighteenth century, speak to us in a direct, dramatic, and personal way. Apart from being historical documents in their own right, they have enabled countless readers to reconstruct the slave experience as well as imaginatively to identify with careers that usually had meager beginnings but finally triumphed over great obstacles.

The most successful and the best written of the early autobiographies (an earlier one, *A Narrative of the Uncommon Sufferings and Surprising Deliverance of Briton Hammon, a Negro Man,* was published in Boston in 1760) was *The Interesting Narrative of the Life of Olaudah Equiano, or Gustavus Vassa, The African,* which appeared in 1789, went through eight editions by 1794 and, following the fortunes of various "Negro revivals," has had many editions ever since. Like Vassa's memoirs, *Narrative of the Life of Frederick Douglass* (1845) was published as part of an abolition campaign. Douglass's first autobiography—a second (1855) and third (1881 and 1892) were expansions and revisions of the first with different titles—marked a new interest in slave narratives. By the time of Booker T. Washington's *The Story of My Life and Work* (1900) —somewhat revised in 1902 as *Up From Slavery*—over a hundred had been published, and a half dozen, including Douglass's *Narrative*, enjoyed brisk sales.

The strength of this heritage has left its mark on almost all of the Negro writers of the twentieth century, and the personal memoir, either in the form of fictionalized biography or "told to" autobiography, persists as an important genre among black writers. W. E. B. Du Bois's writings include at least two autobiographies as do those of James Weldon Johnson. Richard Wright's *Black Boy* (1945), considered by some to be his masterpiece, was written after the success of *Native Son*, and after his publisher suggested he try an autobiography. Langston Hughes continued the tradition in a two-volume work as did James Baldwin in his *Notes of a Native Son* (1955) and, in what could be considered *Black Boy*'s Northern counterpart, *Go Tell It On the Mountain* (1958). One of the most recent and most successful additions to this list is the *Autobiography of Malcolm X*, as told to Alex Haley (1965).

The most enduring of the nineteenth-century narratives is that of Douglass. Four chapters of the 1845 work are reprinted below. When he died, in 1895, Douglass was the most celebrated Negro of his time, and, to later generations of Negroes, he has become a legend. Born into slavery in Tuckahoe, Maryland, in 1817, Frederick was sent to Baltimore as a household servant at the age of nine, a practice that was common in Maryland after 1820 because of the diminishing returns of slave labor in agriculture. In 1833, he was returned to a plantation forty miles from Baltimore. He proved unmanageable in this new setting and, within a year, was hired out to one Edward Covey, a professional slave-breaker. Douglass's treatment at the hands of Covey rekindled the aspirations for freedom that had lain dormant since he first had learned to read. An attempted escape in 1836 failed but, contrary to the usual punishment for this offense, Douglass was sent back to Baltimore and apprenticed to a ship-caulker with a promise of freedom when he reached twenty-five. If compared to those of many others, Douglass's slave years were relatively benign. But his sharply contrasting experiences under different masters kindled his ambition to be totally free of any of them. Even the kindly treatment by Mrs. Auld in Baltimore, which later turned harsh, only reinforced his conviction that the unchecked power of even the best-intentioned slaveholders reduced them to demons.

In 1838, disguised as a sailor, and with borrowed "protection" papers, he boarded a train and escaped to New York. He was joined by Anna, a free Negress he had met in Baltimore, and, after their marriage by the Reverend J. W. C. Pennington (who was also a former slave from Maryland and who later published his own autobiography, *The Fugitive Blacksmith*, London, 1849), they moved to New Bedford, Massachusetts. It was there that Douglass became interested in the abolition movement and, in 1841, that he came to the attention of William Lloyd Garrison. After an extemporaneous speech on Nantucket and some encouragement from Garrison and others, Douglass was hired as an agent of the Massachusetts Anti-Slavery Society. For the next four years, he spoke throughout the North and became the prize exhibit of the Garrisonian abolitionists. Piqued by rumors, based on his considerable oratorical ability and lack of a Southern accent, that he had not actually been a slave, he published his *Narrative* in 1845. To avoid capture, he traveled to Great Britain, and before his return, in 1847, his freedom was purchased by public subscription. He thus returned to his native land a free man.

Within a year, and against the advice of Garrison, Douglass founded his own newspaper, the *North Star*, which, after a final break with Garrison, in 1851, over the proper interpretation of the Constitution, was renamed *Frederick Douglass's Paper*. Douglass's conviction that the Constitution was not a proslavery document put him in the reformist rather than the revolutionary camp of abolitionists. Throughout the rest of his life, he sought a political solution to the problem of slavery and then to the status of the free Negro. Douglass opposed John Brown's raid and even tried to talk him out of it, but because of his known association with Brown he took asylum in Canada briefly in 1859.

Douglass's views finally led him to support Lincoln and the Republicans, and, after the war became linked with emancipation, he was active in organizing Negro troops for service. After the war, he was appointed Assistant Secretary to the Santo Domingo Commission; he was rewarded, in 1877, as Marshal of the District of Columbia, as Recorder of Deeds for the District, in 1881, and as Minister to Haiti, in 1889. Douglass spent his last thirty years as a champion of Negro rights, especially the right of suffrage, in an effort to make the nation live up to the promises of the Fourteenth and Fifteenth Amendments to the Constitution.]

CHAPTER I

I was born in Tuckahoe, near Hillsborough, and about twelve miles from Easton, in Talbot county, Maryland. I have no accurate knowledge of my age, never having seen any authentic record containing it. By far the larger part of the slaves know as little of their ages as horses know of theirs, and it is the wish of most masters within my knowledge to keep their slaves thus ignorant I do not remember to have ever met a slave who could tell of his birthday. They seldom come nearer to it than planting-time, harvest-time, cherry-time, spring-time, or fall-time. A want of information concerning my own was a source of unhappiness to me even during childhood. The white children could tell their ages. I could not tell why I ought to be deprived of the same privilege. I was not allowed to make any inquiries of my master concerning it. He deemed all such inquiries on the part of a slave improper and impertinent, and evidence of a restless spirit. The nearest estimate I can give makes me now between twenty-seven and twenty-eight years of age. I come to this, from hearing my master say, some time during 1835, I was about seventeen years old.

My mother was named Harriet Bailey. She was the daughter of Isaac and Betsey Bailey, both colored, and quite dark. My mother was of a darker complexion than either my grandmother or grandfather.

My father was a white man. He was admitted to be such by all I ever heard speak of my parentage. The opinion was also whispered that my master was my father; but of the correctness of this opinion, I know nothing; the means of knowing was withheld from me. My mother and I were separated when I was but an infant—before I knew her as my mother. It is a common custom, in the part of Maryland from which I ran away, to part children from their mothers at a very early age. Frequently, before the child has reached its twelfth month, its mother is taken from it, and hired out on some farm a considerable distance off, and the child is placed under the care of an old woman, too old for field labor. For what this separation is done, I do not know, unless it be to hinder the development of the child's affection toward its mother, and to blunt and destroy the natural affection of the mother for the child. This is the inevitable result.

I never saw my mother, to know her as such, more than four or five times in my life; and each of these times was very short in duration, and at night. She was hired by a Mr. Stewart, who lived about twelve miles from my home. She made her journeys to see me in the night, travelling the whole distance on foot, after the performance of her day's work. She was a field hand, and a whipping is the penalty of not being in the field at sunrise, unless a slave has special permission from his or her master to the contrary—a permission which they seldom get, and one that gives to him that gives it the proud name of being a kind master. I do not recollect of ever seeing my mother by the light of day. She was with me in the night. She would lie down with me, and get me to sleep, but long before I waked she was gone. Very little communication ever took place between us. Death soon ended what little we could have while she lived, and with it her hardships and suffering. She died when I was about seven years old, on one of my master's farms, near Lee's Mill. I was not allowed to be present during her illness, at her death, or burial. She was gone long before I knew any thing about it. Never having enjoyed, to any considerable extent, her soothing presence, her tender and watchful care, I received the tidings of her death with much the same emotions I should have probably felt at the death of a stranger.

Called thus suddenly away, she left me without the slightest intimation of who my father was. The whisper that my master was my father, may or may not be true; and, true or false, it is of but little consequence to my purpose whilst the fact remains, in all its glaring odiousness, that slaveholders have ordained, and by law established, that the children of slave women shall in all cases follow the condition of their mothers; and this is done too obviously to administer to their own lusts, and make a gratification of their wicked desires profitable as well as pleasurable; for by this cunning arrangement, the slaveholder, in cases not a few, sustains to his slaves the double relation of master and father.

I know of such cases; and it is worthy of remark that such slaves invariably suffer greater hardships, and have more to contend with, than others. They are, in the first place, a constant offence to their mistress. She is ever disposed to find fault with them; they can seldom do any thing to please her; she is never better pleased than when she sees them under the lash, especially when she suspects her husband of showing to his mulatto children favors which he withholds from his black slaves. The master is frequently compelled to sell this class of his slaves, out of deference to the feelings of his white wife; and, cruel as the deed may strike any one to be, for a man to sell his own children to human flesh-mongers, it is often the dictate of humanity for him to do so; for, unless he does this, he must not only whip them himself, but must stand by and see one white son tie up his brother, of but few shades darker complexion than himself, and ply the gory lash to his naked back; and if he lisp one word of disapproval, it is set down to his parental partiality, and only makes a bad matter worse, both for himself and the slave whom he would protect and defend.

Every year brings with it multitudes of this class of slaves. It was doubtless in consequence of a knowledge of this fact, that one great statesman of the south predicted the downfall of slavery by the inevitable laws of population. Whether this prophecy is ever fulfilled or not, it is nevertheless plain that a very different-looking class of people are springing up at the south, and are now held in slavery, from those originally brought to this country from Africa; and if their increase will do no other good, it will do away the force of the argument, that God cursed Ham, and therefore American slavery is right. If the lineal descendants of Ham are alone to be scripturally enslaved, it is certain that slavery at the south must soon become unscriptural; for thousands are ushered into the world, annually, who, like myself, owe their existence to white fathers, and those fathers most frequently their own masters.

I have had two masters. My first master's name was Anthony. I do not remember his first name. He was generally called Captain Anthony—a title which, I presume, he acquired by sailing a craft on the Chesapeake Bay. He was not considered a rich slaveholder. He owned two or three farms, and about thirty slaves. His farms and slaves were under the care of an overseer. The overseer's name was Plummer. Mr. Plummer was a miserable drunkard, a profane swearer, and a savage monster. He always went armed with a cowskin and a heavy cudgel. I have known him to cut and slash the women's heads so horribly, that even master would be enraged at his cruelty, and would threaten to whip him if he did not mind himself. Master, however, was not a humane slaveholder. It required extraordinary barbarity on the part of an overseer to affect him. He was a cruel man, hardened by a long life of slaveholding. He would at times seem to take great pleasure in whipping a slave. I have often been awakened at the dawn of day by the most heart-rending shrieks of an own aunt of mine, whom he used to tie up to a joist, and whip upon her naked back till she was literally covered with blood. No words, no tears, no prayers, from his gory victim, seemed to move his iron heart from its bloody purpose. The louder she screamed, the harder he whipped; and where the blood ran fastest, there he whipped longest. He would whip her to make her scream, and whip her to make her hush; and not until overcome by fatigue, would he cease to swing the blood-clotted cowskin. I remember the first time I ever witnessed this horrible exhibition. I was quite a child, but I well remember it. I never shall forget it whilst I remember any thing. It was the first of a long series of such outrages, of which I was doomed to be a witness and a participant. It struck me with awful force. It was the blood-stained gate, the entrance to the hell of slavery, through which I was about to pass. It was a most terrible spectacle. I wish I could commit to paper the feelings with which I beheld it.

This occurrence took place very soon after I went to live with my old master, and under the following circumstances. Aunt Hester went out one night,—where or for what I do not know,—and happened to be absent when my master desired her presence. He had ordered her not to go out evenings, and warned her that she must never let him catch her in company with a young man, who was paying attention to her belonging to Colonel Lloyd. The young man's name was Ned Roberts, generally called Lloyd's Ned. Why master was so careful of her, may be safely left to conjecture. She was a woman of noble form, and of graceful proportions, having very few equals, and fewer superiors, in personal appearance, among the colored or white women of our neighborhood.

Aunt Hester had not only disobeyed his orders in going out, but had been found in company with Lloyd's Ned; which circumstance, I found, from what he said while whipping her, was the chief offence. Had he been a man of pure morals himself, he might have been thought interested in protecting the innocence of my aunt; but those who knew him will not suspect him of any such virtue. Before he commenced whipping Aunt Hester, he took her into the kitchen, and stripped her from neck to waist, leaving her neck, shoulders, and back, entirely naked. He then told her to cross her hands, calling her at the same time a d——d b——h. After crossing her hands, he tied them with a strong rope, and led her to a stool under a large hook in the joist, put in for the purpose. He made her get upon the stool, and tied her hands to the hook. She now stood fair for his infernal purpose. Her arms were stretched up at their full length, so that she stood upon the ends of her toes. He then said to her, "Now, you d——d b——h, I'll learn you how to disobey my orders!" and after rolling up his sleeves, he commenced to lay on the heavy cowskin, and soon the warm, red blood (amid heart-rending shrieks from her, and horrid oaths from him) came dripping to the floor. I was so terrified and horror-stricken at the sight, that I hid myself in a closet, and dared not venture out till long after the bloody transaction was over. I expected it would be my turn next. It was all new to me. I had never seen any thing like it before. I had always lived with my grandmother on the outskirts of the plantation, where she was put to raise the children of the younger women. I had therefore been, until now, out of the way of the bloody scenes that often occurred on the plantation.

CHAPTER II

My master's family consisted of two sons, Andrew and Richard; one daughter, Lucretia, and her husband, Captain Thomas Auld. They lived in one house, upon the home plantation of Colonel Edward Lloyd. My master was Colonel Lloyd's clerk and superintendent. He was what might be called the overseer of the overseers. I spent two years of childhood on this plantation in my old master's family. It was here that I witnessed the bloody transaction recorded in the first chapter; and as I received my first impressions of slavery on this plantation, I will give some description of it, and of slavery as it there existed. The plantation is about twelve miles north of Easton, in Talbot county, and is situated on the border of Miles River. The principal products raised upon it were tobacco, corn, and wheat. These were raised in great abundance; so that, with the products of this and the other farms belonging to him, he was able to keep in almost constant employment a large sloop, in carrying them to market at Baltimore. This sloop was named Sally Lloyd, in honor of one of the colonel's daughters. My master's son-in-law, Captain Auld, was master of the vessel; she was otherwise manned by the colonel's own slaves. Their names were Peter, Isaac, Rich, and Jake. These were esteemed very highly by the other slaves, and looked upon as the privileged ones of the plantation; for it was no small affair, in the eyes of the slaves, to be allowed to see Baltimore.

Colonel Lloyd kept from three to four hundred slaves on his home plantation, and owned a large number more on the neighboring farms belonging to him. The names of the farms nearest to the home plantation were Wye Town and New Design. "Wye Town" was under the overseership of a man named Noah Willis. New Design was under the overseership of a Mr. Townsend. The overseers of these, and all the rest of the farms, numbering over twenty, received advice and direction from the managers of the home plantation. This was the great business place. It was the seat of government for the whole twenty farms. All disputes among the overseers were settled here. If a slave was convicted of any high misdemeanor, became unmanageable, or evinced a determination to run away, he was brought immediately here, severely whipped, put on board the sloop, carried to Baltimore, and sold to Austin Woolfolk, or some other slave-trader, as a warning to the slaves remaining.

Here, too, the slaves of all the other farms received their monthly allowance of food, and their yearly clothing. The men and women slaves received, as their monthly allowance of food, eight pounds of pork, or its equivalent in fish, and one bushel of corn meal. Their yearly clothing consisted of two coarse linen shirts, one pair of linen trousers, like the shirts, one jacket, one pair of trousers for winter, made of coarse negro cloth, one pair of stockings, and one pair of shoes; the whole of which could not have cost more than seven dollars. The allowance of the slave children was given to their mothers, or the old women having the care of them. The children unable to work in the field had neither shoes, stockings, jackets, nor trousers, given to them; their clothing consisted of two coarse linen shirts per year. When these failed them, they went naked until the next allowance-day. Children from seven to ten years old, of both sexes, almost naked, might be seen at all seasons of the year.

There were no beds given the slaves, unless one coarse blanket be considered such, and none but the men and women had these. This, however, is not considered a very great privation. They find less difficulty from the want of beds, than from the want of time to sleep; for when their day's work in the field is done, the most of them having their washing, mending, and cooking to do, and having few or none of the ordinary facilities for doing either of these, very many of their sleeping hours are consumed in preparing for the field the coming day; and when this is done, old and young, male and female, married and single, drop down side by side, on one common bed,—the cold, damp floor,—each covering himself or herself with their miserable blankets; and here they sleep till they are summoned to the field by the driver's horn. At the sound of this, all must rise, and be off to the field. There must be no halting; every one must be at his or her post; and woe betides them who hear not this morning summons to the field; for if they are not awakened by the sense of hearing, they are by the sense of feeling; no age nor sex finds any favor. Mr. Severe, the overseer, used to stand by the door of the quarter, armed with a large hickory stick and heavy cowskin, ready to whip any one who was so unfortunate as not to hear, or, from any other cause, was prevented from being ready to start for the field at the sound of the horn.

Mr. Severe was rightly named: he was a cruel man. I have seen him whip a woman, causing the blood to run half an hour at the time; and this, too, in the midst of her crying children, pleading for their mother's release. He seemed to take pleasure in manifesting his fiendish barbarity. Added to his cruelty, he was a profane swearer. It was enough to chill the blood and stiffen the hair of an ordinary man to hear him talk. Scarce a sentence escaped him but that was commenced or concluded by some horrid oath. The field was the place to witness his cruelty and profanity. His presence made it both the field of blood and of blasphemy. From the rising till the going down of the sun, he was cursing, raving, cutting, and slashing among the slaves of the field, in the most frightful manner. His career was short. He died very soon after I went to Colonel Lloyd's; and he died as he lived, uttering, with his dying groans, bitter curses and horrid oaths. His death was regarded by the slaves as the result of a merciful providence.

Mr. Severe's place was filled by a Mr. Hopkins. He was a very different man. He was less cruel, less profane, and made less noise, than Mr. Severe. His course was characterized by no extraordinary demonstrations of cruelty. He whipped, but seemed to take no pleasure in it. He was called by the slaves a good overseer.

The home plantation of Colonel Lloyd wore the appearance of a country village. All the mechanical operations for all the farms were performed here. The shoemaking and mending, the blacksmithing, cartwrighting, coopering, weaving, and grain-grinding, were all performed by the slaves on the home plantation. The whole place wore a business-like aspect very unlike the neighboring farms. The number of houses, too, conspired to give it advantage over the neighboring farms. It was called by the slaves the *Great House Farm.* Few privileges were esteemed higher, by the slaves of the out-farms, than that of being selected to do errands at the Great House Farm. It was associated in their minds with greatness. A representative could not be prouder of his election to a seat in the American Congress, than a slave on one of the out-farms would be of his election to do errands at the Great House Farm. They regarded it as evidence of great confidence reposed in them by their overseers; and it was on this account, as well as a constant desire to be out of the field from under the driver's lash, that they esteemed it a high privilege, one worth careful living for. He was called the smartest and most trusty fellow, who had this honor conferred upon him the most frequently. The competitors for this office sought as diligently to please their overseers, as the office-seekers in the political parties seek to please and deceive the people. The same traits of character might be seen in Colonel Lloyd's slaves, as are seen in the slaves of the political parties.

The slaves selected to go to the Great House Farm, for the monthly allowance for themselves and their fellow-slaves, were peculiarly enthusiastic. While on their way, they would make the dense old woods, for miles around, reverberate with their wild songs, revealing at once the highest joy and the deepest sadness. They would compose and sing as they went along, consulting neither time nor tune. The thought that came up, came out—if not in the word, in the sound;—and as frequently in the one as in the other. They would sometimes sing the most pathetic sentiment in the most rapturous tone, and the most rapturous sentiment in the most pathetic tone. Into all of their songs they would manage to weave something of the Great House Farm. Especially would they do this, when leaving home. They would then sing most exultingly the following words:—

> "I am going away to the Great House Farm!
> O, yea! O, yea! O!"

This they would sing, as a chorus, to words which to many would seem unmeaning jargon, but which, nevertheless, were full of meaning to themselves. I have sometimes thought that the mere hearing of those songs would do more to impress some minds with the horrible character of slavery, than the reading of whole volumes of philosophy on the subject could do.

I did not, when a slave, understand the deep meaning of those rude and apparently incoherent songs. I was myself within the circle; so that I neither saw nor heard as those without might see and hear. They told a tale of woe which was then altogether beyond my feeble comprehension; they were tones loud, long, and deep; they breathed the prayer and complaint of souls boiling over with the bitterest anguish. Every tone was a testimony against slavery, and a prayer to God for deliverance from chains. The hearing of those wild notes always depressed my spirit, and filled me with ineffable sadness. I have frequently found myself in tears while hearing them. The mere recurrence to those songs, even now, afflicts me; and while I am writing these lines, an expression of feeling has already found its way down my cheek. To those songs I trace my first glimmering conception of the dehumanizing character of slavery. I can never get rid of that conception. Those songs still follow me, to deepen my hatred of slavery, and quicken my sympathies for my brethren in bonds. If any one wishes to be impressed with the soul-killing effects of slavery, let him go to Colonel Lloyd's plantation, and, on allowance-day, place himself in the deep pine woods, and there let him, in silence, analyze the sounds that shall pass through the chambers of his soul,—and if he is not thus impressed, it will only be because "there is no flesh in his obdurate heart."

I have often been utterly astonished, since I came to the north, to find persons who could speak of the singing, among slaves, as evidence of their contentment and happiness. It is impossible to conceive of a greater mistake. Slaves sing most when they are most unhappy. The songs of the slave represent the sorrows of his heart; and he is relieved by them, only as an aching heart is relieved by its tears. At least, such is my experience. I have often sung to drown my sorrow, but seldom to express my happiness. Crying for joy, and singing for joy, were alike uncommon to me while in the jaws of slavery. The singing of a man cast away upon a desolate island might be as appropriately considered as evidence of contentment and happiness, as the singing of a slave; the songs of the one and of the other are prompted by the same emotion.

CHAPTER VI

My new mistress proved to be all she appeared when I first met her at the door,—a woman of the kindest heart and finest feelings. She had never had a slave under her control previously to myself, and prior to her marriage she had been dependent upon her own industry for a living. She was by trade a weaver; and by constant application to her business, she had been in a good degree preserved from the blighting and dehumanizing effects of slavery. I was utterly astonished at her goodness. I scarcely knew how to behave towards her. She was entirely unlike any other white woman I had ever seen. I could not approach her as I was accustomed to approach other white ladies. My early instruction was all out of place. The crouching servility, usually so acceptable a quality in a slave, did not answer when manifested toward her. Her favor was not gained by it; she seemed to be disturbed by it. She did not deem it impudent or unmannerly for a slave to look her in the face. The meanest slave was put fully at ease in her presence, and none left without feeling better for having seen her. Her face was made of heavenly smiles, and her voice of tranquil music.

But, alas! this kind heart had but a short time to remain such. The fatal poison of irresponsible power was already in her hands, and soon commenced its infernal work. That cheerful eye, under the influence of slavery, soon became red with rage; that voice, made all of sweet accord, changed to one of harsh and horrid discord; and that angelic face gave place to that of a demon.

Very soon after I went to live with Mr. and Mrs. Auld, she very kindly commenced to teach me the A, B, C. After I had learned this, she assisted me in learning to spell words of three or four letters. Just at this point of my progress, Mr. Auld found out what was going on, and at once forbade Mrs. Auld to instruct me further, telling her, among other things, that it was unlawful, as well as unsafe, to teach a slave to read. To use his own words, further, he said, "If you give a nigger an inch, he will take an ell. A nigger should know nothing but to obey his master— to do as he is told to do. Learning would *spoil* the best nigger in the world. Now," said he, "if you teach that nigger (speaking of myself) how to read, there would be no keeping him. It would forever unfit him to be a slave. He would at once become unmanageable, and of no value to his master. As to himself, it could do him no good, but a great deal of harm. It would make him discontented and unhappy." These words sank deep into my heart, stirred up sentiments within that lay slumbering, and called into existence an entirely new train of thought. It was a new and special revelation, explaining dark and mysterious things, with which my youthful understanding had struggled, but struggled in vain. I now understood what had been to me a most perplexing difficulty—to wit, the white man's power to enslave the black man. It was a grand achievement, and I prized it highly. From that moment, I understood the pathway from slavery to freedom. It was just what I wanted, and I got it at a time when I the least expected it. Whilst I was saddened by the thought of losing the aid of my kind mistress, I was gladdened by the invaluable instruction which, by the merest accident, I had gained from my master. Though conscious of the difficulty of learning without a teacher, I set out with high hope, and a fixed purpose, at whatever cost of trouble, to learn how to read. The very decided manner with which he spoke, and strove to impress his wife with the evil consequences of giving me instruction, served to convince me that he was deeply sensible of the truths he was uttering. It gave me the best assurance that I might rely with the utmost confidence on the results which, he said, would flow from teaching me to read. What he most dreaded, that I most desired. What he most loved, that I most hated. That which to him was a great evil, to be carefully shunned, was to me a great good, to be diligently sought; and the argument which he so warmly urged, against my learning to read, only served to inspire me with a desire and determination to learn. In learning to read, I owe almost as much to the bitter opposition of my master, as to the kindly aid of my mistress. I acknowledge the benefit of both.

I had resided but a short time in Baltimore before I observed a marked difference, in the treatment of slaves, from that which I had witnessed in the country. A city slave is almost a freeman, compared with a slave on the plantation. He is much better fed and clothed, and enjoys privileges altogether unknown to the slave on the plantation. There is a vestige of decency, a sense of shame, that does much to curb and check those outbreaks of atrocious cruelty so commonly enacted upon the plantation. He is a desperate slaveholder, who will shock the humanity of his non-slaveholding neighbors with the cries of his lacerated slave. Few are willing to incur the odium attaching to the reputation of being a cruel master; and above all things, they would not be known as not giving a slave enough to eat. Every city slaveholder is anxious to have it known of him, that he feeds his slaves well; and it is due to them to say, that most of them do give their slaves enough to eat. There are, however, some painful exceptions to this rule. Directly opposite to us, on Philpot Street, lived Mr. Thomas Hamilton. He owned two slaves. Their names were Henrietta and Mary. Henrietta was about twenty-two years of age, Mary was about fourteen; and of all the mangled and emaciated creatures I ever looked upon, these two were the most so. His heart must be harder than stone, that could look upon these unmoved. The head, neck, and shoulders of Mary were literally cut to pieces. I have frequently felt her head, and found it nearly covered with festering sores, caused by the lash of her cruel mistress. I do not know that her master ever whipped her, but I have been an eye-witness to the cruelty of Mrs. Hamilton. I used to be in Mr. Hamilton's house nearly every day. Mrs. Hamilton used to sit in a large chair in the middle of the room, with a heavy cowskin always by her side, and scarce an hour passed during the day but was marked by the blood of one of these slaves. The girls seldom passed her without her saying, "Move faster, you *black gip!*" at the same time giving them a blow with the cowskin over the head or shoulders, often drawing the blood. She would then say, "Take that, you *black gip!*"—continuing, "If you don't move faster, I'll move you!" Added to the cruel lashings to which these slaves were subjected, they were kept nearly half-starved. They seldom knew what it was to eat a full meal. I have seen Mary contending with the pigs for the offal thrown into the street. So much was Mary kicked and cut to pieces, that she was oftener called *"pecked"* than by her name.

CHAPTER VII

I lived in Master Hugh's family about seven years. During this time, I succeeded in learning to read and write. In accomplishing this, I was compelled to resort to various stratagems. I had no regular teacher. My mistress, who had kindly commenced to instruct me, had, in compliance with the advice and direction of her husband, not only ceased to instruct, but had set her face against my being instructed by any one else. It is due, however, to my mistress to say of her, that she did not adopt this course of treatment immediately. She at first lacked the depravity indispensable to shutting me up in mental darkness. It was at least necessary for her to have some training in the exercise of irresponsible power, to make her equal to the task of treating me as though I were a brute.

My mistress was, as I have said, a kind and tender-hearted woman; and in the simplicity of her soul she commenced, when I first went to live with her, to treat me as she supposed one human being ought to treat another. In entering upon the duties of a slaveholder, she did not seem to perceive that I sustained to her the relation of a mere chattel, and that for her to treat me as a human being was not only wrong, but dangerously so. Slavery proved as injurious to her as it did to me. When I went there, she was a pious, warm, and tender-hearted woman. There was no sorrow or suffering for which she had not a tear. She had bread for the hungry, clothes for the naked, and comfort for every mourner that came within her reach. Slavery soon proved its ability to divest her of these heavenly qualities. Under its influence, the tender heart became stone, and the lamblike disposition gave way to one of tiger-like fierce-ness. The first step in her downward course was in her ceasing to in-struct me. She now commenced to practise her husband's precepts. She finally became even more violent in her opposition than her husband himself. She was not satisfied with simply doing as well as he had com-manded; she seemed anxious to do better. Nothing seemed to make her more angry than to see me with a newspaper. She seemed to think that here lay the danger. I have had her rush at me with a face made all up of fury, and snatch from me a newspaper, in a manner that fully re-vealed her apprehension. She was an apt woman; and a little experience soon demonstrated, to her satisfaction, that education and slavery were incompatible with each other.

From this time I was most narrowly watched. If I was in a separate room any considerable length of time, I was sure to be suspected of hav-ing a book, and was at once called to give an account of myself. All this, however, was too late. The first step had been taken. Mistress, in teach-ing me the alphabet, had given me the *inch*, and no precaution could prevent me taking the *ell*.

The plan which I adopted, and the one by which I was most successful, was that of making friends of all the little white boys whom I met in the street. As many of these as I could, I converted into teachers. With their kindly aid, obtained at different times and in different places, I finally succeeded in learning to read. When I was sent on errands, I always took my book with me, and by doing one part of my errand quickly, I found time to get a lesson before my return. I used also to carry bread with me, enough of which was always in the house, and to which I was al-ways welcome; for I was much better off in this regard than many of the poor white children in our neighborhood. This bread I used to be-stow upon the hungry little urchins, who, in return, would give me that more valuable bread of knowledge. I am strongly tempted to give the names of two or three of those little boys, as a testimonial of the grati-tude and affection I bear them; but prudence forbids;—not that it would injure me, but it might embarrass them; for it is almost an unpardon-able offence to teach slaves to read in this Christian country. It is enough to say of the dear little fellows, that they lived on Philpot Street, very near Durgin and Bailey's ship-yard. I used to talk this matter of slavery over with them. I would sometimes say to them, I wished I could be as free as they would be when they got to be men. "You will be free as soon as you are twenty-one, *but I am a slave for life!* Have not I as good a right to be free as you have?" These words used to trouble them; they would express for me the liveliest sympathy, and console me with the hope that something would occur by which I might be free.

I was now about twelve years old, and the thought of being *a slave for life* began to bear heavily upon my heart. Just about this time, I got hold of a book entitled "The Columbian Orator." Every opportunity I got, I used to read this book. Among much of other interesting matter, I found in it a dialogue between a master and his slave. The slave was represented as having run away from his master three times. The dia-logue represented the conversation which took place between them, when the slave was retaken the third time. In this dialogue, the whole argument in behalf of slavery was brought forward by the master, all of which was disposed of by the slave. The slave was made to say some very smart as well as impressive things in reply to his master—things which had the desired though unexpected effect; for the conversation resulted in the voluntary emancipation of the slave on the part of the master.

In the same book, I met with one of Sheridan's mighty speeches on and in behalf of Catholic emancipation. These were choice documents to me. I read them over and over again with unabated interest. They gave tongue to interesting thoughts of my own soul, which had frequently flashed through my mind, and died away for want of utterance. The moral which I gained from the dialogue was the power of truth over the conscience of even a slaveholder. What I got from Sheridan was a bold denunciation of slavery, and a powerful vindication of human rights. The reading of these documents enabled me to utter my thoughts, and to meet the arguments brought forward to sustain slavery; but while they relieved me of one difficulty, they brought on another even more painful than the one of which I was relieved. The more I read, the more I was led to abhor and detest my enslavers. I could regard them in no other light than a band of successful robbers, who had left their homes, and gone to Africa, and stolen us from our homes, and in a strange land reduced us to slavery. I loathed them as being the meanest as well as the most wicked of men. As I read and contemplated the subject, behold! that very discontentment which Master Hugh had predicted would follow my learning to read had already come, to torment and sting my soul to unutterable anguish. As I writhed under it, I would at times feel that learning to read had been a curse rather than a blessing. It had given me a view of my wretched condition, without the remedy. It opened my eyes to the horrible pit, but to no ladder upon which to get out. In moments of agony, I envied my fellow-slaves for their stupidity. I have often wished myself a beast. I preferred the condition of the meanest reptile to my own. Any thing, no matter what, to get rid of thinking! It was this everlasting thinking of my condition that tormented me. There was no getting rid of it. It was pressed upon me by every object within sight or hearing, animate or inanimate. The silver trump of freedom had roused my soul to eternal wakefulness. Freedom now appeared, to disappear no more forever. It was heard in every sound, and seen in every thing. It was ever present to torment me with a sense of my wretched condition. I saw nothing without seeing it, I heard nothing without hearing it, and felt nothing without feeling it. It looked from every star, it smiled in every calm, breathed in every wind, and moved in every storm.

I often found myself regretting my own existence, and wishing myself dead; and but for the hope of being free, I have no doubt but that I should have killed myself, or done something for which I should have been killed. While in this state of mind, I was eager to hear any one speak of slavery. I was a ready listener. Every little while, I could hear something about the abolitionists. It was some time before I found what

the word meant. It was always used in such connections as to make it
an interesting word to me. If a slave ran away and succeeded in getting
clear, or if a slave killed his master, set fire to a barn, or did any thing
very wrong in the mind of a slaveholder, it was spoken of as the fruit of
abolition. Hearing the word in this connection very often, I set about
learning what it meant. The dictionary afforded me little or no help. I
found it was "the act of abolishing;" but then I did not know what was
to be abolished. Here I was perplexed. I did not dare to ask any one
about its meaning, for I was satisfied that it was something they wanted
me to know very little about. After a patient waiting, I got one of our
city papers, containing an account of the number of petitions from the
north, praying for the abolition of slavery in the District of Columbia,
and of the slave trade between the States. From this time I understood
the words *abolition* and *abolitionist,* and always drew near when that
word was spoken, expecting to hear something of importance to myself
and fellow-slaves. The light broke in upon me by degrees. I went one day
down on the wharf of Mr. Waters; and seeing two Irishmen unloading a
scow of stone, I went, unasked, and helped them. When we had finished,
one of them came to me and asked me if I were a slave. I told him I was.
He asked, "Are ye a slave for life?" I told him that I was. The good Irishman seemed to be deeply affected by the statement. He said to the other
that it was a pity so fine a little fellow as myself should be a slave for
life. He said it was a shame to hold me. They both advised me to run
away to the north; that I should find friends there, and that I should be
free. I pretended not to be interested in what they said, and treated
them as if I did not understand them; for I feared they might be treacherous. White men have been known to encourage slaves to escape, and
then, to get the reward, catch them and return them to their masters. I
was afraid that these seemingly good men might use me so; but I nevertheless remembered their advice, and from that time I resolved to run
away. I looked forward to a time at which it would be safe for me to
escape. I was too young to think of doing so immediately; besides, I
wished to learn how to write, as I might have occasion to write my own
pass. I consoled myself with the hope that I should one day find a good
chance. Meanwhile, I would learn to write.

The idea as to how I might learn to write was suggested to me by
being in Durgin and Bailey's ship-yard, and frequently seeing the ship
carpenters, after hewing, and getting a piece of timber ready for use,
write on the timber the name of that part of the ship for which it was
intended. When a piece of timber was intended for the larboard side, it
would be marked thus—"L." When a piece was for the starboard side, it
would be marked thus—"S." A piece for the larboard side forward would
be marked thus—"L. F." When a piece was for starboard side forward,
it would be marked thus—"S. F." For larboard aft, it would be marked
thus—"L. A." For starboard aft, it would be marked thus—"S. A." I
soon learned the names of these letters, and for what they were intended
when placed upon a piece of timber in the ship-yard. I immediately commenced copying them, and in a short time was able to make the four
letters named. After that, when I met with any boy who I knew could

write, I would tell him I could write as well as he. The next word would be, "I don't believe you. Let me see you try it." I would then make the letters which I had been so fortunate as to learn, and ask him to beat that. In this way I got a good many lessons in writing, which it is quite possible I should never have gotten in any other way. During this time, my copy-book was the board fence, brick wall, and pavement; my pen and ink was a lump of chalk. With these, I learned mainly how to write. I then commenced and continued copying the Italics in Webster's Spelling Book, until I could make them all without looking on the book. By this time, my little Master Thomas had gone to school, and learned how to write, and had written over a number of copy-books. These had been brought home, and shown to some of our near neighbors, and then laid aside. My mistress used to go to class meeting at the Wilk Street meetinghouse every Monday afternoon, and leave me to take care of the house. When left thus, I used to spend the time in writing in the spaces left in Master Thomas's copy-book, copying what he had written. I continued to do this until I could write a hand very similar to that of Master Thomas. Thus, after a long, tedious effort for years, I finally succeeded in learning how to write.

THE CONDITION, ELEVATION, EMIGRATION, AND DESTINY OF THE COLORED PEOPLE OF THE UNITED STATES

Martin Robison Delany

[Colonization schemes for black Americans in the nineteenth century interested white men for several reasons. Initially, around the time of the Revolution, colonization was conceived as a solution to the black problem by those who wanted to abolish slavery, on religious or political grounds, but who were loath to grant equality, as the logic of political emancipation required, to black freemen. Later, after 1816, such schemes were endorsed by proslavery advocates who feared slave rebellion and looked upon the growing free Negro population as a threat to civil peace. After 1830, when Southern apologists for slavery embraced the position that slavery was just and beneficial (a shift from the previous view that it was a necessary evil), colonization was welcomed not only as a means to deport troublesome blacks but also as a solution to the difficult anomaly of free blacks. For all that, colonization remained an impractical idea, embodying as it did more the hope that the blacks would just go away than any recognition of the difficulty, not to say the arrogance and unfairness, of such proposals.

The separatist solution to the problem of race did not interest really significant numbers of American blacks until the twentieth century. Free Negroes in the North, where slavery had been abolished by 1804, were uniformly opposed to colonization. From the time the American Colonization Society was founded, in 1816, until 1850, the total number of emigrants to Liberia was only about 6,000. Of that total, most came from the South, and over 3,600 were emancipated expressly on the condition that they emigrate.

The free Negro's position deteriorated markedly in the tense decade before the Civil War. The Compromise of 1850, with its new and strengthened Fugitive Slave Law, did nothing to improve his condition. The law made life especially hazardous for blacks who were migrating northward, either legally or illegally. Many thousands had gone to Michigan, Iowa, and California, but the Kansas-Nebraska Act of 1854 opened the possibility that the Western territories would accept slavery; and then, in 1857, the final tragic blow was struck by the Dred Scott decision. In arguing that neither slaves nor the freed descendants of slaves could become citizens of the United States, it cut the ground from under any supposed benefits a general emancipation, if it were to come, could offer and denied, in effect, that Negroes had a right to freedom. But if liberty were an "inalienable right" of human beings, as the Declaration of Independence had said, then this decision asserted, in essence, that Negroes were not human.

Not surprisingly, the same decade saw an increase of interest in colonization among blacks. An additional 5,000—almost as many as in the previous thirty-five years—went off to Liberia, which had become an independent republic in 1847, with the franchise restricted mainly to American colonists. A Haitian emigration movement also began, in 1854, and, within the next eight years, 3,000 went to Haiti.

The emigration even of this relatively small number of blacks was evidence, of course, of their growing realization of the need for some kind of national existence if they were ever to improve their condition. One of the notable spokesmen for this view that emerged in the 1850's was Martin Robison Delany. His *Condition . . . and Destiny of the Colored People of the United States*, the concluding chapter and appendix of which are reprinted here, appeared in 1852. The Africans in America, Delany insisted, were "a nation within a nation." Although he never says so explicitly, his writings reflect an insight that is as old as Aristotle: The state is necessary not for living, but for living well. And blacks in America had never lived well. He, therefore, encouraged them to go to Central America or even to East Africa to form a new state. Initially, he opposed the Liberian experiment because he felt the country would never be free of white influence and, thus, never able to offer real opportunities for black people. For much the same reason, he cautioned against emigration to Canada, which he feared might ultimately be absorbed into the United States. Delany's argument for emigration rested on the presumed equality of social, civil, political, and religious privileges available to blacks in other parts of the Western Hemisphere. He recognized the difficulty of raising children in a society that traditionally assigned their parents (even when nominally free) a permanent place among the lowest social class. The children of the oppressed could never, he felt, break the cycle of degradation into which they were born. If they were to receive the education necessary to aspire to be more than a race of servants, it would be necessary to find "space to rise." The problem was thus seen as one of changing the character of an oppressed people by appealing to their pride. The similarity of Delany's observations to recent discussions of the problems inherent in educating ghetto children is striking. Although the terms of the discussion have changed, it is not a new observation that one cannot educate ghetto children when they see what is happening to their fathers—when they see, that is, what is often tantamount to Ph.D.'s collecting garbage. If it is true that the country is destroying the masses of black children from the cradle, it is not so much that there is a national conspiracy to do this as that the nation has never broken out of the vicious cycle of degradation that is the legacy of slavery.

Delany's enthusiasm for a Negro nation anywhere in the New World waned after 1856, and, in 1859, he journeyed to West Africa to spend six weeks touring the principal cities of Yorubaland. (He had hopes that cotton could be developed as an African crop, to replace Southern cotton on the world market.) On the same trip, he also spent two and a half months in Liberia, where he received a hero's welcome, and his opposition to the Republic finally melted.

When Delany returned to the United States, in December, 1860, there was still considerable interest in emigration among blacks. The Civil War and Emancipation, however, changed the situation of American Negroes. Delany, who had attended Harvard and was a doctor, eventually accepted a major's commission in the Union Army. After the war, he remained in South Carolina, where he ran, unsuccessfully, for lieutenant governor. But, after the end of Reconstruction, he again became interested in Africa and gave support to a group that was promoting an exodus to Liberia.]

A GLANCE AT OURSELVES—CONCLUSION.

With broken hopes—sad devastation;
A race *resigned* to DEGRADATION!

We have said much to our young men and women, about their vocation and calling; we have dwelt much upon the menial position of our people in this country. Upon this point we cannot say too much, because there is a seeming satisfaction and seeking after such positions manifested on their part, unknown to any other people. There appears to be, a want of a sense of propriety or *self-respect*, altogether inexplicable; because young men and women among us, many of whom have good trades and homes, adequate to their support, voluntarily leave them, and seek positions, such as servants, waiting maids, coachmen, nurses, cooks in gentlemens' kitchen, or such like occupations, when they can gain a livelihood at something more respectable, or elevating in character. And the worse part of the whole matter is, that they have become so accustomed to it, it has become so "fashionable," that it seems to have become second nature, and they really become offended, when it is spoken against.

Among the German, Irish, and other European peasantry who come to this country, it matters not what they were employed at before and after they come; just so soon as they can better their condition by keeping shops, cultivating the soil, the young men and women going to night-schools, qualifying themselves for usefulness, and learning trades—they do so. Their first and last care, object and aim is, to better their condition by raising themselves above the condition that necessity places them in. We do not say too much, when we say, as an evidence of the deep degradation of our race, in the United States, that there are those among us, the wives and daughters, some of the *first ladies*, (and who dare say they are not the "first," because they belong to the "first class" and associate where any body among us can?) whose husbands are industrious, able and willing to support them, who voluntarily leave home, and become chamber-maids, and stewardesses, upon vessels and steamboats, in all probability, to enable them to obtain some more fine or costly article of dress or furniture.

We have nothing to say against those whom *necessity* compels to do these things, those who can do no better; we have only to do with those who can, and will not, or do not do better. The whites are always in the advance, and we either standing still or retrograding; as that which does not go forward, must either stand in one place or go back. The father in all probability is a farmer, mechanic, or man of some independent business; and the wife, sons and daughters, are chamber-maids, on vessels, nurses and waiting-maids, or coachmen and cooks in families. This is retrogradation. The wife, sons, and daughters should be elevated above this condition as a necessary consequence.

If we did not love our race superior to others, we would not concern ourself about their degradation; for the greatest desire of our heart is, to see them stand on a level with the most elevated of mankind. No people are ever elevated above the condition of their *females;* hence, the condition of the *mother* determines the condition of the child. To know the position of a people, it is only necessary to know the *condition* of their *females;* and despite themselves, they cannot rise above their level. Then what is our condition? Our *best ladies* being washer-women, chamber-maids, children's traveling nurses, and common house servants, and menials, we are all a degraded, miserable people, inferior to any other people as a whole, on the face of the globe.

These great truths, however unpleasant, must be brought before the minds of our people in its true and proper light, as we have been too delicate about them, and too long concealed them for fear of giving offence. It would have been infinitely better for our race, if these facts had been presented before us half a century ago—we would have been now proportionably benefitted by it.

As an evidence of the degradation to which we have been reduced, we dare premise, that this chapter will give offence to many, very many, and why? Because they may say, "He dared to say that the occupation of a *servant* is a degradation." It is not necessarily degrading; it would not be, to one or a few people of a kind; but a *whole race of servants* are a degradation to that people.

Efforts made by men of qualifications for the toiling and degraded millions among the whites, neither gives offence to that class, nor is it taken unkindly by them; but received with manifestations of gratitude; to know that they are thought to be, equally worthy of, and entitled to stand on a level with the elevated classes; and they have only got to be informed of the way to raise themselves, to make the effort and do so as far as they can. But how different with us. Speak of our position in society, and it at once gives insult. Though we are servants; among ourselves we claim to be *ladies* and *gentlemen*, equal in standing, and as the popular expression goes, "Just as good as any body"—and so believing, we make no efforts to raise above the common level of menials; because the *best* being in that capacity, all are content with the position. We cannot at the same time, be domestic and lady; servant and gentleman. We must be the one or the other. Sad, sad indeed, is the thought, that hangs drooping in our mind, when contemplating the picture drawn before us. Young men and women, "we write these things unto you, because ye are strong," because the writer, a few years ago, gave unpardonable offence to many of the young people of Philadelphia and other places, because he dared to tell them, that he thought too much of them, to be content with seeing them the servants of other people. Surely, she that could be the mistress, would not be the maid; neither would he that could be the master, be content with being the servant; then why be offended, when we point out to you, the way that leads from the menial to the mistress or the master. All this we seem to reject with fixed determination, repelling with anger, every effort on the part of our intelligent men and women to elevate us, with true Israelitish degradation, in reply to any suggestion or proposition that may be offered, "Who made thee a ruler and judge?"

The writer is no "Public Man," in the sense in which this is understood among our people, but simply an humble individual, endeavoring to seek a livelihood by a profession obtained entirely by his own efforts, without relatives and friends able to assist him; except such friends as he gained by the merit of his course and conduct, which he here gratefully acknowledges; and whatever he has accomplished, other young men may, by making corresponding efforts, also accomplish.

We have advised an emigration to Central and South America, and even to Mexico and the West Indies, to those who prefer either of the last named places, all of which are free countries, Brazil being the only real slave-holding State in South America—there being nominal slavery in Dutch Guiana, Peru, Buenos Ayres, Paraguay, and Uraguay, in all of which places colored people have equality in social, civil, political, and religious privileges; Brazil making it punishable with death to import slaves into the empire.

Our oppressors, when urging us to go to Africa, tell us that we are better adapted to the climate than they—that the physical condition of the constitution of colored people better endures the heat of warm climates than that of the whites; this we are willing to *admit*, without argument, without adducing the physiological reason why, that colored people can and do stand warm climates better than whites; and find an answer fully to the point in the fact, that they also stand *all other* climates, cold, temperate, and modified, that white people can stand; therefore, according to our oppressors' own showing, we are a *superior race*, being endowed with properties fitting us for *all parts* of the earth, while they are only adapted to *certain* parts. Of course, this proves our right and duty to live wherever we may *choose;* while the white race may only live where they *can*. We are content with the fact, and have ever claimed it. Upon this rock, they and we shall ever agree.

Of the West India Islands, Santa Cruz, belonging to Denmark; Porto Rico, and Cuba with its little adjuncts, belonging to Spain, are the only slave-holding Islands among them—three-fifths of the whole population of Cuba being colored people, who cannot and will not much longer endure the burden and the yoke. They only want intelligent leaders of their own color, when they are ready at any moment to charge to the conflict—to liberty or death. The remembrance of the noble mulatto, PLACIDO, the gentleman, scholar, poet, and intended Chief Engineer of the Army of Liberty and Freedom in Cuba; and the equally noble black, CHARLES BLAIR, who was to have been Commander-in-Chief, who were shamefully put to death in 1844, by that living monster, Captain General O'Donnell, is still fresh and indelible to the mind of every bondman of Cuba.

In our own country, the United States, there are *three million five hundred thousand slaves;* and we, the nominally free colored people, are *six hundred thousand* in number; estimating one-sixth to be men, we have *one hundred thousand* able bodied freemen, which will make a powerful auxiliary in any country in which we may become adopted—an ally not to be despised by any power on earth. We love our country, dearly love her, but she don't love us—she despises us, and bids us begone, driving us from her embraces; but we shall not go where she desires us; but when we do go, whatever love we have for her, we shall love the country none the less that receives us as her adopted children.

For the want of business habits and training, our energies have become paralyzed; our young men never think of business, any more than if they were so many bondmen, without the right to pursue any calling they may think most advisable. With our people in this country, dress and good appearances have been made the only test of gentlemen and lady-ship, and that vocation which offers the best opportunity to dress and appear well, has generally been preferred, however menial and degrading, by our young people, without even, in the majority of cases, an effort to do better; indeed, in many instances, refusing situations equally lucrative, and superior in position; but which would not allow as much display of dress and personal appearance. This, if we ever expect to rise, must be discarded from among us, and a high and respectable position assumed.

One of our great temporal curses is our consummate poverty. We are the poorest people, as a class, in the world of civilized mankind—abjectly, miserably poor, no one scarcely being able to assist the other. To this, of course, there are noble exceptions; but that which is common to, and the very process by which white men exist, and succeed in life, is unknown to colored men in general. In any and every considerable community may be found, some one of our white fellow-citizens, who is worth more than all the colored people in that community put together. We consequently have little or no efficiency. We must have means to be practically efficient in all the undertakings of life; and to obtain them, it is necessary that we should be engaged in lucrative pursuits, trades, and general business transactions. In order to be thus engaged, it is necessary that we should occupy positions that afford the facilities for such pursuits. To compete now with the mighty odds of wealth, social and religious preferences, and political influences of this country, at this advanced stage of its national existence, we never may expect. A new country, and new beginning, is the only true, rational, politic remedy for our disadvantageous position; and that country we have already pointed out, with triple golden advantages, all things considered, to that of any country to which it has been the province of man to embark.

Every other than we, have at various periods of necessity, been a migratory people; and all when oppressed, shown a greater abhorrence of oppression, if not a greater love of liberty, than we. We cling to our oppressors as the objects of our love. It is true that our enslaved brethren are here, and we have been led to believe that it is necessary for us to remain, on that account. Is it true, that all should remain in degradation, because a part are degraded? We believe no such thing. We believe it to be the duty of the Free, to elevate themselves in the most speedy and effective manner possible; as the redemption of the bondman depends entirely upon the elevation of the freeman; therefore, to elevate the free colored people of America, anywhere upon this continent; forebodes the speedy redemption of the slaves. We shall hope to hear no more of so fallacious a doctrine—the necessity of the free remaining in degradation, for the sake of the oppressed. Let us apply, first, the lever to ourselves; and the force that elevates us to the position of manhood's considerations and honors, will cleft the manacle of every slave in the land.

When such great worth and talents—for want of a better sphere—of men like Rev. Jonathan Robinson, Robert Douglass, Frederick A. Hinton, and a hundred others that might be named, were permitted to expire in a barber-shop; and such living men as may be found in Boston, New York, Philadelphia, Baltimore, Richmond, Washington City, Charleston, (S. C.) New Orleans, Cincinnati, Louisville, St. Louis, Pittsburg, Buffalo, Rochester, Albany, Utica, Cleveland, Detroit, Milwaukie, Chicago, Columbus, Zanesville, Wheeling, and a hundred other places, confining themselves to Barber-shops and waiterships in Hotels; certainly the necessity of such a course as we have pointed out, must be cordially acknowledged; appreciated by every brother and sister of oppression; and not rejected as heretofore, as though they preferred inferiority to equality.

These minds must become "unfettered," and have "space to rise." This cannot be in their present positions. A continuance in any position, becomes what is termed "Second Nature;" it begets an *adaptation*, and *reconciliation* of *mind* to such condition. It changes the whole physiological condition of the system, and adapts man and woman to a higher or lower sphere in the pursuits of life. The offsprings of slaves and peasantry, have the general characteristics of their parents; and nothing but a different course of training and education, will change the character.

The slave may become a lover of his master, and learn to forgive him for continual deeds of maltreatment and abuse; just as the Spaniel would couch and fondle at the feet that kick him; because he has been taught to reverence them, and consequently, becomes adapted in body and mind to his condition. Even the shrubbery-loving Canary, and lofty-soaring Eagle, may be tamed to the cage, and learn to love it from habit of confinement. It has been so with us in our position among our oppressors; we have been so prone to such positions, that we have learned to love them. When reflecting upon this all important, and to us, all absorbing subject; we feel in the agony and anxiety of the moment, as though we could cry out in the language of a Prophet of old: "Oh that my head were waters, and mine eyes a fountain of tears, that I might weep day and night for the" degradation "of my people! Oh that I had in the wilderness a lodging place of way-faring men; that I might leave my people, and go from them!"

The Irishman and German in the United States, are very different persons to what they were when in Ireland and Germany, the countries of their nativity. There their spirits were depressed and downcast; but the instant they set their foot upon unrestricted soil; free to act and untrammeled to move; their physical condition undergoes a change, which in time becomes physiological, which is transmitted to the offspring, who when born under such circumstances, is a decidedly different being to what it would have been, had it been born under different circumstances.

A child born under oppression, has all the elements of servility in its constitution; who when born under favorable circumstances, has to the contrary, all the elements of freedom and independence of feeling. Our children then, may not be expected, to maintain that position and manly bearing; born under the unfavorable circumstances with which we are surrounded in this country; that we so much desire. To use the language of the talented Mr. Whipper, "they cannot be raised in this country, without being stoop shouldered." Heaven's pathway stands unobstructed, which will lead us into a Paradise of bliss. Let us go on and possess the land, and the God of Israel will be our God.

The lessons of every school book, the pages of every history, and columns of every newspaper, are so replete with stimuli to nerve us on to manly aspirations, that those of our young people, who will now refuse to enter upon this great theatre of Polynesian adventure, and take their position on the stage of Central and South America, where a brilliant engagement, of certain and most triumphant success, in the drama of human equality awaits them; then, with the blood of *slaves*, write upon the lintel of every door in sterling Capitals, to be gazed and hissed at by every passer by—

> Doomed by the Creator
> To servility and degradation;
> The SERVANT of the *white man*,
> And despised of every nation!

A PROJECT FOR AN EXPEDITION OF ADVENTURE, TO THE EASTERN COAST OF AFRICA

Every people should be the originators of their own designs, the projector of their own schemes, and creators of the events that lead to their destiny—the consummation of their desires.

Situated as we are, in the United States, many, and almost insurmountable obstacles present themselves. We are four-and-a-half millions in numbers, free and bond; six hundred thousand free, and three-and-a-half millions bond.

We have native hearts and virtues, just as other nations; which in their pristine purity are noble, potent, and worthy of example. We are a nation within a nation;—as the Poles in Russia, the Hungarians in Austria, the Welsh, Irish, and Scotch in the British dominions.

But we have been, by our oppressors, despoiled of our purity, and corrupted in our native characteristics, so that we have inherited their vices, and but few of their virtues, leaving us in character, really a *broken people.*

Being distinguished by complexion, we are still singled out—although having merged in the habits and customs of our oppressors—as a distinct nation of people; as the Poles, Hungarians, Irish, and others, who still retain their native peculiarities, of language, habits, and various other traits. The claims of no people, according to established policy and usage, are respected by any nation, until they are presented in a national capacity.

To accomplish so great and desirable an end, there should be held, a great representative gathering of the colored people of the United States; not what is termed a National Convention, represented en masse, such as have been, for the last few years, held at various times and places; but a true representation of the intelligence and wisdom of the colored freemen; because it will be futile and an utter failure, to attempt such a project without the highest grade of intelligence.

No great project was ever devised without the consultation of the most mature intelligence, and discreet discernment and precaution.

To effect this, and prevent intrusion and improper representation, there should be a CONFIDENTIAL COUNCIL held; and circulars issued, only to such persons as shall be *known* to the projectors to be equal to the desired object.

The authority from whence the call should originate, to be in this wise:—The originator of the scheme, to impart the contemplated Confidential Council, to a limited number of known, worthy gentlemen, who agreeing with the project, endorse at once the scheme, when becoming joint proprietors in interest, issue a *Confidential Circular*, leaving blanks for *date, time,* and *place* of *holding* the Council; sending them to trusty, worthy, and suitable colored freemen, in all parts of the United States, and the Canadas, inviting them to attend; who when met in Council, have the right to project any scheme they may think proper for the general good of the whole people—provided, that the project is laid before them after its maturity.

By this Council to be appointed, a Board of Commissioners, to consist of three, five, or such reasonable number as may be decided upon, one of whom shall be chosen as Principal or Conductor of the Board, whose duty and business shall be, to go on an expedition to the EASTERN COAST OF AFRICA, to make researches for a suitable location on that section of the coast, for the settlement of colored adventurers from the United States, and elsewhere. Their mission should be to all such places as might meet the approbation of the people; as South America, Mexico, the West Indies, &c.

The Commissioners all to be men of decided qualifications, to embody among them, the qualifications of physician, botanist, chemist, geologist, geographer, and surveyor,—having a sufficient knowledge of these sciences, for practical purposes.

Their business shall be, to make a topographical, geographical, geological, and botanical examination, into such part or parts as they may select, with all other useful information that may be obtained; to be recorded in a journal kept for that purpose.

The Council shall appoint a permanent Board of Directors, to manage and supervise the doings of the Commissioners, and to whom they shall be amenable for their doings, who shall hold their offices until successors shall be appointed.

A National Confidential Council, to be held once in three years; and sooner, if necessity or emergency should demand it; the Board of Directors giving at least three months' notice, by circulars and newspapers. And should they fail to perform their duty, twenty-five of the representatives from any six States, of the former Council, may issue a call, authentically bearing their names, as sufficient authority for such a call. But when the Council is held for the reception of the report of the Commissioners, a general mass convention should then take place, by popular representation.

Manner of Raising Funds

The National Council shall appoint one or two Special Commissioners, to England and France, to solicit, in the name of the Representatives of a Broken Nation, of four-and-a-half millions, the necessary outfit and support, for any period not exceeding three years, of such an expedition. Certainly, what England and France would do, for a little nation—mere nominal nation, of five thousand civilized Liberians, they would be willing and ready to do, for five millions; if they be but authentically represented, in a national capacity. What was due to Greece, enveloped by

Turkey, should be due to us, enveloped by the United States; and we believe would be respected, if properly presented. To England and France, we should look for sustenance, and the people of those two nations—as they would have every thing to gain from such an adventure and eventual settlement on the EASTERN COAST OF AFRICA—the opening of an immense trade being the consequence. The whole Continent is rich in minerals, and the most precious metals, as but a superficial notice of the topographical and geological reports from that country, plainly show to any mind versed in the least, in the science of the earth.

The Eastern Coast of Africa has long been neglected, and never but little known, even to the ancients; but has ever been our choice part of the Continent. Bounded by the Red Sea, Arabian Sea, and Indian Ocean, it presents the greatest facilities for an immense trade, with China, Japan, Siam, Hindoostan, in short, all the East Indies—of any other country in the world. With a settlement of enlightened freemen, who with the immense facilities, must soon grow into a powerful nation. In the Province of Berbera, south of the Strait of Babelmandel, or the great pass, from the Arabian to the Red Sea, the whole commerce of the East must touch this point.

Also, a great rail road could be constructed from here, running with the Mountains of the Moon, clearing them entirely, except making one mountain pass, at the western extremity of the Mountains of the Moon, and the southeastern terminus of the Kong Mountains; entering the Province of Dahomey, and terminating on the Atlantic Ocean West; which would make the GREAT THOROUGHFARE for all the trade with the East Indies and Eastern Coast of Africa, and the Continent of America. All the world would pass through Africa upon this rail road, which would yield a revenue infinitely greater than any other investment in the world.

The means for prosecuting such a project—as stupendous as it may appear—will be fully realised in the prosecution of the work. Every mile of the road, will thrice pay for itself, in the development of the rich treasures that now lie hidden in the bowels of the earth. There is no doubt, that in some one section of twenty-five miles, the developments of gold would more than pay the expenses of any one thousand miles of the work. This calculation may, to those who have never given this subject a thought, appear extravagant, and visionary; but to one who has had his attention in this direction for years, it is clear enough. But a few years will witness a development of gold, precious metals, and minerals in Eastern Africa, the Moon and Kong Mountains, ten-fold greater than all the rich productions of California.

There is one great physiological fact in regard to the colored race—which, while it may not apply to all colored persons, is true of those having black skins—that they can bear *more different* climates than the white race. They bear *all* the temperates and extremes, while the other can only bear the temperates and *one* of the extremes. The black race is endowed with natural properties, that adapt and fit them for temperate, cold, and hot climates; while the white race is only endowed with properties that adapt them to temperate and cold climates; being unable to stand the warmer climates; in them, the white race cannot work, but become perfectly indolent, requiring somebody to work for them—and these, are always people of the black race.

The black race may be found, inhabiting in healthful improvement, every part of the globe where the white race reside; while there are parts of the globe where the black race reside, that the white race cannot live in health.

What part of mankind is the "denizen of every soil, and the lord of terrestrial creation," if it be not the black race? The Creator has indisputably adapted us for the "denizens of *every soil*," all that is left for us to do, is to *make* ourselves the *"lords* of terrestrial creation." The land is ours—there it lies with inexhaustible resources; let us go and possess it. In Eastern Africa must rise up a nation, to whom all the world must pay commercial tribute.

SPEECH AT THE ATLANTA EXPOSITION AND WHAT I AM TRYING TO DO

Booker T. Washington

[By the 1880's, with Reconstruction a thing of the past, Negro hopes for equality foundered more obviously than ever on the color bar. The promise of the Fourteenth and Fifteenth Amendments to the Constitution was being whittled away by state laws and Supreme Court decisions. Negro participation in all phases of American life was qualified by prejudice, and many avenues of economic improvement remained closed. The tireless agitation of a Frederick Douglass kept Negro grievances before the public. "Who would be free," Douglass counseled in 1883, "themselves must strike the first blow. We do not believe, as we are often told, that the Negro is the ugly child of the national family, and the more he is kept out of sight the better it will be for him. You know that liberty given is never so precious as liberty sought for and fought for." But the views of Douglass were not to prevail until a later time.

In the year Douglass died, 1895, another leader, Booker T. Washington, on September 18, delivered an address at the Cotton States and International Exposition in Atlanta, Georgia. Rufus Bullock, a former governor, introduced Washington as a "representative of Negro enterprise and Negro civilization." In the speech, which is reprinted below, Washington urged a moderate course while stressing the need for moral and economic improvement. His phrase "separate as the fingers, yet one as the hand in all things essential to mutual progress," which has been variously interpreted by his supporters and detractors ever since, allayed any fears his white audience might have had about the ambitions of the Southern Negro. The speech made Washington a national figure (replacing Douglass in that role) to the point where he became public property and his words were taken as representative of Negro thought for a generation afterward. Whatever the merits of his position, Washington's ideas on social separateness could not have had a more receptive audience. A year after the speech, as if to sanction his thought, Justice Henry B. Brown handed down the landmark decision in *Plessy* v. *Ferguson*, which sanctioned segregation in the South as well as in the North for nearly sixty years.

Washington's plan, spelled out more explicitly in the 1913 magazine article also reprinted here, was to elicit white support in making the Negro useful to society and to delay demands for equality until the race as a whole had advanced as freemen. He believed that, to accomplish this end, he had to convince the white society that it was in their own interest to educate the Negro. Washington's ideas on Negro progress and education were embodied in Tuskegee Institute, which he founded in 1881. The school was organized around vocational training—farming, industrial mechanics, domestic service—and was instilled with the notion that labor was a spiritual and edifying force. From the very beginning, the students cooperated in whatever work needed to be done, including the construction of the early buildings and the raising of their own food. Indeed, the cultivation and ownership of land comprised a large part of Washington's hopes for providing the Negro with an economic foothold in American life.

Washington's critics have regularly pointed out that his program, while serving the interests of white society, finally accomplished very little for the Negro. In the 1890's, Southern white aspirations for the Negro, even at their best, harbored a thinly veiled belief in the natural inferiority of the Negro. Henry Grady, for example, the editor of the *Atlanta Constitution*, who courted the industrialists with rousing speeches in the North and did his best to paint a picture of Negro progress, was adamant that white society should maintain its position of political supremacy. Whatever else Grady meant, he clearly made a condition of any alliance between Northern industry and Southern agriculture that there should be no agitation on the question of equal political rights for the Negro. If one compares Washington's policies with Grady's program for the "New South," it is difficult not to notice the hand-in-glove fit; nor should one be surprised at the ready acceptance by whites of what could easily be seen as a solution that would provide a "place" for the Negro in American society. But if Washington's conciliatory position made him a white man's Negro leader, this had been no less true of Douglass, for all his rhetoric about equality. And it is doubtful if even a Douglass could have accomplished what Washington did, in the atmosphere of race hatred that accompanied the demise of Reconstruction.]

SPEECH AT THE ATLANTA EXPOSITION

Mr. President and Gentlemen of the Board of Directors and Citizens:

One-third of the population of the South is of the Negro race. No enterprise seeking the material, civil, or moral welfare of this section can disregard this element of our population and reach the highest success. I but convey to you, Mr. President and Directors, the sentiment of the masses of my race when I say that in no way have the value and manhood of the American Negro been more fittingly and generously recognized than by the managers of this magnificent exposition at every stage of its progress. It is a recognition that will do more to cement the friendship of the two races than any occurrence since the dawn of our freedom.

Not only this, but the opportunity here afforded will awaken among us a new era of industrial progress. Ignorant and inexperienced, it is not strange that in the first years of our new life we began at the top instead of at the bottom; that a seat in Congress or the state legislature was more sought than real estate or industrial skill; that the political convention or stump speaking had more attractions than starting a dairy farm or truck garden.

A ship lost at sea for many days suddenly sighted a friendly vessel. From the mast of the unfortunate vessel was seen a signal: "Water, water; we die of thirst!" The answer from the friendly vessel at once came back: "Cast down your bucket where you are." A second time the signal, "Water, water, send us water!" ran up from the distressed vessel, and was answered: "Cast down your bucket where you are." And a third and fourth signal for water was answered: "Cast down your bucket where you are." The captain of the distressed vessel, at last heeding the injunction, cast down his bucket, and it came up full of fresh, sparkling water from the mouth of the Amazon River.

To those of my race who depend on bettering their condition in a foreign land or who underestimate the importance of cultivating friendly relations with the Southern white man, who is their next-door neighbor, I would say: Cast down your bucket where you are; cast it down in making friends, in every manly way, of the people of all races by whom we are surrounded. Cast it down in agriculture, mechanics, in commerce, in domestic service, and in the professions. And in this connection it is well to bear in mind that whatever other sins the South may be called to bear, when it comes to business, pure and simple, it is in the South that the Negro is given a man's chance in the commercial world, and in nothing is this exposition more eloquent than in emphasizing this chance.

Our greatest danger is that, in the great leap from slavery to freedom, we may overlook the fact that the masses of us are to live by the productions of our hands and fail to keep in mind that we shall prosper in proportion as we learn to dignify and glorify common labor, and put brains and skill into the common occupations of life; shall prosper in proportion as we learn to draw the line between the superficial and the substantial, the ornamental gewgaws of life and the useful. No race can prosper till it learns that there is as much dignity in tilling a field as in writing a poem. It is at the bottom of life we must begin, and not at the top. Nor should we permit our grievances to overshadow our opportunities.

To those of the white race who look to the incoming of those of foreign birth and strange tongue and habits for the prosperity of the South, were I permitted I would repeat what I say to my own race, "Cast down your bucket where you are." Cast it down among the 8 million Negroes whose habits you know, whose fidelity and love you have tested in days when to have proved treacherous meant the ruin of your firesides. Cast down your bucket among these people who have, without strikes and labor wars, tilled your fields, cleared your forests, builded your railroads and cities, and brought forth treasures from the bowels of the earth and helped make possible this magnificent representation of the progress of the South. Casting down your bucket among my people, helping and encouraging them as you are doing on these grounds, and, with education of head, hand, and heart, you will find that they will buy your surplus land, make blossom the waste places in your fields, and run your factories.

While doing this, you can be sure in the future, as in the past, that you and your families will be surrounded by the most patient, faithful, law-abiding, and unresentful people that the world has seen, As we have proved our loyalty to you in the past, in nursing your children, watching by the sickbed of your mothers and fathers, and often following them with tear-dimmed eyes to their graves, so in the future, in our humble way, we shall stand by you with a devotion that no foreigner can approach, ready to lay down our lives, if need be, in defense of yours; interlacing our industrial, commercial, civil, and religious life with yours in a way that shall make the interests of both races one. In all things that are purely social we can be as separate as the fingers, yet one as the hand in all things essential to mutual progress.

There is no defense or security for any of us except in the highest intelligence and development of all. If anywhere there are efforts tending to curtail the fullest growth of the Negro, let these efforts be turned into stimulating, encouraging, and making him the most useful and intelligent citizen. Effort or means so invested will pay a thousand percent interest. These efforts will be twice blessed—"blessing him that gives and him that takes."

There is no escape, through law of man or God, from the inevitable:

> The laws of changeless justice bind
> Oppressor with oppressed;
> And close as sin and suffering joined
> We march to fate abreast

Nearly 16 millions of hands will aid you in pulling the load upward, or they will pull against you the load downward. We shall constitute one-third and more of the ignorance and crime of the South, or one-third its intelligence and progress; we shall contribute one-third to the business and industrial prosperity of the South, or we shall prove a veritable body of death, stagnating, depressing, retarding every effort to advance the body politic.

Gentlemen of the exposition, as we present to you our humble effort at an exhibition of our progress, you must not expect overmuch. Starting thirty years ago with ownership here and there in a few quilts and pumpkins and chickens (gathered from miscellaneous sources), remember: the path that has led from these to the invention and production of agricultural implements, buggies, steam engines, newspapers, books, statuary, carving, paintings, the management of drugstores and banks, has not been trodden without contact with thorns and thistles. While we take pride in what we exhibit as a result of our independent efforts, we do not for a moment forget that our part in this exhibition would fall far short of your expectations but for the constant help that has come to our educational life, not only from the Southern states but especially from Northern philanthropists who have made their gifts a constant stream of blessing and encouragement.

The wisest among my race understand that the agitation of questions of social equality is the extremest folly, and that progress in the enjoyment of all the privileges that will come to us must be the result of severe and constant struggle rather than of artificial forcing. No race that has anything to contribute to the markets of the world is long in any degree ostracized. It is important and right that all privileges of the law be ours, but it is vastly more important that we be prepared for the exercise of these privileges. The opportunity to earn a dollar in a factory just now is worth infinitely more than the opportunity to spend a dollar in an opera house.

In conclusion, may I repeat that nothing in thirty years has given us more hope and encouragement and drawn us so near to you of the white race as this opportunity offered by the exposition; and here bending, as it were, over the altar that represents the results of the struggles of your race and mine, both starting practically empty-handed three decades ago, I pledge that, in your effort to work out the great and intricate problem which God has laid at the doors of the South, you shall have at all times the patient, sympathetic help of my race; only let this be constantly in mind that, while from representations in these buildings of the product of field, of forest, of mine, of factory, letters, and art, much good will come—yet far above and beyond material benefits will be that higher good, that let us pray God will come, in a blotting out of sectional differences and racial animosities and suspicions, in a determination to administer absolute justice, in a willing obedience among all classes to the mandates of law. This, coupled with our material prosperity, will bring into our beloved South a new heaven and a new earth.

WHAT I AM TRYING TO DO

Soon after I settled down for my life's work near the little town of Tuskegee, Ala., I made up my mind to do as an individual that which I am striving to get my race to do throughout the United States. I resolved to make myself, so far as I was able, so useful to the community, and the state that every man, woman, and child, white and black, would respect me and want me to live among them.

I foresaw, before I reached Tuskegee, that I should be classed as an "educated Negro," and I knew that this meant that people would expect me to be a kind of artificial being, living in the community but not a part of it in either my dress, talk, work, or in my general interests. My first duty, therefore, was to convince the people that I did not have "education," but only a head and heart to serve.

This personal illustration will, perhaps, suggest one thing that I am striving to do, that is, to get the Negro race as a whole to make itself so valuable and so necessary to the community in which it lives that it will not merely be tolerated, like a poor relation, but rather welcomed and sought after. To do this I learned years ago from my great teacher of Hampton Institute, Gen. S. C. Armstrong, that it would first be necessary to get out of the Negro's mind the idea that education unfitted a man for any kind of labor, whether with the hand or head. So from the first I have striven to get the educated Negro to feel that it was just as honorable and dignified for him to use his education in the field, the shop, the kitchen, or the laundry as to use it in teaching school or preaching the gospel.

The most difficult and delicate task that Tuskegee, in common with institutions like Hampton and others, had to perform has been to convince members of my race that in preparing them to use their knowledge of chemistry, mathematics, or any other form of knowledge, to improve the soil, develop the mineral resources, to construct a house or prepare and serve a meal, it was not necessary to limit or circumscribe their mental growth or to assign them to any special or narrow sphere of life. I have constantly urged upon them that we must begin at the bottom instead of at the top; that there will be little permanent gain by "short cut" methods; that we must stick to that which is fundamental and enduring—and we must overcome evil with good.

But in all this I have not sought to confine the ambitions, nor to set limits to the progress of the race. I have never felt that the Negro was bound to behave in any manner different from that of any other race in the same stage of development. I have merely insisted that we should do the first things first; that we should lay the foundation before we sought to erect the superstructure.

At one time, when I was a young boy working in the coal mines of West Virginia, I came out of the mine after a hard day's work feeling tired, sick, and discouraged. A neighbor, wishing to cheer me up and make me feel better, offered me a large red stick of candy. That candy looked good to me and I took it eagerly. My mother, who knew my condition and needs, told me that it was not candy that I needed, but a good big dose of vermifuge, which is about the worst tasting and smelling medicine, I firmly believe, that was ever concocted. However, it was in general use in those days for almost every real and imaginary ailment. In fact, vermifuge was about the only medicine on sale at that time in the coal mining districts of West Virginia.

Contrary to my mother's advice I took the candy and put the vermifuge aside. The next day I came out of the coal mine feeling no better, and the next day I was still worse. Finally I decided to follow the advice of mother and take my medicine. So I threw back my head and held my nose while my mother forced the nasty stuff down with a large spoon. The next day, however, I felt fine.

Now, in my experience in working with my race I have found that the Negro meets with two classes of advisers, each of which is equally well-meaning and kindly disposed. One class of advisers hands him the red candy and the other offers the vermifuge. Very often it has been a hard task for me to make certain kinds of colored people see that it is the vermifuge the race needs rather than the red candy. Still, the Negro is learning this lesson, and nothing gives me more genuine satisfaction at the present time than to note that the great masses of my race, in every part of this country, are willing to take the vermifuge in place of the red candy.

I recall another experience that I had while working in the coal mine that has helped me in trying to lead my race in the direction of things that are permanent and lasting rather than the things that are merely showy and temporary. As a boy I long cherished a desire to own a suit of "store" clothes. I worked hard in the mine and finally saved enough to gratify this desire. It was a flashy, showy suit with many colors, called, in those days, I think, a Dolly Varden suit. It cost at wholesale, I suppose, about five dollars. At any rate, I purchased it for ten or twelve. The following Sunday I wore it with great pride to church. On my way home, however, a heavy rain came that drenched both me and the suit. Monday morning I put the suit out in the sun to dry. Presently I noticed that the colors had begun to flow. In fact, they had gotten all mixed up with one another and the whole suit seemed to be in a process of disintegration. My mother had advised me that it would be wiser to spend my money in buying some "homespun" cloth which she promised would make into a good, sensible, and serviceable suit. Eventually she did make me a "homespun" suit which was far from being showy. However, I wore it for several years.

The lesson which I learned in this simple fashion at home was of great value to me when, later on, I went away to school, for though I learned many new and interesting things at Hampton Institute, it did not take me long to discover that, back of all else, the lesson which General Armstrong was trying to teach us was the same that my mother had taught me. He stated it in other words, and gave it a deeper and broader significance, but what I learned at Hampton, through the medium of books and tools and through contact with my teachers, was at bottom what I had learned at home, namely, to distinguish between the real and the sham, to choose the substance rather than the shadow, to seek the permanent good rather than the passing pleasant. And so it is a source of great satisfaction to me to observe throughout the whole country that my race is beginning to prefer "homespun" to "Dolly Varden."

It is not easy to teach a new people, just out of slavery, the kind of lessons I have described. For a number of years the purposes of General Armstrong and of Hampton were misunderstood by a number of the

Negro people. The same has been true at Tuskegee. I have had some mighty interesting experiences, both in school and out, in trying to teach the members of my race some of those simple but fundamental lessons, the meaning and significance of which I learned at Hampton Institute.

At one time, while stopping for a day in one of the border states, I visited a colored family whose son had recently graduated and returned home from college. The mother of the young man was naturally very proud of her son and told me with great satisfaction how he had learned to speak Latin, but lamented the fact that there was no one in the neighborhood who was able to talk Latin with him. She had heard that I had some education and felt rather confident that I would be able to converse in the Latin language with him. When I was obliged to confess that I could not, her feathers fell, and I do not believe she ever afterward had the same respect for me. However, I got acquainted with the son, and, as I knew more of the young man, learned to like him. He was an ambitious, high strung young fellow, who had studied books, but he had not studied man. He had learned a great deal about the ancient world, but he knew very little of the world right about him. He had studied about things, through the medium of books, but had not studied things themselves. In a word, he had been infected with the college bacillus and displayed the usual symptoms. However, I had seen cases of this kind before and felt sure that he would in time recover.

This young man was exceedingly sensitive concerning the "rights" of his race, and propounded to me the very popular theory that the only reason the Negro did not have all the rights coming to him was that he did not protest whenever these rights were infringed upon. He determined to put this theory into practice and so wrote a very learned lecture which he delivered on every possible occasion. The subject of his lecture was "Manhood Rights." As he was really a rather brilliant speaker he was able to work up an audience with this lecture to a high pitch of enthusiasm and indignation in regard to the wrongs committed against the Negro race.

For a season this lecture was quite popular and the author was in some demand as a lecturer. During this time he was invariably present at every indignation meeting that was called to pass resolutions condemning some wrong meted out to members of the race. Here, again, his eloquence and burning words could excite an audience to the highest degree of indignation. This was especially true when he quoted some striking passage from Demosthenes or Cicero.

Like most young colored orators he was strong on quotations from people who have been a long time dead. At the same time he forgot the fact that most of the men he quoted never so much as dreamed that the average man had any rights at all, and he totally overlooked the really thrilling fact that never in the history of the world before were there ten million black men who possessed so many rights and enjoyed so many opportunities as the ten millions of Negroes in the United States to-day. I mention this, let me add, not because I want to minimize or make light of the injustices which my race has suffered and still suffers, but because I believe that it is important that we view our present situation in its true light and see things in their proper perspective. In no other way can we gain the courage, the wisdom, and the patience that will help us to go forward, not only steadily and persistently, but cheerfully.

In the course of time it gradually began to dawn upon my young friend and his mother that neither indignation meetings, the passing of resolutions, nor his lecture on "Manhood Rights" were providing him or the family with shelter, food, or clothes. For a while the old mother was quite puzzled to know why it was that neither eloquence nor Latin quotations would provide the family with the common necessities of every-day life. The young man himself grew morose, peevish, and miserable. He could neither eat nor sleep properly, because he was constantly thinking of the wrongs of his race. He was not only unhappy himself but he made everyone he came in contact with unhappy. Nevertheless, for a number of years, he went on in the way that he had started. Finally he seemed to have struck bottom. He found himself face to face with, not a book world, but an actual world. Home, food, clothes, rent were now pressing so hard that something had to be done.

At this point I had an opportunity to renew my acquaintance with him. In fact, he called to see me. He had now become quite softened, mellowed, and even sweet, but I could discern that he was still troubled about the "rights" of his race, and he ventured to suggest a little vaguely once or twice that he would be willing to "die for his race." I noticed, however that he was not quite so emphatic in his desire to "die for his race" as he had been a year or two before, when I heard him pouring out his soul before a small but enthusiastic audience. In one of the first conversations I had with him after the mellowing process had set in, I ventured to suggest to him rather mildly that there were other methods by which he could help the Negro race to secure those rights and opportunities which both he and I were so anxious they should possess and enjoy.

At first he was rather taken aback at the thought that I was just as much interested in the rights of the race as he was, and he was still further surprised when I told him that I felt just as indignant and outraged when my race was insulted and persecuted as he did. This opened the way for a heart to heart talk, which was followed by others, all which resulted in a changed life for my young friend, a change not in the end that he was seeking, but rather in the method of seeking that end.

The story of the young college man that I have just tried to sketch is not different, except in particular circumstances, from that of many other young men that I have known. Several of these young men I have come to know intimately and, as we came to understand one another, they have become faithful friends and supporters of the work I am trying to do. Let me now relate as briefly as possible the sequel of the young college man's story.

After several backsets, my friend persuaded his mother to sell her little property and invest the proceeds in a farm some miles from the city. Here my friend began a new career. He began to study the soil, to observe and study animals, birds, and trees. Soon he became so absorbed in his new life and work that he forgot that he had ever been to college.

After a time, however, it began to dawn upon him that his college education could be serviceable in the highest degree by applying all that he had
learned to the development of the soil, and so he proceeded to do this.
Th result was that for the first time in his life he experienced real joy
and satisfaction in living. In finding that he could apply his education he
had found out what education really is.

He has continued to prosper as a farmer and is looked up to as the
leader among his people in his community. He has the respect and confidence of his white neighbors as well as of those of his own race.
Although he lives in a county where it is not common for colored people
to vote, my friend votes regularly and his white neighbors seem glad to
have him do so. He has not only made himself a useful citizen but has
become a large taxpayer and keeps a considerable balance in the local
bank. He has a wholesome and happy family. Through his influence the
local school has become, instead of a mere form, a real power for good
in the community. My friend has become so influential in his own community that his word or wish controls the colored church. He virtually
decides who shall teach the public school, what wage shall be paid, and
how many months the school shall continue in session. He is not only the
leader in church and school, but he is president of the farmers' institute,
and has control of the county fair. If difficulties arise between white and
black people, his advice and counsel are invariably sought. His children,
with better preparation than he had, will perhaps attend the college
from which he graduated.

I do not pretend that my friend has secured all the rights and privileges
that he thinks belong to him. What man of any race or color ever does?
Some of the most miserable and ineffective people that I ever met are
those who, when viewed from a distance, seem to have all the privileges
that the world can confer. No man ever enjoys privileges in the highest
sense until he has had the experience of having privileges withheld from
him. The people who get the most enjoyment out of wealth are those
who have experienced poverty. Sometimes people ask me how I can get
so much happiness out of my work and my surroundings when I must
be conscious of the suffering and wrongs endured by my race. I usually
reply that I am happy because I can compare the present with the past,
that I know the depths from which we have come as well as the heights
to which we have attained.

During a recent trip through Europe for the purpose of studying the
condition of the poorer classes in that part of the world, it was a source
of encouragement to me that, wherever I found misery, almost without
exception the people told me that things were better than they used to
be, that people were looking up, not down. It is not so much what we
have as it is the upward look, the knowledge that we are making
progress, which makes life worth living.

And so it is with my friend as I observe him to-day. Instead of being
miserable he is happy. He is happy because he is engaged in a definite,
vital, and constructive work, and through this work, and because of it,
he exerts a larger social and political influence than would ever come to
him by pursuing the mistaken course on which he first set out. In fact,

with all his handicaps, I believe I am safe in saying that he exerts more real influence than nine out of every ten persons of the white or colored people either in the North or in the South.

As the solution of the problems of the individual colored man consists very largely in turning his attention from abstract questions to the concrete problems of daily life—consists, in other words, in interesting and connecting himself with the local, practical, commonplace work and interests of the people among whom he lives—so, too, the solution of the Negro schools consists in connecting the studies in the classroom with the absorbing and inspiring problems of actual life.

Another thing that I am trying to do, therefore, is to get people to see that education in books and in the schoolroom can be articulated into the life and activities of the community surrounding the schoolroom in a way to make the local activities the basis for much of the mental training that is supposed to be furnished by the old traditional and abstract education. In using the local and practical activities as a means of education nothing is sacrificed in culture and discipline, and much is gained in interest and understanding and in earnestness. Children who hate the schoolroom and love the fishing pond, the berry patch, or the peach orchard frequently do so because one is artificial and the other real life. There is often a better opportunity to do this kind of work, I am convinced, with a new race as mine is, whose ancestors for generations have not been educated in the old formal methods, than with a race that has much to unlearn.

I have had some experiences in helping teachers to connect schoolroom work with real life. Often so simple a thing as a button can be used to make this connection. I have often referred to the "button" connection. Early in my experience as a teacher in Alabama I was called into a community to help compromise between parents and teacher. The parents wanted their children educated. The teacher was earnest and a hard worker, but somehow she was at "outs" with the parents and the parents were at "outs" with the teacher. One of the complaints was the far-reaching one that the school did not seem to accomplish any good.

On my first visit to this community I spent some time in the schoolroom listening to the recitations, which were of the usual sort. But, as I have said, the teacher was in earnest, and, in the effort to be of service, she had got hold of a text book on embroidery which she had seen advertised somewhere. The children were first required to read some lessons from this text book on embroidery a number of times; then they were instructed in the art of embroidery in the most up-to-date and approved fashion. There was about as much difference between the garments which the people actually wore in their homes and the embroidery the children were making as there is between the pictures that you sometimes see in a fashion magazine and an actual human being.

In the first place, about half of the children in the school were more than half naked, and so, as I told the teacher, embroidery was not what they needed most. The teacher complained that although she had gone to considerable expense to prepare to teach embroidery the people showed no interest in what she was trying to do for them. Looking the school over, I noted that there were few buttons on the clothes of any of the children, even of those who were fully dressed. That suggested to me a point of attack upon the situation. As gently and tactfully as I could, I suggested to the teacher that she had missed a step in the evolution of the people in this community and that from almost no garments to embroidery was too sudden a transition. I suggested that she defer her lessons in embroidery for eight or ten years until she could work the people up by gradual processes to the point when they needed embroidered garments and the other things that go with them. She readily consented. Then we began on the "button" connection. The teacher asked the children to count the missing buttons on their garments. The number was amazing. Here was an interesting problem in mathematics.

After that the teacher asked every pupil to get permission from his parents to bring to the school the next day all the garments from home that needed buttons sewed on, and what was her surprise to find that we had about all the spare clothing in that community in the school. When the hour for the sewing lesson came it was a mighty interesting hour, one that pupils and teacher looked forward to, because every child felt that the lesson in sewing on buttons was of vital interest to him and to his family. When the clothes were taken home by the pupils at the close of the day, with all the buttons in their places, the parents for the first time in their lives began to understand what education meant; for the first time in the history of the community a vital connection had been made between the schoolroom and the home. As a result new interest was awakened in the subject of education. The parents now felt that the school was a part of themselves. The teacher found that her work in the schoolroom was no longer a burden, that it was no longer a treadmill of dull routine, but a living reality. The reason was that she was touching and teaching life. Instead of dreading the hour for the reopening of school; pupils and teacher were impatient for the hour to come. It was the "button" connection that did it all. The school continued to grow and expand in the directions which the teaching had taken. Garments that needed darning and patching were regularly brought to the school to be mended. Later, vegetables were raised by the pupils in the school garden and the pupils were permitted to carry home specimens of vegetables that they themselves had raised. Some of them were better vegetables than their parents had ever raised. Still later, the pupils were encouraged to have their own plots at home for the growing of vegetables, and after a while one of the teachers was appointed to make weekly visits to the homes of the pupils to inspect the vegetable plots.

On these activities as the basis, real problems in arithmetic were constructed—problems as to the cost of cloth, of buttons, the time required to sew on the buttons or to do the darning and patching; compositions were written describing how parents, teachers, and pupils had worked together in bringing about these results. The children no longer dreaded the sound of the word "composition," because in a natural, simple way they were describing something that they were all genuinely interested in.

Another thing that I have tried to do has been to bring the white people in the Southern States and throughout the country into what seems to me a proper and practical attitude toward the Negro and his efforts to go forward and make progress. I am seeking to do this not only in the interest of my race, but also in the interest of the white race.

There are in the Southern States nine million Negroes. There are three million Negro children of school age. Fifty-three per cent, or more than half, never go to school. Many of these Negro children, particularly in the country districts, are in school only from three to four months in the year. I am trying to get the white people to see that, both from an economic point of view and as a matter of justice and fair play, these conditions must be changed. I am trying to get the white people to see that sending ignorant Negroes to jails and penitentiaries, putting them in the chain gang, hanging and lynching them does not civilize, but on the contrary, though it brutalizes the Negro, it at the same time blunts and dulls the conscience of the white man.

I want the white people to see that it is unfair to expect a black man who goes to school only three months in the year to produce as much on the farm as a white man who has been in school eight or nine months in the year; that it is unjust to let the Negro remain ignorant, with nothing between him and the temptation to fill his body with whiskey and cocaine, and then expect him, in his ignorance, to be able to know the law and be able to exercise that degree of self-control which shall enable him to keep it.

Still another thing that I am trying to get the people of the whole country to realize is that the education of the Negro should be considered not so much as a matter of charity, but as a matter of business, that, like any other business, should be thoroughly studied, organized, and systematized. The money that has already been spent by states, institutions, and individuals would have done vastly more good if there had been, years ago, more thorough organization and coöperation between the different isolated and detached members of the Negro school system in the Southern States.

I am trying to get the white people to realize that since no color line is drawn in the punishment for crime, no color line should be drawn in the preparation for life, in the kind of education, in other words, that makes for useful, clean living. I am trying to get the white people to see that in hundreds of counties in the South it is costing more to punish colored people for crime than it would cost to educate them. I am trying to get all to see that ignorance, poverty, and weakness invite and encourage the stronger race to act unjustly toward the weak, and that so long as this condition remains the young white men of the South will have a fearful handicap in the battle of life.

OF MR. BOOKER T. WASHINGTON AND OTHERS AND THE COLORED WORLD WITHIN

W. E. Burghardt Du Bois

[With his Atlanta Ex-
position Address of 1895, Booker T. Washington inherited the mantle of
Frederick Douglass, and, for two decades, he was considered by whites
to be the spokesman of the supposed Negro monolith; but, within five
years after the speech that W. E. Burghardt Du Bois was to characterize
as the "Atlanta compromise," Washington was the center of a raging
controversy among blacks. Having grown restive under what seemed the
folly of the old priest-king, a group of aspiring hierophants, led by William Monroe Trotter in Boston, sought to bring forth a new dispensation.

Trotter, a Harvard graduate who founded the *Boston Guardian* to
combat the heresies of the Tuskegeeian, was able to attract a fellow
alumnus to the cause. Du Bois was the first Negro Ph.D. to be graduated
from Harvard, receiving his degree in the year of Washington's Atlanta
speech, and was the author of a pioneering sociological study of race
relations in a Northern city, *The Philadelphia Negro* (1899). His book
The Souls of Black Folk (1903) immediately made him the leading intellect in Black America, a role he was to retain for many years. In the
third chapter of the book, which was devoted to Washington and is
reprinted below, Du Bois exposed the shortcomings of vocational educa-

tion, when used as the sole means of Negro elevation, and the political consequences (by 1900, Negroes had been virtually disfranchised in the South) of postponing the demand for civil rights. The rift with the Washingtonians was now out in the open, and the contending forces rushed to align themselves in what proved to be an increasingly hostile debate.

In 1905, Du Bois called a conference—attended by twenty-nine ministers, lawyers, editors, teachers, and businessmen, all of whom were critics of Washington—which met in the vicinity of Niagara Falls in July and launched the "Niagara Movement." The manifesto issued from Niagara contained eighteen paragraphs of complaint, demand, and protest, most of them implied criticisms of Washington. On July 30 of the same year, Washington gave a speech in Boston; the affair, because of the agitation of Trotter, ended in a general disturbance. Reports of a "Boston riot" resulted in more converts for both sides. The Niagara Movement had dissipated by 1910, but it did establish a national organization and lay the foundations for the National Association for the Advancement of Colored People (NAACP), an interracial group for whom Du Bois edited the *Crisis* until the mid-1930's.

The conflict between self-improvement and equal political rights, between vocational training and higher education, that marked the controversy between Washington and Du Bois was only symptomatic of a larger issue in Du Bois's mind. Du Bois relied heavily on the possibility of developing the potentialities of a talented Negro elite—the so-called talented tenth—who would then not only be in a position to solve the problems of, but would also reflect back their achievements on, the large mass of black people. Even at this date, his vision of the future was not confined to the Negroes in America. "The problem of the twentieth century," he reiterated in *Souls of Black Folk*, "is the problem of the color-line—the relation of the darker to the lighter races of men in Asia and Africa, in America and the islands of the sea." The larger issue in Du Bois's mind was the survival of black folk in a white world that, at the turn of the century, dominated the darker peoples of the earth.

Du Bois never lost this perspective, though his thought followed various paths over the decades. He restated the problem in an autobiography, *Dusk of Dawn* (1940), of which one chapter, devoted largely to a new departure in his thinking, is also reprinted below. In 1934, Du Bois had launched an attack in the *Crisis* on the whole liberal program of the NAACP, a program that he himself had been influential in formulating. Much of the controversy centered on the merits of a carefully planned segregation, which, contrary to NAACP policy, Du Bois was now defending as a temporary measure. The measure, he felt, was necessary until a majority of Americans became converted to the Negro cause. He commented in *Dusk of Dawn:*

> Of course, I soon realized, that in this matter of segregation I was touching an old and bleeding sore in Negro thought. From the eighteenth century down the Negro intelligentsia has regarded segregation as the visible badge of their servitude and as the object of their unceasing attack. The upper class Negro has almost never been nationalistic. He has never planned or thought of a Negro state or a Negro church or a Negro school. This solution has always been a thought up-surging from the mass, because of pressure which they could not withstand and which compelled a racial institution or chaos. . . . American Negroes have always feared with perfect fear their

eventual expulsion from America. They have been willing to submit to caste rather than face this. . . . As the Negro develops from an easily exploitable profit-furnishing laborer to an intelligent independent self-supporting citizen, the possibilities of his being pushed out of his American fatherland may easily be increased rather than diminished. . . . Whether self-segregation for his protection, for inner development and growth in intelligence and social efficiency, will increase his acceptability to white Americans or not, that growth must go on.

Du Bois had indeed touched a bleeding sore in Negro thought, and black leaders were having none of his shift to nationalism at the time. By June 1934, Du Bois had resigned as the editor of the *Crisis* and accepted a post at Atlanta University. The nascent nationalism of the masses did not emerge until Malcolm X began to reach thousands of blacks through television. Then, for the first time, a significant number of black intellectuals also turned to nationalism.]

OF MR. BOOKER T. WASHINGTON AND OTHERS

Easily the most striking thing in the history of the American Negro since 1876 is the ascendancy of Mr. Booker T. Washington. It began at the time when war memories and ideals were rapidly passing; a day of astonishing commercial development was dawning; a sense of doubt and hesitation overtook the freedmen's sons,—then it was that his leading began. Mr. Washington came, with a single definite programme, at the psychological moment when the nation was a little ashamed of having bestowed so much sentiment on Negroes, and was concentrating its energies on Dollars. His programme of industrial education, conciliation of the South, and submission and silence as to civil and political rights, was not wholly original; the Free Negroes from 1830 up to wartime had striven to build industrial schools, and the American Missionary Association had from the first taught various trades; and Price and others had sought a way of honorable alliance with the best of the Southerners. But Mr. Washington first indissolubly linked these things; he put enthusiasm, unlimited energy, and perfect faith into this programme, and changed it from a by-path into a veritable Way of Life. And the tale of the methods by which he did this is a fascinating study of human life.

It startled the nation to hear a Negro advocating such a programme after many decades of bitter complaint; it startled and won the applause of the South, it interested and won the admiration of the North; and after a confused murmur of protest, it silenced if it did not convert the Negroes themselves.

To gain the sympathy and coöperation of the various elements comprising the white South was Mr. Washington's first task; and this, at the time Tuskegee was founded, seemed, for a black man, well-nigh impossible. And yet ten years later it was done in the word spoken at Atlanta: "In all things purely social we can be as separate as the five fingers, and yet one as the hand in all things essential to mutual progress." This "Atlanta Compromise" is by all odds the most notable thing in Mr. Washington's career. The South interpreted it in different ways: the radicals received it as a complete surrender of the demand for civil and political equality; the conservatives, as a generously conceived working basis for mutual understanding. So both approved it, and to-day its author is certainly the most distinguished Southerner since Jefferson Davis, and the one with the largest personal following.

Next to this achievement comes Mr. Washington's work in gaining place and consideration in the North. Others less shrewd and tactful had formerly essayed to sit on these two stools and had fallen between them; but as Mr. Washington knew the heart of the South from birth and training, so by singular insight he intuitively grasped the spirit of the age which was dominating the North. And so thoroughly did he learn the speech and thought of triumphant commercialism, and the ideals of material prosperity, that the picture of a lone black boy poring over a French grammar amid the weeds and dirt of a neglected home soon seemed to him the acme of absurdities. One wonders what Socrates and St. Francis of Assisi would say to this.

And yet this very singleness of vision and thorough oneness with his age is a mark of the successful man. It is as though Nature must needs make men narrow in order to give them force. So Mr. Washington's cult has gained unquestioning followers, his work has wonderfully prospered, his friends are legion, and his enemies are confounded. To-day he stands as the one recognized spokesman of his ten million fellows, and one of the most notable figures in a nation of seventy millions. One hesitates, therefore, to criticise a life which, beginning with so little, has done so much. And yet the time is come when one may speak in all sincerity and utter courtesy of the mistakes and shortcomings of Mr. Washington's career, as well as of his triumphs, without being thought captious or envious, and without forgetting that it is easier to do ill than well in the world.

The criticism that has hitherto met Mr. Washington has not always been of this broad character. In the South especially has he had to walk warily to avoid the harshest judgments,—and naturally so, for he is dealing with the one subject of deepest sensitiveness to that section. Twice—once when at the Chicago celebration of the Spanish-American War he alluded to the color-prejudice that is "eating away the vitals of the South," and once when he dined with President Roosevelt—has the resulting Southern criticism been violent enough to threaten seriously his popularity. In the North the feeling has several times forced itself into words, that Mr. Washington's counsels of submission overlooked certain elements of true manhood, and that his educational programme was unnecessarily narrow. Usually, however, such criticism has not found open expression, although, too, the spiritual sons of the Abolition-ists have not been prepared to acknowledge that the schools founded before Tuskegee, by men of broad ideals and self-sacrificing spirit, were wholly failures or worthy of ridicule. While, then, criticism has not failed to follow Mr. Washington, yet the prevailing public opinion of the land has been but too willing to deliver the solution of a wearisome problem into his hands, and say, "If that is all you and your race ask, take it."

Among his own people, however, Mr. Washington has encountered the strongest and most lasting opposition, amounting at times to bitterness, and even to-day continuing strong and insistent even though largely silenced in outward expression by the public opinion of the nation. Some of this opposition is, of course, mere envy; the disappointment of dis-placed demagogues and the spite of narrow minds. But aside from this, there is among educated and thoughtful colored men in all parts of the land a feeling of deep regret, sorrow, and apprehension at the wide cur-rency and ascendancy which some of Mr. Washington's theories have gained. These same men admire his sincerity of purpose, and are willing to forgive much to honest endeavor which is doing something worth the doing. They coöperate with Mr. Washington as far as they conscientiously can; and, indeed, it is no ordinary tribute to this man's tact and power that, steering as he must between so many diverse interests and opinions, he so largely retains the respect of all.

But the hushing of the criticism of honest opponents is a dangerous thing. It leads some of the best of the critics to unfortunate silence and paralysis of effort, and others to burst into speech so passionately and intemperately as to lose listeners. Honest and earnest criticism from those whose interests are most nearly touched,—criticism of writers by readers, of government by those governed, of leaders by those led,—this is the soul of democracy and the safeguard of modern society. If the best of the American Negroes receive by outer pressure a leader whom they had not recognized before, manifestly there is here a certain palpable gain. Yet there is also irreparable loss,—a loss of that peculiarly valuable education which a group receives when by search and criticism it finds and commissions its own leaders. The way in which this is done is at once the most elementary and the nicest problem of social growth. His-tory is but the record of such group-leadership; and yet how infinitely changeful is its type and character! And of all types and kinds, what can be more instructive than the leadership of a group within a group?—that curious double movement where real progress may be negative and actual advance be relative retrogression. All this is the social student's inspiration and despair.

Now in the past the American Negro has had instructive experience in the choosing of group leaders, founding thus a peculiar dynasty which in the light of present conditions is worth while studying. When sticks and stones and beasts form the sole environment of a people, their attitude is largely one of determined opposition to and conquest of natural forces. But when to earth and brute is added an environment of men and ideas, then the attitude of the imprisoned group may take three main forms,—a feeling of revolt and revenge; an attempt to adjust all thought and action to the will of the greater group; or, finally, a determined effort at self-realization and self-development despite environing opinion. The influence of all of these attitudes at various times can be traced in the history of the American Negro, and in the evolution of his successive leaders.

Before 1750, while the fire of African freedom still burned in the veins of the slaves, there was in all leadership or attempted leadership but the one motive of revolt and revenge,—typified in the terrible Maroons, the Danish blacks, and Cato of Stono, and veiling all the Americas in fear of insurrection. The liberalizing tendencies of the latter half of the eighteenth century brought, along with kindlier relations between black and white, thoughts of ultimate adjustment and assimilation. Such aspiration was especially voiced in the earnest songs of Phyllis, in the martyrdom of Attucks, the fighting of Salem and Poor, the intellectual accomplishments of Banneker and Derham, and the political demands of the Cuffes.

Stern financial and social stress after the war cooled much of the previous humanitarian ardor. The disappointment and impatience of the Negroes at the persistence of slavery and serfdom voiced itself in two movements. The slaves in the South, aroused undoubtedly by vague rumors of the Haitian revolt, made three fierce attempts at insurrection,—in 1800 under Gabriel in Virginia, in 1822 under Vesey in Carolina, and in 1831 again in Virginia under the terrible Nat Turner. In the Free States, on the other hand, a new and curious attempt at self-development was made. In Philadelphia and New York color-prescription led to a withdrawal of Negro communicants from white churches and the formation of a peculiar socio-religious institution among the Negroes known as the African Church,—an organization still living and controlling in its various branches over a million of men.

Walker's wild appeal against the trend of the times showed how the world was changing after the coming of the cotton-gin. By 1830 slavery seemed hopelessly fastened on the South, and the slaves thoroughly cowed into submission. The free Negroes of the North, inspired by the mulatto immigrants from the West Indies, began to change the basis of their demands; they recognized the slavery of slaves, but insisted that they themselves were freemen, and sought assimilation and amalgamation with the nation on the same terms with other men. Thus, Forten and Purvis of Philadelphia, Shad of Wilmington, Du Bois of New Haven, Barbadoes of Boston, and others, strove singly and together as men, they said, not as slaves; as "people of color," not as "Negroes." The trend of the times, however, refused them recognition save in individual and exceptional cases, considered them as one with all the despised blacks, and they soon found themselves striving to keep even the rights they formerly had of voting and working and moving as freemen. Schemers of migration and colonization arose among them; but these they refused to entertain, and they eventually turned to the Abolition movement as a final refuge.

Here, led by Remond, Nell, Wells-Brown, and Douglass, a new period of self-assertion and self-development dawned. To be sure, ultimate freedom and assimilation was the ideal before the leaders, but the assertion of the manhood rights of the Negro by himself was the main reliance, and John Brown's raid was the extreme of its logic. After the war and emancipation, the great form of Frederick Douglass, the greatest of American Negro leaders, still led the host. Self-assertion, especially in political lines, was the main programme, and behind Douglass came Elliot, Bruce, and Langston, and the Reconstruction politicians, and, less conspicuous but of greater social significance Alexander Crummell and Bishop Daniel Payne.

Then came the Revolution of 1876, the suppression of the Negro votes, the changing and shifting of ideals, and the seeking of new lights in the great night. Douglass, in his old age, still bravely stood for the ideals of his early manhood,—ultimate assimilation *through* self-assertion, and on no other terms. For a time Price arose as a new leader, destined, it seemed, not to give up, but to re-state the old ideals in a form less repugnant to the white South. But he passed away in his prime. Then came the new leader. Nearly all the former ones had become leaders by the silent suffrage of their fellows, had sought to lead their own people alone, and were usually, save Douglass, little known outside their race. But Booker T. Washington arose as essentially the leader not of one race but of two,—a compromiser between the South, the North, and the Negro. Naturally the Negroes resented, at first bitterly, signs of compromise which surrendered their civil and political rights, even though this was to be exchanged for larger chances of economic development. The rich and dominating North, however, was not only weary of the race problem, but was investing largely in Southern enterprises, and welcomed any method of peaceful coöperation. Thus, by national opinion, the Negroes began to recognize Mr. Washington's leadership; and the voice of criticism was hushed.

Mr. Washington represents in Negro thought the old attitude of adjustment and submission; but adjustment at such a peculiar time as to make his programme unique. This is an age of unusual economic development, and Mr. Washington's programme naturally takes an economic cast, becoming a gospel of Work and Money to such an extent as apparently almost completely to overshadow the higher aims of life. Moreover, this is an age when the more advanced races are coming in closer contact with the less developed races, and the race-feeling is therefore intensified; and Mr. Washington's programme practically accepts the alleged inferiority of the Negro races. Again, in our own land, the reaction from the sentiment of war time has given impetus to race-prejudice against Negroes, and Mr. Washington withdraws many of the high demands of Negroes as men and American citizens. In other periods of intensified prejudice all the Negro's tendency to self-assertion has been called forth; at this period a policy of submission is advocated. In the history of nearly all other races and peoples the doctrine preached at such crises has been that manly self-respect is worth more than lands and houses, and that a people who voluntarily surrender such respect, or cease striving for it, are not worth civilizing.

In answer to this, it has been claimed that the Negro can survive only through submission. Mr. Washington distinctly asks that black people give up, at least for the present, three things,—

First, political power,

Second, insistence on civil rights,

Third, higher education of Negro youth,—

and concentrate all their energies on industrial education, the accumulation of wealth, and the conciliation of the South. This policy has been courageously and insistently advocated for over fifteen years, and has been triumphant for perhaps ten years. As a result of this tender of the palm-branch, what has been the return? In these years there have occurred:

1. The disfranchisement of the Negro
2. The legal creation of a distinct status of civil inferiority for the Negro
3. The steady withdrawal of aid from institutions for the higher training of the Negro

These movements are not, to be sure, direct results of Mr. Washington's teachings; but his propaganda has, without a shadow of doubt, helped their speedier accomplishment. The question then comes: Is it possible, and probable, that nine millions of men can make effective progress in economic lines if they are deprived of political rights, made a servile caste, and allowed only the most meager chance for developing their exceptional men? If history and reason give any distinct answer to these questions, it is an emphatic *No*. And Mr. Washington thus faces the triple paradox of his career:

1. He is striving nobly to make Negro artisans business men and property-owners; but it is utterly impossible, under modern competitive methods, for workingmen and property-owners to defend their rights and exist without the right of suffrage.
2. He insists on thrift and self-respect, but at the same time counsels a silent submission to civic inferiority such as is bound to sap the manhood of any race in the long run.
3. He advocates common-school and industrial training, and depreciates institutions of higher learning; but neither the Negro common-schools, nor Tuskegee itself, could remain open a day were it not for teachers trained in Negro colleges, or trained by their graduates.

This triple paradox in Mr. Washington's position is the object of criticism by two classes of colored Americans. One class is spiritually descended from Toussaint the Savior, through Gabriel, Vesey, and Turner, and they represent the attitude of revolt and revenge; they hate the white South blindly and distrust the white race generally, and so far as they agree on definite action, think that the Negro's only hope lies in emigration beyond the borders of the United States. And yet, by the irony of fate, nothing has more effectually made this programme seem hopeless than the recent course of the United States toward weaker and darker peoples in the West Indies, Hawaii, and the Philippines,—for where in the world may we go and be safe from lying and brute force?

The other class of Negroes who cannot agree with Mr. Washington has hitherto said little aloud. They deprecate the sight of scattered counsels, of internal disagreement; and especially they dislike making their just criticism of a useful and earnest man an excuse for a general discharge of venom from small-minded opponents. Nevertheless, the questions involved are so fundamental and serious that it is difficult to see how men like the Grimkes, Kelly Miller, J. W. E. Bowen, and other representatives of this group, can much longer be silent. Such men feel in conscience bound to ask of this nation three things:

1. The right to vote
2. Civic equality
3. The education of youth according to ability

They acknowledge Mr. Washington's invaluable service in counselling patience and courtesy in such demands; they do not ask that ignorant black men vote when ignorant whites are debarred, or that any reasonable restrictions in the suffrage should not be applied; they know that the low social level of the mass of the race is responsible for much discrimination against it, but they also know, and the nation knows, that relentless color-prejudice is more often a cause than a result of the Negro's degradation; they seek the abatement of this relic of barbarism, and not its systematic encouragement and pampering by all agencies of social power from the Associated Press to the Church of Christ. They advocate, with Mr. Washington, a broad system of Negro common schools supplemented by thorough industrial training; but they are surprised that a man of Mr. Washington's insight cannot see that no such educational system ever has rested or can rest on any other basis than that of the well-equipped college and university, and they insist that there is a demand for a few such institutions throughout the South to train the best of the Negro youth as teachers, professional men, and leaders.

This group of men honor Mr. Washington for his attitude of conciliation toward the white South; they accept the "Atlanta Compromise" in its broadest interpretation; they recognize, with him, many signs of promise, many men of high purpose and fair judgment, in this section; they know that no easy task has been laid upon a region already tottering under heavy burdens. But, nevertheless, they insist that the way to truth and right lies in straightforward honesty, not in indiscriminate flattery; in praising those of the South who do well and criticising uncompromisingly those who do ill; in taking advantage of the opportunities at hand and urging their fellows to do the same, but at the same time in remembering that only a firm adherence to their higher ideals and aspirations will ever keep those ideals within the realm of possibility. They do not expect that the free right to vote, to enjoy civic rights, and to be educated, will come in a moment; they do not expect to see the bias and prejudices of years disappear at the blast of a trumpet; but they are absolutely certain that the way for a people to gain their reasonable rights is not by voluntarily throwing them away and insisting that they do not want them; that the way for a people to gain respect is not by continually belittling and ridiculing themselves; that, on the contrary,

Negroes must insist continually, in season and out of season, that voting is necessary to modern manhood, that color discrimination is barbarism, and that black boys need education as well as white boys.'

In failing thus to state plainly and unequivocally the legitimate demands of their people, even at the cost of opposing an honored leader, the thinking classes of American Negroes would shirk a heavy responsibility,—a responsibility to themselves, a responsibility to the struggling masses, a responsibility to the darker races of men whose future depends so largely on this American experiment, but especially a responsibility to this nation,—this common Fatherland. It is wrong to encourage a man or a people in evil-doing; it is wrong to aid and abet a national crime simply because it is unpopular not to do so. The growing spirit of kindliness and reconciliation between the North and South after the frightful difference of a generation ago ought to be a source of deep congratulation to all, and especially to those whose mistreatment caused the war; but if that reconciliation is to be marked by the industrial slavery and civic death of those same black men, with permanent legislation into a position of inferiority, then those black men, if they are really men, are called upon by every consideration of patriotism and loyalty to oppose such a course by all civilized methods, even though such opposition involves disagreement with Mr. Booker T. Washington. We have no right to sit silently by while the inevitable seeds are sown for a harvest of disaster to our children, black and white.

First, it is the duty of black men to judge the South discriminatingly. The present generation of Southerners are not responsible for the past, and they should not be blindly hated or blamed for it. Furthermore, to no class is the indiscriminate endorsement of the recent course of the South toward Negroes more nauseating than to the best thought of the South. The South is not "solid"; it is a land in the ferment of social change, wherein forces of all kinds are fighting for supremacy; and to praise the ill the South is to-day perpetrating is just as wrong as to condemn the good. Discriminating and broad-minded criticism is what the South needs,—needs it for the sake of her own white sons and daughters, and for the insurance of robust, healthy mental and moral development.

To-day even the attitude of the Southern whites toward the blacks is not, as so many assume, in all cases the same; the ignorant Southerner hates the Negro, the workingmen fear his competition, the money-makers wish to use him as a laborer, some of the educated see a menace in his upward development, while others—usually the sons of the masters— wish to help him to rise. National opinion has enabled this last class to maintain the Negro common schools, and to protect the Negro partially in property, life, and limb. Through the pressure of the money-makers, the Negro is in danger of being reduced to semi-slavery, especially in the country districts; the workingmen, and those of the educated who fear the Negro, have united to disfranchise him, and some have urged his deportation; while the passions of the ignorant are easily aroused to lynch and abuse any black man. To praise this intricate whirl of thought and prejudice is nonsense; to inveigh indiscriminately against "the

South" is unjust; but to use the same breath in praising Governor Aycock, exposing Senator Morgan, arguing with Mr. Thomas Nelson Page, and denouncing Senator Ben Tillman, is not only sane, but the imperative duty of thinking black men.

It would be unjust to Mr. Washington not to acknowledge that in several instances he has opposed movements in the South which were unjust to the Negro; he sent memorials to the Louisiana and Alabama constitutional conventions, he has spoken against lynching, and in other ways has openly or silently set his influence against sinister schemes and unfortunate happenings. Notwithstanding this, it is equally true to assert that on the whole the distinct impression left by Mr. Washington's propaganda is, first, that the South is justified in its present attitude toward the Negro because of the Negro's degradation; secondly, that the prime cause of the Negro's failure to rise more quickly is his wrong education in the past; and, thirdly, that his future rise depends primarily on his own efforts. Each of these propositions is a dangerous half-truth. The supplementary truths must never be lost sight of: first, slavery and race-prejudice are potent if not sufficient causes of the Negro's position; second, industrial and common-school training were necessarily slow in planting because they had to await the black teachers trained by higher institutions,—it being extremely doubtful if any essentially different development was possible, and certainly a Tuskegee was unthinkable before 1880; and, third, while it is a great truth to say that the Negro must strive and strive mightily to help himself, it is equally true that unless his striving be not simply seconded, but rather aroused and encouraged, by the initiative of the richer and wiser environing group, he cannot hope for great success.

In his failure to realize and impress this last point, Mr. Washington is especially to be criticised. His doctrine has tended to make the whites, North and South, shift the burden of the Negro problem to the Negro's shoulders and stand aside as critical and rather pessimistic spectators; when in fact the burden belongs to the nation, and the hands of none of us are clean if we bend not our energies to righting these great wrongs.

The South ought to be led, by candid and honest criticism, to assert her better self and do her full duty to the race she has cruelly wronged and is still wronging. The North—her co-partner in guilt—cannot salve her conscience by plastering it with gold. We cannot settle this problem by diplomacy and suaveness, by "policy" alone. If worse comes to worst, can the moral fibre of this country survive the slow throttling and murder of nine millions of men?

The black men of America have a duty to perform, a duty stern and delicate,—a forward movement to oppose a part of the work of their greatest leader. So far as Mr. Washington preaches Thrift, Patience, and Industrial Training for the masses, we must hold up his hands and strive with him, rejoicing in his honors and glorying in the strength of this Joshua called of God and of man to lead the headless host. But so far as Mr. Washington apologizes for injustice, North or South, does not rightly value the privilege and duty of voting, belittles the emasculating effects of caste distinctions, and opposes the higher training and ambition of our brighter minds,—so far as he, the South, or the Nation, does this,—we must unceasingly and firmly oppose them. By every civilized and peaceful method we must strive for the rights which the world accords to men, clinging unwaveringly to those great words which the sons of the Fathers would fain forget: "We hold these truths to be self-evident: That all men are created equal; that they are endowed by their Creator with certain unalienable rights; that among these are life, liberty, and the pursuit of happiness."

THE COLORED WORLD WITHIN

Not only do white men but also colored men forget the facts of the Negro's double environment. The Negro American has for his environment not only the white surrounding world, but also, and touching him usually much more nearly and compellingly, is the environment furnished by his own colored group. There are exceptions, of course, but this is the rule. The American Negro, therefore, is surrounded and conditioned by the concept which he has of white people and he is treated in accordance with the concept they have of him. On the other hand, so far as his own people are concerned, he is in direct contact with individuals and facts. He fits into this environment more or less willingly. It gives him a social world and mental peace. On the other hand and especially if in education and ambition and income he is above the average culture of his group, he is often resentful of its environing power; partly because he does not recognize its power and partly because he is determined to consider himself part of the white group from which, in fact, he is excluded. This weaving of words does not make the situation entirely clear and yet it does point toward its complications.

It is true, as I have argued, that Negroes are not inherently ugly nor congenitally stupid. They are not naturally criminal and their poverty and ignorance today have clear and well-known and remediable causes. All this is true; and yet what every colored man living today knows is that by practical present measurement Negroes today are inferior to whites. The white folk of the world are richer and more intelligent; they live better; have better government; have better legal systems; have built more impressive cities, larger systems of communication and they control a larger part of the earth than all the colored peoples together.

Against this colored folk may certainly bring many countervailing considerations. But putting these aside, there remains the other fact that the mass of the colored peoples in Asia and Africa, in North America and the West Indies and in South America and in the South Sea Islands are in the mass ignorant, diseased, and inefficient; that the governments which they have evolved, even allowing for the interested interference of the white world, have seldom reached the degree of efficiency of modern European governments; and that particularly in the use, increase, and distribution of wealth, in the regulation of human services, they have at best fallen behind the accomplishment of modern England, France and the United States.

It may be said, and with very strong probability back of such assertion, there is no reason to doubt, that whatever white folk have accomplished, black, brown and yellow folk might have done possibly in differing ways with different results. Certainly modern civilization is too new and has steered too crooked a course and been too much a matter of chance and fate to make any final judgment as to the abilities of humankind.

All this I strongly believe and yet today we are faced by these uncomforting facts: the ignorance, poverty and inefficiency of the darker peoples; the wealth, power and technical triumph of the whites. It is not enough when the colored people face this situation, that they decry resulting attitudes of the white world. There is a strong suspicion among themselves and a probability often asserted among whites, that were conditions reversed, blacks would have done everything to white people that white people have done to blacks; or going less far afield than this: if yellow folk in the future gain the domination of the world, their program might not be more philanthropic than that of the whites. But here again, this is not the question. Granting its possible truth, it is no answer to the present plight.

The present question is: What is the colored world going to do about the current situations? Present Negro attitudes can be illuminated by turning our attention for a space to colored America, to an average group of Negroes, say, in Harlem, not in their role of agitation and reform, but in their daily human intercourse and play. Imagine a conversation like this, of which I have heard dozens:

"Just like niggers!"
"This is what colored people always do."
"What can you expect of the 'brother'?"
"I wish to God I had been born white!"

This interchange takes place at midnight. There are no white persons present. Four persons have spent an evening playing bridge, and now are waiting until a fifth, the hostess, brings in the supper. The apartment is small but comfortable; perhaps a little too full of conventional furniture, which does not altogether agree in pattern; but evidently the home of fairly well-to-do people who like each other and are enjoying themselves. But, of course, they have begun to discuss "the problem" which no group of American colored people can long keep from discussing. It is and must be the central interest of their lives.

There is a young colored teacher from the public schools of New York—well-paid and well-dressed with a comely form and an arresting personality. She is from the South. Her mother had been servant and housekeeper in a wealthy Southern white family. Her grandmother had been a slave of their own grandfather. This teacher is complaining bitterly of her walk through Harlem that night; of the loud and vulgar talking; of the way in which the sidewalks were blocked; of the familiarity and even insults of dark loafers; of the insistent bad manners and resentful attitude of so many of these Harlem black folk.

The lawyer lights a cigar. "It certainly is a question where to live," he says. He had been educated at Fisk University and brought in contact for eight years with Northern white teachers. Then he had gone West and eventually studied law at the University of Michigan. He is big, dark, good-natured and well-dressed. He complains of the crowded conditions of living in Harlem; of the noise and dirt in any Negro community; of the fact that if you went out to a better class white neighborhood you could not rent, you had to buy; if you did buy, first you could place no mortgage; then the whites made your life a hell; if you survived this, the whites became panicky, sold to anyone for anything: pretty soon, in two, three, five years, people of all sorts and kinds came crowding in. Homes were transformed into lodging houses; undesirable elements became your neighbors. "I moved to a nice apartment on Sugar Hill last year. It had just been turned over to colored people. The landlord promised everything. I started out of the apartment last night; there was a pool of blood in front of my door, where there had been a drunken brawl and cutting the night before."

A young, slim, cream-colored physician, native of New York and a graduate of its schools, but compelled to go to Howard in order to finish the clinical work of his medical education, looked uncomfortable. "I don't mind going with colored people; I prefer it, if they are my kind; but if I go out to lunch here in Harlem, I get pork chops and yams which I do not like, served on a table cloth which is not clean, set down negligently by indifferent waiters. In the movies uptown here I find miscellaneous and often ill-smelling neighbors. On my vacation, where shall I—where can I go? The part of Atlantic City open to me, I continue to frequent, because I see so many charming friends of mine from all over the land; but always I get sick at heart not only at the discrimination on the boardwalk, in the restaurants, on the beach, in the amusements— that is bad enough; but I gag at the kind of colored people always in evidence, against whom I want to discriminate myself. We tried to support a colored section of the beach; see who crowded in; we failed."

"Yes, but that is all pleasure or convenience," says the fourth man. He was an insurance agent, playing a difficult game of chance with people who made weekly payments to him and then tried to beat him by malingering; or with others who paid promptly and had their claims disallowed by the higher-ups. "What I am bothered about," he says, "is this poverty, sickness and crime; the cheating of Negroes not only by whites, but by Negroes themselves; the hold-ups and murders of colored people by colored people. I am afraid to go to some places to make my collections. I don't know what is going to become of Negroes at this rate."

Just then, the fifth member of the party, the wife of the insurance agent, emerges from the kitchen where she has been arranging the lunch. She is pretty and olive, a little inclined to be fat. She was the daughter of dark laborers who had gone to Boston after emancipation. There she had been educated in the public schools and was a social worker there before she married. She knew how to cook and liked to, and is accompanied through the swinging door by a delicious aroma of coffee, hot biscuits and fried chicken. She has been listening to the conversation from outside and she came in saying, "What's got me worried to death, is where I am going to send Junior to school. Junior is bright and has got nice manners, if I do say it; but I just can't send him to these Harlem schools. I was visiting them yesterday; dirt, noise, bad manners, filthy tales, no discipline, over-crowded. The teachers aren't half trying. They purposely send green teachers to Harlem for experience. I just can't send Junior there; but where can I send him?"

This is a fairly characteristic colored group of the better class and they are voicing that bitter inner criticism of Negroes directed in upon themselves, which is widespread. It tends often to fierce, angry, contemptuous judgment of nearly all that Negroes do, say, and believe. Of course these words are seldom voiced in the presence of white folk. Every one of these persons, in the presence of whites, would eagerly and fiercely defend their "race."

Such complaints are the natural reaction of people toward the low average of culture among American Negroes. There is some exaggeration here, which the critics themselves, if challenged, would readily admit; and yet, there is sound basis for much of this criticism. Similar phenomena may be noticed always among undeveloped or suppressed peoples or groups undergoing extraordinary experience. None have more pitilessly castigated Jews than the Jewish prophets, ancient and modern. It is the Irish themselves who rail at "dirty Irish tricks." Nothing could exceed the self-abasement of the Germans during the *Sturm und Drang.*

Negro self-criticism recognizes a perfectly obvious fact and that fact is that most Negroes in the United States today occupy a low cultural status; both low in itself and low as compared with the national average in the land. There are cultured individuals and groups among them. All Negroes do not fall culturally below all whites. But if one selects any one of the obviously low culture groups in the United States, the proportion of Negroes who belong to it will be larger than the Negro proportion in the total population. Nor is there anything singular about it; the real miracle would be if this were not so. Former slavery, present poverty and ignorance, with the inevitable resulting sickness and crime, are adequate social explanation.

This low social condition of the majority of Negroes is not solely a problem of the whites; a question of historic guilt in slavery and labor exploitation and of present discrimination; it is not merely a matter of the social uplifting of an alien group within their midst; a problem of social contact and political power. Howsoever it may be thus rationalized and explained, it must be, at any current moment, primarily an inner problem of the Negro group itself, a condition from which they themselves are prime sufferers, and a problem with which this group is forced itself to grapple. No matter what the true reasons are, or where the blame lies, the fact remains that among twelve million American Negroes, there are today poverty, ignorance, bad manners, disease, and crime.

A determined fight has been made upon Negro ignorance, both within and without the group, and the results have been notable. Nevertheless, this is still an ignorant people. One in every six Negroes ten years of age and over admitted in 1930 that he could not read and write. It is probable that one in every three would have been justified in confessing to practical illiteracy, to inexperience and lack of knowledge of the meaning of the modern world. In the South not one-half the colored children from five to sixteen are regularly in school and the majority of these schools are not good schools. Any poor, ignorant people herded by themselves, filled with more or less articulate resentment, are bound to be bad-mannered, for manners are a matter of social environment; and the mass of American Negroes have retrograded in this respect.

There has been striking improvement in the Negro death rate. It was better than that of most South American countries, of Italy, Japan and Spain even before the war. Nevertheless it is still bad and costly, and the toll in tuberculosis, pneumonia, heart disease, syphilis, and homicide is far too high. It is hard to know just what the criminal tendencies of the American Negroes are, for our crime statistics are woefully inadequate. We do know that in proportion to population three times as many Negroes are arrested as whites, but to what extent this measures prejudice and to what extent anti-social ills, who shall say? Many of these ought never to have been arrested; most of them are innocent of grave crimes; but the transgression of the poor and sick is always manifest among Negroes: disorder of all sorts, theft and burglary, fighting, breaking the gambling and liquor laws and especially fighting with and killing each other.

Above all the Negro is poor: poor by heritage from two hundred forty-four years of chattel slavery, by emancipation without land or capital and by seventy-five years of additional wage exploitation and crime peonage. Sudden industrial changes like the Civil War, the World War and the spree in speculation during the twenties have upset him. The Negro worker has been especially hard hit by the current depression. Of the nearly three million Negro families in the United States today, probably the breadwinners of a million are unemployed and another million on the lower margin of decent subsistence. Assuming a gradual restoration of fairly normal conditions it is probable that not more than two per cent of the Negro families in the United States would have an income of $2,500 a year and over; while fifty-eight per cent would have incomes between $500 and $2,500.

This social degradation is intensified and emphasized by discrimination; inability to get work, discrimination in pay, improbability of promotion, and more fundamentally, spiritual segregation from contact with manners, customs, incentives to effort despite handicaps. By outer pressure in most cases, Negroes must live among themselves; neighbors to their own people in segregated parts of the city, in segregated country districts. The segregation is not complete and most of it is customary rather than legal. Nevertheless, most Negroes live with Negroes, in what are on the whole the least pleasant dwelling places, although not necessarily always bad places in themselves.

This means that Negroes live in districts of low cultural level; that their contacts with their fellow men involve contacts with people largely untrained and ignorant, frequently diseased, dirty, and noisy, and sometimes antisocial. These districts are not usually protected by the police—

rather victimized and tyrannized over by them. No one who does not know can realize what tyranny a low-grade white policeman can exercise in a colored neighborhood. In court his unsupported word cannot be disputed and the only defense against him is often mayhem and assassination by black criminals, with resultant hue and cry. City services of water, sewage, garbage-removal, street-cleaning, lighting, noise and traffic regulation, schools and hospitalization are usually neglected or withheld. Saloons, brothels, and gambling seek these areas with open or tacit consent. No matter in what degree or in what way the action of the white population may increase or decrease these social problems, they remain the present problems which must be faced by colored people themselves and by colored people of widely different status.

It goes without saying that while Negroes are thus manifestly of low average culture, in no place nor at any time do they form a homogeneous group. Even in the country districts of the lower South, Allison Davis likens the group to a steeple with wide base tapering to a high pinnacle. This means that while the poor, ignorant, sick and anti-social form a vast foundation, that upward from that base stretch classes whose highest members, although few in number, reach above the average not only of the Negroes but of the whites, and may justly be compared to the better-class white culture. The class structure of the whites, on the other hand, resembles a tower bulging near the center with the lowest classes small in number as compared with the middle and lower middle classes; and the highest classes far more numerous in proportion than those among blacks. This, of course, is what one would naturally expect, but it is easily forgotten. The Negro group is spoken of continually as one undifferentiated low-class mass. The culture of the higher whites is often considered as typical of all the whites.

American Negroes again are of differing descent, from parents with varied education, born in many parts of the land and under all sorts of conditions. In differing degrees these folk have come through periods of great and vital social change; emancipation from slavery, migration from South to North, from country to city; changes in income and intelligence. Above this they have experienced widely different contacts with their own group and with the whites. For instance, during slavery the dark house servant came into close and intimate contact with the master class. This class itself differed in all degree from cultured aristocrats to brutal tyrants. Many of the Negroes thus received ideals of gracious manners, of swaggering self-assertion, of conspicuous consumption. Later cultural contact came to the best of the Negroes through the mission schools in the South succeeding the war: the more simple and austere intellectual life of New England with its plain living and high thinking; its cleanliness and conscience; this was brought into direct contact with educated Negro life. Its influence is still felt among the descendants of those trained at Fisk and Atlanta, Hampton and Talladega and a score of other schools.

These contacts between the white and colored groups in the United States have gradually changed. On the whole the better cultural contacts have lessened in breadth and time, and greater cultural segregation by race has ensued. The old bonds between servants and masters in the South disappeared. The white New England teachers gradually withdrew from the Southern schools partly by white Southern caste pressure, partly to make place for Negroes whom the Northern teachers had trained. The bonds that replaced these older contacts were less direct, more temporary and casual; and yet, these still involve considerable numbers of persons. In Northern public schools and colleges, numbers of white and colored youth come into direct contact, knowledge and sympathy. Various organizations, movements, and meetings bring white and colored people together; in various occupations they work side by side and in large numbers of cases they meet as employers and employed. Deliberate interracial movements have brought some social contacts in the South.

Thus considerable intercourse between white and black folk in America is current today; and yet on the whole, the more or less clearly defined upper layers of educated and ambitious Negroes find themselves for the most part largely segregated and alone. They are unable, or at least unwilling on the terms offered, to share the social institutions of the cultured whites of the nation, and are faced with inner problems of contact with their own lower classes with which they have few or no social institutions capable of dealing.

The Negro of education and income is jammed beside the careless, ignorant and criminal. He recoils from appeal to the white city even for physical protection against his anti-social elements, for this, he feels, is a form of self-accusation, of attack on the Negro race. It invites the smug rejoinder: "Well, if you can't live with niggers, how do you expect us to?" For escape of the Negro cultured to areas of white culture, with the consequent acceleration of acculturation, there is small opportunity. There is little or no chance for a Negro family to remove to a quiet neighborhood, to a protected suburb or a college town. I tried once to buy a home in the Sage Foundation development at Forest Hills, Long Island. The project was designed for the class of white-collar workers to which I belonged. Robert De Forest and his directors hesitated, but finally and definitely refused, simply and solely because of my dark skin.

What now is the practical path for the solution of the problem? Usually it has been assumed in such cases that the culture recruits rising from a submerged group will be received more or less willingly by corresponding classes of neighboring or enveloping groups. Of course it is clear in the case of immigrant groups and other disadvantaged clusters of folk that this process is by no means easy or natural. Much bitter frustration and social upheaval continually arise from the refusal of the upper social layers to receive recruits from below. Nevertheless, in the United States it has been impossible long or entirely to exclude the better classes of the Irish, the Italians, the Southern poor whites. In the case of the Negro, the unwillingness is greater and public opinion supports it to such a degree, that admission of black folk to cultured circles is slow and difficult. It still remains possible in the United States for a white American to be a gentleman and a scholar, a Christian and a man of integrity, and yet flatly and openly refuse to treat as a fellow human being any person who has Negro ancestry.

The inner contradiction and frustration which this involves is curious. The younger educated Negroes show here vastly different interpretations. One avoids every appearance of segregation. He will not sit in a street car beside a Negro; he will not frequent a Negro church; he will join few, if any, Negro organizations. On the other hand he will take every opportunity to join in the political and cultural life of the whites. But he pays for this and pays dearly. He so often meets actual insult or more or less veiled rebuffs from the whites that he becomes nervous and truculent through expectation of dislike, even when its manifestation does not always appear. And on the other hand, Negroes more or less withdraw from associating with him. They suspect that he is "ashamed of his race."

Another sort of young educated Negro forms and joins Negro organizations; prides himself on living with "his people"; withdraws from contact with whites, unless there is no obvious alternative. He too pays. His cultural contacts sink of necessity to a lower level. He becomes provincial in his outlook. He attributes to whites a dislike and hatred and racial prejudice of which many of them are quite unconscious and guiltless.

Between these two extremes range all sorts of interracial patterns, and all of them theoretically follow the idea that Negroes must only submit to segregation "when forced." In practically all cases the net result is a more or less clear and definite crystallization of the culture elements among colored people into their own groups for social and cultural contact.

The resultant path which commends itself to many whites is deliberate and planned cultural segregation of the upper classes of Negroes not only from the whites of all classes, but from their own masses. It has been said time and time again: if certain classes of Negroes do not like the squalor, filth and crime of Negro slums, instead of trying to escape to better class white neighborhoods, why do they not establish their own exclusive neighborhoods? In other words, why does not the Negro race build up a class structure of its own, parallel to that of the whites, but separate; and including its own social, economic and religious institutions?

The arresting thing about this advice and program is that even when not planned, this is exactly what Negroes are doing and must do even in the case of those who theoretically resent it. The group with whose conversation this chapter started is a case in point. They form a self-segregated culture group. They have come to know each other partly by chance, partly by design, but form a small integrated clique because of similar likes and ideas, because of corresponding culture. This is happening all over the land among these twelve million Negroes. It is not a matter yet of a few broad super-imposed social classes, but rather of smaller cliques and groups gradually integrating and extending out of their neighborhoods into neighboring districts and cities. In this way a distinct social grouping has long been growing among American Negroes and recent studies have emphasized what we all knew, and that is that the education and acculturation of the Negro child is more largely the result of the training through contact with these cultural groups than it is of the caste-conditioned contacts with whites.

The question now comes as to how far this method of acculturation should and could go, and by what conscious planning the uplift of the Negro race can be accomplished through this means. Is cultural separation in the same territory feasible? To force a group of various levels of culture to segregate itself, will certainly retard its advance, since it must put energy not simply into social advance, but in the vast and intricate effort to duplicate, evolve, and contrive new social institutions to maintain their advance and guard against retrogression.

There can be two theories here: one that the rise of a talented tenth within the Negro race, whether or not it succeeds in escaping to the higher cultural classes of the white race, is a threat to the development of the whole Negro group and hurts their chances for salvation. Or it may be said that the rise of classes within the Negro group is precisely a method by which the level of culture in the whole group is going to be raised. But this depends upon the relations that develop between these masses and the cultural aims of the higher classes.

Many assume that an upper social class maintains its status mainly by reason of its superior culture. It may, however, maintain its status because of its wealth and political power and in that case its ranks can be successfully invaded only by the wealthy. In white America, it is in this direction that we have undoubtedly changed the older pattern of social hierarchy. Birth and culture still count, but the main avenue to social power and class domination is wealth: income and oligarchic economic power, the consequent political power and the prestige of those who own and control capital and distribute credit. This makes a less logical social hierarchy and one that can only be penetrated by the will and permission of the ruling oligarchy or the chances of gambling. Education, thrift, hard work and character undoubtedly are influential, but they are implemented with power only as they gain wealth; and as land, natural resources, credit and capital are increasingly monopolized, they gain wealth by permission of the dominating wealthy class.

If now American Negroes plan a vertical parallel of such a structure and such processes, they will find it practically impossible. First of all, they have not the wealth; secondly, they have not the political power which wealth manipulates, and in the realm of their democratic power they are not only already partly disfranchised by law and custom, but they suffer the same general limitation of democratic power in income and industry, in which the white masses are imprisoned.

There would be greater possibility of the Negro imitating the class structure of the white race if those whites who advise and encourage it were ready to help in its accomplishment, ready to furnish the Negro the broadest opportunity for cultural development and in addition to this to open the way for them to accumulate such wealth and receive such income as would make the corresponding structure secure. But, of course, those who most vehemently tell the Negro to develop his own classes and social institutions, have no plan or desire for such help. First of all, and often deliberately, they curtail the education and cultural advantage of black folk and they do this because they are not convinced of the cultural ability or gift of Negroes and have no hope nor wish that the mass of Negroes can be raised even as far as the mass of whites have been. It is this insincere attitude which especially arouses the ire and resentment of the culture groups among American Negroes.

When the Negro despairs of duplicating white development, his despair is not always because the paths to this development are shut in his face, but back of this lurks too often a lack of faith in essential Negro possibilities, parallel to similar attitudes on the part of the whites. Instead of this proving anything concerning the truth, it is simply a natural phenomenon. Negroes, particularly the better class Negroes, are brought up like other Americans despite the various separations and segregations. They share, therefore, average American culture and current American prejudices. It is almost impossible for a Negro boy trained in a white Northern high school and a white college to come out with any high idea of his own people or any abiding faith in what they can do; or for a Negro trained in the segregated schools of the South wholly to escape the deadening environment of insult and caste, even if he happens to have the good teachers and teaching facilities, which poverty almost invariably denies him. He may rationalize his own individual status as exceptional. He can well believe that there are many other exceptions, but he cannot ordinarily believe that the mass of Negro people have possibilities equal to the whites.

It is this sort of thing that leads to the sort of self-criticism that introduces this chapter. My grandfather, Alexander Du Bois, was pushed into the Negro group. He resented it. He wasn't a "Negro," he was a man. He would not attend Negro picnics or join a Negro church, and yet he had to. Now, his situation in 1810 was much different from mine, in 1940, because the Negro group today is much more differentiated and has distinct cultural elements. He could go to a Negro picnic today and associate with interesting people of his own level. So much so, indeed, that some Negro thinkers are beginning to be afraid that we will become so enamored of our own internal social contacts, that we will cease to hammer at the doors of the larger group, with all the consequent loss of breadth through lack of the widest cultural contact; and all the danger of ultimate extinction through exacerbated racial repulsions and violence. For any building of a segregated Negro culture in America in those areas where it is by law or custom the rule and where neglect to take positive action would mean a slowing down or stoppage or even retrogression of Negro advance, unusual and difficult and to some extent unprecedented action is called for.

To recapitulate: we cannot follow the class structure of America; we do not have the economic or political power, the ownership of machines and materials, the power to direct the process of industry, the monopoly of capital and credit. On the other hand, even if we cannot follow this method of structure, nevertheless we must do something. We cannot stand still; we cannot permit ourselves simply to be the victims of exploitation and social exclusion. It is from this paradox that arises the present frustration among American Negroes.

Historically, beginning with their thought in the eighteenth century and coming down to the twentieth, Negroes have tended to choose between these difficulties and emphasize two lines of action: the *first* is exemplified in Walker's Appeal, that tremendous indictment of slavery by a colored man published in 1829, and resulting very possibly in the murder of the author; and coming down through the work of the Niagara Movement and the National Association for the Advancement of Colored People in our day. This program of organized opposition to the action and attitude of the dominant white group, includes ceaseless agitation and insistent demand for equality: the equal right to work, civic and political equality, and social equality. It involves the use of force of every sort: moral suasion, propaganda and where possible even physical resistance.

There are, however, manifest difficulties about such a program. First of all it is not a program that envisages any direct action of Negroes themselves for the uplift of their socially depressed masses; in the very conception of the program, such work is to be attended to by the nation and Negroes are to be the subjects of uplift forces and agencies to the extent of their numbers and need. Another difficulty is that the effective organization of this plan of protest and agitation involves a large degree of inner union and agreement among Negroes. Now for obvious reasons of ignorance and poverty, and the natural envy and bickering of any disadvantaged group, this unity is difficult to achieve. In fact the efforts to achieve it through the Negro conventions of 1833 and thereafter during the fifties; during Reconstruction, and in the formation of the early Equal Rights League and Afro-American Council, were only partly successful.

The largest measure of united effort in the demand for Negro rights was attempted by the NAACP in the decade between 1914 and 1924. The difficulty even in that case was the matter of available funds. The colored people are not today able to furnish enough funds for the kind of campaign against Negro prejudice which is demanded; or at least the necessity of large enough contributions is not clear to a sufficient number of Negroes. Moreover, even if there were the necessary unity and resources available, there are two assumptions usually made in such a campaign, which are not quite true; and that is the assumption on one hand that most race prejudice is a matter of ignorance to be cured by information; and on the other hand that much discrimination is a matter of deliberate deviltry and unwillingness to be just. Admitting widespread ignorance concerning the guilt of American whites for the plight of the Negroes; and the undoubted existence of sheer malevolence, the present attitude of the whites is much more the result of inherited customs and of those irrational and partly subconscious actions of men which control so large a proportion of their deeds. Attitudes and habits thus built up cannot be changed by sudden assault. They call for a long, patient, well-planned and persistent campaign of propaganda.

Moreover, until such a campaign has had a chance to do its work, the minority which is seeking emancipation must remember that they are facing a powerful majority. There is no way in which the American Negro can force this nation to treat him as equal until the unconscious cerebration and folkways of the nation, as well as its rational deliberate thought among the majority of whites, are willing to grant equality.

In the meantime of course the agitating group may resort to a campaign of countermoves. They may organize and collect resources and by every available means teach the white majority and appeal to their sense of justice; but at the very best this means a campaign of waiting and the colored group must be financially able to afford to wait and patient to endure without spiritual retrogression while they wait.

The *second* group effort to which Negroes have turned is more extreme and decisive. One can see it late in the eighteenth century when the Negro union of Newport, Rhode Island, in 1788 proposed to the Free African Society of Philadelphia a general exodus to Africa on the part at least of free Negroes. This "back to Africa" movement has recurred time and time again in the philosophy of American Negroes and has commended itself not simply to the inexperienced and to demagogues, but to the prouder and more independent type of Negro; to the black man who is tired of begging for justice and recognition from folk who seem to him to have no intention of being just and do not propose to recognize Negroes as men. This thought was strong during the active existence of the Colonization Society and succeeded in convincing leading Negroes like John Russworm, the first Negro college graduate, and Lott Carey, the powerful Virginia preacher. Then it fell into severe disrepute when the objects of the Colonization Society were shown by the Abolitionists to be the perpetuation rather than the amelioration of American slavery.

Later, just before the Civil War, the scheme of migration to Africa or elsewhere was revived and agents sent out to South America, Haiti and Africa. After the Civil War and the disappointments of Reconstruction came Bishop Turner's proposal and recently the crazy scheme of Marcus Garvey. The hard facts which killed all these proposals were first lack of training, education and habits on the part of ex-slaves which unfitted them to be pioneers; and mainly that tremendous industrial expansion of Europe which made colonies in Africa or elsewhere about the last place where colored folk could successfully seek freedom and equality.

These extreme plans tended always to fade to more moderate counsel. First came the planned inner migration of the Negro group: to Canada, to the North, to the West, to cities everywhere. This has been a vast and continuing movement, affecting millions and changing and modifying the Negro problems. One result has been a new system of racial integrations. Groups of Negroes in their own clubs and organizations, in their own neighborhoods and schools, were formed, and were not so much the result of deliberate planning as the rationalization of the segregation into which they were forced by racial prejudice. These groups became physical and spiritual cities of refuge, where sometimes the participants were inspired to efforts for social uplift, learning and ambition; and sometimes reduced to sullen wordless resentment. It is toward this sort of group effort that the thoughts and plans of Booker T. Washington led. He did not advocate a deliberate and planned segregation, but advised submission to segregation in settlement and in work, in order that this bending to the will of a powerful majority might bring from that majority gradually such sympathy and sense of justice that in the long run the best interests of the Negro group would be served; particularly as those interests, were, he thought, inseparable from the best interests of the dominant group. The difficulty here was that unless the dominant group saw its best interests bound up with those of the black minority, the situation was hopeless; and in any case the danger was that if the minority ceased to agitate and resist oppression it would grow to accept it as normal and inevitable.

A *third* path of the advance which lately I have been formulating and advocating can easily be mistaken for a program of complete racial segregation and even nationalism among Negroes. Indeed it has been criticized as such. This is a misapprehension. First, ignoring other racial separations, I have stressed the economic discrimination as fundamental and advised concentration of planning here. We need sufficient income for health and home; to supplement our education and recreation; to fight our own crime problem; and above all to finance a continued, planned and intelligent agitation for political, civil and social equality. How can we Negroes in the United States gain such average income as to be able to attend to these pressing matters? The cost of this program must fall first and primarily on us, ourselves. It is silly to expect any large number of whites to finance a program which the overwhelming majority of whites today fear and reject. Setting up as a bogey-man an assumed proposal for an absolute separate Negro economy in America, it has been easy for colored philosophers and white experts to dismiss the matter with a shrug and a laugh. But this is not so easily dismissed. In the first place we have already got a partially segregated Negro economy in the United States. There can be no question about this. We not only build and finance Negro churches, but we furnish a considerable part of the funds for our segregated schools. We furnish most of our own professional services in medicine, pharmacy, dentistry and law. We furnish some part of our food and clothes, our home building and repairing and many retail services. We furnish books and newspapers; we furnish endless personal services like those of barbers, beauty shop keepers, hotels, restaurants. It may be said that this inner economy of the Negro serves but a small proportion of its total needs; but it is growing and expanding in various ways; and what I propose is to so plan and guide it as to take advantage of certain obvious facts.

It is of course impossible that a segregated economy for Negroes in the United States should be complete. It is quite possible that it could never cover more than the smaller part of the economic activities of Negroes. Nevertheless, it is also possible that this smaller part could be so important and wield so much power that its influence upon the total economy of Negroes and the total industrial organization of the United States would be decisive for the great ends towards which the Negro moves.

We are of course obsessed with the vastness of the industrial machine in America, and with the way in which organized wealth dominates our whole government, our education, our intellectual life and our art. But despite this, the American economic class structure—that system of domination of industry and the state through income and monopoly—is breaking down; not simply in America but in the world. We have reached the end of an economic era, which seemed but a few years ago omnipotent and eternal. We have lived to see the collapse of capitalism. It makes no difference what we may say, and how we may boast in the United States of the failures and changed objectives of the New Deal, and the prospective rehabilitation of the rule of finance capital; that is but wishful thinking. In Europe and in the United States as well as in Russia the whole organization and direction of industry is changing. We are not called upon to be dogmatic as to just what the end of this change will be and what form the new organization will take. What we are sure of is the present fundamental change.

There faces the American Negro therefore an intricate and subtle problem of combining into one object two difficult sets of facts; his present racial segregation which despite anything he can do will persist for many decades; and his attempt by carefully planned and intelligent action to fit himself into the new economic organization which the world faces.

This plan of action would have for its ultimate object, full Negro rights and Negro equality in America; and it would most certainly approve, as one method of attaining this, continued agitation, protest and propaganda to that end. On the other hand my plan would not decline frankly to face the possibility of eventual emigration from America of some considerable part of the Negro population, in case they could find a chance for free and favorable development unmolested and unthreatened, and in case the race prejudice in America persisted to such an extent that it would not permit the full development of the capacities and aspirations of the Negro race. With its eyes open to the necessity of agitation and to possible migration, this plan would start with the racial grouping that today is inevitable and proceed to use it as a method of progress along which we have worked and are now working. Instead of letting this segregation remain largely a matter of chance and unplanned development, and allowing its objects and results to rest in the hands of the white majority or in the accidents of the situation, it would make the segregation a matter of careful thought and intelligent planning on the part of Negroes.

The object of that plan would be two-fold: first to make it possible for the Negro group to await its ultimate emancipation with reasoned patience, with equitable temper and with every possible effort to raise the social status and increase the efficiency of the group. And secondly and just as important, the ultimate object of the plan is to obtain admission of the colored group to cooperation and incorporation into the white group on the best possible terms.

This planned and deliberate recognition of self-segregation on the part of colored people involves many difficulties which have got to be faced.

First of all, in what lines and objects of effort should segregation come? This choice is not wide, because so much segregation is compulsory: most colored children, most colored youth, are educated in Negro schools and by Negro teachers. There is more education by race today than there was in the latter part of the nineteenth century; partly because of increased racial consciousness, and partly because more Negroes are applying for education and this would call for larger social contact than ever before, if whites and Negroes went to the same school.

On the other hand this educational segregation involves, as Negroes know all too well, poorer equipment in the schools and poorer teaching than colored children would have if they were admitted to white schools and treated with absolute fairness. It means that their contact with the better-trained part of the nation, a contact which spells quicker acculturation, is lessened and shortened; and that above all, less money is spent upon their schools. They must submit to double taxation in order to have a minimum of decent equipment. The Rosenwald school houses involved such double taxation on the Negro. The Booker T. Washington High School in Atlanta raises thousands of dollars each year by taxation upon colored students and parents, while city funds furnish only salaries, buildings, books and a minimum of equipment. This is the pattern throughout the South. On the other hand with the present attitude of teachers and the public, even if colored students were admitted to white schools, they would not in most cases receive decent treatment nor real education.

It is not then the theory but a fact that faces the Negro in education. He has group education in large proportion and he must organize and plan these segregated schools so that they become efficient, well-housed, well-equipped, with the best of teachers and with the best results on the children; so that the illiteracy and bad manners and criminal tendencies of young Negroes can be quickly and effectively reduced. Most Negroes would prefer a good school with properly paid colored teachers for educating their children, to forcing their children into white schools which met them with injustice and humiliation and discouraged their efforts to progress.

So too in the church, the activities for ethical teaching, character-building, and organized charity and neighborliness, which are largely concentrated in religious organizations, are segregated racially more completely than any other human activity; a curious and eloquent commentary upon modern Christianity. These are the facts and the colored church must face them. It is facing them only in part today because a large proportion of the intelligent colored folk do not co-operate with the church and leave the ignorant to make the church a seat of senseless dogma and meaningless ceremonies together with a multitude of activities which have no social significance and lead to no social betterment. On the other hand the Negro church does do immense amounts of needed works of charity and mercy among the poor; but here again it lacks funds.

There has been a larger movement on the part of the Negro intelligentsia toward racial grouping for the advancement of art and literature.

There has been a distinct plan for reviving ancient African art through an American Negro art movement; and more especially a thought to use the extremely rich and colorful life of the Negro in America and elsewhere as a basis for painting, sculpture and literature. This has been partly nullified by the fact that if these new artists expect support for their art from the Negro group itself, that group must be deliberately trained and schooled in art appreciation and in willingness to accept new canons of art and in refusal to follow the herd instinct of the nation. Instead of this artistic group following such lines, it has largely tried to get support for the Negro art movement from the white public often with disastrous results. Most whites want Negroes to amuse them; they demand caricature; they demand jazz; and torn between these allegiances: between the extraordinary reward for entertainers of the white world, and meager encouragement to honest self-expression, the artistic movement among American Negroes has accomplished something, but it has never flourished and never will until it is deliberately planned. Perhaps its greatest single accomplishment is Carter Woodson's "Negro History Week."

In the same way there is a demand for a distinct Negro health movement. We have few Negro doctors in proportion to our population and the best training of Negro doctors has become increasingly difficult because of their exclusion from the best medical schools of America. Hospitalization among Negroes is far below their reasonable health needs and the individual medical practitioner depending upon fees is the almost universal pattern in this group. What is needed is a carefully planned and widely distributed system of Negro hospitals and socialized medicine with an adequate number of doctors on salary, with the object of social health and not individual income. "Negro Health Week," originating in Tuskegee, is a step in this direction. The whole planned political program of intelligent Negroes is deliberate segregation of their vote for Negro welfare. William L. Dawson, former alderman of Chicago, recently said, "I am not playing Party politics but race politics"; he urged, irrespective of party, adherence to political groups interested in advancing the political and economic rights of the Negro.

The same need is evident in the attitude of Negroes toward Negro crime; obsessed by the undoubted fact that crime is increased and magnified by race prejudice, we ignore the other fact that we have crime and a great deal of it and that we ourselves have got to do something about it; what we ought to do is to cover the Negro group with the services of legal defense organizations in order to counteract the injustice of the police and of the magistrate courts; and then we need positive organized effort to reclaim young and incipient malefactors. There is little organized effort of that sort among Negroes today, save a few Negro reformatories with meager voluntary support and grudging state aid.

From all the foregoing, it is evident that economic planning to insure adequate income is the crying need of Negroes today. This does not involve plans that envisage a return to the old patterns of economic organization in America and the world. This is the American Negro's present danger. Most of the well-to-do with fair education do not realize the imminence of profound economic change in the modern world. They are thinking in terms of work, thrift, investment and profit. They hope with the late Booker T. Washington to secure better economic conditions for Negroes by wider chances of employment and higher wages. They believe in savings and investment in Negro and in general business, and in the gradual evolution of a Negro capitalist class which will exploit both Negro and white labor.

The younger and more intelligent Negroes, realizing in different degrees and according to their training and acquaintance with the modern world the profound economic change through which the world is passing and is destined to pass, have taken three different attitudes: first, they have been confronted with the Communist solution of present social difficulties. The Communist philosophy was a program for a majority, not for a relatively small minority; it presupposed a class structure based on exploitation of the overwhelming majority by an exploiting minority; it advised the seizure of power by this majority and the future domination of the state by and for this majority through the dictation of a trusted group, who would hold power until the people were intelligent and experienced enough to rule themselves by democratic methods.

This philosophy did not envisage a situation where instead of a horizontal division of classes, there was a vertical fissure, a complete separation of classes by race, cutting square across the economic layers. Even if on one side this color line, the dark masses were overwhelmingly workers, with but an embryonic capitalist class, nevertheless the split between white and black workers was greater than that between white workers and capitalists; and this split depended not simply on economic exploitation but on a racial folk-lore grounded on centuries of instinct, habit and thought and implemented by the conditioned reflex of visible color. This flat and incontrovertible fact, imported Russian Communism ignored, would not discuss. American Negroes were asked to accept a complete dogma without question or alteration. It was first of all emphasized that all racial thought and racial segregation must go and that Negroes must put themselves blindly under the dictatorship of the Communist Party.

American Communists did thoroughly and completely obliterate the color bar within their own party ranks, but by so doing, absolutely blocked any chance they might have had to attract any considerable number of white workers to their ranks. The movement consequently did not get far. First, because of the natural fear of radical action in a group made timid through the heredity of slavery; but also and mainly because the attempt to abolish American race prejudice by a phrase was impossible even for the Communist Party. One result of Communistic agitation among Negroes was, however, far-reaching; and that was to impress the younger intellectuals with the fact that American Negroes were overwhelmingly workers, and that their first duty was to associate themselves with the white labor movement, and thus seek to bridge the gap of color, and eradicate the deep-seated racial instincts.

This formed a second line of action, more in consonance with conservative Negro thought. In accordance with this thought and advice and the pressure of other economic motives, Negro membership in labor unions has increased and is still increasing. This is an excellent development, but it has difficulties and pitfalls. The American labor movement varies from closed skilled labor groups, who are either nascent capitalists or stooges, to masses of beaten, ignorant labor outcasts, quite as helpless as the Negroes. Moreover among the working white masses the same racial repulsion persists as in the case of other cultural contacts. This is only natural. The white laborer has been trained to dislike and fear black labor; to regard the Negro as an unfair competitor, able and willing to degrade the price of labor; and even if the Negro prove a good union man, his treatment as an equal would involve equal status, which the white laborer through his long cultural training bitterly resents as a degradation of his own status. Under these circumstances the American Negro faces in the current labor movement, especially in the A F of L and also even in the CIO, the current racial patterns of America.

To counteract this, a recent study of Negro unionism suggests that like the Jews with their United Hebrew Trades, so the Negroes with a United Negro Trades should fight for equality and opportunity within the labor ranks. This illustrates exactly my plan to use the segregation technique for industrial emancipation. The Negro has but one clear path: to enter the white labor movement wherever and whenever he can; but to enter fighting still within labor ranks for recognition and equal treatment. Certainly unless the Negro by his organization and discipline is in position to bring to the movement something beside ignorance, poverty and ill-health, unionization in itself is no panacea.

There has come a third solution which is really a sophisticated attempt to dodge the whole problem of color in economic change; this proposal says that Negroes should join the labor movement, and also so far as possible should join themselves to capital and become capitalists and employers; and in this way, gradually the color line will dissolve into a class line between employers and employees.

Of course this solution ignores the impending change in capitalist society and hopes whatever that change may be, Negroes will benefit along with their economic class. The difficulty here is threefold: not only would there be the same difficulties of the color line in unions, but additional difficulties and exclusion when Negroes as small capitalists seek larger power through the use of capital and credit. The color bar there is beyond present hope of scaling. But in addition to that, this plan will have inserted into the ranks of the Negro race a new cause of division, a new attempt to subject the masses of the race to an exploiting capitalist class of their own people. Negro labor will be estranged from its own intelligentsia, which represents black labor's own best blood; upper class Negroes and Negro labor will find themselves cutting each other's throats on opposite sides of a desperate economic battle, which will be but [a] replica of the old battle which the white world is seeking to outgrow. Instead of forging ahead to a new relation of capital and labor, we would relapse into the old discredited pattern.

It seems to me that all three of these solutions are less hopeful than a fourth solution and that is a racial attempt to use the power of the Negro as a consumer not only for his economic uplift but in addition to that, for his economic education. What I propose is that into the interstices of this collapse of the industrial machine, the Negro shall search intelligently and carefully and farsightedly plan for his entrance into the new economic world, not as a continuing slave but as an intelligent free man with power in his hands.

I see this chance for planning in the role which the Negro plays as a consumer. In the future reorganization of industry the consumer as against the producer is going to become the key man. Industry is going to be guided according to his wants and needs and not exclusively with regard to the profit of the producers and transporters. Now as a consumer the Negro approaches economic equality much more nearly than he ever has as producer. Organizing then and conserving and using intelligently the power which twelve million people have through what they buy, it is possible for the American Negro to help in the rebuilding of the economic state.

The American Negro is primarily a consumer in the sense that his place and power in the industrial process is low and small. Nevertheless, he still has a remnant of his political power and that is growing not only in the North but even in the South. He has in addition to that his economic power as a consumer, as one who can buy goods with some discretion as to what goods he buys. It may truly be said that his discretion is not large but it does exist and it may be made the basis of a new instrument of democratic control over industry.

The cultural differentiation among American Negroes has considerably outstripped the economic differences, which sets this group aside as unusual and at the same time opens possibilities for institutional development and changes of great importance. Fundamental in such change would be the building up of new economic institutions suited to minority groups without wide economic differences, and with distinct cultural possibilities.

The fact that the number of Negro college graduates has increased from 215 between 1876 and 1880 to 10,000 between 1931 and 1935 shows that the ability is there if it can act. In addition to mental ability there is demanded an extraordinary moral strength, the strength to endure discrimination and not become discouraged; to face almost universal disparagement and keep one's soul; and to sacrifice for an ideal which the present generation will hardly see fulfilled. This is an unusual demand and no one can say off-hand whether or not the present generation of American Negroes is equal to it. But there is reason to believe that if the high emotional content of the Negro soul could once be guided into channels that promise success, the end might be accomplished.

Despite a low general level of income, Negroes probably spend at least one hundred and fifty million a month under ordinary circumstances, and they live in an era when gradually economic revolution is substituting the consumer as the decisive voice in industry rather than the all-powerful producer of the past. Already in the Negro group the consumer interest is dominant. Outside of agriculture the Negro is a producer only so far as he is an employee and usually a subordinate employee of large interests dominated almost entirely by whites. His social institutions, therefore, are almost entirely the institutions of consumers and it is precisely along the development of these institutions that he can move in general accordance with the economic development of his time and of the larger white group, and also in this way evolve unified organiza-tion for his own economic salvation.

The fact is, as the Census of 1930 shows, there is almost no need that a modern group has which Negro workers already trained and at work are not able to satisfy. Already Negroes can raise their own food, build their own homes, fashion their own clothes, mend their own shoes, do much of their repair work, and raise some raw materials like tobacco and cotton. A simple transfer of Negro workers, with only such addi-tional skills as can easily be learned in a few months, would enable them to weave their own cloth, make their own shoes, slaughter their own meat, prepare furniture for their homes, install electrical appliances, make their own cigars and cigarettes.

Appropriate direction and easily obtainable technique and capital would enable Negroes further to take over the whole of their retail dis-tribution, to raise, cut, mine and manufacture a considerable proportion of the basic raw material, to man their own manufacturing plants, to process foods, to import necessary raw materials, to invent and build machines. Processes and monopolized natural resources they must con-tinue to buy, but they could buy them on just as advantageous terms as their competitors if they bought in large quantities and paid cash, instead of enslaving themselves with white usury.

Large numbers of other Negroes working as miners, laborers in in-dustry and transportation, could without difficulty be transferred to productive industries designed to cater to Negro consumers. The matter of skill in such industries is not as important as in the past, with in-dustrial operations massed and standardized.

Without doubt, there are difficulties in the way of this program. The Negro population is scattered. The mouths which the Negro farmers might feed might be hundreds or thousands of miles away, and car-penters and mechanics would have to be concentrated and guaranteed a sufficiency of steady employment. All this would call for careful planning and particularly for such an organization of consumers as would elimi-nate unemployment, risk and profit. Demand organized and certain must precede the production and transportation of goods. The waste of advertising must be eliminated. The difference between actual cost and selling price must disappear, doing away with exploitation of labor which is the source of profit.

All this would be a realization of democracy in industry led by con-sumers' organizations and extending to planned production. Is there any reason to believe that such democracy among American Negroes could evolve the necessary leadership in technique and the necessary social in-stitutions which would so guide and organize the masses that a new economic foundation could be laid for a group which is today threatened with poverty and social subordination?

In this process it will be possible to use consumers' organizations already established among the whites. There are such wholesale and manufacturing plants and they welcome patronage; but the Negro co-operative movement cannot rest here. If it does, it will find that quite unconsciously and without planning, Negroes will not be given places of authority or perhaps even of ordinary co-operation in these wider institutions; and the reason will be that white co-operators will not conceive it probable that Negroes could share and guide this work. This the Negro must prove in his own wholesale and manufacturing establishments. Once he has done this and done it thoroughly, there will gradually disappear much of the discrimination in the wider co-operative movement. But that will take a long time.

Meantime, this integration of the single consumers' co-operative into wholesales and factories will intensify the demand for selected leaders and intelligent democratic control over them—for the discovery of ability to manage, of character, of absolute honesty, of inspirational push not toward power but toward efficiency, of expert knowledge in the technique of production and distribution and of scholarship in the past and present of economic development. Nor is this enough. The eternal tendency of such leadership is, once it is established, to assume its own technocratic right to rule, to begin to despise the mass of people who do not know, who have no idea of difficulties of machinery and processes, who succumb to the blandishments of the glib talker, and are willing to select people not because they are honest and sincere but because they wield the glad hand.

Now these people must not be despised, they must be taught. They must be taught in long and lingering conference, in careful marshaling of facts, in the willingness to come to decision slowly and the determination not to tyrannize over minorities. There will be minorities that do not understand. They must patiently be taught to understand. There will be minorities who are stubborn, selfish, self-opinionated. Their real character must be so brought out and exhibited until the overwhelming mass of people who own the co-operative movement and whose votes guide and control it will be able to see just exactly the principles and persons for which they are voting.

The group can socialize most of its professional activities. Certain general and professional services they could change from a private profit to a mutual basis. They could mutualize in reality and not in name, banking and insurance, law and medicine. Health can be put upon the same compulsory basis that we have tried in the case of education, with universal service under physicians paid if possible by the state, or helped by the state, or paid entirely by the group. Hospitals can be as common as churches and used to far better advantage. The legal profession can be socialized and instead of being, as it is now, a defense of property and of the anti-social aggressions of wealth, it can become as it should be, the defense of the young, poor, ignorant and careless

Banking should be so arranged as to furnish credit to the honest in emergencies or to put unneeded savings to useful and socially necessary work. Banking should not be simply and mainly a method of gambling, theft, tyranny, exploitation and profit-making. Our insurance business should cease to be, as it so largely is, a matter of deliberate gambling and become a co-operative service to equalize the incidence of misfortune equitably among members of the whole group without profit to anybody.

Negroes could not only furnish pupils for their own schools and colleges, but could control their teaching force and policies, their textbooks and ideals. By concentrating their demand, by group buying and by their own plants they could get Negro literature issued by the best publishers without censorship upon expression and they could evolve Negro art for its own sake and for its own beauty and not simply for the entertainment of white folk.

The American Negro must remember that he is primarily a consumer; that as he becomes a producer, it must be at the demand and under the control of organized consumers and according to their wants; that in this way he can gradually build up the absolutely needed co-operation in occupations. Today we work for others at wages pressed down to the limit of subsistence. Tomorrow we may work for ourselves, exchanging services, producing an increasing proportion of the goods which we consume and being rewarded by a living wage and by work under civilized conditions. This will call for self-control. It will eliminate the millionaire and even the rich Negro; it will put the Negro leader upon a salary which will be modest as American salaries go and yet sufficient for a life under modern standards of decency and enjoyment. It will eliminate also the pauper and the industrial derelict.

To a degree, but not completely, this is a program of segregation. The consumer group is in important aspects a self-segregated group. We are now segregated largely without reason. Let us put reason and power beneath this segregation. Here comes tremendous opportunity in the Negro housing projects of New York, Chicago, Atlanta and a dozen other centers; in re-settlement projects like the eight all-Negro farmers' colonies in six Southern states and twenty-three rural projects in twelve states. Rail if you will against the race segregation here involved and condoned, but take advantage of it by planting secure centers of Negro co-operative effort and particularly of economic power to make us spiritually free for initiative and creation in other and wider fields, and for eventually breaking down all segregation based on color or curl of hair.

There are unpleasant eventualities which we must face even if we succeed. For instance, if the Negro in America is successful in welding a mass or large proportion of his people into groups working for their own betterment and uplift, they will certainly, like the Jews, be suspected of sinister designs and inner plotting; and their very success in cultural advance be held against them and used for further and perhaps fatal segregation. There is, of course, always the possibility that the plan of a minority group may be opposed to the best interests of a neighboring or enveloping or larger group; or even if it is not, the larger and more powerful group may think certain policies of a minority are inimical to the national interests. The possibility of this happening must be taken into account.

The Negro group in the United States can establish, for a large proportion of its members, a co-operative commonwealth, finding its authority in the consensus of the group and its intelligent choice of inner leadership. It can see to it that not only no action of this inner group is opposed to the real interests of the nation, but that it works for and in conjunction with the best interests of the nation. It need draw no line of exclusion so long as the outsiders join in the consensus. Within its own group it can, in the last analysis, expel the anti-social and hand him over to the police force of the nation. On the other hand it can avoid all appearance of conspiracy, of seeking goals incompatible with the general welfare of the nation, it can court publicity, it can exhibit results, it can plead for co-operation. Its great advantage will be that it is no longer as now attempting to march face forward into walls of prejudice. If the wall moves, we can move with it; and if it does not move it cannot, save in extreme cases, hinder us.

Have we the brains to do this?

Here in the past we have easily landed into a morass of criticism, without faith in the ability of American Negroes to extricate themselves from their present plight. Our former panacea emphasized by Booker T. Washington was flight of class from mass in wealth with the idea of escaping the masses or ruling the masses through power placed by white capitalists into the hands of those with larger income. My own panacea of earlier days was flight of class from mass through the development of a Talented Tenth; but the power of this aristocracy of talent was to lie in its knowledge and character and not in its wealth. The problem which I did not then attack was that of leadership and authority within the group, which by implication left controls to wealth—a contingency of which I never dreamed. But now the whole economic trend of the world has changed. That mass and class must unite for the world's salvation is clear. We who have had least class differentiation in wealth, can follow in the new trend and indeed lead it.

Most Negroes do not believe that this can be done. They not only share American public opinion in distrusting the inherent ability of the Negro group, but they see no way in which the present classes who have proven their intelligence and efficiency can gain leadership over their own people. On the contrary, they fear desperately a vulgarization of emerging culture among them, by contact with the ignorant and anti-social mass. This fear has been accentuated by recent radical agitation; unwashed and unshaven black demagogues have scared and brow-beaten cultured Negroes; have convinced them that their leadership can only be secured through demagoguery. It is for this reason that we see in large Northern centers like Chicago and New York, intelligent, efficient Negroes conniving with crime, gambling and prostitution, in order to secure control of the Negro vote and gain place and income for black folk. Their procedure is not justified by the fact that often excellent and well-trained Negro officials are thus often raised to power. The price paid is deliberate surrender of any attempt at acculturation of the mass in exchange for increased income among the few.

Yet American Negroes must know that the advance of the Negro people since emancipation has been the extraordinary success in education, technique and character among a small number of Negroes and that the emergence of these exceptional men has been largely a matter of chance; that their triumph proves that down among the mass, ten times their number with equal ability could be discovered and developed, if sustained effort and sacrifice and intelligence were put to this task. That, on the contrary, today poverty, sickness and crime are choking the paths to Negro uplift, and that salvation of the Negro race is to come by planned and sustained efforts to open ways of development to those who now form the unrisen mass of the Negro group.

That this can be done by force, by the power of wealth and of the police is true. Along that path of progress most of the nineteenth century acculturation of the masses of men has come; but it has been an unsatisfactory, unsteady method. It has not developed the majority of men to anywhere near the top of their possibilities, and it has pitifully submerged certain groups among whites, and colored groups, like Negroes in America, the West Indies and Africa. Here comes then a special chance for a new trial of democratic development without force among some of the worst victims of force. How can it be done? It can be done through consumers' groups and the mutual interests that these members have in the success of the groups. It can bring the cultured face to face with the untrained and it can accomplish by determined effort and planned foresight the acculturation of the many through the few, rather than the opposite possibility of pulling the better classes down through ignorance, carelessness, and crime.

It is to be admitted this will be a real battle. There are chances of failure, but there are also splendid chances of success. In the African communal group, ties of family and blood, of mother and child, of group relationship, made the group leadership strong, even if not always toward the highest culture. In the case of the more artificial group among American Negroes, there are sources of strength in common memories of suffering in the past; in present threats of degradation and extinction; in common ambitions and ideals; in emulation and the determination to prove ability and desert. Here in subtle but real ways the communalism of the African clan can be transferred to the Negro American group, implemented by higher ideals of human accomplishment through the education and culture which have arisen and may further arise through contact of black folk with the modern world. The emotional wealth of the American Negro, the nascent art in song, dance, and drama can all be applied, not to amuse the white audience, but to inspire and direct the acting Negro group itself. I can conceive no more magnificent nor promising crusade in modern times. We have a chance here to teach industrial and cultural democracy to a world that bitterly needs it.

A nation can depend on force and therefore carry through plans of capitalistic industry, or state socialism, or co-operative commonwealth, despite the opposition of large and powerful minorities. They can use police and the militia to enforce their will, but this is dangerous. In the long run force defeats itself. It is only the consensus of the intelligent men of good will in a community or in a state that really can carry out a great program with absolute and ultimate authority. And by that same token, without the authority of the state, without force of police and army, a group of people who can attain such consensus is able to do anything to which the group agrees.

It is too much to expect that any such guiding consensus will entirely eliminate dissent, but it will make agreement so overwhelming that eventual clear irrational dissent can safely be ignored. When real and open democratic control is intelligent enough to select of its own accord on the whole the best, most courageous, most expert and scholarly leadership, then the problem of democracy within the Negro group is solved and by that same token the possibility of American Negroes entering into world democracy and taking their rightful place according to their knowledge and power is also sure. Here then is the economic ladder by which the American Negro, achieving new social institutions, can move pari passu with the modern world into a new heaven and a new earth.

PHILOSOPHY AND OPINIONS

Marcus Garvey

[For six hectic years before he was finally imprisoned and then deported, Marcus Garvey preached a gospel of "Africa for Africans" to a following that some estimated, perhaps overgenerously, at 4 million people. Garvey came to the United States from Jamaica in 1916 and, within a year, had organized the Universal Negro Improvement Association (UNIA) in New York. His initial following was among fellow Jamaicans but, amidst the rising tide of race consciousness in the American Negro after World War I, Garvey's appeal reached thousands in Harlem and other urban areas. In January, 1918, he launched the *Negro World*, a newspaper that Claude McKay, another Jamaican, dubbed "the best edited colored weekly in New York." In 1919, an attack on his life led to further publicity for Garvey as a persecuted martyr. In the same year, Garvey founded the Black Star Line, a shipping venture that eventually led to his prosecution for mail fraud. In August, 1920, the UNIA held a highly successful international convention in New York. There were parades featuring the African Legion and the Black Cross Nurses, and 25,000 gathered at Madison Square Garden to hear Garvey speak. At the peak of his influence, in 1921, Garvey had organized the largest movement of Negroes in American history.

The material reprinted here, which is taken from an edition of his writings and speeches edited by his second wife, Amy Jacques-Garvey, in 1923, is typical of the African nationalism for which he has remained famous. Garvey's critics, of whom there were many even at the peak of his power, have always pointed out that his desire to form an African nation of the world's 400 million black people was an unrealistic dream. Even in the United States, where Garvey had his largest following, there was probably not a very high percentage who wanted to leave the country. If this opinion was correct, it left unexplained his program's enormous appeal, which has usually been attributed to the growing frustration of the thousands of Negroes who migrated North after the turn of the century. American blacks were aware of the economic and political exploitation of their group as a whole, their exclusion from the "mobility" and status available to white members of society, and their disproportionately small share of the wealth. As the years after emancipation wore on, Negroes, many of whom faced quiet hopelessness year after year, became cynical over the good will of white folk, and were increasingly torn between escape and angry, though perforce silent, accommodation. Garvey's success could, thus, be seen as a measure of the deep dissatisfaction and unrest in the Negro community.

The criticism of Garvey by Negro intellectuals mellowed somewhat after he passed from the scene. James Weldon Johnson wrote in 1930:

> Garvey failed, yet he might have succeeded with more than moderate success. He had energy and daring and the Napoleonic personality. . . . He stirred the imagination of the Negro masses as no Negro ever had. He raised more money in a few years than any other Negro organization dreamed of. He had great power and great possibilities within his grasp. But his deficiencies as a leader outweighed his abilities. . . . As he grew in power, he fought every other Negro rights organization in the country, especially the National Association for the Advancement of Colored People.

W. E. B. Du Bois, who had engaged in several bitter exchanges with Garvey and whose promotion of Pan-African congresses was sometimes confused with the Garvey movement, wrote in 1940:

> It was a grandiose and bombastic scheme, utterly impracticable as a whole, but it was sincere and had some practical features; and Garvey proved not only an astonishing popular leader, but a master of propaganda. Within a few years, news of his movement, of his promises and plans, reached Europe and Asia, and penetrated every corner of Africa.

Garvey returned to Jamaica after he was deported in 1927 and later centered his activities in London. He was never able to repeat his American success, but his reputation as the father of African nationalism has steadily increased since his death in 1940.]

SHALL THE NEGRO BE EXTERMINATED?

The Negro now stands at the cross roads of human destiny. He is at the place where he must either step forward or backward. If he goes backward he dies; if he goes forward it will be with the hope of a greater life. Those of us who have developed our minds scientifically are compelled, by duty, to step out among the millions of the unthinking masses and convince them of the seriousness of the age in which we live.

From Adam and Eve

We are either on the way to a higher racial existence or racial extermination. This much is known and realized by every thoughtful race and nation; hence, we have the death struggle of the different races of Europe and Asia in the scramble of the survival of the fittest race.

As we look at things we see that the great world in which we live has undergone much change since the time of the creation. When God created the world, and all therein, He handed His authority over to the two beings He created in His own image; namely, Adam and Eve. From the time of Adam and Eve the human race has multiplied by leaps and bounds. Where we once had two persons to exercise authority over the world, we to-day have one billion five hundred millions claiming authority and possession of the same world that was once the property of the two.

The Tragedy of Race Extinction

When the Colonists of America desired possession of the land they saw that a weak aboriginal race was in their way. What did they do? They got hold of them, killed them, and buried them underground. This is a fair indication of what will happen to the weaker peoples of the world in another two or three hundred years when the stronger races will have developed themselves to the position of complete mastery of all things material. They will not then as they have not in the past, allow a weak and defenceless race to stand in their way, especially if in their doing so they will endanger their happiness, their comfort and their pleasures. These are the things that strike the thoughtful Negro as being dangerous, and these are the things that cause us who make up the Universal Negro Improvement Association to be fighting tenaciously for the purpose of building up a strong Negro race, so as to make it impossible for us to be exterminated in the future to make room for the stronger races, even as the North American Indian has been exterminated to make room for the great white man on this North American continent.

The illiterate and shallow-minded Negro who can see no farther than his nose is now the greatest stumbling block in the way of the race. He tells us that we must be satisfied with our condition; that we must not think of building up a nation of our own, that we must not seek to organize ourselves racially, but that we must depend upon the good feeling of the other fellow for the solution of the problem that now confronts us. This is a dangerous policy and it is my duty to warn the four hundred million Negroes of the world against this kind of a leadership— a leadership that will try to make Negroes believe that all will be well without their taking upon themselves the task of bettering their condition politically, industrially, educationally and otherwise.

The time has come for those of us who have the vision of the future to inspire our people to a closer kinship, to a closer love of self, because it is only through this appreciation of self will we be able to rise to that higher life that will make us not an extinct race in the future, but a race of men fit to survive.

The Price of Leadership

Those of us who are blazing the way in this new propaganda of the Universal Negro Improvement Association to enlighten our people everywhere are at times very much annoyed and discouraged by the acts of our own people in that consciously or unconsciously they do so many things to hurt our deeper feeling of loyalty and love for the race. But what can we do? Can we forsake them because they hurt our feelings? Surely not. Painful though it may be to be interfered with and handicapped in the performance of the higher sense of duty, yet we must, martyr-like, make up our minds and our hearts to pay the price of leadership. We must be sympathetic, we must be forgiving, we must really have forbearance, so that when the ignorant and illiterate fellow who happens to be a member of your own race stands up to block the passage of some cause that you believe would be to his benefit and to yours as a people you will be able to overlook him, even though he fosters his opposition with the greatest amount of insult to your intelligence and to your dignity.

The excuse that some of our most brilliant men give for not identifying themselves with race movements is, that they cannot tolerate the interference of the illiterate Negro, who, being a member of the same organization will attempt to dictate what you should do in the interest of the race, when his act is based upon no deeper judgment than his like or dislike for the person he is opposing, or the satisfaction it would give him to embarrass the person he feels like opposing. Many an able leader is lost to his race because of this fear, and sometimes we must admit the reasonableness of this argument; but as I have said leadership means martyrdom, leadership means sacrifice, leadership means giving up one's personality, giving up of everything for the cause that is worth while. It is only because of that feeling that I personally continue to lead the Universal Negro Improvement Association, because like every other leader, I have had to encounter the opposition, the jealousy, the plotting of men who take advantage of the situation, simply because they happen to be members of the organization, and that we may have to depend upon their vote one way or the other for the good of the cause. Not that some of us care one row of pins about what the other fellow thinks, but when it is considered that we can only achieve success through harmony and unity, then it can be realized how much one has to sacrifice as a leader for getting that harmony that is necessary to bring about the results that are desired.

The White Race

We desire harmony and unity to-day more than ever, because it is only through the bringing together of the four hundred million Negroes into one mighty bond that we can successfully pilot our way through the avenues of opposition and the oceans of difficulties that seem to confront us. When it is considered that the great white race is making a herculean struggle to become the only surviving race of the centuries, and when it is further considered that the great yellow race under the leadership of Japan is making a like struggle, then more than ever the seriousness of the situation can be realized as far as our race is concerned. If we sit supinely by and allow the great white race to lift itself in numbers and in power, it will mean that in another five hundred years this full grown race of white men will in turn exterminate the weaker race of black men for the purpose of finding enough room on this limited mundane sphere to accommodate that race which will have numerically multiplied itself into many billions. This is the danger point. What will become of the Negro in another five hundred years if he does not organize now to develop and to protect himself? The answer is that he will be exterminated for the purpose of making room for the other races that will be strong enough to hold their own against the oppositions of all and sundry.

An Appeal to the Intelligentsia

The leadership of the Negro of to-day must be able to locate the race, and not only for to-day but for all times. It is in the desire to locate the Negro in a position of prosperity and happiness in the future that the Universal Negro Improvement Association is making this great fight for the race's emancipation everywhere and the founding of a great African government. Every sober-minded Negro will see immediately the reason why we should support a movement of this kind. If we will survive then it must be done through our own effort, through our own energy. No race of weaklings can survive in the days of tomorrow, because they will be hard and strenuous days fraught with many difficulties.

I appeal to the higher intelligence as well as to the illiterate groups of our race. We must work together. Those of us who are better positioned intellectually must exercise forbearance with the illiterate and help them to see the right. If we happen to be members of the same organization, and the illiterate man tries to embarras you, do not become disgusted, but remember that he does it because he does not know better, and it is your duty to forbear and forgive because the ends that we serve are not of self, but for the higher development of the entire race. It is on this score, it is on this belief, that I make the sacrifice of self to help this downtrodden race of mine. Nevertheless, I say there is a limit to human patience, and we should not continue to provoke the other fellow against his human feelings for in doing so we may be but bringing down upon our own heads the pillars of the temple.

AFRICA FOR THE AFRICANS

For five years the Universal Negro Improvement Association has been advocating the cause of Africa for the Africans—that is, that the Negro peoples of the world should concentrate upon the object of building up for themselves a great nation in Africa.

When we started our propaganda toward this end several of the so-called intellectual Negroes who have been bamboozling the race for over half a century said that we were crazy, that the Negro peoples of the western world were not interested in Africa and could not live in Africa. One editor and leader went so far as to say at his so-called Pan-African Congress that American Negroes could not live in Africa, because the climate was too hot. All kinds of arguments have been adduced by these Negro intellectuals against the colonization of Africa by the black race. Some said that the black man would ultimately work out his existence alongside of the white man in countries founded and established by the latter. Therefore, it was not necessary for Negroes to seek an independent nationality of their own. The old time stories of "African fever," "African bad climate," "African mosquitos," "African savages," have been repeated by these "brainless intellectuals" of ours as a scare against our people in America and the West Indies taking a kindly interest in the new program of building a racial empire of our own in our Motherland. Now that years have rolled by and the Universal Negro Improvement Association has made the circuit of the world with its propaganda, we find eminent statesmen and leaders of the white race coming out boldly advocating the cause of colonizing Africa with the Negroes of the western world. A year ago Senator MacCullum (*sic*) of the Mississippi Legislature introduced a resolution in the House for the purpose of petitioning the Congress of the United States of America and the President to use their good influence in securing from the Allies sufficient territory in Africa in liquidation of the war debt, which territory should be used for the establishing of an independent nation for American Negroes. About the same time Senator France of Maryland gave expression to a similar desire in the Senate of the United States. During a speech on the "Soldiers' Bonus." He said: "We owe a big debt to Africa and one which we have too long ignored. I need not enlarge upon our peculiar interest in the obligation to the people of Africa. Thousands of Americans have for years been contributing to the missionary work which has been carried out by the noble men and women who have been sent out in that field by the churches of America."

Germany to the Front

This reveals a real change on the part of prominent statesmen in their attitude on the African question. Then comes another suggestion from Germany, for which Dr. Heinrich Schnee, a former Governor of German East Africa, is author. This German statesman suggests in an interview given out in Berlin, and published in New York, that America takes over the mandatories of Great Britain and France in Africa for the colonization of American Negroes. Speaking on the matter, he says "As regards the attempt to colonize Africa with the surplus American colored population, this would in a long way settle the vexed problem, and under the plan such as Senator France has outlined, might enable France and Great Britain to discharge their duties to the United States, and simultaneously ease the burden of German reparations which is paralyzing economic life."

With expressions as above quoted from prominent world statesmen, and from the demands made by such men as Senators France and McCullum, it is clear that the question of African nationality is not a far-fetched one, but is as reasonable and feasible as was the idea of an American nationality.

A "Program" at Last

I trust that the Negro peoples of the world are now convinced that the work of the Universal Negro Improvement Association is not a visionary one, but very practical, and that it is not so far fetched, but can be realized in a short while if the entire race will only co-operate and work toward the desired end. Now that the work of our organization has started to bear fruit we find that some of these "doubting Thomases" of three and four years ago are endeavoring to mix themselves up with the popular idea of rehabilitating Africa in the interest of the Negro. They are now advancing spurious "programs" and in a short while will endeavor to force themselves upon the public as advocates and leaders of the African idea.

It is felt that those who have followed the career of the Universal Negro Improvement Association will not allow themselves to be deceived by these Negro opportunists who have always sought to live off the ideas of other people.

The Dream of a Negro Empire

It is only a question of a few more years when Africa will be completely colonized by Negroes, as Europe is by the white race. What we want is an independent African nationality, and if America is to help the Negro peoples of the world establish such a nationality, then we welcome the assistance.

It is hoped that when the time comes for American and West Indian Negroes to settle in Africa, they will realize their responsibility and their duty. It will not be to go to Africa for the purpose of exercising an over-lordship over the natives, but it shall be the purpose of the Universal Negro Improvement Association to have established in Africa that brotherly co-operation which will make the interests of the African native and the American and West Indian Negro one and the same, that is to say, we shall enter into a common partnership to build up Africa in the interests of our race.

Oneness of Interests

Everybody knows that there is absolutely no difference between the native African and the American and West Indian Negroes, in that we are descendants from one common family stock. It is only a matter of accident that we have been divided and kept apart for over three hundred years, but it is felt that when the time has come for us to get back together, we shall do so in the spirit of brotherly love, and any Negro who expects that he will be assisted here, there or anywhere by the Universal Negro Improvement Association to exercise a haughty superiority over the fellows of his own race, makes a tremendous mistake. Such men had better remain where they are and not attempt to become in any way interested in the higher development of Africa.

The Negro has had enough of the vaunted practice of race superiority as inflicted upon him by others, therefore he is not prepared to tolerate a similar assumption on the part of his own people. In America and the West Indies, we have Negroes who believe themselves so much above their fellows as to cause them to think that any readjustment in the affairs of the race should be placed in their hands for them to exercise a kind of an autocratic and despotic control as others have done to us for centuries. Again I say, it would be advisable for such Negroes to take their hands and minds off the now popular idea of colonizing Africa in the interest of the Negro race, because their being identified with this new program will not in any way help us because of the existing feeling among Negroes everywhere not to tolerate the infliction of race or class superiority upon them, as is the desire of the self-appointed and self-created race leadership that we have been having for the last fifty years.

The Basis of an African Aristocracy

The masses of Negroes in America, the West Indies, South and Central America are in sympathetic accord with the aspirations of the native Africans. We desire to help them build up Africa as a Negro Empire, where every black man, whether he was born in Africa or in the Western world, will have the opportunity to develop on his own lines under the protection of the most favorable democratic institutions.

It will be useless, as before stated, for bombastic Negroes to leave America and the West Indies to go to Africa, thinking that they will have privileged positions to inflict upon the race that bastard aristocracy that they have tried to maintain in this Western world at the expense of the masses. Africa shall develop an aristocracy of its own, but it shall be based upon service and loyalty to race. Let all Negroes work toward that end. I feel that it is only a question of a few more years before our program will be accepted not only by the few statesmen of America who are now interested in it, but by the strong statesmen of the world, as the only solution to the great race problem. There is no other way to avoid the threatening war of the races that is bound to engulf all mankind, which has been prophesied by the world's greatest thinkers; there is no better method than by apportioning every race to its own habitat.

The time has really come for the Asiatics to govern themselves in Asia, as the Europeans are in Europe and the Western world, so also is it wise for the Africans to govern themselves as home, and thereby bring peace and satisfaction to the entire human family.

THE FUTURE AS I SEE IT

It comes to the individual, the race, the nation, once in a life time to decide upon the course to be pursued as a career. The hour has now struck for the individual Negro as well as the entire race to decide the course that will be pursued in the interest of our own liberty.

We who make up the Universal Negro Improvement Association have decided that we shall go forward, upward and onward toward the great goal of human liberty. We have determined among ourselves that all barriers placed in the way of our progress must be removed, must be cleared away for we desire to see the light of a brighter day.

The Negro Is Ready

The Universal Negro Improvement Association for five years has been proclaiming to the world the readiness of the Negro to carve out a pathway for himself in the course of life. Men of other races and nations have become alarmed at this attitude of the Negro in his desire to do things for himself and by himself. This alarm has become so universal that organizations have been brought into being here, there and everywhere for the purpose of deterring and obstructing this forward move of our race. Propaganda has been waged here, there and everywhere for the purpose of misinterpreting the intention of this organization; some have said that this organization seeks to create discord and discontent among the races; some say we are organized for the purpose of hating other people. Every sensible, sane and honest-minded person knows that the Universal Negro Improvement Association has no such intention. We are organized for the absolute purpose of bettering our condition, industrially, commercially, socially, religiously and politically. We are organized not to hate other men, but to lift ourselves, and to demand respect of all humanity. We have a program that we believe to be righteous; we believe it to be just, and we have made up our minds to lay down ourselves on the altar of sacrifice for the realization of this great hope of ours, based upon the foundation of righteousness. We declare to the world that Africa must be free, that the entire Negro race must be emancipated from industrial bondage, peonage and serfdom; we make no compromise, we make no apology in this our declaration. We do not desire to create offense on the part of other races, but we are determined that we shall be heard, that we shall be given the rights to which we are entitled.

The Propaganda of Our Enemies

For the purpose of creating doubts about the work of the Universal Negro Improvement Association, many attempts have been made to cast shadow and gloom over our work. They have even written the most uncharitable things about our organization; they have spoken so unkindly of our effort, but what do we care? They spoke unkindly and uncharitably about all the reform movements that have helped in the betterment of humanity. They maligned the great movement of the Christian religion; they maligned the great liberation movements of America, of France, of England, of Russia; can we expect, then, to escape being maligned in this, our desire for the liberation of Africa and the freedom of four hundred million Negroes of the world?

We have unscrupulous men and organizations working in opposition to us. Some trying to capitalize the new spirit that has come to the Negro to make profit out of it to their own selfish benefit; some are trying to set back the Negro from seeing the hope of his own liberty, and thereby poisoning our people's mind against the motives of our organization; but every sensible far-seeing Negro in this enlightened age knows what propaganda means. It is the medium of discrediting that which you are opposed to, so that the propaganda of our enemies will be of little avail as soon as we are rendered able to carry to our peoples scattered throughout the world the true message of our great organization.

"Crocodiles" as Friends

Men of the Negro race, let me say to you that a greater future is in store for us; we have no cause to lose hope, to become faint-hearted. We must realize that upon ourselves depend our destiny, out future; we must carve out that future, that destiny, and we who make up the Universal Negro Improvement Association have pledged ourselves that nothing in the world shall stand in our way, nothing in the world shall discourage us, but opposition shall make us work harder, shall bring us closer together so that as one man the millions of us will march on toward that goal that we have set for ourselves. The new Negro shall not be deceived. The new Negro refuses to take advice from anyone who has not felt with him, and suffered with him. We have suffered for three hundred years, therefore we feel that the time has come when only those who have suffered with us can interpret our feelings and our spirit. It takes the slave to interpret the feelings of the slave; it takes the unfortunate man to interpret the spirit of his unfortunate brother; and so it takes the suffering Negro to interpret the spirit of his comrade. It is strange that so many people are interested in the Negro now, willing to advise him how to act, and what organizations he should join, yet nobody was interested in the Negro to the extent of not making him a slave for two hundred and fifty years, reducing him to industrial peonage and serfdom after he was freed; it is strange that the same people can be so interested in the Negro now, as to tell him what organization he should follow and what leader he should support.

Whilst we are bordering on a future of brighter things, we are also at our danger period, when we must either accept the right philosophy, or go down by following deceptive propaganda which has hemmed us in for many centuries.

Deceiving the People

There is many a leader of our race who tells us that everything is well, and that all things will work out themselves and that a better day is coming. Yes, all of us know that a better day is coming; we all know that one day we will go home to Paradise, but whilst we are hoping by our Christian virtues to have an entry into Paradise we also realize that we are living on earth, and that the things that are practiced in Paradise are not practiced here. You have to treat this world as the world treats you; we are living in a temporal, material age, an age of activity, an age of racial, national selfishness. What else can you expect but to give back to the world what the world gives to you, and we are calling upon the four hundred million Negroes of the world to take a decided stand, a determined stand, that we shall occupy a firm position; that position shall be an emancipated race and a free nation of our own. We are determined that we shall have a free country; we are determined that we shall have a flag; we are determined that we shall have a government second to none in the world.

An Eye for an Eye

Men may spurn the idea, they may scoff at it; the metropolitan press of this country may deride us; yes, white men may laugh at the idea of Negroes talking about government; but let me tell you there is going to be a government, and let me say to you also that whatsoever you give, in like measure it shall be returned to you. The world is sinful, and therefore man believes in the doctrine of an eye for an eye, a tooth for a tooth. Everybody believes that revenge is God's, but at the same time we are men, and revenge sometimes springs up, even in the most Christian heart.

Why should man write down a history that will react against him? Why should man perpetrate deeds of wickedness upon his brother which will return to him in like measure? Yes, the Germans maltreated the French in the Franco-Prussian war of 1870, but the French got even with the Germans in 1918. It is history, and history will repeat itself. Beat the Negro, brutalize the Negro, kill the Negro, burn the Negro, imprison the Negro, scoff at the Negro, deride the Negro, it may come back to you one of these fine days, because the supreme destiny of man is in the hands of God. God is no respecter of persons, whether that person be white, yellow or black. Today the one race is up, tomorrow it has fallen; today the Negro seems to be the footstool of the other races and nations of the world; tomorrow the Negro may occupy the highest rung of the great human ladder.

But, when we come to consider the history of man, was not the Negro a power, was he not great once? Yes, honest students of history can recall the day when Egypt, Ethiopia and Timbuctoo towered in their civilizations, towered above Europe, towered above Asia. When Europe was inhabited by a race of cannibals, a race of savages, naked men, heathens and pagans, Africa was peopled with a race of cultured black men, who were masters in art, science and literature; men who were cultured and refined; men who, it was said, were like the gods. Even the great poets of old sang in beautiful sonnets of the delight it afforded the gods to be in companionship with the Ethiopians. Why, then, should we lose hope? Black men, you were once great; you shall be great again. Lose not courage, lose not faith, go forward. The thing to do is to get organized; keep separated and you will be exploited, you will be robbed, you will be killed. Get organized, and you will compel the world to respect you. If the world fails to give you consideration, because you are black men, because you are Negroes, four hundred millions of you shall, through organization, shake the pillars of the universe and bring down creation, even as Samson brought down the temple upon his head and upon the heads of the Philistines.

An Inspiring Vision

So Negroes, I say, through the Universal Negro Improvement Association, that there is much to live for. I have a vision of the future, and I see before me a picture of a redeemed Africa, with her dotted cities, with her beautiful civilization, with her millions of happy children, going to and fro. Why should I lose hope, why should I give up and take a back place in this age of progress? Remember that you are men, that God created you Lords of this creation. Lift up yourselves, men, take yourselves out of the mire and hitch your hopes to the stars; yes, rise as high as the very stars themselves. Let no man pull you down, let no man destroy your ambition, because man is but your companion, your equal; man is your brother; he is not your lord; he is not your sovereign master.

We of the Universal Negro Improvement Association feel happy; we are cheerful. Let them connive to destroy us; let them organize to destroy us; we shall fight the more. Ask me personally the cause of my success, and I say opposition; oppose me, and I fight the more, and if you want to find out the sterling worth of the Negro, oppose him, and under the leadership of the Universal Negro Improvement Association he shall fight his way to victory, and in the days to come, and I believe not far distant, Africa shall reflect a splendid demonstration of the worth of the Negro, of the determination of the Negro, to set himself free and to establish a government of his own.

THE NEW NEGRO

Alain Locke

[The beginning of
the Harlem Renaissance is generally agreed to have been marked by the
appearance of Claude McKay's "If We Must Die," which was inspired by
the widespread race riots of the summer of 1919. Other writers, of
course, had preceded McKay. The novels and stories of Charles W. Ches-
nutt, the poems of Paul Lawrence Dunbar, the writings of W. E. B. Du
Bois, and James Weldon Johnson's *Autobiography of an Ex-Coloured
Man* had all anticipated the awakening of the 1920's. But the Renaissance
was real enough. It marked the first time in American history that a
school of Negro writing had been recognized by whites, and the first
time, too, that the works of black writers had been considered as com-
parable to those of whites.

Johnson, whose book did not become a popular success until it was
reissued in 1927, remarked that the so-called Renaissance would be better
termed a "birth" than a "rebirth." This was not altogether correct; for
example, the antislavery movement of the nineteenth century had acted
as a kind of midwife for Negro literary talent. What was true was that
Negro artists of the 1920's commanded a sizable white audience for the
first time and that they were sensitive to the attention that was being
focused on them. Johnson saw another element that was new. As he
wrote in 1928:

> A number of approaches to the heart of the race problem have been tried,
> religious, educational, political, industrial, ethical, economic, sociological. . . .
> Today a newer approach is being tried, an approach which discards most
> of the older methods. . . . It depends more upon what the Negro himself
> does than upon what someone else does for him. It is the approach along
> the line of intellectual and artistic achievement by Negroes and may be
> called the art approach to the Negro problem. . . . The results of this
> method seem to carry a high degree of finality, to be the thing itself that
> was to be demonstrated.

Johnson, who was secretary of the NAACP from 1916 to 1930, felt that the Renaissance was evidence of a changing attitude on the part of the American people, a change for which the Negro artist and intellectual, by undermining assumptions about black inferiority, was directly responsible. His hopes that the artist was the key to better race relations were shared by Alain Locke, whose essay "The New Negro" is reprinted here. It was the opening essay in a book with the same title, edited by Locke at the height of the Renaissance, in 1925. The book was a collection of pieces by the best talents that had led the revival. Locke was a Harvard graduate, a Rhodes Scholar, and professor of philosophy at Howard University from 1913 until his death in 1952. His nationalism was of the cultural sort. He was extremely sensitive to the deep feeling of race that was becoming the "mainspring of Negro life," but, unlike Garvey, to whom he devoted very little attention, he did not base his hopes for Negro advancement on separation. His essay, among other things, is one of the best statements of the position that Negro nationalism is compatible with the true realization of the American mission.]

In the last decade something beyond the watch and guard of statistics has happened in the life of the American Negro and the three norns who have traditionally presided over the Negro problem have a changeling in their laps. The Sociologist, the Philanthropist, the Race-leader are not unaware of the New Negro, but they are at a loss to account for him. He simply cannot be swathed in their formulæ. For the younger generation is vibrant with a new psychology; the new spirit is awake in the masses, and under the very eyes of the professional observers is transforming what has been a perennial problem into the progressive phases of contemporary Negro life.

Could such a metamorphosis have taken place as suddenly as it has appeared to? The answer is no; not because the New Negro is not here, but because the Old Negro had long become more of a myth than a man. The Old Negro, we must remember, was a creature of moral debate and historical controversy. He has been a stock figure perpetuated as an historical fiction partly in innocent sentimentalism, partly in deliberate reactionism. The Negro himself has contributed his share to this through a sort of protective social mimicry forced upon him by the adverse circumstances of dependence. So for generations in the mind of America, the Negro has been more of a formula than a human being—a something to be argued about, condemned or defended, to be "kept down," or "in his place," or "helped up," to be worried with or worried over, harassed or patronized, a social bogey or a social burden. The thinking Negro even has been induced to share this same general attitude, to focus his attention on controversial issues, to see himself in the distorted perspective of a social problem. His shadow, so to speak, has been more real to him than his personality. Through having had to appeal from the unjust stereotypes of his oppressors and traducers to those of his liberators, friends and benefactors he has had to subscribe to the traditional positions from which his case has been viewed. Little true social or self-understanding has or could come from such a situation.

But while the minds of most of us, black and white, have thus burrowed in the trenches of the Civil War and Reconstruction, the actual march of development has simply flanked these positions, necessitating a sudden reorientation of view. We have not been watching in the right direction; set North and South on a sectional axis, we have not noticed the East till the sun has us blinking.

Recall how suddenly the Negro spirituals revealed themselves; suppressed for generations under the stereotypes of Wesleyan hymn harmony, secretive, half-ashamed, until the courage of being natural brought them out—and behold, there was folk-music. Similarly the mind of the Negro seems suddenly to have slipped from under the tyranny of social intimidation and to be shaking off the psychology of imitation and implied inferiority. By shedding the old chrysalis of the Negro problem we are achieving something like a spiritual emancipation. Until recently, lacking self-understanding, we have been almost as much of a problem to ourselves as we still are to others. But the decade that found us with a problem has left us with only a task. The multitude perhaps feels as yet only a strange relief and a new vague urge, but the thinking few know that in the reaction the vital inner grip of prejudice has been broken.

With this renewed self-respect and self-dependence, the life of the Negro community is bound to enter a new dynamic phase, the buoyancy from within compensating for whatever pressure there may be of conditions from without. The migrant masses, shifting from countryside to city, hurdle several generations of experience at a leap, but more important, the same thing happens spiritually in the life-attitudes and self-expression of the Young Negro, in his poetry, his art, his education and his new outlook, with the additional advantage, of course, of the poise and greater certainty of knowing what it is all about. From this comes the promise and warrant of a new leadership. As one of them has discerningly put it:

> We have tomorrow
> Bright before us
> Like a flame.
>
> Yesterday, a night-gone thing
> A sun-down name.
>
> And dawn today
> Broad arch above the road we came.
> We march!

This is what, even more than any "most creditable record of fifty years of freedom," requires that the Negro of to-day be seen through other than the dusty spectacles of past controversy. The day of "aunties," "uncles" and "mammies" is equally gone. Uncle Tom and Sambo have passed on, and even the "Colonel" and "George" play barnstorm rôles from which they escape with relief when the public spotlight is off. The popular melodrama has about played itself out, and it is time to scrap the fictions, garret the bogeys and settle down to a realistic facing of facts.

First we must observe some of the changes which since the traditional lines of opinion were drawn have rendered these quite obsolete. A main change has been, of course, that shifting of the Negro population which has made the Negro problem no longer exclusively or even predominantly Southern. Why should our minds remain sectionalized, when the problem itself no longer is? Then the trend of migration has not only been toward the North and the Central Midwest, but city-ward and to the great centers of industry—the problems of adjustment are new, practical, local and not peculiarly racial. Rather they are an integral part of the large industrial and social problems of our present-day democracy. And finally, with the Negro rapidly in process of class differentiation, if it ever was warrantable to regard and treat the Negro *en masse* it is becoming with every day less possible, more unjust and more ridiculous.

In the very process of being transplanted, the Negro is becoming transformed.

The tide of Negro migration, northward and city-ward, is not to be fully explained as a blind flood started by the demands of war industry coupled with the shutting off of foreign migration, or by the pressure of poor crops coupled with increased social terrorism in certain sections of the South and Southwest. Neither labor demand, the boll-weevil nor the Ku Klux Klan is a basic factor, however contributory any or all of them may have been. The wash and rush of this human tide on the beach line of the northern city centers is to be explained primarily in terms of a new vision of opportunity, of social and economic freedom, of a spirit to seize, even in the face of an extortionate and heavy toll, a chance for the improvement of conditions. With each successive wave of it, the movement of the Negro becomes more and more a mass movement toward the larger and the more democratic chance—in the Negro's case a deliberate flight not only from countryside to city, but from medieval America to modern.

Take Harlem as an instance of this. Here in Manhattan is not merely the largest Negro community in the world, but the first concentration in history of so many diverse elements of Negro life. It has attracted the African, the West Indian, the Negro American; has brought together the Negro of the North and the Negro of the South; the man from the city and the man from the town and village; the peasant, the student, the business man, the professional man, artist, poet, musician, adventurer and worker, preacher and criminal, exploiter and social outcast. Each group has come with its own separate motives and for its own special ends, but their greatest experience has been the finding of one another.

Proscription and prejudice have thrown these dissimilar elements into a common area of contact and interaction. Within this area, race sympathy and unity have determined a further fusing of sentiment and experience. So what began in terms of segregation becomes more and more, as its elements mix and react, the laboratory of a great race-welding. Hitherto, it must be admitted that American Negroes have been a race more in name than in fact, or to be exact, more in sentiment than in experience. The chief bond between them has been that of a common condition rather than a common consciousness; a problem in common rather than a life in common. In Harlem, Negro life is seizing upon its first chances for group expression and self-determination. It is—or promises at least to be—a race capital. That is why our comparison is taken with those nascent centers of folk-expression and self-determination which are playing a creative part in the world to-day. Without pretense to their political significance, Harlem has the same rôle to play for the New Negro as Dublin has had for the New Ireland or Prague for the New Czechoslovakia.

Harlem, I grant you, isn't typical—but it is significant, it is prophetic. No sane observer, however sympathetic to the new trend, would contend that the great masses are articulate as yet, but they stir, they move, they are more physically restless. The challenge of the new intellectuals among them is clear enough—the "race radicals" and realists who have broken with the old epoch of philanthropic guidance, sentimental appeal and protest. But are we after all only reading into the stirrings of a sleeping giant the dreams of an agitator? The answer is in the migrating peasant. It is the "man farthest down" who is most active in getting up. One of the most characteristic symptoms of this is the professional man himself migrating to recapture his constituency after a vain effort to maintain in some Southern corner what for years back seemed an established living and clientele. The clergyman following his errant flock, the physician or lawyer trailing his clients, supply the true clues. In a real sense it is the rank and file who are leading, and the leaders who are following. A transformed and transforming psychology permeates the masses.

When the racial leaders of twenty years ago spoke of developing race-pride and stimulating race-consciousness, and of the desirability of race solidarity, they could not in any accurate degree have anticipated the abrupt feeling that has surged up and now pervades the awakened centers. Some of the recognized Negro leaders and a powerful section of white opinion identified with "race work" of the older order have indeed attempted to discount this feeling as a "passing phase," an attack of "race nerves" so to speak, an "aftermath of the war," and the like. It has not abated, however, if we are to gauge by the present tone and temper of the Negro press, or by the shift in popular support from the officially recognized and orthodox spokesmen to those of the independent, popular, and often radical type who are unmistakable symptoms of a new order. It is a social disservice to blunt the fact that the Negro of the Northern centers has reached a stage where tutelage, even of the most interested and well-intentioned sort, must give place to new relationships, where positive self-direction must be reckoned with in ever increasing measure. The American mind must reckon with a fundamentally changed Negro.

The Negro too, for his part, has idols of the tribe to smash. If on the one hand the white man has erred in making the Negro appear to be that which would excuse or extenuate his treatment of him, the Negro, in turn, has too often unnecessarily excused himself because of the way he has been treated. The intelligent Negro of to-day is resolved not to make discrimination an extenuation for his shortcomings in performance, individual or collective; he is trying to hold himself at par, neither inflated by sentimental allowances nor depreciated by current social discounts. For this he must know himself and be known for precisely what he is, and for that reason he welcomes the new scientific rather than the old sentimental interest. Sentimental interest in the Negro has ebbed. We used to lament this as the falling off of our friends; now we rejoice and pray to be delivered both from self-pity and condescension. The mind of each racial group has had a bitter weaning, apathy or hatred on one side matching disillusionment or resentment on the other; but they face each other to-day with the possibility at least of entirely new mutual attitudes.

It does not follow that if the Negro were better known, he would be better liked or better treated. But mutual understanding is basic for any subsequent coöperation and adjustment. The effort toward this will at least have the effect of remedying in large part what has been the most unsatisfactory feature of our present stage of race relationships in America, namely the fact that the more intelligent and representative elements of the two race groups have at so many points got quite out of vital touch with one another.

The fiction is that the life of the races is separate, and increasingly so. The fact is that they have touched too closely at the unfavorable and too lightly at the favorable levels.

While inter-racial councils have sprung up in the South, drawing on forward elements of both races, in the Northern cities manual laborers may brush elbows in their everyday work, but the community and business leaders have experienced no such interplay or far too little of it. These segments must achieve contact or the race situation in America becomes desperate. Fortunately this is happening. There is a growing realization that in social effort the co-operative basis must supplant long-distance philanthropy, and that the only safeguard for mass relations in the future must be provided in the carefully maintained contacts of the enlightened minorities of both race groups. In the intellectual realm a renewed and keen curiosity is replacing the recent apathy; the Negro is being carefully studied, not just talked about and discussed. In art and letters, instead of being wholly caricatured, he is being seriously portrayed and painted.

To all of this the New Negro is keenly responsive as an augury of a new democracy in American culture. He is contributing his share to the new social understanding. But the desire to be understood would never in itself have been sufficient to have opened so completely the protectively closed portals of the thinking Negro's mind. There is still too much possibility of being snubbed or patronized for that. It was rather the necessity for fuller, truer self-expression, the realization of the unwisdom of allowing social discrimination to segregate him mentally, and a counter-attitude to cramp and fetter his own living—and so the "spite-wall" that the intellectuals built over the "color-line" has happily been taken down. Much of this reopening of intellectual contacts has centered in New York and has been richly fruitful not merely in the enlarging of personal experience, but in the definite enrichment of American art and letters and in the clarifying of our common vision of the social tasks ahead.

The particular significance in the re-establishment of contact between the more advanced and representative classes is that it promises to off-set some of the unfavorable reactions of the past, or at least to re-surface race contacts somewhat for the future. Subtly the conditions that are molding a New Negro are molding a new American attitude.

However, this new phase of things is delicate; it will call for less charity but more justice; less help, but infinitely closer understanding. This is indeed a critical stage of race relationships because of the likelihood, if the new temper is not understood, of engendering sharp group antagonism and a second crop of more calculated prejudice. In some quarters, it has already done so. Having weaned the Negro, public opinion cannot continue to paternalize. The Negro to-day is inevitably moving forward under the control largely of his own objectives. What are these objectives? Those of his outer life are happily already well and finally formulated, for they are none other than the ideals of American institutions and democracy. Those of his inner life are yet in process of formation, for the new psychology at present is more of a consensus of feeling than of opinion, of attitude rather than of program. Still some points seem to have crystallized.

Up to the present one may adequately describe the Negro's "inner objectives" as an attempt to repair a damaged group psychology and re-shape a warped social perspective. Their realization has required a new mentality for the American Negro. And as it matures we begin to see its effects; at first, negative, iconoclastic, and then positive and constructive. In this new group psychology we note the lapse of sentimental appeal, then the development of a more positive self-respect and self-reliance; the repudiation of social dependence, and then the gradual recovery from hypersensitiveness and "touchy" nerves, the repudiation of the double standard of judgment with its special philanthropic allowances and then the sturdier desire for objective and scientific appraisal; and finally the rise from social disillusionment to race pride, from the sense of social debt to the responsibilities of social contribution, and offsetting the necessary working and commonsense acceptance of restricted conditions, the belief in ultimate esteem and recognition. Therefore the Negro to-day wishes to be known for what he is, even in his faults and shortcomings, and scorns a craven and precarious survival at the price of seeming to be what he is not. He resents being spoken of as a social ward or minor, even by his own, and to be regarded a chronic patient for the sociological clinic, the sick man of American Democracy. For the same reasons, he himself is through with those social nostrums and panaceas, the so-called "solutions" of his "problem," with which he and the country have been so liberally dosed in the past. Religion, freedom, education, money—in turn, he has ardently hoped for and peculiarly trusted these things; he still believes in them, but not in blind trust that they alone will solve his life-problem.

Each generation, however, will have its creed, and that of the present is the belief in the efficacy of collective effort, in race co-operation. This deep feeling of race is at present the mainspring of Negro life. It seems to be the outcome of the reaction to proscription and prejudice; an attempt, fairly successful on the whole, to convert a defensive into an offensive position, a handicap into an incentive. It is radical in tone, but not in purpose and only the most stupid forms of opposition, misunderstanding or persecution could make it otherwise. Of course, the thinking Negro has shifted a little toward the left with the world-trend, and there is an increasing group who affiliate with radical and liberal movements. But fundamentally for the present the Negro is radical on race matters, conservative on others, in other words, a "forced radical," a social protestant rather than a genuine radical. Yet under further pressure and injustice iconoclastic thought and motives will inevitably increase. Harlem's quixotic radicalisms call for their ounce of democracy to-day lest to-morrow they be beyond cure.

The Negro mind reaches out as yet to nothing but American wants, American ideas. But this forced attempt to build his Americanism on race values is a unique social experiment, and its ultimate success is impossible except through the fullest sharing of American culture and institutions. There should be no delusion about this. American nerves in sections unstrung with race hysteria are often fed the opiate that the trend of Negro advance is wholly separatist, and that the effect of its operation will be to encyst the Negro as a benign foreign body in the body politic. This cannot be—even if it were desirable. The racialism of the Negro is no limitation or reservation with respect to American life; it is only a constructive effort to build the obstructions in the stream of his progress into an efficient dam of social energy and power. Democracy itself is obstructed and stagnated to the extent that any of its channels are closed. Indeed they cannot be selectively closed. So the choice is not between one way for the Negro and another way for the rest, but between American institutions frustrated on the one hand and American ideals progressively fulfilled and realized on the other.

There is, of course, a warrantably comfortable feeling in being on the right side of the country's professed ideals. We realize that we cannot be undone without America's undoing. It is within the gamut of this attitude that the thinking Negro faces America, but with variations of mood that are if anything more significant than the attitude itself. Sometimes we have it taken with the defiant ironic challenge of McKay:

> Mine is the future grinding down to-day
> Like a great landslip moving to the sea,
> Bearing its freight of debris far away

> Where the green hungry waters restlessly
> Heave mammoth pyramids, and break and roar
> Their eerie challenge to the crumbling shore.

Sometimes, perhaps more frequently as yet, it is taken in the fervent and almost filial appeal and counsel of Weldon Johnson's:

> O Southland, dear Southland!
> Then why do you still cling
> To an idle age and a musty page,
> To a dead and useless thing?

But between defiance and appeal, midway almost between cynicism and hope, the prevailing mind stands in the mood of the same author's *To America*, an attitude of sober query and stoical challenge:

> How would you have us, as we are?
> Or sinking 'neath the load we bear,
> Our eyes fixed forward on a star,
> Or gazing empty at despair?
>
> Rising or falling? Men or things?
> With dragging pace or footsteps fleet?
> Strong, willing sinews in your wings,
> Or tightening chains about your feet?

More and more, however, an intelligent realization of the great discrepancy between the American social creed and the American social practice forces upon the Negro the taking of the moral advantage that is his. Only the steadying and sobering effect of a truly characteristic gentleness of spirit prevents the rapid rise of a definite cynicism and counter-hate and a defiant superiority feeling. Human as this reaction would be, the majority still deprecate its advent, and would gladly see it forestalled by the speedy amelioration of its causes. We wish our race pride to be a healthier, more positive achievement than a feeling based upon a realization of the shortcomings of others. But all paths toward the attainment of a sound social attitude have been difficult; only a relatively few enlightened minds have been able as the phrase puts it "to rise above" prejudice. The ordinary man has had until recently only a hard choice between the alternatives of supine and humiliating submission and stimulating but hurtful counter-prejudice. Fortunately from some inner, desperate resourcefulness has recently sprung up the simple expedient of fighting prejudice by mental passive resistance, in other words by trying to ignore it. For the few, this manna may perhaps be effective, but the masses cannot thrive upon it.

Fortunately there are constructive channels opening out into which the balked social feelings of the American Negro can flow freely.

Without them there would be much more pressure and danger than there is. These compensating interests are racial but in a new and enlarged way. One is the consciousness of acting as the advance-guard of the African peoples in their contact with Twentieth Century civilization; the other, the sense of a mission of rehabilitating the race in world esteem from that loss of prestige for which the fate and conditions of slavery have so largely been responsible. Harlem, as we shall see, is the center of both these movements; she is the home of the Negro's "Zionism." The pulse of the Negro world has begun to beat in Harlem. A Negro newspaper carrying news material in English, French and Spanish, gathered from all quarters of America, the West Indies and Africa has maintained itself in Harlem for over five years. Two important magazines, both edited from New York, maintain their news and circulation consistently on a cosmopolitan scale. Under American auspices and backing, three pan-African congresses have been held abroad for the discussion of common interests, colonial questions and the future cooperative development of Africa. In terms of the race question as a world problem, the Negro mind has leapt, so to speak, upon the parapets of prejudice and extended its cramped horizons. In so doing it has linked up with the growing group consciousness of the dark-peoples and is gradually learning their common interests. As one of our writers has recently put it: "It is imperative that we understand the white world in its relations to the non-white world." As with the Jew, persecution is making the Negro international.

As a world phenomenon this wider race consciousness is a different thing from the much asserted rising tide of color. Its inevitable causes are not of our making. The consequences are not necessarily damaging to the best interests of civilization. Whether it actually brings into being new Armadas of conflict or argosies of cultural exchange and enlightenment can only be decided by the attitude of the dominant races in an era of racial change. With the American Negro, his new internationalism is primarily an effort to recapture contact with the scattered peoples of African derivation. Garveyism may be a transient, if spectacular, phenomenon, but the possible role of the American Negro in the future development of Africa is one of the most constructive and universally helpful missions that any modern people can lay claim to.

Constructive participation in such causes cannot help giving the Negro valuable group incentives, as well as increased prestige at home and abroad. Our greatest rehabilitation may possibly come through such channels, but for the present, more immediate hope rests in the revaluation by white and black alike of the Negro in terms of his artistic endowments and cultural contributions, past and prospective. It must be increasingly recognized that the Negro has already made very substantial contributions, not only in his folk-art, music especially, which has always found appreciation, but in larger, though humbler and less acknowledged ways. For generations the Negro has been the peasant matrix of that section of America which has most undervalued him, and here he has contributed not only materially in labor and in social patience, but spiritually as well. The South has unconsciously absorbed the gift of his folk-temperament. In less than half a generation it will be easier to recognize this, but the fact remains that a leaven of humor, sentiment, imagination and tropic nonchalance has gone into the making of the South from a humble, unacknowledged source. A second crop of the Negro's gifts promises still more largely. He now becomes a conscious contributor and lays aside the status of a beneficiary and ward for that of a collaborator and participant in American civilization. The great social gain in this is the releasing of our talented group from the arid fields of controversy and debate to the productive fields of creative expression. The especially cultural recognition they win should in turn prove the key to that revaluation of the Negro which must precede or accompany any considerable further betterment of race relationships. But whatever the general effect, the present generation will have added the motives of self-expression and spiritual development to the old and still unfinished task of making material headway and progress. No one who understandingly faces the situation with its substantial accomplishment or views the new scene with its still more abundant promise can be entirely without hope. And certainly, if in our lifetime the Negro should not be able to celebrate his full initiation into American democracy, he can at least, on the warrant of these things, celebrate the attainment of a significant and satisfying new phase of group development, and with it a spiritual Coming of Age.

THE NEGRO ARTIST AND THE RACIAL MOUNTAIN

Langston Hughes

[Black artists, even when their work has been molded in the white artistic tradition, have reflected their group experience of oppression, unique in America.

The Negro folk-tradition, which preserved the stories, the spirituals, and the dance forms that have been the source of much creative art of the twentieth century, was the product of the suffering and aspirations of a people bent but not broken under the yoke of slavery. The slave, in his nondeliberate art, expressed a yearning for things as they ought to have been but were not. His art taught lessons, aroused emotions, and afforded pleasures that are a testimony to the preservation of his humanity.

The conscious Negro artist, as he emerged in the twentieth century, struggled with a dilemma that is still unresolved. As W. E. B. Du Bois wrote at the turn of the century:

> The Negro is a sort of a seventh son, born with a veil, and gifted with second-sight in this American world—a world which yields him no true self-consciousness, but only lets him see himself through the revelation of the other world. . . . One ever feels his twoness—an American, a Negro; two souls, two thoughts, two unreconciled strivings; two warring ideals in one dark body, whose dogged strength alone keeps it from being torn asunder.

This dilemma of "twoness" is best exemplified in the literary upheaval, often called the Negro Renaissance, that occurred in the 1920's and in a similar artistic revolt that began about forty years later. The "new"

Negro of the 1920's had a number of things in common with the "new" black of the 1960's. Both were concerned to make of Negro history a revelation of the way things were. Both turned to poetry and drama to exemplify the way things should be. Both celebrated the folk tradition, with its heritage of rhythm and warmth, which had achieved new levels of irony and humor in the blues and in jazz; and both explored an identification with Africa.

The literary credo of Langston Hughes, which is reprinted here from a 1926 issue of the *Nation*, reflects a new sympathy for the lives of the Negro masses and is an indication that the Negro artist was overcoming his sense of inferiority. The artist, if successful, would emancipate himself and his people. By emancipating himself from white critical opinion and, thus, from white symbols and imagery, the artist would not be trapped by the familiar stereotypes and pat situations that a white audience demanded. By writing about real Negroes he could free those of his people who were still acting more or less in conformity with the stereotypes and, therefore, helping to perpetuate a white mythology. The dilemma of "twoness" was, thus, reformulated as a dilemma of writing either for a white or for a black audience.

Forty years later, the problem was seen as similar, but much more drastic. The rising race-consciousness had reached flood tide. Black writers and artists were no longer afraid of the reactions of a white audience. The white man, it was claimed, was dead or was dying along with the Negro middle class, which, insofar as it tried to assimilate, was also white. For example, LeRoi Jones stressed, in 1963, that the Negro's isolation from the American mainstream, however painful it may have been, offers the black writer an opportunity denied to members of other groups. It is not just that the black writer has been outside the mainstream. He has been outside and inside at the same time. "The paradox of the Negro experience in America," Jones had written a year earlier, "is that it is a separate experience, but inseparable from the complete fabric of American life."

Much of Hughes's writing is lighthearted, but this does not hide the fact that his characters reflect the suffering inherent in centuries of oppression. Hughes followed his credo for the rest of his long career. In the process, he created, in his dramatic characters, an invaluable portrait of Negro life that has exerted a steady influence on Negro writers.]

One of the most promising of the young Negro poets said to me once, "I want to be a poet—not a Negro poet," meaning, I believe, "I want to write like a white poet"; meaning subconsciously, "I would like to be a white poet"; meaning behind that, "I would like to be white." And I was sorry the young man said that, for no great poet has ever been afraid

of being himself. And I doubted then that, with his desire to run away
spiritually from his race, this boy would ever be a great poet. But this
is the mountain standing in the way of any true Negro art in America
—this urge within the race toward whiteness, the desire to pour racial
individuality into the mold of American standardization, and to be as
little Negro and as much American as possible.

But let us look at the immediate background of this young poet. His
family is of what I suppose one would call the Negro middle class: people who are by no means rich yet never uncomfortable nor hungry—
smug, contented, respectable folk, members of the Baptist church. The
father goes to work every morning. He is a chief steward at a large
white club. The mother sometimes does fancy sewing or supervises
parties for the rich families of the town. The children go to a mixed
school. In the home they read white papers and magazines. And the
mother often says "Don't be like niggers" when the children are bad. A
frequent phrase from the father is, "Look how well a white man does
things." And so the word white comes. to be unconsciously a symbol of
all the virtues. It holds for the children beauty, morality, and money.
The whisper of "I want to be white" runs silently through their minds.
This young poet's home is, I believe, a fairly typical home of the colored
middle class. One sees immediately how difficult it would be for an artist
born in such a home to interest himself in interpreting the beauty of
his own people. He is never taught to see that beauty. He is taught
rather not to see it, or if he does, to be ashamed of it when it is not according to Caucasian patterns.

For racial culture the home of a self-styled "high-class" Negro has
nothing better to offer. Instead there will perhaps be more aping of
things white than in a less cultured or less wealthy home. The father is
perhaps a doctor, lawyer, landowner, or politician. The mother may be
a social worker, or a teacher, or she may do nothing and have a maid.
Father is often dark but he has usually married the lightest woman he
could find. The family attend a fashionable church where few really
colored faces are to be found. And they themselves draw a color line. In
the North they go to white theaters and white movies. And in the South
they have at least two cars and a house "like white folks." Nordic manners, Nordic faces, Nordic hair, Nordic art (if any), and an Episcopal
heaven. A very high mountain indeed for the would-be racial artist to
climb in order to discover himself and his people.

But then there are the low-down folks, the so-called common element,
and they are the majority—may the Lord be praised. The people who
have their nip of gin on Saturday nights and are not too important to
themselves or the community, or too well fed, or too learned to watch
the lazy world go round. They live on Seventh Street in Washington or
State Street in Chicago and they do not particularly care whether they
are like white folks or anybody else. Their joy runs, bang! into ecstasy.
Their religion soars to a shout. Work maybe a little today, rest a little
tomorrow. Play awhile. Sing awhile. O, let's dance! These common people are not afraid of spirituals, as for a long time their more intellectual
brethren were, and jazz is their child. They furnish a wealth of colorful,

distinctive material for any artist because they still hold their own individuality in the face of American standardizations. And perhaps these common people will give to the world its truly great Negro artist, the one who is not afraid to be himself. Whereas the better-class Negro would tell the artist what to do, the people at least let him alone when he does appear. And they are not ashamed of him—if they know he exists at all. And they accept what beauty is their own without question.

Certainly there is, for the American Negro artist who can escape the restrictions the more advanced among his own group would put upon him, a great field of unused material ready for his art. Without going outside his race, and even among the better classes with their "white" culture and conscious American manners, but still Negro enough to be different, there is sufficient matter to furnish a black artist with a lifetime of creative work. And when he chooses to touch on the relations between Negroes and whites in this country with their innumerable overtones and undertones, surely, and especially for literature and the drama, there is an inexhaustible supply of themes at hand. To these the Negro artist can give his racial individuality, his heritage of rhythm and warmth, and his incongruous humor that is often, as in the Blues, becomes ironic laughter mixed with tears. But let us look again at the mountain.

A prominent Negro clubwoman in Philadelphia paid eleven dollars to hear Raquel Meller sing Andalusian popular songs. But she told me a few weeks before she would not think of going to hear "that woman," Clara Smith, a great black artist, sing Negro folksongs. And many an upper-class Negro church, even now, would not dream of employing a spiritual in its services. The drab melodies in white folks' hymnbooks are much to be preferred. "We want to worship the Lord correctly and quietly. We don't believe in 'shouting.' Let's be dull like the Nordics," they say, in effect.

The road for the serious black artist, then, who would produce a racial art is most certainly rocky and the mountain is high. Until recently he received almost no encouragement for his work from either white or colored people. The fine novel of Chestnutt go out of print with neither race noticing their passing. The quaint charm and humor of Dunbar's dialect verse brought to him, in his day, largely the same kind of encouragement one would give a sideshow freak (A colored man writing poetry! How odd!) or a clown (How amusing!).

The present vogue in things Negro, although it may do as much harm as good for the budding colored artist, has at least done this: it has brought him forcibly to the attention of his own people among whom for so long, unless the other race had noticed him beforehand, he was a prophet with little honor. I understand that Charles Gilpin acted for years in Negro theaters without any special acclaim from his own, but when Broadway gave him eight curtain calls, Negroes, too, began to beat a tin pan in his honor. I know a young colored writer, a manual worker by day, who had been writing well for the colored magazines for some years, but it was not until he recently broke into the white publications and his first book was accepted by a prominent New York publisher that the "best" Negroes in his city took the trouble to discover that he lived there. Then almost immediately they decided to give a grand dinner for him. But the society ladies were careful to whisper to his mother that perhaps she'd better not come. They were not sure she would have an evening gown.

The Negro artist works against an undertow of sharp criticism and misunderstanding from his own group and unintentional bribes from the whites. "O, be respectable, write about nice people, show how good we are," say the Negroes. "Be stereotyped, don't go too far, don't shatter our illusions about you, don't amuse us too seriously. We will pay you," say the whites. Both would have told Jean Toomer not to write "Cane." The colored people did not praise it. The white people did not buy it. Most of the colored people who did read "Cane" hate it. They are afraid of it. Although the critics gave it good reviews the public remained indifferent. Yet (excepting the work of DuBois) "Cane" contains the finest prose written by a Negro in America. And like the singing of Robeson, it is truly racial.

But in spite of the Nordicized Negro intelligentsia and the desires of some white editors we have an honest American Negro literature already with us. Now I await the rise of the Negro theater. Our folk music, having achieved world-wide fame, offers itself to the genius of the great individual American Negro composer who is to come. And within the next decade I expect to see the work of a growing school of colored artists who paint and model the beauty of dark faces and create with new technique the expressions of their own soul-world. And the Negro dancers who will dance like flame and the singers who will continue to carry our songs to all who listen—they will be with us in even greater numbers tomorrow.

Most of my own poems are racial in theme and treatment, derived from the life I know. In many of them I try to grasp and hold some of the meanings and rhythms of jazz. I am sincere as I know how to be in these poems and yet after every reading I answer questions like these from my own people: Do you think Negroes should always write about Negroes? I wish you wouldn't read some of your poems to white folks. How do you find anything interesting in a place like a cabaret? Why do you write about black people? You aren't black. What makes you do so many jazz poems?

But jazz to me is one of the inherent expressions of Negro life in America: the eternal tom-tom beating in the Negro soul—the tom-tom of revolt against weariness in a white world, a world of subway trains, and work, work, work; the tom-tom of joy and laughter, and pain swallowed in a smile. Yet the Philadelphia clubwoman is ashamed to say that her race created it and she does not like me to write about it. The old sub-conscious "white is best" runs through her mind. Years of study under white teachers, a life-time of white books, pictures, and papers, and white manners, morals, and Puritan standards made her dislike the spirituals. And now she turns up her nose at jazz and all its manifesta-tions—likewise almost everything else distinctly racial. She doesn't care for the Winold Reiss portraits of Negroes because they are "too Negro."

She does not want a true picture of herself from anybody. She wants the artist to flatter her, to make the white world believe that all Negroes are as smug and as near white in soul as she wants to be. But, to my mind, it is the duty of the younger Negro artist, if he accepts any duties at all from outsiders, to change through the force of his art that old whispering "I want to be white," hidden in the aspirations of his people, to "Why should I want to be white? I am a Negro—and beautiful!"

So I am ashamed for the black poet who says, "I want to be a poet, not a Negro poet," as though his own racial world were not as interesting as any other world. I am ashamed, too, for the colored artist who runs from the painting of Negro faces to the painting of sunsets after the manner of the academicians because he fears the strange un-whiteness of his own features. An artist must be free to choose what he does, certainly, but he must also never be afraid to do what he might choose.

Let the blare of Negro jazz bands and the bellowing voice of Bessie Smith singing Blues penetrate the closed ears of the colored near-intellectuals until they listen and perhaps understand. Let Paul Robeson singing Water Boy, and Rudolph Fisher writing about the streets of Harlem, and Jean Toomer holding the heart of Georgia in his hands, and Aaron Douglas drawing strange black fantasies cause the smug Negro middle class to turn from their white, respectable, ordinary books and papers to catch a glimmer of their own beauty. We younger Negro artists who create now intend to express our individual dark-skinned selves without fear or shame. If white people are pleased we are glad. If they are not, it doesn't matter. We know we are beautiful. And ugly too. The tom-tom cries and the tom-tom laughs. If colored people are pleased we are glad. If they are not, their displeasure doesn't matter either. We build our temples for tomorrow, strong as we know how, and we stand on top of the mountain, free within ourselves.

HOW "BIGGER" WAS BORN

Richard Wright

[Richard Wright was the first black literary figure with enough talent to make apparent the strain in the critical assumption underlying the category "Negro writer." *Native Son,* his second major work, was published in 1940 and was an immediate success. It became a Book-of-the-Month Club selection; a dramatic version, under the direction of Orson Welles, ran briefly on Broadway; and a movie, starring the author, was later made in Argentina (Wright had refused the film rights to Hollywood because they wanted to make the characters white). The essay reprinted here also appeared in 1940. It was a defense and explanation by the author of what he was about in the creation of Bigger Thomas, the hero of the novel.

The story of Bigger revolves around two killings. The first victim is Mary Dalton, the daughter of his white employer. Bigger has reluctantly escorted her to her room after an evening in which he has acted as guide to Chicago's South Side for Mary and her boyfriend. At evening's end, Mary is too drunk to manage by herself, and, when her blind mother appears at the door of the room, Bigger finds himself in a predicament that usually has spelled death for a black man. To preclude her crying out, he covers Mary's face with a pillow, and she suffocates. His life is now transformed:

> Though he had killed by accident, not once did he feel the need to tell himself that it had been an accident. He was black and he had been alone in a room where a white girl had been killed; therefore, he had killed her. That was what everybody would say anyhow, no matter what he said. . . . The hidden meaning of his life—a meaning which others did not see and which he had always tried to hide—had spilled out.

Bigger confides in Bessie, his own girlfriend, and the revelation drives him to kill her, too. If the first killing is accidental, the second is willful murder by someone rejoicing in the hatred that has given significance to his life. Bigger is pursued over the ghetto rooftops before being caught by the police. His conviction at the subsequent trial brings a death sentence, which his lawyer, in a long summary indictment of society's injustices against the Negro, tries unsuccessfully to avert.

The drama of Bigger's life, Wright felt, was produced by three centuries of oppression; Bigger's actions and feelings, he also felt, would be encountered on a vaster scale in the future. In the more extended analysis of "How 'Bigger' Was Born," Wright explored the circumstances that led to Bigger's anger. The black man's alternatives, Wright noted prophetically, were circumscribed by the need to respond to the closeness of and the incentives offered by white society; they lay between "blind rebellion . . . [and] a sweet otherworldly submissiveness." Bigger's fear and hatred of the society that excluded him made him a "nationalist," and his rejection of religion, combined with his need for fuufillment, drove him to rebellion, finally turning his anger against his own.

In retrospect, these alternatives can be seen as the same ones that faced a Malcolm X or a Martin Luther King; and Bigger himself can be seen as the embodiment of later theories that celebrated self-realization through violence. Wright's essay also focused on another aspect of Bigger's character that is often ignored. Bigger, in his aspirations and ideals, was also an American—a deprived American, to be sure, but one who was responding to the national rhetoric of freedom and opportunity that motivates all of us. But his "disinheritance" was such as to make him not even a "lukewarm supporter of the status quo." A dispossessed man in a land of plenty, Bigger, thus, carried within himself the potentialities for either Communism (a revolutionary redistribution of wealth) or Fascism (a felt need for a leader who would respond to the Negro's need for solidarity) as well as that striving for self-realization that was motivated by a need for a whole, fulfilled life. The complexities of Bigger were sufficient to make Wright hope he could create a figure that was symbolic of American life, or at least of the Bigger that is present in all Americans, white or black. Whether or not he succeeded, Wright captured the horror and the tragedy of the Negro's past in America with a universality that dwarfed his predecessors and inspired many future native sons.

Wright published another book, *Black Boy*, before leaving for Paris in 1946. His self-imposed exile, which lasted until his death in 1960, was as much owing to his disenchantment with the "money-grabbing, industrial civilization" in the United States as to his unwillingness to live where the Negro remained oppressed. The appearance of *Native Son* also marked the beginning of the end of Wright's flirtation with Communism, although he remained sympathetic to its ideology. He left the Party in 1944. His life in Paris introduced him to the writings of Kierkegaard and Jaspers, Sartre and Camus. The title of his next novel, *The Outsider* (1953), could have been a translation of Camus's *L'Etranger*. The protagonist, Cross Damon, abandons the middle-class aspirations that even Bigger harbored.

Wright also wrote nonfiction. *Black Power* (1954), *The Color Curtain* (1956), and *White Man, Listen!* (1957) are testimony to his attempt to cope with the estrangement of black people from the world political situation and from the dominant white culture. Wright's later fiction, most critics, both black and white, maintain, never equaled the power and drama of *Native Son*, and his major contribution still appears to be his deep understanding of racial issues in America.]

I am not so pretentious as to imagine that it is possible for me to account completely for my own book, *Native Son*. But I am going to try to account for as much of it as I can, the sources of it, the material that went into it, and my own years' long changing attitude toward that material.

In a fundamental sense, an imaginative novel represents the merging of two extremes; it is an intensely intimate expression on the part of a consciousness couched in terms of the most objective and commonly known events. It is at once something private and public by its very nature and texture. Confounding the author who is trying to lay his cards on the table is the dogging knowledge that his imagination is a kind of community medium of exchange: what he has read, felt, thought, seen, and remembered is translated into extensions as impersonal as a worn dollar bill.

The more closely the author thinks of why he wrote, the more he comes to regard his imagination as a kind of self-generating cement which glued his facts together, and his emotions as a kind of dark and obscure designer of those facts. Always there is something that is just beyond the tip of the tongue that could explain it all. Usually, he ends up by discussing something far afield, an act which incites skepticism and suspicion in those anxious for a straight-out explanation.

Yet the author is eager to explain. But the moment he makes the attempt his words falter, for he is confronted and defied by the inexplicable array of his own emotions. Emotions are subjective and he can communicate them only when he clothes them in objective guise; and how can he ever be so arrogant as to know when he is dressing up the right emotion in the right Sunday suit? He is always left with the uneasy notion that maybe *any* objective drapery is as good as *any* other for any emotion.

And the moment he does dress up an emotion, his mind is confronted with the riddle of that "dressed up" emotion, and he is left peering with eager dismay back into the dim reaches of his own incommunicable life. Reluctantly, he comes to the conclusion that to account for his book is to account for his life, and he knows that that is impossible. Yet, some curious, wayward motive urges him to supply the answer, for there is the feeling that his dignity as a living being is challenged by something within him that is not understood.

So, at the outset, I say frankly that there are phases of *Native Son* which I shall make no attempt to account for. There are meanings in my book of which I was not aware until they literally spilled out upon the paper. I shall sketch the outline of how I *consciously* came into possession of the materials that went into *Native Son*, but there will be many things I shall omit, not because I want to, but simply because I don't know them.

The birth of Bigger Thomas goes back to my childhood, and there was not just one Bigger, but many of them, more than I could count and more than you suspect. But let me start with the first Bigger, whom I shall call Bigger No. 1.

When I was a bareheaded, barefoot kid in Jackson, Mississippi, there was a boy who terrorized me and all of the boys I played with. If we were playing games, he would saunter up and snatch from us our balls, bats, spinning tops, and marbles. We would stand around pouting, sniffling, trying to keep back our tears, begging for our playthings. But Bigger would refuse. We never demanded that he give them back; we were afraid, and Bigger was bad. We had seen him clout boys when he was angry and we did not want to run that risk. We never recovered our toys unless we flattered him and made him feel that he was superior to us. Then, perhaps, if he felt like it, he condescended, threw them at us and then gave each of us a swift kick in the bargain, just to make us feel his utter contempt.

That was the way Bigger No. 1 lived. His life was a continuous challenge to others. At all times he *took* his way, right or wrong, and those who contradicted him had him to fight. And never was he happier than when he had someone cornered and at his mercy; it seemed that the deepest meaning of his squalid life was in him at such times.

I don't know what the fate of Bigger No. 1 was. His swaggering personality is swallowed up somewhere in the amnesia of my childhood. But I suspect that his end was violent. Anyway, he left a marked impression upon me; maybe it was because I longed secretly to be like him and was afraid. I don't know.

If I had known only one Bigger I would not have written *Native Son*. Let me call the next one Bigger No. 2; he was about seventeen and tougher than the first Bigger. Since I, too, had grown older, I was a little less afraid of him. And the hardness of this Bigger No. 2 was not directed toward me or the other Negroes, but toward the whites who ruled the South. He bought clothes and food on credit and would not pay for them. He lived in the dingy shacks of the white landlords and refused to pay rent. Of course, he had no money, but neither did we. We did without the necessities of life and starved ourselves, but he never would. When we asked him why he acted as he did, he would tell us (as though we were little children in a kindergarten) that the white folks had everything and he had nothing. Further, he would tell us that we were fools not to get what we wanted while we were alive in this world. We would listen and silently agree. We longed to believe and act as he did, but we were afraid. We were Southern Negroes and we were hungry and we wanted to live, but we were more willing to tighten our belts than risk conflict. Bigger No. 2 wanted to live and he did; he was in prison the last time I heard from him.

There was Bigger No. 3, whom the white folks called a "bad nigger." He carried his life in his hands in a literal fashion. I once worked as a ticket-taker in a Negro movie house (all movie houses in Dixie are Jim Crow; there are movies for whites and movies for blacks), and many times Bigger No. 3 came to the door and gave my arm a hard pinch and walked into the theater. Resentfully and silently, I'd nurse my bruised arm. Presently, the proprietor would come over and ask how things were going, I'd point into the darkened theater and say: "Bigger's in there." "Did he pay?" the proprietor would ask. "No, sir," I'd answer. The proprietor would pull down the corners of his lips and speak through his teeth: "We'll kill that goddamn nigger one of these days." And the episode would end right there. But later on Bigger No. 3 was killed during the days of Prohibition: while delivering liquor to a customer he was shot through the back by a white cop.

And then there was Bigger No. 4, whose only law was death. The Jim Crow laws of the South were not for him. But as he laughed and cursed and broke them, he knew that some day he'd have to pay for his freedom. His rebellious spirit made him violate all the taboos and consequently he always oscillated between moods of intense elation and depression. He was never happier than when he had outwitted some foolish customs, and he was never more melancholy then when brooding over the impossibility of his ever being free. He had no job, for he regarded digging ditches for fifty cents a day as slavery. "I can't live on that," he would say. Oft-times I'd find him reading a book; he would stop and in a joking, wistful, and cynical manner ape the antics of the white folks. Generally, he'd end his mimicry in a depressed state and say: "The white folks won't let us do nothing." Bigger No. 4 was sent to the asylum for the insane.

Then there was Bigger No. 5, who always rode the Jim Crow streetcars without paying and sat wherever he pleased. I remember one morning his getting into a streetcar (all streetcars in Dixie are divided into two sections: one section is for whites and is labeled—FOR WHITES; the other section is for Negroes and is labeled—FOR COLORED) and sitting in the white section. The conductor went to him and said: "Come on, nigger. Move over where you belong. Can't you read?" Bigger answered: "Naw, I can't read." The conductor flared up: "Get out of that seat!" Bigger took out his knife, opened it, held it nonchalantly in his hand, and replied: "Make me." The conductor turned red, blinked, clenched his fists, and walked away, stammering: "The goddam scum of the earth!" A small angry conference of white men took place in the front of the car and the Negroes sitting in the Jim Crow section overheard: "That's that Bigger Thomas nigger and you'd better leave 'im alone." The Negroes experienced an intense flash of pride and the streetcar moved on its journey without incident. I don't know what happened to Bigger No. 5. But I can guess.

The Bigger Thomases were the only Negroes I know of who consistently violated the Jim Crow laws of the South and got away with it, at least for a sweet brief spell. Eventually, the whites who restricted their lives made them pay a terrible price. They were shot, hanged, maimed, lynched, and generally hounded until they were either dead or their spirits broken.

There were many variations to this behavioristic pattern. Later on I encountered other Bigger Thomases who did not react to the locked-in Black Belts with this same extremity and violence. But before I use Bigger Thomas as a springboard for the examination of milder types, I'd better indicate more precisely the nature of the environment that produced these men, or the reader will be left with the impression that they were essentially and organically bad.

In Dixie there are two worlds, the white world and the black world, and they are physically separated. There are white schools and black schools, white churches and black churches, white businesses and black businesses, white graveyards and black graveyards, and, for all I know, a white God and a black God. . . .

This separation was accomplished after the Civil War by the terror of the Ku Klux Klan, which swept the newly freed Negro through arson, pillage, and death out of the United States Senate, the House of Representatives, the many state legislatures, and out of the public, social, and economic life of the South. The motive for this assault was simple and urgent. The imperialistic tug of history had torn the Negro from his African home and had placed him ironically upon the most fertile plantation areas of the South; and, when the Negro was freed, he outnumbered the whites in many of these fertile areas. Hence, a fierce and bitter struggle took place to keep the ballot from the Negro, for had he had a chance to vote, he would have automatically controlled the richest lands of the South and with them the social, political, and economic destiny of a third of the Republic. Though the South is politically a part of America, the problem that faced her was peculiar and the struggle between the whites and the blacks after the Civil War was in essence a struggle for power, ranging over thirteen states and involving the lives of tens of millions of people.

But keeping the ballot from the Negro was not enough to hold him in check; disfranchisement had to be supplemented by a whole panoply of rules, taboos, and penalties designed not only to insure peace (complete submission), but to guarantee that no real threat would ever arise. Had the Negro lived upon a common territory, separate from the bulk of the white population, this program of oppression might not have assumed such a brutal and violent form. But this war took place between people who were neighbors, whose homes adjoined, whose farms had common boundaries. Guns and disfranchisement, therefore, were not enough to make the black neighbor keep his distance. The white neighbor decided to limit the amount of education his black neighbor could receive; decided to keep him off the police force and out of the local national guards; to segregate him residentially; to Jim Crow him in public places; to restrict his participation in the professions and jobs; and to build up a vast, dense ideology of racial superiority that would justify any act of violence taken against him to defend white dominance; and further, to

condition him to hope for little and to receive that little without re-
belling.

But, because the blacks were so *close* to the very civilization which
sought to keep them out, because they could not *help* but react in
some way to its incentives and prizes, and because the very tissue of
their consciousness received its tone and timbre from the strivings of
that dominant civilization, oppression spawned among them a myriad
variety of reactions, reaching from outright blind rebellion to a sweet,
otherworldly submissiveness.

In the main, this delicately balanced state of affairs has not greatly
altered since the Civil War, save in those parts of the South which have
been industrialized or urbanized. So volatile and tense are these relations
that if a Negro rebels against rule and taboo, he is lynched and the reason for the lynching is usually called "rape," that catchword which has
garnered such vile connotations that it can rise a mob anywhere in the
South pretty quickly, even today.

Now for the variations in the Bigger Thomas pattern. Some of the
Negroes living under these conditions got religion, felt that Jesus would
redeem the void of living, felt that the more bitter life was in the present the happier it would be in the hereafter. Others, clinging still to
that brief glimpse of post-Civil War freedom, employed a thousand ruses
and stratagems of struggle to win their rights. Still others projected their
hurts and longings into more naive and mundane forms—blues, jazz,
swing—and, without intellectual guidance, tried to build up a compensa-
tory nourishment for themselves. Many labored under hot suns and then
killed the restless ache with alcohol. Then there were those who strove
for an education, and when they got it, enjoyed the financial fruits of it
in the style of their bourgeois oppressors. Usually they went hand in
hand with the powerful whites and helped to keep their groaning brothers in line, for that was the safest course of action. Those who did this
called themselves "leaders." To give you an idea of how completely these
"leaders" worked with those who oppressed, I can tell you that I lived
the first seventeen years of my life in the South without so much as
hearing of or seeing one act of rebellion from *any* Negro, save the Bigger
Thomases.

But why did Bigger revolt? No explanation based upon a hard and
fast rule of conduct can be given. But there were always two factors
psychologically dominant in his personality. First, through some quirk
of circumstance, he had become estranged from the religion and the
folk culture of his race. Second, he was trying to react to and answer
the call of the dominant civilization whose glitter came to him through
the newspapers, magazines, radios, movies, and the mere imposing sight
and sound of daily American life. In many respects his emergence as a
distinct type was inevitable.

As I grew older, I became familiar with the Bigger Thomas condi-
tioning and its numerous shadings no matter where I saw it in Negro
life. It was not, as I have already said, as blatant or extreme as in the
originals; but it was there, nevertheless, like an undeveloped negative.

Sometimes, in areas far removed from Mississippi, I'd hear a **Negro** say: "I wish I didn't have to live this way. I feel like I want to burst." Then the anger would pass; he would go back to his job and try to eke out a few pennies to support his wife and children.

Sometimes I'd hear a Negro say: "God, I wish I had a flag and a country of my own." But that mood would soon vanish and he would go his way placidly enough.

Sometimes I'd hear a Negro ex-soldier say: "What in hell did I fight in the war for? They segregated me even when I was offering my life for my country." But he, too, like the others, would soon forget, would become caught up in the tense grind of struggling for bread.

I've even heard Negroes, in moments of anger and bitterness, praise what Japan is doing in China, not because they believed in oppression (being objects of oppression themselves), but because they would suddenly sense how empty their lives were when looking at the dark faces of Japanese generals in the rotogravure supplements of the Sunday newspapers. They would dream of what it would be like to live in a country where they could forget their color and play a responsible role in the vital processes of the nation's life.

I've even heard Negroes say that maybe Hitler and Mussolini are all right; that maybe Stalin is all right. They did not say this out of any intellectual comprehension of the forces at work in the world, but because they felt that these men "did things," a phrase which is charged with more meaning than the mere words imply. There was in the back of their minds, when they said this, a wild and intense longing (wild and intense because it was suppressed!) to belong, to be identified, to feel that they were alive as other people were, to be caught up forgetfully and exultingly in the swing of events, to feel the clean, deep, organic satisfaction of doing a job in common with others.

It was not until I went to live in Chicago that I first thought seriously of writing of Bigger Thomas. Two items of my experience combined to make me aware of Bigger as a meaningful and prophetic symbol. First, being free of the daily pressure of the Dixie environment, I was able to come into possession of my own feelings. Second, my contact with the labor movement and its ideology made me see Bigger clearly and feel what he meant.

I made the discovery that Bigger Thomas was not black all the time; he was white, too, and there were literally millions of him, everywhere. The extension of my sense of the personality of Bigger was the pivot of my life; it altered the complexion of my existence. I became conscious, at first dimly, and then later on with increasing clarity and conviction, of a vast, muddied pool of human life in America. It was as though I had put on a pair of spectacles whose power was that of an x-ray enabling me to see deeper into the lives of men. Whenever I picked up a newspaper, I'd no longer feel that I was reading of the doings of whites alone (Negroes are rarely mentioned in the press unless they've committed some crime!), but of a complex struggle for life going on in my country, a struggle in which I was involved. I sensed, too, that the Southern scheme of oppression was but an appendage of a far vaster and in many respects more ruthless and impersonal commodity-profit machine.

Trade-union struggles and issues began to grow meaningful to me. The flow of goods across the seas, buoying and depressing the wages of men, held a fascination. The pronouncements of foreign governments, their policies, plans, and acts were calculated and weighed in relation to the lives of people about me. I was literally overwhelmed when, in reading the works of Russian revolutionists, I came across descriptions of the "holiday energies of the masses," "the locomotives of history," "the conditions prerequisite for revolution," and so forth. I approached all of these new revelations in the light of Bigger Thomas, his hopes, fears, and despairs; and I began to feel far-flung kinships, and sense, with fright and abashment, the possibilities of *alliances* between the American Negro and other people possessing a kindred consciousness.

As my mind extended in this general and abstract manner, it was fed with even more vivid and concrete examples of the lives of Bigger Thomas. The urban environment of Chicago, affording a more stimulating life, made the Negro Bigger Thomases react more violently than even in the South. More than ever I began to see and understand the environmental factors which made for this extreme conduct. It was not that Chicago segregated Negroes more than the South, but that Chicago had more to offer, that Chicago's physical aspect—noisy, crowded, filled with the sense of power and fulfillment—did so much more to dazzle the mind with a taunting sense of possible achievement that the segregation it did impose brought forth from Bigger a reaction more obstreperous than in the South.

So the concrete picture and the abstract linkages of relationships fed each other, each making the other more meaningful and affording my emotions an opportunity to react to them with success and understanding. The process was like a swinging pendulum, each to and fro motion throwing up its tiny bit of meaning and significance, each stroke helping to develop the dim negative which had been implanted in my mind in the South.

During this period the shadings and nuances which were filling in Bigger's picture came, not so much from Negro life, as from the lives of whites I met and grew to know. I began to sense that they had their own kind of Bigger Thomas behavioristic pattern which grew out of a more subtle and broader frustration. The waves of recurring crime, the silly fads and crazes, the quicksilver changes in public taste, the hysteria and fears—all of these had long been mysteries to me. But now I looked back on them and felt the pinch and pressure of the environment that gave them their pitch and peculiar kind of being. I began to feel with my mind the inner tensions of the people I met. I don't mean to say that I think that environment *makes* consciousness (I suppose God makes that, if there is a God), but I do say that I felt and still feel that the environment supplies the instrumentalities through which the organism expresses itself, and if that environment is warped or tranquil, the mode and manner of behavior will be affected toward deadlocking tensions or orderly fulfillment and satisfaction.

Let me give examples of how I began to develop the dim negative of Bigger. I met white writers who talked of their responses, who told me how whites reacted to this lurid American scene. And, as they talked, I'd translate what they said in terms of Bigger's life. But what was more important still, I read their novels. Here for the first time, I found ways and techniques of gauging meaningfully the effects of American civilization upon the personalities of people. I took these techniques, these ways of seeing and feeling, and twisted them, bent them, adapted them, until they became *my* ways of apprehending the locked-in life of the Black Belt areas. This association with white writers was the life preserver of my hope to depict Negro life in fiction, for my race possessed no fictional works dealing with such problems, had no background in such sharp and critical testing of experience, no novels that went with a deep and fearless will down to the dark roots of life.

Here are examples of how I culled information relating to Bigger from my reading:

There is in me a memory of reading an interesting pamphlet telling of the friendship of Gorky and Lenin in exile. The booklet told of how Lenin and Gorky were walking down a London street. Lenin turned to Gorky and, pointing, said: "Here is *their* Big Ben." "There is *their* Westminster Abbey." "There is *their* library." And at once, while reading that passage, my mind stopped, teased, challenged with the effort to remember, to associate widely disparate but meaningful experiences in my life. For a moment nothing would come, but I remained convinced that I had heard the meaning of those words sometime, somewhere before. Then, with a sudden glow of satisfaction of having gained a little more knowledge about the world in which I lived, I'd end up by saying: "That's Bigger. That's the Bigger Thomas reaction."

In both instances the deep sense of exclusion was identical. The feeling of looking at things with a painful and unwarrantable nakedness was an experience, I learned, that transcended national and racial boundaries. It was this intolerable sense of feeling and understanding so much, and yet living on a plane of social reality where the look of a world which one did not make or own struck one with a blinding objectivity and tangibility, that made me grasp the revolutionary impulse in my life and the lives of those about me and far away.

I remember reading a passage in a book dealing with old Russia which said: "We must be ready to make endless sacrifices if we are to be able to overthrow the Czar." And again I'd say to myself: "I've heard that somewhere, sometime before." And again I'd hear Bigger Thomas, far away and long ago, telling some white man who was trying to impose upon him: "I'll kill you and go to hell and pay for it." While living in America I heard from far away Russia the bitter accents of tragic calculation of how much human life and suffering it would cost a man to live as a man in a world that denied him the right to live with dignity. Actions and feelings of men ten thousand miles from home helped me to understand the moods and impulses of those walking the streets of Chicago and Dixie.

I am not saying that I heard any talk of revolution in the South when I was a kid there. But I did hear the lispings, the whispers, the mutters which some day, under one stimulus or another, will surely grow into open revolt unless the conditions which produce Bigger Thomases are changed.

In 1932 another source of information was dramatically opened up to me and I saw data of a surprising nature that helped to clarify the personality of Bigger. From the moment that Hitler took power in Germany and began to oppress the Jews, I tried to keep track of what was happening. And on innumerable occasions I was startled to detect, either from the side of the Fascists or from the side of the oppressed, reactions, moods, phrases, attitudes that reminded me strongly of Bigger, that helped to bring out more clearly the shadowy outlines of the negative that lay in the back of my mind.

I read every account of the Fascist movement in Germany I could lay my hands on, and from page to page I encountered and recognized familiar emotional patterns. What struck me with particular force was the Nazi preoccupation with the construction of a society in which there would exist among all people (*German* people, of course!) *one* solidarity of ideals, *one* continuous circulation of fundamental beliefs, notions, and assumptions. I am not now speaking of the popular idea of regimenting people's thought; I'm speaking of the implicit, almost unconscious, or pre-conscious, assumptions and ideals upon which whole nations and races act and live. And while reading these Nazi pages I'd be reminded of the Negro preacher in the South telling of a life beyond this world, a life in which the color of men's skins would not matter, a life in which each man would know what was deep down in the hearts of his fellow man. And I could hear Bigger Thomas standing on a street corner in America expressing his agonizing doubts and chronic suspicions, thus: "I ain't going to trust nobody. Everything is a racket and everybody is out to get what he can for himself. Maybe if we had a true leader, we could do something." And I'd know that I was still on the track of learning about Bigger, still in the midst of the modern struggle for solidarity among men.

When the Nazis spoke of the necessity of a highly ritualized and symbolized life, I could hear Bigger Thomas on Chicago's South Side saying: "Man, what we need is a leader like Marcus Garvey. We need a nation, a flag, an army of our own. We colored folks ought to organize into groups and have generals, captains, lieutenants, and so forth. We ought to take Africa and have a national home." I'd know, while listening to these childish words, that a white man would smile derisively at them. But I could not smile, for I knew the truth of those simple words from the facts of my own life. The deep hunger in those childish ideas was like a flash of lightning illuminating the whole dark inner landscape of Bigger's mind. Those words told me that the civilization which had given birth to Bigger contained no spiritual sustenance, had created no culture which could hold and claim his allegiance and faith, had sensitized him and had left him stranded, a free agent to roam the streets of our cities, a hot and whirling vortex of undisciplined and unchannelized impulses. The results of these observations made me feel more than ever estranged from the civilization in which I lived, and more than ever resolved toward the task of creating with words a scheme of images and symbols

One of the most significant phases in the black-American experience was the period that has been called the Age of Booker T. Washington. It dated from his famous speech at Atlanta in 1895 and lasted for nearly two decades. Unlike Frederick Douglass, Washington played down the black American's grievances. He believed that it was impractical for blacks to study science, mathematics, history, and so on. He advocated instead the type of vocational education that was given at Hampton Institute, where he had studied, and at Tuskegee Institute, the school he established in 1881. At both institutions, men were taught farming, carpentry, and plumbing, while women were instructed in such skills as cooking, sewing, and nursing.

Wide World Photos

STUDENTS AT HAMPTON

New York Public Library
Picture Collection

STUDENTS AT TUSKEGEE

New York Public Library
Picture Collection

Washington's program was acclaimed by many whites who saw in it a formula that would settle, once and for all, the matter of the black man's place in American society. But many blacks felt that it did little more than reinforce economic and social inequality. In 1905, W. E. B. Du Bois, who had received his Ph.D. from Harvard in 1895, founded the Niagara movement, which called for aggressive action to achieve the abolition of racial discrimination and the recognition of the principles of human brotherhood. The movement later developed into the NAACP.

Wide World Photos

In 1919, America experienced the greatest period of racial strife it had ever known. During the last six months of the year—the "Red Summer"—the country was rocked by more than twenty race riots of unprecedented violence and savagery. During the next few years, as riots continued on a smaller scale, it became clear that a new element had been introduced into the racial problem: the increased racial pride and cohesiveness of black Americans and their willingness to defend themselves. Out of these conditions emerged Marcus Garvey, who, with his appeal to race pride and self-determination, organized the largest movement of black Americans in history.

*New York Public Library
Picture Collection*

The Great Depression severely affected the lives of millions of black Americans. In urban centers, many lost their jobs to whites, while in rural areas black farm workers were reduced to near starvation. Racial discrimination was present even in relief activities. Some of the soup kitchens established for the poor by charitable organizations were for whites only, and agencies in Southern states offering relief work generally paid blacks less than whites. Measures instituted by the New Deal relieved, to a degree, the conditions of scores of black Americans, but black agricultural workers in the South derived little benefit from them.

Farm Security
Administration
Photo by: Lee

One of the most significant aspects of the New Deal was the political recognition accorded to black Americans by President Franklin Delano Roosevelt. Other Presidents had occasionally sought advice from one or more blacks, but Roosevelt had what was known as a "Black Cabinet," a group of highly qualified people chosen to perform specific tasks in relation to problems affecting black Americans.

New York Public Library Picture Collection

Richard Wright was the first black writer to receive serious attention as a major American literary figure. During and after the Depression, many black writers had evoked the horror and frustrations of life in the ghettos, but Wright succeeded in giving the racial theme a universality that dwarfed his predecessors. Bigger Thomas, the main character in Wright's first novel, *Native Son,* which was published in 1940, a year before the United States entered World War II, was seen as more than just an angry young black living in an urban slum; he was seen as representative of deprived Americans, black or white, who, in a land of plenty, respond to the same rhetoric of freedom and opportunity that motivates all Americans.

Schomburg Collection
New York Public Library

In the decade following World War II, substantial progress was made in the drive for full equality of black Americans. One of the most significant events was the Supreme Court school-desegregation decision handed down in 1954, which reversed the "separate but equal" doctrine that had been officially sanctioned for more than fifty years. Though the decision was limited to education, it implied that blacks must be treated as citizens in the fullest sense. One of the lawyers who argued the case on which the Court based its decision was Thurgood Marshall, then chief counsel for the NAACP. In 1967, Marshall became a Supreme Court Justice.

Wide World Photos

The broad implications of the Supreme Court's decision were not lost on a single black American, and new leaders emerged to demand that they be translated into realities. But the non-violent civil rights movement that was to spread across the nation was touched off by a person who was neither a brilliant spokesman nor a leader. Though a college graduate, Mrs. Rosa Parks was a seamstress, active only in church affairs. On December 1, 1955, when she refused to yield her seat on a downtown bus in Montgomery, Alabama, to a white man, she was arrested. Black citizens of Montgomery, stirred by the action against this quiet, religious woman, formed a protest organization, with the Reverend Martin Luther King, Jr., as president.

Wide World Photos

The Supreme Court's decision concerning school desegregation was widely opposed in the South. In 1957, Governor Orval Faubus, of Arkansas, called out the National Guard to turn away black students who tried to enter a previously all-white school in Little Rock. The students were admitted after President Eisenhower sent federal troops to the city, but the harsh treatment the blacks suffered from white students and their parents was a portent of the bitterness to come as more attempts were made to implement the Court's decision.

New York Public Library Picture Collection

In the 1960's, several new organizations rose to prominence as new tactics were developed to secure equal rights for black Americans. But one group remained aloof from all participation in the civil rights struggle. The Black Muslims, founded in 1930, had slowly gained considerable support in black ghettos in the North by undertaking programs that gave a sense of dignity and worth to some of the most neglected members of the black community. Though the Muslims bitterly denounce racism, they believe that it is impossible for blacks to enjoy full rights in America.

BLACK MUSLIM WOMEN

*New York Public Library
Picture Collection*

In 1963, the centennial year of the Emancipation Proclamation, a wave of civil rights demonstrations swept the country. But the demonstration that Martin Luther King, Jr., initiated in Birmingham, Alabama, on April 13 was a turning point in the civil rights struggle. For leading the protest against court orders, King was sentenced to five days in jail. When the sentence was handed down, he and his associates left Atlanta, Georgia, where they had been engaged in other civil rights activities, to serve the jail term in Birmingham.

Wide World Photos

During the month-long demonstrations in Birmingham, there were more than a thousand arrests, but the protests did not become violent until fire hoses and snarling dogs were used against the demonstrators, who retaliated by throwing rocks and bottles. The violence spread, and sympathy demonstrations were staged in various parts of the country. On August 28, 1963, to dramatize the plight of black Americans, more than 200,000 people, of all races and from all walks of life, converged on Washington, D.C., in what was, up to that time, the largest demonstration in American history.

Wide World Photos

Malcolm X was one of the most striking leaders of the 1960's. As first "national minister" of the Black Muslims, he mercilessly condemned white America and advocated black nationalism. But the Muslims' insistence on separatism and their aloofness from the civil rights struggle gradually alienated him; and, in 1964, he left the movement and launched his own group. Though he did not accept Martin Luther King's doctrine of nonviolence, he conceded that much good could come out of civil rights groups and that whites could join in the black American's struggle. In his short career, Malcolm X earned the devotion of millions of blacks and the quiet admiration of many whites. His assassination in 1965 and that of Martin Luther King, Jr., three years later, marked the end of an era.

Wide World Photos

A new period in the black-American experience began in 1966, when the term "black power" was used for the first time by Stokely Carmichael, head of the Student Nonviolent Coordinating Committee (SNCC), at a rally in Jackson, Mississippi. At first, the term seemed to be another rallying cry for civil rights groups; but, during the summer and, particularly, the fall of that year, when Carmichael spoke at a conference organized by the predominantly white Students for a Democratic Society (SDS), it became clear that "black power" had several more important connotations. It stood for a militant political and economic movement with an emphasis on black pride. It stressed black control of civil rights organizations and urged white policy-makers in such organizations to resign and concentrate on fighting racism among other whites.

Wide World Photos

One of the most important meanings of "black power" is to be found in the development of a broad cultural nationalism among black Americans, especially among the young. It is reflected in the abandonment of the word "Negro" for "black," a term that ten years ago was insulting. It is evident in the black American's acceptance of his inherent physical characteristics as beautiful and in his new interest and pride in black culture. LeRoi Jones, the poet and playwright, is the most noted spokesman for this cultural nationalism, which, though at times strident, seeks to build rather than destroy.

Wide World Photos

whose direction could enlist the sympathies, loyalties, and yearnings of the millions of Bigger Thomases in every land and race. . . .

But more than anything else, as a writer, I was fascinated by the similarity of the emotional tensions of Bigger in America and Bigger in Nazi Germany and Bigger in old Russia. All Bigger Thomases, white and black, felt tense, afraid, nervous, hysterical, and restless. From far away Nazi Germany and old Russia had come to me items of knowledge that told me that certain modern experiences were creating types of personalities whose existence ignored racial and national lines of demarcation, that these personalities carried with them a more universal drama-element than anything I'd ever encountered before; that these personalities were mainly imposed upon men and women living in a world whose fundamental assumptions could no longer be taken for granted: a world ridden with national and class strife; a world whose metaphysical meanings had vanished; a world in which God no longer existed as a daily focal point of men's lives; a world in which men could no longer retain their faith in an ultimate hereafter. It was a highly geared world whose nature was conflict and action, a world whose limited area and vision imperiously urged men to satisfy their organisms, a world that existed on a plane of animal sensation alone.

It was a world in which millions of men lived and behaved like drunkards, taking a stiff drink of hard life to lift them up for a thrilling moment, to give them a quivering sense of wild exultation and fulfillment that soon faded and let them down. Eagerly they took another drink, wanting to avoid the dull, flat look of things, then still another, this time stronger, and then they felt that their lives had meaning. Speaking figuratively, they were soon chronic alcoholics, men who lived by violence, through extreme action and sensation, through drowning daily in a perpetual nervous agitation.

From these items I drew my first political conclusions about Bigger: I felt that Bigger, an American product, a native son of this land, carried within him the potentialities of either Communism or Fascism. I don't mean to say that the Negro boy I depicted in *Native Son* is either a Communist or a Fascist. He is not either. But he is product of a dislocated society; he is a dispossessed and disinherited man; he is all of this, and he lives amid the greatest possible plenty on earth and he is looking and feeling for a way out. Whether he'll follow some gaudy, hysterical leader who'll promise rashly to fill the void in him, or whether he'll come to an understanding with the millions of his kindred fellow workers under trade-union or revolutionary guidance depends upon the future drift of events in America. But, granting the emotional state, the tensity, the fear, the hate, the impatience, the sense of exclusion, the ache for violent action, the emotional and cultural hunger, Bigger Thomas, conditioned as his organism is, will not become an ardent, or even a lukewarm, supporter of the *status quo*.

The difference between Bigger's tensity and the German variety is that Bigger's, due to America's educational restrictions on the bulk of her Negro population, is in a nascent state, not yet articulate. And the difference between Bigger's longing for self-identification and the Russian principle of self-determination is that Bigger's, due to the effects of American oppression, which has not allowed for the forming of deep ideas of solidarity among Negroes, is still in a state of individual anger and hatred. Here, I felt was *drama!* Who will be the first to touch off these Bigger Thomases in America, white and black?

For a long time I toyed with the idea of writing a novel in which a Negro Bigger Thomas would loom as a symbolic figure of American life, a figure who would hold within him the prophecy of our future. I felt strongly that he held within him, in a measure which perhaps no other contemporary type did, the outlines of action and feeling which we would encounter on a vast scale in the days to come. Just as one sees when one walks into a medical research laboratory jars of alcohol containing abnormally large or distorted portions of the human body, just so did I see and feel that the conditions of life under which Negroes are forced to live in America contain the embryonic emotional prefigurations of how a large part of the body politic would react under stress.

So, with this much knowledge of myself and the world gained and known, why should I not try to work out on paper the problem of what will happen to Bigger? Why should I not, like a scientist in a laboratory, use my imagination and invent test-tube situations, place Bigger in them, and, following the guidance of my own hopes and fears, what I had learned and remembered, work out in fictional form an emotional statement and resolution of this problem?

But several things militated against my starting to work. Like Bigger himself, I felt a mental censor—product of the fears which a Negro feels from living in America—standing over me, draped in white, warning me not to write. This censor's warnings were translated into my own thought processes thus: "What will white people think if I draw the picture of such a Negro boy? Will they not at once say: 'See, didn't we tell you all along the niggers are like that? Now, look, one of their own kind has come along and drawn the picture for us!'" I felt that if I drew the picture of Bigger truthfully, there would be many reactionary whites who would try to make of him something I did not intend. And yet, and this was what made it difficult, I knew that I could not write of Bigger convincingly if I did not depict him as he *was:* that is, resentful toward whites, sullen, angry, ignorant, emotionally unstable, depressed and unaccountably elated at times, and unable even, because of his own lack of inner organization which American oppression has fostered in him, to unite with the members of his own race. And would not whites misread Bigger and, doubting his authenticity, say: "This man is preaching hate against the whole white race"?

The more I thought of it the more I became convinced that if I did not write of Bigger as I saw and felt him, if I did not try to make him a living personality and at the same time a symbol of all the larger things I felt and saw in him, I'd be reacting as Bigger himself reacted: that is, I'd be acting out of *fear* if I let what I thought whites would say constrict and paralyze me.

As I contemplated Bigger and what he meant, I said to myself: "I must write this novel, not only for others to read, but to free *myself* of this sense of shame and fear." In fact, the novel, as time passed, grew upon me to the extent that it became a necessity to write it; the writing of it turned into a way of living for me.

Another thought kept me from writing. What would my own white and black comrades in the Communist party say? This thought was the most bewildering of all. Politics is a hard and narrow game; its policies represent the aggregate desires and aspirations of millions of people. Its goals are rigid and simply drawn, and the minds of the majority of politicians are set, congealed in terms of daily tactical maneuvers. How could I create such complex and wide schemes of associational thought and feeling, such filigreed webs of dreams and politics, without being mistaken for a "smuggler of reaction," "an ideological confusionist," or "an individualistic and dangerous element"? Though my heart is with the collectivist and proletarian ideal, I solved this problem by assuring myself that honest politics and honest feeling in imaginative representation ought to be able to meet on common healthy ground without fear, suspicion, and quarreling. Further, and more importantly, I steeled myself by coming to the conclusion that whether politicians accepted or rejected Bigger did not really matter; my task, as I felt it, was to free myself of this burden of impressions and feelings, recast them into the image of Bigger and make him *true*. Lastly, I felt that a right more immediately deeper than that of politics or race was at stake; that is, a *human* right, the right of a man to think and feel honestly. And especially did this personal and human right bear hard upon me, for temperamentally I am inclined to satisfy the claims of my own ideals rather than the expectations of others. It was this obscure need that had pulled me into the labor movement in the beginning and by exercising it I was but fulfilling what I felt to be the laws of my own growth.

There was another constricting thought that kept me from work. It deals with my own race. I asked myself: "What will Negro doctors, lawyers, dentists, bankers, school teachers, social workers and business men, think of me if I draw such a picture of Bigger?" I knew from long and painful experience that the Negro middle and professional classes were the people of my own race who were more than others ashamed of Bigger and what he meant. Having narrowly escaped the Bigger Thomas reaction pattern themselves—indeed, still retaining traces of it within the confines of their own timid personalities—they would not relish being publicly reminded of the lowly, shameful depths of life above which they enjoyed their bourgeois lives. Never did they want people, especially *white* people, to think that their lives were so much touched by anything so dark and brutal as Bigger.

Their attitude toward life and art can be summed up in a single paragraph: "But, Mr. Wright, there are so many of us who are *not* like Bigger? Why don't you portray in your fiction the *best* traits of our race, something that will show the white people what we have done in spite of oppression? Don't represent anger and bitterness. Smile when a white person comes to you. Never let him feel that you are so small that what he has done to crush you has made you hate him! Oh, above all, save your *pride!*"

But Bigger won over all these claims; he won because I felt that I was hunting on the trail of more exciting and thrilling game. What Bigger meant had claimed me because I felt with all of my being that he was more important than what any person, white or black, would say or try to make of him, more important than any political analysis designed to explain or deny him, more important, even, than my own sense of fear, shame, and diffidence.

But Bigger was still not down upon paper. For a long time I had been writing of him in my mind, but I had yet to put him into an image, a breathing symbol draped out in the guise of the only form of life my native land had allowed me to know intimately, that is, the ghetto life of the American Negro. But the basic reason for my hesitancy was that another and far more complex problem had risen to plague me. Bigger, as I saw and felt him, was a snarl of many realities; he had in him many levels of life.

First, there was his personal and private life, that intimate existence that is so difficult to snare and nail down in fiction, that elusive core of being, that individual data of consciousness which in every man and woman is like that in no other. I had to deal with Bigger's dreams, his fleeting, momentary sensations, his yearning, visions, his deep emotional responses.

Then I was confronted with that part of him that was dual in aspect, dim, wavering, that part of him which is so much a part of *all* Negroes and *all* whites that I realized that I could put it down upon paper only by feeling out its meaning first within the confines of my own life. Bigger was attracted and repelled by the American scene. He was an American, because he was a native son; but he was also a Negro nationalist in a vague sense because he was not allowed to live as an American. Such was his way of life and mine; neither Bigger nor I resided fully in either camp.

Of this dual aspect of Bigger's social consciousness, I placed the nationalistic side first, not because I agreed with Bigger's wild and intense hatred of white people, but because his hate had placed him, like a wild animal at bay, in a position where he was most symbolic and explainable. In other words, his nationalist complex was for me a concept through which I could grasp more of the total meaning of his life than I could in any other way. I tried to approach Bigger's *snarled* and *confused* nationalist feelings with *conscious* and *informed* ones of my own. Yet, Bigger was not nationalist enough to feel the need of religion or the folk culture of his own people. What made Bigger's social consciousness most complex was the fact that he was hovering unwanted between two worlds—between powerful America and his own stunted place in life— and I took upon myself the task of trying to make the reader feel this No Man's Land. The most that I could say of Bigger was that he felt the *need* for a whole life and *acted* out of that need; that was all.

Above and beyond all this, there was that American part of Bigger which is the heritage of us all, that part of him which we get from our seeing and hearing, from school, from the hopes and dreams of our friends; that part of him which the common people of America never talk of but take for granted. Among millions of people the deepest convictions of life are never discussed openly: they are felt, implied, hinted at tacitly and obliquely in their hopes and fears. We live by idealism that makes us believe that the Constitution is a good document of government, that the Bill of Rights is a good legal and humane principle to safeguard our civil liberties, that every man and woman should have the opportunity to realize himself, to seek his own individual fate and goal, his own peculiar and untranslatable destiny. I don't say that Bigger knew this in the terms in which I'm speaking of it; I don't say that any such thought ever entered his head. His emotional and intellectual life was never that articulate. But he knew it emotionally, intuitively, for his emotions and his desires were developed, and he caught it, as most of us do, from the mental and emotional climate of our time. Bigger had all of this in him, dammed up, buried, implied, and I had to develop it in fictional form.

There was still another level of Bigger's life that I felt bound to account for and render, a level as elusive to discuss as it was to grasp in writing. Here again, I had to fall back upon my own feeling as a guide, for Bigger did not offer in his life any articulate verbal explanations. There seems to hover somewhere in that dark part of all our lives, in some more than in others, an objectless, timeless, spaceless element of primal fear and dread, stemming, perhaps, from our birth (depending upon whether one's outlook upon personality is Freudian or non-Freudian!), a fear and dread which exercises an impelling influence upon our lives all out of proportion to its obscurity. And, accompanying this *first fear*, is, for the want of a better name, a reflex urge toward ecstasy, complete submission, and trust. The springs of religion are here, and also the origins of rebellion. And in a boy like Bigger, young, unschooled, whose subjective life was clothed in the tattered rags of American "culture," this primitive fear and ecstasy were naked, exposed, unprotected by religion or a framework of government or a scheme of society whose final faiths would gain his love and trust; unprotected by trade or profession, faith or belief; opened to every trivial blast of daily or hourly circumstance.

There was yet another level of reality in Bigger's life: the impliedly political. I've already mentioned that Bigger had in him impulses which I had felt were present in the vast upheavals of Russia and Germany. Well, somehow, I had to make these political impulses felt by the reader in terms of Bigger's daily actions, keeping in mind as I did so the probable danger of my being branded as a propagandist by those who would not like the subject matter.

Then there was Bigger's relationship with white America, both North and South, which I had to depict, which I had to make known once again, alas; a relationship whose effects are carried by every Negro, like scars, somewhere in his body and mind.

I had also to show what oppression had done to Bigger's relationships with his own people, how it had split him off from them, how it had baffled him; how oppression seems to hinder and stifle in the victim those very qualities of character which are so essential for an effective struggle against the oppressor.

Then there was the fabulous city in which Bigger lived, an indescribable city, huge, roaring, dirty, noisy, raw, stark, brutal; a city of extremes: torrid summers and sub-zero winters, white people and black people, the English language and strange tongues, foreign born and native born, scabby poverty and gaudy luxury, high idealism and hard cynicism! A city so young that, in thinking of its short history, one's mind, as it travels backward in time, is stopped abruptly by the barren stretches of wind-swept prairie! But a city old enough to have caught within the homes of its long, straight streets the symbols and images of man's age-old destiny, of truths as old as the mountains and seas, of dramas as abiding as the soul of man itself! A city which has become the pivot of the Eastern, Western, Northern, and Southern poles of the nation. But a city whose black smoke clouds shut out the sunshine for seven months of the year; a city in which, on a fine balmy May morning one can sniff the stench of the stockyards; a city where people have grown so used to gangs and murders and graft that they have honestly forgotten that government can have a pretense of decency!

With all of this thought out, Bigger was still unwritten. Two events, however, came into my life and accelerated the process, made me sit down and actually start work on the typewriter, and just stop the writing of Bigger in my mind as I walked the streets.

The first event was my getting a job in the South Side Boys' Club, an institution which tried to reclaim the thousands of Negro Bigger Thomases from the dives and the alleys of the Black Belt. Here, on a vast scale, I had an opportunity to observe Bigger in all of his moods, actions, haunts. Here I felt for the first time that the rich folk who were paying my wages did not really give a good goddamn about Bigger, that their kindness was prompted at the bottom by a selfish motive. They were paying me to distract Bigger with ping-pong, checkers, swimming, marbles, and baseball in order that he might not roam the streets and harm the valuable white property which adjoined the Black Belt. I am not condemning boys' clubs and ping-pong as such; but these little stopgaps were utterly inadequate to fill up the centuries-long chasm of emptiness which American civilization had created in these Biggers. I felt that I was doing a kind of dressed-up police work, and I hated it.

I would work hard with these Biggers, and when it would come time for me to go home I'd say to myself under my breath so that no one could hear: "Go to it, boys! Prove to the bastards that gave you these games that life is stronger than ping-pong. . . . Show them that full-blooded life is harder and hotter than they suspect, even though that life is draped in a black skin which at heart they despise. . . ."

They did. The police blotters of Chicago are testimony to how *much* they did. That was the only way I could contain myself for doing a job I hated; for a moment I'd allow myself, vicariously, to feel as Bigger felt—not much, just a little, just a *little*—but, still, there it was.

The second event that spurred me to write of Bigger was more personal and subtle. I had written a book of short stories which was published under the title of *Uncle Tom's Children*. When the reviews of that book began to appear, I realized that I had made an awfully naive mistake. I found that I had written a book which even bankers' daughters could read and weep over and feel good about. I swore to myself that if I ever wrote another book, no one would weep over it; that it would be so hard and deep that they would have to face it without the consolation of tears. It was this that made me get to work in dead earnest.

Now, until this moment I did not stop to think very much about the plot of *Native Son*. The reason I did not is because I was not for one moment ever worried about it. I had spent years learning about Bigger, what had made him, what he meant; so, when the time came for writing, *what had made him and what he meant* constituted my plot. But the far-flung items of his life had to be couched in imaginative terms, terms known and acceptable to a common body of readers, terms which would, in the course of the story, manipulate the deepest held notions and convictions of their lives. That came easy. The moment I began to write, the plot fell out, so to speak. I'm not trying to oversimplify or make the process seem oversubtle. At bottom, what happened is very easy to explain.

Any Negro who has lived in the North or the South knows that times without number he has heard of some Negro boy being picked up on the streets and carted off to jail and charged wth "rape." This thing happens so often that to my mind it had become a representative symbol of the Negro's uncertain position in America. Never for a second was I in doubt as to what kind of social reality or dramatic situation I'd put Bigger in, what kind of test-tube I'd set up to evoke his deepest reactions. Life had made the plot over and over again, to the extent that I knew it by heart. So frequently do these acts recur that when I was halfway through the first draft of *Native Son* a case paralleling Bigger's flared forth in the newspapers of Chicago. (Many of the newspaper items and some of the incidents in *Native Son* are but fictionalized versions of the Robert Nixon case and rewrites of news stories from the *Chicago Tribune*.) Indeed, scarcely was *Native Son* off the press before Supreme Court Justice Hugo L. Black gave the nation a long and vivid account of the American police methods of handling Negro boys.

Let me describe this stereotyped situation: A crime wave is sweeping a city and citizens are clamoring for police action. Squad cars cruise the Black Belt and grab the first Negro boy who seems to be unattached and homeless. He is held for perhaps a week without charge or bail, without the privilege of communicating with anyone, including his own relatives. After a few days this boy "confesses" anything that he is asked to confess, any crime that handily happens to be unsolved and on the calendar. Why does he confess? After the boy has been grilled night and day, hanged up by his thumbs, dangled by his feet out of twenty-story windows, and beaten (in places that leave no scars—cops have found a way to do that), he signs the papers before him, papers which are usually accompanied by a verbal promise to the boy that he will not go to the electric chair. Of course, he ends up by being executed or sentenced for life. If you think I'm telling tall tales, get chummy with some white cop who works in a Black Belt district and ask him for the lowdown.

When a black boy is carted off to jail in such a fashion, it is almost impossible to do anything for him. Even well-disposed Negro lawyers find it difficult to defend him, for the boy will plead guilty one day and then not guilty the next, according to the degree of pressure and persuasion that is brought to bear upon his frightened personality from one side or the other. Even the boy's own family is scared to death; sometimes fear of police intimidation makes them hesitate to acknowledge that the boy is blood relation of theirs.

Such has been America's attitude toward these boys that if one is picked up and confronted in a police cell with ten white cops, he is intimidated almost to the point of confessing anything. So far removed are these practices from what the average American citizen encounters in his daily life that it takes a huge act of his imagination to believe that it is true; yet, this same average citizen, with his kindness, his American sportsmanship and good will, would probably act with the mob if a self-respecting Negro family moved into his apartment building to escape the Black Belt and its terrors and limitations. . . .

Now, after all this, when I sat down to the typewriter, I could not work; I could not think of a good opening scene for the book. I had definitely in mind the kind of emotion I wanted to evoke in the reader in that first scene, but I could not think of the type of concrete event that would convey the motif of the entire scheme of the book, that would sound, in varied form, the note that was to be resounded throughout its length, that would introduce to the reader just what kind of an organism Bigger's was and the environment that was bearing hourly upon it. Twenty or thirty times I tried and failed; then I argued that if I could not write the opening scene, I'd start with the scene that followed. I did. The actual writing of the book began with the scene in the pool room.

Now, for the writing. During the years in which I had met all of those Bigger Thomases, those varieties of Bigger Thomases, I had not consciously gathered material to write of them; I had not kept a notebook record of their sayings and doings. Their actions had simply made impressions upon my sensibilities as I lived from day to day, impressions which crystallized and coagulated into clusters and configurations of memory, attitudes, moods, ideas. And these subjective states, in turn, were automatically stored away somewhere in me. I was not even aware of the process. But, excited over the book which I had set myself to write, under the stress of emotion, these things came surging up, tangled, fused, knotted, entertaining me by the sheer variety and potency of their meaning and suggestiveness.

With the whole theme in mind, in an attitude almost akin to prayer, I gave myself up to the story. In an effort to capture some phase of Bigger's life that would not come to me readily, I'd jot down as much of it as I could. Then I'd read it over and over, adding each time a word, a phrase, a sentence until I felt that I had caught all the shadings of reality I felt dimly were there. With each of these rereadings and rewritings it seemed that I'd gather in facts and facets that tried to run away. It was an act of concentration, of trying to hold within one's center of attention all of that bewildering array of facts which science, politics, experience, memory, and imagination were urging upon me. And, then, while writing, a new and thrilling relationship would spring up under the drive of emotion, coalescing and telescoping alien facts into a known and felt truth. That was the deep fun of the job: to feel within my body that I was pushing out to new areas of feeling, strange landmarks of emotion tramping upon foreign soil, compounding new relationships of perceptions, making new and—until that very split second of time!—unheard-of and unfelt effects with words. It had a buoying and tonic impact upon me; my senses would strain and seek for more and more of such relationships; my temperature would rise as I worked. That is writing as I feel it, a kind of significant living.

The first draft of the novel was written in four months, straight through, and ran to some 576 pages. Just as a man rises in the morning to dig ditches for his bread, so I'd work daily. I'd think of some abstract principle of Bigger's conduct and at once my mind would turn it into some act I'd seen Bigger perform, some act which I hoped would be familiar enough to the American reader to gain his credence. But in the writing of scene after scene I was guided by but one criterion: to tell the truth as I saw it and felt it. That is, to objectify in words some insight derived from my living in the form of action, scene, and dialogue. If a scene seemed improbable to me, I'd not tear it up, but ask myself: "Does it reveal enough of what I feel to stand in spite of its unreality?" If I felt it did, it stood. If I felt that it did not, I ripped it out. The degree of morality in my writing depended upon the degree of felt life and truth I could put down upon the printed page. For example, there is a scene in *Native Son* where Bigger stands in a cell with a Negro preacher, Jan, Max, the State's Attorney, Mr. Dalton, Mrs. Dalton, Bigger's mother, his sister, Al, Gus, and Jack. While writing the scene, I knew that it was unlikely that so many people would ever be allowed to come into a murderer's cell. But I wanted those people in that cell to elicit a certain important emotional response from Bigger. And so the scene stood. I felt that what I wanted that scene to say to the reader was *more important than its surface reality or plausibility.*

Always, as I wrote, I was both reader and writer, both the conceiver of the action and the appreciator of it. I tried to write so that, in the same instant of time, the objective and subjective aspects of Bigger's life would be caught in a focus of prose. And always I tried to *render,* *depict,* not merely to tell the story. If a thing was cold, I tried to make the reader *feel cold,* and not just tell about it. In writing in this fashion, sometimes I'd find it necessary to use a stream of consciousness technique, then rise to an interior monologue, descend to a direct rendering of a dream state, then to a matter-of-fact depiction of what Bigger was saying, doing, and feeling. Then I'd find it impossible to say what I wanted to say without stepping in and speaking outright on my own; but when doing this I always made an effort to retain the mood of the story, explaining everything only in terms of Bigger's life and, if possible, in the rhythms of Bigger's thought (even though the words would be mine).

Again, at other times, in the guise of the lawyer's speech and the news-paper items, or in terms of what Bigger would overhear or see from afar, I'd give what others were saying and thinking of him. But always, from the start to finish, it was Bigger's story, Bigger's fears, Bigger's flight, and Bigger's fate that I tried to depict. I wrote with the conviction in mind (I don't know if this is right or wrong; I only know that I'm tem-peramentally inclined to feel this way) that the main burden of all seri-ous fiction consists almost wholly of character-destiny and the items, social, political, and personal, of that character-destiny.

As I wrote I followed, almost unconsciously, many principles of the novel which my reading of the novels of other writers had made me feel were necessary for the building of a well-constructed book. For the most part the novel is rendered in the present; I wanted the reader to feel that Bigger's story was happening *now*, like a play upon the stage or a movie unfolding upon the screen. Action follows action, as in a prize fight. Wherever possible, I told of Bigger's life in close-up, slow-motion, giving the feel of the grain in the passing of time. I had long had the feeling that this was the best way to "enclose" the reader's mind in a new world, to blot out all reality except that which I was giving him.

Then again, as much as I could, I restricted the novel to what Bigger saw and felt, to the limits of his feeling and thoughts, even when I was conveying *more* than that to the reader. I had the notion that such a manner of rendering made for a sharper effect, a more pointed sense of the character, his peculiar type of being and consciousness. Throughout there is but one point of view: Bigger's. This, too, I felt, made for a richer illusion of reality.

I kept out of the story as much as possible, for I wanted the reader to feel that there was nothing between him and Bigger; that the story was a special *première* given in his own private theater.

I kept the scenes long, made as much happen within a short space of time as possible; all of which, I felt, made for greater density and rich-ness of effect.

In a like manner I tried to keep a unified sense of background through-out the story; the background would change, of course, but I tried to keep before the eyes of the reader at all times the forces and elements against which Bigger was striving.

And because I had limited myself to rendering only what Bigger saw and felt, I gave no more reality to the other characters than that which Bigger himself saw.

This, honestly, is all I can account for in the book. If I attempted to account for scenes and characters, to tell why certain scenes were written in certain ways, I'd be stretching facts in order to be pleasantly intelligi-ble. All else in the book came from my feelings reacting upon the ma-terial, and any honest reader knows as much about the rest of what is in the book as I do; that is, if, as he reads, he is willing to let his emotions and imagination become as influenced by the materials as I did. As I wrote, for some reason or other, one image, symbol, character, scene, mood, feeling evoked its opposite, its parallel, its complimentary, and its ironic counterpart. Why? I don't know. My emotions and imagination just

like to work that way. One can account for just so much of life, and then
no more. At least, not yet.

With the first draft down, I found that I could not end the book sat-
isfactorily. In the first draft I had Bigger going smack to the electric
chair; but I felt that two murders were enough for one novel. I cut the
final scene and went back to worry about the beginning. I had no luck.
The book was one-half finished, with the opening and closing scenes
unwritten. Then, one night, in desperation—I hope that I'm not disclosing
the hidden secrets of my craft!—I sneaked out and got a bottle. With the
help of it, I began to remember many things which I could not remember before. One of them was that Chicago was overrun with rats. I re-
called that I'd seen many rats on the streets, that I'd heard and read of
Negro children being bitten by rats in their beds. At first I rejected the
idea of Bigger battling a rat in his room; I was afraid that the rat would
"hog" the scene. But the rat would not leave me; he presented himself
in many attractive guises. So, cautioning myself to allow the rat scene to
disclose *only* Bigger, his family, their little room, and their relationships,
I let the rat walk in, and he did his stuff.

Many of the scenes were torn out as I reworked the book. The mere
rereading of what I'd written made me think of the possibility of developing themes which had been only hinted at in the first draft. For
example, the entire guilt theme that runs through *Native Son* was woven
in *after* the first draft was written.

At last I found out how to end the book; I ended it just as I had begun
it, showing Bigger living dangerously, taking his life into his hands,
accepting what life had made him. The lawyer, Max, was placed in Bigger's cell at the end of the novel to register the moral—or what *I* felt
was the moral—horror of Negro life in the United States.

The writing of *Native Son* was to me an exciting, enthralling, and even
a romantic experience. With what I've learned in the writing of this
book, with all of its blemishes, imperfections, with all of its unrealized
potentialities, I am launching out upon another novel, this time about
the status of women in modern American society. This book, too, goes
back to my childhood just as Bigger went, for, while I was storing away
impressions of Bigger, I was storing away impressions of many other
things that made me think and wonder. Some experience will ignite
somewhere deep down in me the smoldering embers of new fires and
I'll be off again to write yet another novel. It is good to live when one
feels that such as that will happen to one. Life becomes sufficient unto
life; the rewards of living are found in living.

I don't know if *Native Son* is a good book or a bad book. And I don't
know if the book I'm working on now will be a good book or a bad book.
And I really don't care. The mere writing of it will be more fun and a
deeper satisfaction than any praise or blame from anybody.

I feel that I'm lucky to be alive to write novels today, when the whole
world is caught in the pangs of war and change. Early American writers,
Henry James and Nathaniel Hawthorne, complained bitterly about the
bleakness and flatness of the American scene. But I think that if they
were alive, they'd feel at home in modern America. True, we have no great

church in America; our national traditions are still of such a sort that we are not wont to brag of them; and we have no army that's above the level of mercenary fighters; we have no group acceptable to the whole of our country upholding certain humane values; we have no rich symbols, no colorful rituals. We have only a money-grabbing, industrial civilization. But we do have in the Negro the embodiment of a past tragic enough to appease the spiritual hunger of even a James; and we have in the oppression of the Negro a shadow athwart our national life dense and heavy enough to satisfy even the gloomy broodings of a Hawthorne. And if Poe were alive, he would not have to invent horror; horror would invent him.

BROWN ET AL. V. BOARD OF EDUCATION OF TOPEKA ET AL.

Earl Warren

[The "separate but equal" doctrine in education originated in the decision of Justice Lemuel Shaw in the Massachusetts case of *Sarah C. Roberts* v. *The City of Boston* (1850). The case had been brought by Sarah's father, Benjamin F. Roberts, after several attempts to enroll his daughter in a white school had been unsuccessful. The case for Roberts was argued by Charles Sumner in December, 1849. Despite praise from the court, the decision was in favor of continuing the city's separate school policy. Benjamin Roberts continued his efforts after the case by circulating a petition urging a new law for the whole state. A significant portion of the opposition to Roberts came from the Negro population of Boston, which, in 1850, numbered about 2,000. Those favoring separation circulated their own petition, which, according to the *Liberator* of February 15, 1850, was signed by 170 Negroes. "We believe colored schools to be institutions," the correspondent urged, "when properly conducted, of great advantage to the colored people. We believe society imperatively requires their existence among us." Massachusetts abolished segregated schools by state law in 1855. Most other states did not, even in the North; and even where state laws were passed, *de facto* segregation was often in effect. In the South, after Reconstruction, school segregation became official.

The separate but equal doctrine became national policy in 1896, with the Supreme Court's decision in *Plessy* v. *Ferguson*, a case involving segregation of transportation facilities but one that was widely interpreted as applying to educational facilities as well. A single protesting voice was heard against the decision, that of Justice John Marshall Harlan, who, in dissent, declared that the Constitution is color-blind. The separate but equal doctrine remained the law of the land for fifty-eight years, although, of course, separation was not mandatory, and some Northern states—for example, New York in 1900—passed antisegregation statutes.

The decision of the Court in *Brown* v. *Board of Education*, handed down in May, 1954, marked a highly significant change in racial policy. The legal battles of the preceding half century had been aimed at upholding the "equal" part of the doctrine, without disturbing the doctrine itself. But now the Court found itself agreeing with Justice Harlan, and disagreeing with his eight colleagues. Indeed, Chief Justice Warren now spoke for a unanimous Court in holding that segregated schools were "inherently unequal." This unity was in no small measure owing to Warren himself, who, in the five months that preceded the decision, had worked hard to bring it about. The Court left the question of adjustment to the law open to argument, but the next year decreed that segregation should end "with all deliberate speed." The significance of the ruling, which was aimed at the heart of the race problem (namely, different treatment based on a difference in color), was not lost on a single black man in America.

The pattern of separation of the races had, of course, preceded the decision in *Plessy* v. *Ferguson*. It had become firmly established in social gatherings long before emancipation. The founding of all-Negro churches in the seventeenth and early eighteenth centuries was, indeed, a reaction to the unwillingness of whites to hold religious services with blacks. And legal restrictions that isolated free Negroes, which began before the Revolution and steadily increased until the Civil War, were only interrupted by the Reconstruction imposed by the Army. The colonization schemes of the nineteenth century were openly tied to the idea of separateness and inequality. And the Supreme Court's decision in *Dred Scott* v. *Sanford* (1857), which officially stated that Africans and their descendants could not become citizens of the United States, only voiced the unofficial sentiment that had hardened to that view fifty years earlier.

In many ways, *Brown* v. *Board of Education* was more directly a reversal of *Dred Scott* v. *Sanford* than of *Plessy* v. *Ferguson*. The earlier decision was unequivocal in its implication that the United States was intended to be a white man's country. Much of the argument in the Dred Scott case was designed to show that the Constitution and the Declaration of Independence had never meant to include African peoples either as citizens or as a part of the "people" of the new nation. But even more significantly, Justice Taney's logic would have precluded for Scott the civil right of a trial even if his temporary residence in free territory was construed as manumission, which, of course, it was not. Scott had no rights because he was black. And blacks, whether free or not, could never become citizens. The no man's land in which blacks were thus placed was not overcome by the insistence on separateness in *Plessy* v. *Ferguson*. But the broad implication of *Brown* v. *Board of Education*, even though it focused on education, was that political equality, that is, citizenship, could never be achieved by a separatist philosophy. The Warren decision demanded that blacks be treated as citizens in the fullest sense. Although the decision was limited to schools, it was clear, because of the reflexive nature of the school problem, that a common education could make inroads into all the other areas of social inequality. The hope that it would do this, in any case, reflected the democratic faith in education to solve social and political problems.

The extent of the faith the Negro has placed in education is revealed by the exuberant response of even the most alienated blacks at the time of the Warren ruling. Eldridge Cleaver, whose image of the color line was the line between mind and body, wrote, in the 1960's, that the

> . . . decision in the case of *Brown* v. *Board of Education,* demolishing the principle of segregation of the races in public education . . . was a major surgical operation performed by nine men in black robes on the racial Maginot Line which is embedded as deep as sex or the lust for lucre in the schismatic American psyche. This piece of social surgery, if successful, . . . was meant to graft the nation's Mind back onto its Body and vice versa.

The operation, he felt at the time, had been successful and "a way station on a slow route travelled with all deliberate speed" had been reached. Others went so far as to suggest that the NAACP Legal Defense and Educational Fund, which had engineered the attack in the courts under the leadership of Thurgood Marshall, was no longer necessary and could close up shop.

It remained to be seen what effects the surgery would have on Cleaver's patient. Much disillusionment followed the 1954 decision. Compliance was generally slow, and Southern opposition to the ruling quickly solidified into massive resistance. Five states adopted forty-two segregation measures, and some Virginia counties closed down their public schools rather than integrate. In the late summer of 1957, Governor Orval Faubus ordered the Arkansas National Guard to prevent Negro children from attending white schools. A federal judge ordered the troops withdrawn, but mobs of whites refused to allow Negro students to enter a high school in Little Rock. On September 24, President Eisenhower took command of the Arkansas Guard and ordered it and federal marshals to enforce integration. After this show of force wide-scale resistance to the law diminished, but many blacks concluded that the spirit of the law had been nullified.

After twelve years of negligible compliance with the Warren decision, and, after the demise of the Civil Rights movement of the early 1960's, some blacks, like Stokely Carmichael, denounced integration as a subterfuge to maintain white supremacy. What was more important, Carmichael argued, was that black people control the schools in which their children were taught. In 1969, some Southern states, still opposed to the law on the ground that "mixed schools" would lead to "mixed blood," retreated once again from desegregation. They received the support of the Nixon Administration, which granted desegregation delays to thirty Mississippi school districts. But the Supreme Court, in a ruling that pronounced the "all deliberate speed" doctrine obsolete, declared that separate school systems should be immediately abolished. The decision (*Beatrice Alexander* v. *Holmes County Board of Education,* October, 1969) was an attempt by the Court to recapture the momentum of the 1954 case, which had been criticized in some quarters for allowing the opponents of integration time to marshal their ranks. In 1969, Southern reaction to the new ruling was more temperate than it had been fifteen years earlier. The law, Southern governors and senators announced, would be obeyed; but most predicted a collapse of the public school system. In the early 1970's, new legal battles, centering around the use of federal funds for public schools, were taking shape as Southern whites threatened to withdraw into a private school system.]

These cases come to us from the states of Kansas, South Carolina, Virginia, and Delaware. They are premised on different facts and different local conditions, but a common legal question justifies their consideration together in this consolidated opinion.[1]

In each of the cases, minors of the Negro race, through their legal representatives, seek the aid of the courts in obtaining admission to the public schools of their community on a nonsegregated basis. In each instance, they had been denied admission to schools attended by white children under laws requiring or permitting segregation according to race. This segregation was alleged to deprive the plaintiffs of the equal protection of the laws under the Fourteenth Amendment. In each of the cases other than the Delaware case, a three-judge federal District Court denied relief to the plaintiffs on the so-called "separate but equal" doctrine announced by this Court in *Plessy* v. *Ferguson*, 163 U.S. 537. Under that doctrine, equality of treatment is accorded when the races are provided substantially equal facilities, even though these facilities be separate. In the Delaware case, the Supreme Court of Delaware adhered to that doctrine, but ordered that the plaintiffs be admitted to the white schools because of their superiority to the Negro schools.

The plaintiffs contend that segregated public schools are not "equal" and cannot be made "equal," and that hence they are deprived of the equal protection of the laws. Because of the obvious importance of the question presented, the Court took jurisdiction.[2] Argument was heard in the 1952 Term, and reargument was heard this Term on certain questions propounded by the court.[3]

Reargument was largely devoted to the circumstances surrounding the adoption of the Fourteenth Amendment in 1868. It covered exhaustively consideration of the amendment in Congress, ratification by the states, then-existing practices in racial segregation, and the views of proponents and opponents of the amendment. This discussion and our own investigation convince us that, although these sources cast some light, it is not enough to resolve the problem with which we are faced. At best, they are inconclusive. The most avid proponents of the postwar amendments undoubtedly intended them to remove all legal distinctions among "all persons born or naturalized in the United States." Their opponents, just as certainly, were antagonistic to both the letter and the spirit of the amendments and wished them to have the most limited effect. What others in Congress and the state legislatures had in mind cannot be determined with any degree of certainty.

An additional reason for the inconclusive nature of the amendment's history, with respect to segregated schools, is the status of public education at that time.[4] In the South, the movement toward free common schools, supported by general taxation, had not yet taken hold. Education of white children was largely in the hands of private groups. Education of Negroes was almost nonexistent, and practically all of the race were illiterate. In fact, any education of Negroes was forbidden by law in some states. Today, in contrast, many Negroes have achieved oustanding success in the arts and sciences as well as the business and professional world. It is true that public-school education at the time of the amendment had advanced further in the North, but the effect of the amendment on Northern states was generally ignored in the congressional debates.

Even in the North, the conditions of public education did not approximate those existing today. The curriculum was usually rudimentary; ungraded schools were common in rural areas; the school term was but three months a year in many states; and compulsory school attendance was virtually unknown. As a consequence, it is not surprising that there should be so little in the history of the Fourteenth Amendment relating to its intended effect on public education.

In the first cases in this Court construing the Fourteenth Amendment, decided shortly after its adoption, the Court interpreted it as proscribing all state-imposed discriminations against the Negro race.[5] The doctrine of "separate but equal" did not make its appearance in this Court until 1896 in the case of *Plessy* v. *Ferguson, supra,* involving not education but transportation.[6] American courts have since labored with the doctrine for over half a century.

In this Court there have been six cases involving the "separate but equal" doctrine in the field of public education.[7] In *Cumming* v. *County Board of Education,* 175 U. S. 528, and *Gong Lum* v. *Rice,* 275 U. S. 78, the validity of the doctrine itself was not challenged. In more recent cases, all on the graduate-school level, inequality was found in that specific benefits enjoyed by white students were denied to Negro students of the same educational qualifications. *Missouri ex rel. Gaines* v. *Canada,* 305 U. S. 337; *Sipuel* v. *Oklahoma,* 332 U. S. 631; *Sweatt* v. *Painter,* 339 U. S. 629; *McLaurin* v. *Oklahoma State Regents,* 339 U. S. 637. In none of these cases was it necessary to reexamine the doctrine to grant relief to the Negro plaintiff. And in *Sweatt* v. *Painter, supra,* the Court expressly reserved decision on the question whether *Plessy* v. *Ferguson* should be held inapplicable to public education.

In the instant cases, that question is directly presented. Here, unlike *Sweatt* v. *Painter,* there are findings below that the Negro and white schools involved have been equalized, or are being equalized, with respect to buildings, curricula, qualifications and salaries of teachers, and other "tangible" factors.[9] Our decision, therefore, cannot turn on merely a comparison of these tangible factors in the Negro and white schools involved in each of the cases. We must look instead to the effect of segregation itself on public education.

In approaching this problem, we cannot turn the clock back to 1868 when the amendment was adopted, or even to 1896 when *Plessy* v. *Ferguson* was written. We must consider public education in the light of its full development and its present place in American life throughout the nation. Only in this way can it be determined if segregation in public schools deprives these plaintiffs of the equal protection of the laws.

Today, education is perhaps the most important function of state and local governments. Compulsory school-attendance laws and the great expenditures for education both demonstrate our recognition of the importance of education to our democratic society. It is required in the performance of our most basic public responsibilities, even service in the armed forces. It is the very foundation of good citizenship. Today it is a principal instrument in awakening the child to cultural values, in preparing him for later professional training, and in helping him to adjust normally to his environment. In these days, it is doubtful that any child may reasonably be expected to succeed in life if he is denied the opportunity of an education. Such an opportunity, where the state has undertaken to provide it, is a right which must be made available to all on equal terms.

We come then to the question presented: Does segregation of children in public schools solely on the basis of race, even though the physical facilities and other "tangible" factors may be equal, deprive the children of the minority group of equal educational opportunities? We believe that it does.

In *Sweatt* v. *Painter, supra,* in finding that a segregated law school for Negroes could not provide them equal educational opportunities, this Court relied in large part on "those qualities which are incapable of objective measurement but which make for greatness in a law school." In *McLaurin* v. *Oklahoma State Regents, supra,* the Court, in requiring that a Negro admitted to a white graduate school be treated like all other students, again resorted to intangible considerations: " . . . his ability to study, to engage in discussions and exchange views with other students, and, in general, to learn his profession." Such considerations apply with added force to children in grade and high schools. To separate them from others of similar age and qualifications solely because of their race generates a feeling of inferiority as to their status in the community that may affect their hearts and minds in a way unlikely ever to be undone. The effect of this separation on their educational opportunities was well stated by a finding in the Kansas case by a court which nevertheless felt compelled to rule against the Negro plaintiffs:

> Segregation of white and colored children in public schools has a detrimental effect upon the colored children. The impact is greater when it has the sanction of the law; for the policy of separating the races is usually interpreted as denoting the inferiority of the Negro group. A sense of

inferiority affects the motivation of a child to learn. Segregation with the sanction of law, therefore, has a tendency to [retard] the educational and mental development of Negro children and to deprive them of some of the benefits they would receive in a racial[ly] integrated school system.[10]

Whatever may have been the extent of psychological knowledge at the time of *Plessy* v. *Ferguson*, this finding is amply supported by modern authority.[11] Any language in *Plessy* v. *Ferguson* contrary to this finding is rejected.

We conclude that in the field of public education the doctrine of "separate but equal" has no place. Separate educational facilities are inherently unequal. Therefore, we hold that the plaintiffs and others similarly situated for whom the actions have been brought are, by reason of the segregation complained of, deprived of the equal protection of the laws guaranteed by the Fourteenth Amendment. This disposition makes unnecessary any discussion whether such segregation also violates the due process clause of the Fourteenth Amendment.[12]

Because these are class actions, because of the wide applicability of this decision, and because of the great variety of local conditions, the formulation of decrees in these cases presents problems of considerable complexity. On reargument, the consideration of appropriate relief was necessarily subordinated to the primary question—the constitutionality of segregation in public education. We have now announced that such segregation is a denial of the equal protection of the laws. In order that we may have the full assistance of the parties in formulating decrees, the cases will be restored to the docket, and the parties are requested to present further argument on Questions 4 and 5 previously propounded by the Court for the reargument this Term.[13] The attorney general of the United States is again invited to participate. The attorneys general of the states requiring or permitting segregation in public education will also be permitted to appear as *amici curiae* upon request to do so by Sept. 15, 1954, and submission of briefs by Oct. 1, 1954.[14]

NOTES

1. In the Kansas case, *Brown* v. *Board of Education*, the plaintiffs are Negro children of elementary-school age residing in Topeka. They brought this action in the United States District Court for the District of Kansas to enjoin enforcement of a Kansas statute which permits, but does not require, cities of more than 15,000 population to maintain separate school facilities for Negro and white students. Kan. Gen. Stat. Sec. 72-1724 (1949). Pursuant to that authority, the Topeka Board of Education elected to establish segregated elementary schools. Other public schools in the community, however, are operated on a nonsegregated basis. The three-judge District Court convened under 28 U.S.C. Sec. 2281 and 2284, found that segregation in public education has a detrimental effect upon Negro children, but denied relief on the ground that the Negro and white schools were substantially equal with respect to buildings, transportation, curricula, and educational qualifications of teachers. 98 F. Supp. 797. The case is here on direct appeal under 28 U.S.C. Sec. 1253.

In the South Carolina case, *Briggs* v. *Elliott*, the plaintiffs are Negro children of both elementary and high school age residing in Clarendon County. They brought this action in the United States District Court for the Eastern District of South Carolina to enjoin enforcement of provisions in the state constitution and statutory code which require the segregation of Negroes and whites in public schools. S.C. Const., Art. XI, Sec. 7; S.C Code Sec. 5377 (1942). The three-judge District Court, convened under 28 U.S.C. Sec. 2281 and 2284, denied the requested relief. The court found that the Negro schools were inferior to the white schools and ordered the defendants to begin immediately to equalize the facilities. But the court sustained the validity of the contested provisions and denied the plaintiffs admission to the white schools during the equalization program. 98 F. Supp. 529. This Court vacated the District Court's judgment and remanded the case for the purpose of obtaining the court's views on a report filed by the defendants concerning the progress made in the equalization program. 342 U.S. 350. On remand, the District Court found that substantial equality had been achieved except for buildings and that the defendants were proceeding to rectify this inequality as well. 103 F. Supp. 920. The case is again here on direct appeal under 28 U.S.C. Sec. 1253.

In the Virginia case, *Davis* v. *County School Board*, the plaintiffs are Negro children of high-school age residing in Prince Edward County. They brought this action in the United States District Court for the Eastern District of Virginia to enjoin enforcement of provisions in the state constitution and statutory code which require the segregation of Negroes and whites in public schools. Va. Const., Sec. 140; Va. Code Sec. 22-221 (1950). The three-judge District Court, convened under 28 U.S.C. Sec. 2281 and 2284, denied the requested relief. The court found the Negro school inferior in physical plant, curricula, and transportation, and ordered the defendants forthwith to provide substantially equal curricula and transportation and to "proceed with all reasonable diligence and dispatch to remove" the inequality in physical plant. But, as in the South Carolina case, the court sustained the validity of the contested provisions and denied the plaintiffs admission to the white schools during the equalization program. 103 F. Supp. 337. The case is here on direct appeal under 28 U.S.C. Sec. 1253. In the Delaware case, *Gebhart* v. *Belton*, the plaintiffs are Negro children of both elementary and high-school age residing in New Castle County. They brought this action in the Delaware Court of Chancery to enjoin enforcement of provisions in the state constitution and statutory code which require the segregation of Negroes and whites in public schools. Del. Const., Art. X, Sec. 2; Del. Rev. Code Sec. 2631 (1935). The chancellor gave judgment for the plaintiffs and ordered their immediate admission to schools previously attended only by white children on the ground that the Negro schools were inferior with respect to teacher training, pupil-teacher ratio, extracurricular activities, physcial plant, and time and distance involved in travel. 87 A. 2d 862. The chancellor also found that segregation itself results in an inferior education for Negro children (see note 10, *infra*), but did not rest his decision on that ground. *Id.*, at 865. The chancellor's decree was affirmed by the Supreme Court of Delaware, which intimated, however, that the defendants might be able to obtain a modification of the decree after equalization of the Negro and white schools had been accomplished. 91 A. 2nd 137, 152. The defendants, contending only that the Delaware courts had erred in ordering the immediate admission of the Negro plaintiffs to the white schools, applied to this Court for certiorari. The writ was granted, 344 U.S. 891. The plaintiffs, who were successful below, did not submit a cross-petition.

2. 344 U.S. 1, 141, 891.

3. 345 U.S. 972. The attorney general of the United States participated both Terms as *amicus curiae.*

4. For a general study of the development of public education prior to the amendment, see Butts and Cremin, *A History of Education in American Culture* (1953), Pts. I, II; Cubberley, *Public Education in the United States* (1934 ed.), cc. II-XII. School practices current at the time of the adoption of the Fourteenth Amendment are described in Butts and Cremin, *supra*, at 269-275; Cubberley, *supra*, at 288-339, 408-431; Knight, *Public Education in the South* (1922), cc. VIII, IX. See also H. Ex. Doc. No. 315, 41st Cong., 2nd Sess. (1871). Although the demand for free public schools followed substantially the same pattern in both the North and the South, the development in the South did not begin to gain momentum until about 1850, some twenty years after that in the North. The reasons for the somewhat slower development in the South (*e.g.*, the rural character of the South and the different regional attitudes toward state assistance) are well explained in Cubberley, *supra*, at 408-423. In the country as a whole, but particularly in the South, the war virtually stopped all progress in public education. *Id.*, at 427-428. The low status of Negro education in all sections of the country, both before and immediately after the war, is described in Beale, *A History of Freedom of Teaching in American Schools* (1941), 112-132, 175-195. Compulsory school-attendance laws were not generally adopted until after the ratification of the Fourteenth Amendment, and it was not until 1918 that such laws were in force in all the states. Cubberley, *supra*, at 563-565.

5. *Slaughter-House Cases*, 16 Wall. 36, 67-72 (1873); *Strauder* v. *West Virginia*, 100 U.S. 303, 307-308 (1880): "It ordains that no state shall deprive any person of life, liberty, or property, without due process of law, or deny to any person within its jurisdiction the equal protection of the laws. What is this but declaring that the law in the states shall be the same for the black as for the white; that all persons, whether colored or white, shall stand equal before the laws of the states, and, in regard to the colored race, for whose protection the amendment was primarily designed, that no discrimination shall be made against them by law because of their color? The words of the amendment, it is true, are prohibitory, but they contain a necessary implication of a positive immunity, or right, most valuable to the colored race—the right to exemption from unfriendly legislation against them distinctively as colored—exemption from legal discriminations, implying inferiority in civil society, lessening the security of their enjoyment of the rights which others enjoy, and discriminations which are steps toward reducing them to the condition of a subject race." See also *Virginia* v. *Rives*, 100 U.S. 313, 318 (1880); *Ex parte Virginia*, 100 U.S. 339, 344-345 (1880).

6. The doctrine apparently originated in *Roberts* v. *City of Boston*, 59 Mass. 198, 206

(1850), upholding school segregation against attack as being violative of a state constitutional guarantee of equality. Segregation in Boston public schools was eliminated in 1855. Mass. Acts 1855, c. 256. But elsewhere in the North, segregation in public education has persisted in some communities until recent years. It is apparent that such segregation has long been a nationwide problem, not merely one of sectional concern.

7. See also *Berea College* v. *Kentucky*, 211 U.S. 45 (1908).

8. In the *Cumming* case, Negro taxpayers sought an injunction requiring the defendant school board to discontinue the operation of a high school for white children until the board resumed operation of a high school for Negro children. Similarly, in the *Gong Lum* case, the plaintiff, a child of Chinese descent, contended only that state authorities had misapplied the doctrine by classifying him with Negro children and requiring him to attend a Negro school.

9. In the Kansas case, the court below found substantial equality as to all such factors. 98 F. Supp. 797, 798. In the South Carolina case, the court below found that the defendants were proceeding "promptly and in good faith to comply with the court's decree." 103 F. Supp. 920, 921. In the Virginia case, the court below noted that the equalization program was already "afoot and progressing" (103 F. Supp. 337, 341); since then, we have been advised, in the Virginia attorney general's brief on reargument, that the program has now been completed. In the Delaware case, the court below similarly noted that the state's equalization program was well under way. 91 A. 2d 137, 149.

10. A similar finding was made in the Delaware case: "I conclude from the testimony that, in our Delaware society, state-imposed segregation in education itself results in the Negro children, as a class, receiving educational opportunities which are substantially inferior to those available to white children otherwise similarly situated." 87 A. 2d 862, 865.

11. K. B. Clark, *Effect of Prejudice and Discrimination on Personality Development* (Midcentury White House Conference on Children and Youth, 1950); Witmer and Kotinsky, *Personality in the Making* (1952), c. VI; Deutscher and Chein, "The Psychological Effects of Enforced Segregation: A Survey of Social Science Opinion," 26 *J. Psychol.* 259 (1948); Chein, "What are the Psychological effects of Segregation Under Conditions of Equal Facilities?" 3 *Int. J. Opinion and Attitude Res.* 229 (1949); Brameld, *Educational Costs, in Discrimination and National Welfare* (MacIver, ed., 1949), 44-48; Frazier, *The Negro in the United States* (1949), 674-681. And see generally Myrdal, *An American Dilemma* (1944).

12. See *Bolling* v. *Sharpe, post.* p. 497, concerning the due process clause of the Fifth Amendment.

13. "4. Assuming it is decided that segregation in public schools violates the Fourteenth Amendment.

"(a) would a decree necessarily follow providing that, within the limits set by normal geographic school districting, Negro children should forthwith be admitted to schools of their choice, or

"(b) may this Court, in the exercise of its equity powers, permit an effective gradual adjustment to be brought about from existing segregated systems to a system not based on color distinctions?

"5. On the assumption on which questions 4 (a) and (b) are based, and assuming further that this Court will exercise its equity powers to the end described in question 4 (b),

"(a) should this Court formulate detailed decrees in these cases;

"(b) if so, what specific issues should the decrees reach;

"(c) should this Court appoint a special master to hear evidence with a view to recommending specific terms for such decrees;

"(d) should this Court remand to the courts of first instance with directions to frame decrees in these cases, and if so what general directions should the decrees of this Court include and what procedures should the courts of first instance follow in arriving at the specific terms of more detailed decrees?"

14. See Rule 42, Revised Rules of this Court (effective July 1, 1954).

BLACK BOURGEOISIE

E. Franklin Frazier

[E. Franklin Frazier's
Black Bourgeoisie, the concluding chapter of which is reprinted here,
was first written in French and published in Paris in 1955, the same year
that Rosa Parks's defiance of Southern custom precipitated a fifty-five-
week bus boycott by the Negroes in Montgomery, Alabama, and inspired,
seemingly, a new age of protest. The English version of the book, which
was published in the United States in 1957, was to have a similar effect
among Negro intellectuals and Negro youth, many of whom had become
dissatisfied with the polite leadership of the previous generation.

Although a sociological study, Frazier's book was a polemic against the
Negro middle class, which Frazier had characterized as early as 1925 as
"a strange mixture of the peasant and the gentleman," and whose ancestry was the mixed-blood aristocracy that was free before the Civil
War. "Two hundred years of enforced labor," he had written in his first
article on the subject, "with no incentive in its just reward, more than
any inherent traits, explain why the Negro has for so long been concerned with consumption rather than production. Peasant virtues are
middle class faults. And so are the gentleman's; and the Negro has come
by these in curious but inevitable ways." It was precisely this peasant-
cum-gentleman who was most shocked by the book and who felt that
Frazier, himself a Negro, had betrayed the Negro community.

Frazier's concern for the Negro middle class—the Negro, he felt, lacked
a true upper class—grew out of his interest in the traditions of the Negro family. It was this interest that had led to his major work, *The Negro Family in the United States* (1939), a kind of natural history of the
Negro family as it evolved through slavery and emancipation. Throughout his work, Frazier assumed that the family structure grew as a peculiar response to the environment in which it flourished.

Frazier was convinced that the Negro family, which had become oriented largely to the values of American culture, had assured the survival of the Negro in American society. The development by Negroes of an institutional family in the space of about 175 years, Frazier said, telescoped the agelong evolution of the human family. The last conclusion is especially interesting as it reinforces the view that African tradition has disappeared among American Negroes. The matriarchal organization, for example, where it exists, is both a response to the conditions of the American environment and a repetition of one of the archetypal ways of organizing a human family. It is not, Frazier felt, a perpetuation of or a reversion to a matriarchal tradition in the African heritage. Similarly, polygamous patterns among Negro males, where they exist, are not a carry-over from an ancient heritage; they reflect, rather, the lack of a deeply rooted family tradition, a lack traceable to the ugly facts of slavery. Frazier was convinced, that is, that the African cultural heritage perished because no social organization was formed to perpetuate it. The only social institution that existed for the Negro during slavery was the plantation system, and the only cultural heritage that this provided was European and not African.

Black Bourgeoisie supports Frazier's general view that the African cultural heritage has been completely sloughed off, a view that continues to generate much controversy. The predicament of the bourgeoisie was that they were running away from both the folk culture of the Negro masses and the remnants of the genteel tradition. They were thus living in a vacuum, devoting their lives to fatuities, conspicuous consumption, and a world of make believe, aided in this, of course, by their rejection by the white world. Frazier's book was welcomed by a new generation of blacks who did not aspire to become the hollow men and women that Frazier portrayed and who, in keeping with the swelling nationalist tide, celebrated the cultural values of the Negro masses.]

BEHIND THE MASKS

Since the Black Bourgeoisie live largely in a world of make-believe, the masks which they wear to play their sorry roles conceal the feelings of inferiority and of insecurity and the frustrations that haunt their inner lives. Despite their attempt to escape from real identification with the masses of Negroes, they can not escape the mark of oppression any more than their less favored kinsmen. In attempting to escape identification with the black masses, they have developed a self-hatred that reveals itself in their deprecation of the physical and social characteristics of Negroes. Likewise, their feelings of inferiority and insecurity are revealed in their pathological struggle for status within the isolated Negro world and craving for recognition in the white world. Their escape into a world of make-believe with its sham "society" leaves them with a feeling of emptiness and futility which causes them to constantly seek an escape in new delusions.

1. The Mark of Oppression

There is an attempt on the part of the parents in middle-class families to shield their children against racial discrimination and the contempt of whites for colored people. Sometimes the parents go to fantastic extremes, such as prohibiting the use of the words "Negro" or "colored" in the presence of their children. They sometimes try to prevent their children from knowing that they can not enter restaurants or other public places because they are Negroes, or even that the schools they attend are segregated schools for Negroes. Despite such efforts to insulate their children against a hostile white world, the children of the black bourgeoisie can not escape the mark of oppression. This is strikingly revealed in the statement of a seventeen-year-old middle-class Negro youth. When asked if he felt inferior in the presence of white people, he gave the following answer—which was somewhat unusual for its frankness but typical of the attitude of the black bourgeoisie:

> Off-hand, I'd say no, but actually knowing all these things that are thrown up to you about white people being superior—that they look more or less down upon all Negroes—that we have to look to them for everything we get—that they'd rather think of us as mice than men–I don't believe I or any other Negro can help but feel inferior. My father says that it isn't so— that we only feel inferior to those whom we feel are superior. But I don't believe we can feel otherwise. Around white people until I know them a while I feel definitely out of place. Once I played a ping-pong match with a white boy whose play I know wasn't as good as mine, and boys he managed to beat with ease, but I just couldn't get it out of my mind that I was playing a white boy. Sort of an Indian sign on me, you know.

The statement of this youth reveals how deep-seated is the feeling of inferiority, from which even the most favored elements among Negroes can not escape. However much some middle-class Negroes may seek to soothe their feeling of inferiority in an attitude which they often express in the adage, "it is better to reign in hell than serve in heaven," they are still conscious of their inferior status in American society. They may say, as did a bewildered middle-class youth, that they are proud of being a Negro or proud of being a member of the upper stratum in the Negro community and feel sorry for the Negro masses "stuck in the mud," but they often confess, as did this youth:

> However, knowing that there are difficulties that confront us all as Negroes, if I could be born again and had my choice I'd really want to be a white boy—I mean white or my same color, providing I could occupy the same racial and economic level I now enjoy. I am glad I am this color—I'm frequently taken for a foreigner. I wouldn't care to be lighter or darker and be a Negro. I am the darkest one in the family due to my constant outdoor activities. I realize of course that there are places where I can't go despite

my family or money just because I happen to be a Negro. With my present education, family background, and so forth, if I was only white I could go places in life. A white face holds supreme over a black one despite its economic and social status. Frankly, it leaves me bewildered.

Not all middle-class Negroes consciously desire, as this youth, to be white in order to escape from their feelings of inferiority. In fact, the majority of middle-class Negroes would deny having the desire to be white, since this would be an admission of their feeling of inferiority. Within an intimate circle of friends some middle-class Negroes may admit that they desire to be white, but publicly they would deny any such wish. The black bourgeoisie constantly boast of their pride in their identification as Negroes. But when one studies the attitude of this class in regard to the physical traits or the social characteristics of Negroes, it becomes clear that the black bourgeoisie do not really wish to be identified with Negroes.

2. Insecurities and Frustrations

Since the black bourgeoisie can not escape identification with Negroes, they experience certain feelings of insecurity because of their feeling of inferiority. Their feeling of inferiority is revealed in their fear of competition with whites. There is first a fear of competition with whites for jobs. Notwithstanding the fact that middle-class Negroes are the most vociferous in demanding the right to compete on equal terms with whites, many of them still fear such competition. They prefer the security afforded by their monopoly of certain occupations within the segregated Negro community. For example, middle-class Negroes demand that the two Negro medical schools be reserved for Negro students and that a quota be set for white students, though Negro students are admitted to "white" medical schools. Since the Supreme Court of the United States has ruled against segregated public schools, many Negro teachers, even those who are well-prepared, fear that they can not compete with whites for teaching positions. Although this fear stems principally from a feeling of inferiority which is experienced generally by Negroes, it has other causes.

The majority of the black bourgeoisie fear competition with whites partly because such competition would mean that whites were taking them seriously, and consequently they would have to assume a more serious and responsible attitude towards their work. Middle-class Negroes, who are notorious for their inefficiency in the management of various Negro institutions, excuse their inefficiency on the grounds that Negroes are a "young race" and, therefore, will require time to attain the efficiency of the white man. The writer has heard a Negro college president, who has constantly demanded that Negroes have equality in American life, declare before white people in extenuation of the shortcomings of his own administration, that Negroes were a "child race" and that they had "to crawl before they could walk." Such declarations, while flattering to the whites, are revealing in that they manifest the black bourgeoisie's contempt for the Negro masses, while excusing its own deficiencies by attributing them to the latter. Yet it is clear that the black workers who must gain a living in a white man's mill or factory and in competition with white workers cannot offer any such excuse for his inefficiency.

The fear of competition with whites is probably responsible for the black bourgeoisie's fear of competence and first-rate performance within his own ranks. When a Negro is competent and insists upon first-rate work it appears to this class that he is trying to be a white man, or that he is insisting that Negroes measure up to white standards. This is especially true where the approval of whites is taken as a mark of competence and first-rate performance. In such cases the black bourgeoisie reveal their ambivalent attitudes toward the white world. They slavishly accept the estimate which almost any white man places upon a Negro or his work, but at the same time they fear and reject white standards. For example, when a group of Negro doctors were being shown the modern equipment and techniques of a white clinic, one of them remarked to a Negro professor in a medical school, "This is the white man's medicine. I never bother with it and still I make $30,000 a year." Negroes who adopt the standards of the white world create among the black bourgeoisie a feeling of insecurity and often become the object of both the envy and hatred of this class.

Among the women of the black bourgeoisie there is an intense fear of the competition of white women for Negro men. They often attempt to rationalize their fear by saying that the Negro man always occupies an inferior position in relation to the white woman or that he marries much below his "social" status. They come nearer to the source of their fear when they confess that there are not many eligible Negro men and that these few should marry Negro women. That such rationalizations conceal deep-seated feelings of insecurity is revealed by the fact that generally they have no objection to the marriage of white men to Negro women, especially if the white man is reputed to be wealthy. In fact, they take pride in the fact and attribute these marriages to the "peculiar" charms of Negro women. In fact, the middle-class Negro woman's fear of the competition of white women is based often upon the fact that she senses her own inadequacies and shortcomings. Her position in Negro "society" and in the larger Negro community is often due to some adventitious factor, such as a light complexion or a meager education, which has pushed her to the top of the social pyramid. The middle-class white woman not only has a white skin and straight hair, but she is generally more sophisticated and interesting because she has read more widely and has a larger view of the world. The middle-class Negro woman may make fun of the "plainness" of her white competitor and the latter's lack of "wealth" and interest in "society"; nevertheless she still feels insecure when white women appear as even potential competitors.

Both men and women among the black bourgeoisie have a feeling of insecurity because of their constant fear of the loss of status. Since they have no status in the larger American society, the intense struggle for status among middle-class Negroes is, as we have seen, an attempt to compensate for the contempt and low esteem of the whites. Great value is, therefore, placed upon all kinds of status symbols. Academic degrees, both real and honorary, are sought in order to secure status. Usually the symbols are of a material nature implying wealth and conspicuous consumption. Sometimes Negro doctors do not attend what are supposedly scientific meetings because they do not have a Cadillac or some other expensive automobile. School teachers wear mink coats and maintain homes beyond their incomes for fear that they may lose status. The extravagance in "social" life generally is due to an effort not to lose status. But in attempting to overcome their fear of loss of status they are often beset by new feelings of insecurity. In spite of their pretended wealth, they are aware that their incomes are insignificant and that they must struggle to maintain their mortgaged homes and the show of "wealth" in lavish "social" affairs. Moreover, they are beset by a feeling of insecurity because of their struggles to maintain a show of wealth through illegal means. From time to time "wealthy" Negro doctors are arrested for selling narcotics and performing abortions. The life of many a "wealthy" Negro doctor is shortened by the struggle to provide diamonds, minks, and an expensive home for his wife.

There is much frustration among the black bourgeoisie despite their privileged position within the segregated Negro world. Their "wealth" and "social" position can not erase the fact that they are generally segregated and rejected by the white world. Their incomes and occupations may enable them to escape the cruder manifestations of racial prejudice, but they can not insulate themselves against the more subtle forms of racial discrimination. These discriminations cause frustrations in Negro men because they are not allowed to play the "masculine role" as defined by American culture. They can not assert themselves or exercise power as white men do. When they protest against racial discrimination there is always the threat that they will be punished by the white world. In spite of the movement toward the wider integration of the Negro into the general stream of American life, middle-class Negroes are still threatened with the loss of positions and earning power if they insist upon their rights. After the Supreme Court of the United States ruled that segregation in public education was illegal, Negro teachers in some parts of the South were dismissed because they would not sign statements supporting racial segregation in education.

As one of the results of not being able to play the "masculine role," middle-class Negro males have intended to cultivate their "personalities" which enable them to exercise considerable influence among whites and achieve distinction in the Negro world. Among Negroes they have been noted for their glamour. In this respect they resemble women who use their "personalities" to compensate for their inferior status in relation to men. This fact would seem to support the observation of an American sociologist that the Negro was "the lady among the races," if he had restricted his observation to middle-class males among American Negroes.

In the South the middle-class Negro male is not only prevented from playing a masculine role, but generally he must let Negro women assume leadership in any show of militancy. This reacts upon his status in the home where the tradition of female dominance, which is widely established among Negroes, has tended to assign a subordinate role to the male. In fact, in middle-class families, especially if the husband has risen in social status through his own efforts and married a member of an "old" family or a "society" woman, the husband is likely to play a pitiful role. The greatest compliment that can be paid such a husband is that he "worships his wife," which means that he is her slave and supports all her extravagances and vanities. But, of course, many husbands in such positions escape from their frustrations by having extra-marital sex relations. Yet the conservative and conventional middle-class husband presents a pathetic picture. He often sits at home alone, impotent physically and socially, and complains that his wife has gone crazy about poker and "society" and constantly demands money for gambling and expenditures which he can not afford. Sometimes he enjoys the sympathy of a son or daughter who has not become a "socialite." Such children often say that they had a happy family life until "mamma took to poker."

Preoccupation with poker on the part of the middle-class woman is often an attempt to escape from a frustrated life. Her frustration may be bound up with her unsatisfactory sexual life. She may be married to a "glamorous" male who neglects her for other women. For among the black bourgeoisie, the glamour of the male is often associated with his sexual activities. The frustration of many Negro women has a sexual origin. Even those who have sought an escape from frustration in sexual promiscuity may, because of satiety or deep psychological reasons, become obsessed with poker in order to escape from their frustrations. One "society" woman, in justification of her obsession with poker remarked that it had taken the place of her former preoccupation with sex. Another said that to win at poker was similar to a sexual orgasm.

The frustration of the majority of the women among the black bourgeoisie is probably due to the idle or ineffectual lives which they lead. Those who do not work devote their time to the frivolities of Negro "society." When they devote their time to "charity" or worth-while causes, it is generally a form of play or striving for "social" recognition. They are constantly forming clubs which ostensibly have a serious purpose, but in reality are formed in order to consolidate their position in "society" or to provide additional occasions for playing poker. The idle, overfed women among the black bourgeoisie are generally, to use their language, "dripping with diamonds." They are forever dieting and reducing only to put on more weight (which is usually the result of the food that they consume at their club meetings). Even the women among the black bourgeoisie who work exhibit the same frustrations. Generally, they have no real interest in their work and only engage in it in order to be able to provide the conspicuous consumption demanded by "society." As we have indicated, the women as well as the men among the black bourgeoisie read very little and have no interest in music, art or the theater. They are constantly restless and do not know how to relax. They are generally dull people and only become animated when "social" matters are discussed, especially poker games. They are afraid to be alone and constantly seek to be surrounded by their friends, who enable them to escape from their boredom.

The frustrated lives of the black bourgeoisie are reflected in the attitudes of parents towards their children. Middle-class Negro families as a whole have few children, while among the families that constitute Negro "society" there are many childless couples. One finds today, as an American observed over forty years ago, that "where the children are few, they are usually spoiled" in middle-class Negro families. There is often not only a deep devotion to their one or two children, but a subservience to them. It is not uncommon for the only son to be called and treated as the "boss" in the family. Parents cater to the transient wishes of their children and often rationalize their behavior towards them on the grounds that children should not be "inhibited." They spend large sums of money on their children for toys and especially for clothes. They provide their children with automobiles when they go to college. All of this is done in order that the children may maintain the status of the parents and be eligible to enter the "social" set in Negro colleges. When they send their children to northern "white" colleges they often spend more time in preparing them for what they imagine will be their "social" life than in preparing them for the academic requirements of these institutions.

In their fierce devotion to their children, which generally results in spoiling them, middle-class Negro parents are seemingly striving at times to establish a human relationship that will compensate for their own frustrations in the realm of human relationships. Devotion to their children often becomes the one human tie that is sincere and free from the competition and artificiality of the make-believe world in which they live. Sometimes they may project upon their children their own frustrated professional ambitions. But usually, even when they send their children to northern "white" universities as a part of their "social" striving within the Negro community, they seem to hope that their children will have an acceptance in the white world which has been denied them.

3. Self-Hatred and Guilt Feelings

One of the chief frustrations of the middle-class Negro is that he can not escape identification with the Negro race and consequently is subject to the contempt of whites. Despite his "wealth" in which he has placed so much faith as a solvent of racial discrimination, he is still subject to daily insults and is excluded from participation in white American society. Middle-class Negroes do not express their resentment against discrimination and insults in violent outbreaks, as lower-class Negroes often do. They constantly repress their hostility toward whites and seek to soothe their hurt self-esteem in all kinds of rationalizations. They may boast of their wealth and culture as compared with the condition of the poor whites. Most often they will resort to any kind of subterfuge in order to avoid contact with whites. For example, in the South they often pay their bills by mail rather than risk unpleasant contacts with representatives of white firms. The daily repression of resentment and the constant resort to means of avoiding contacts with whites do not relieve them of their hostility toward whites. Even middle-class Negroes who gain a reputation for exhibiting "objectivity" and a "statesmanlike" attitude on racial discrimination harbor deep-seated hostilities toward whites. A Negro college president who has been considered such an interracial "statesman" once confessed to the writer that some day he was going to "break loose" and tell white people what he really thought. However, it is unlikely that a middle-class Negro of his standing will ever "break loose." Middle-class Negroes generally express their aggressions against whites by other means, such as deceiving whites and utilizing them for their own advantage.

Because middle-class Negroes are unable to indulge in aggression against whites as such, they will sometimes make other minority groups the object of their hostilities. For example, they may show hostility against Italians, who are also subject to discrimination. But more often middle-class Negroes, especially those who are engaged in a mad scramble to accumulate money, will direct their hostilities against Jews. They are constantly expressing their anti-semitism within Negro circles, while pretending publicly to be free from prejudice. They blame the Jew for the poverty of Negroes and for their own failures and inefficiencies in their business undertakings. In expressing their hostility towards Jews, they are attempting at the same time to identify with the white American majority.

The repressed hostilities of middle-class Negroes to whites are not only directed towards other minority groups but inward toward themselves. This results in self-hatred, which may appear from their behavior to be directed towards the Negro masses but which in reality is directed against themselves. While pretending to be proud of being a Negro, they ridicule Negroid physical characteristics and seek to modify or efface them as much as possible. Within their own groups they constantly proclaim that "niggers" make them sick. The very use of the term "nigger," which they claim to resent, indicates that they want to disassociate themselves from the Negro masses. They talk condescendingly of Africans and of African culture, often even objecting to African sculpture in their homes. They are insulted if they are identified with Africans. They refuse to join organizations that are interested in Africa. If they are of mixed ancestry, they may boast of the fact that they have Indian ancestry. When making compliments concerning the beauty of Negroes of mixed ancestry, they generally say, for example, "She is beautiful; she looks like an Indian." On the other hand, if a black woman has European features, they will remark condescendingly, "Although she is black, you must admit that she is good looking." Some middle-class Negroes of mixed ancestry like to wear Hindu costumes—while they laugh at the idea of wearing an African costume. When middle-class Negroes travel, they studiously avoid association with other Negroes, especially if they themselves have received the slightest recognition by whites. Even when they can not "pass" for white they fear that they will lose this recognition if they are identified as Negroes. Therefore, nothing pleases them more than to be mistaken for a Puerto Rican, Philippino, Egyptian or Arab or any ethnic group other than Negro.

The self-hatred of middle-class Negroes is often revealed in the keen competition which exists among them for status and recognition. This keen competition is the result of the frustrations which they experience in attempting to obtain acceptance and recognition by whites. Middle-class Negroes are constantly criticizing and belittling Negroes who achieve some recognition or who acquire a status above them. They prefer to submit to the authority of whites than to be subordinate to other Negroes. For example, Negro scholars generally refuse to seek the advice and criticism of competent Negro scholars and prefer to turn to white scholars for such co-operation. In fact, it is difficult for middle-class Negroes to co-operate in any field of endeavor. This failure in social relations is, as indicated in an important study, because "in every Negro he encounters his own self-contempt." It is as if he said, "You are only a Negro like myself; so why should you be in a position above me?"

This self-hatred often results in guilt feelings on the part of the Negro who succeeds in elevating himself above his fellows. He feels unconsciously that in rising above other Negroes he is committing an act of aggression which will result in hatred and revenge on their part. The act of aggression may be imagined, but very often it is real. This is the case when middle-class Negroes oppose the economic and social welfare of Negroes because of their own interests. In some American cities, it has been the black bourgeoisie and not the whites who have opposed the building of lowcost public housing for Negro workers. In one city two wealthy Negro doctors, who have successfully opposed public housing projects for Negro workers, own some of the worst slums in the United States. While their wives, who wear mink coats, "drip with diamonds" and are written up in the "society" columns of Negro newspapers, ride in Cadillacs, their Negro tenants sleep on the dirt floors of hovels unfit for human habitation. The guilt feelings of the middle-class Negro are not always unconscious. For example, take the case of the Negro leader who proclaimed over the radio in a national broadcast that the Negro did not want social equity. He was conscious of his guilt feelings and his self-hatred in playing such a role, for he sent words privately to the writer that he never hated so much to do anything in his life, but that it was necessary because of his position as head of a state college which was under white supervision. The self-hatred of the middle-class Negro arises, then, not only from the fact that he does not want to be a Negro but also because of his sorry role in American society.

4. Escape into Delusions

The black bourgeoisie, as we have seen, has created a world of make-believe to shield itself from the harsh economic and social realities of American life. This world of make-believe is created out of the myth of Negro business, the reports of the Negro press on the achievements and wealth of Negroes, the recognition accorded them by whites, and the fabulous life of Negro "society." Some of the middle-class Negro intellectuals are not deceived by the world of make-believe. They will have nothing to do with Negro "society" and refuse to waste their time in frivolities. They take their work seriously and live in relative obscurity

so far as the Negro world is concerned. Others seek an escape from their
frustrations by developing, for example, a serious interest in Negro
music—which the respectable black bourgeoisie often pretend to despise.
In this way these intellectuals achieve some identification with the Negro masses and with the traditions of Negro life. But many more middle-
class Negroes, who are satisfied to live in the world of make-believe but
must find a solution to the real economic and social problems which
they face, seek an escape in delusions.

They seek an escape in delusions involving wealth. This is facilitated
by the fact that they have had little experience with the real meaning of
wealth and that they lack a tradition of saving and accumulation. Wealth
to them means spending money without any reference to its source.
Hence, their behavior generally reflects the worst qualities of the gentleman and peasant from whom their only vital traditions spring. Therefore, their small accumulations of capital and the income which they
receive from professional services within the Negro community make
them appear wealthy in comparison with the low economic status of the
majority of Negroes. The delusion of wealth is supported by the myth of
Negro business. Moreover, the attraction of the delusion of wealth is en-
hanced by the belief that wealth will gain them acceptance in American
life. In seeking an escape in the delusion of wealth, middle-class Negroes
make a fetish of material things or physical possessions. They are constantly buying things—houses, automobiles, furniture and all sorts of
gadgets, not to mention clothes. Many of the furnishings and gadgets
which they acquire are never used; nevertheless they continue to accumulate things. The homes of many middle-class Negroes have the appearance of museums for the exhibition of American manufactures and
spurious art objects. The objects which they are constantly buying are
always on display. Negro school teachers who devote their lives to "society" like to display twenty to thirty pairs of shoes, the majority of
which they never wear. Negro professional men proudly speak of the
two automobiles which they have acquired when they need only one. The
acquisition of objects which are not used or needed seems to be an attempt to fill some void in their lives.

The delusion of power also appears to provide an escape for middle-
class Negroes from the world of reality which pierces through the world
of make-believe of the black bourgeoisie. The positions of power which
they occupy in the Negro world often enable them to act autocratically
towards other Negroes, especially when they have the support of the
white community. In such cases the delusion of power may provide an
escape from their frustrations. It is generally, however, when middle-
class Negroes hold positions enabling them to participate in the white
community that they seek in the delusion of power an escape from their
frustrations. Although their position may be only a "token" of the integration of the Negro into American life, they will speak and act as if
they were a part of the power structure of American society. Negro advisers who are called into council by whites to give advice about Negroes
are especially likely to find an escape from their feelings of inferiority
in the delusion of power. Negro social workers, who are dependent upon

white philanthropy, have often gained the reputation, with the support of the Negro press, of being powerful persons in American communities.

However, the majority of the black bourgeoisie who seek an escape from their frustrations in delusions seemingly have not been able to find it in the delusion of wealth or power. They have found it in magic or chance, and in sex and alcohol. Excessive drinking and sex seems to provide a means for narcotizing the middle-class Negro against a frustrating existence. A "social" function is hardly ever considered a success unless a goodly number of the participants "pass out." But gambling, especially poker, which has become an obsession among many middle-class Negroes, offers the chief escape into delusion. Among the black bourgeoisie it is not simply a device for winning money. It appears to be a magical device for enhancing their self-esteem through overcoming fate. Although it often involves a waste of money which many middle-class Negroes can not afford, it has an irresistible attraction which they often confess they can not overcome.

Despite the tinsel, glitter and gaiety of the world of make-believe in which middle-class Negroes take refuge, they are still beset by feelings of insecurity, frustration and guilt. As a consequence, the free and easy life which they appear to lead is a mask for their unhappy existence.

Conclusion

When viewed in the broad perspective of the changes which are occurring in the western world, this study of the black bourgeoisie reveals in an acute form many of the characteristics of modern bourgeois society, especially in the United States. Hence it was difficult to resist the temptation to compare the black bourgeoisie with the same class among white Americans. However, it was not the purpose of this study to isolate and analyze the common characteristics of this class in the modern world. Our task was less ambitious and therefore more restricted. Our purpose was to treat the black bourgeoisie as a case study of a middle-class group which had emerged during the changing adjustment of a racial minority to modern industrial society. From this stand-point our study may have a broader significance than the group which we have studied. It may have some relevance for the study of the emergence of a middle class in colonial societies, especially in African societies at present undergoing rapid changes. The characteristics of this class in the various societies will have to be studied in each case in relation to its history and the economic and social forces which are responsible for its development.

The black bourgeoisie in the United States is an essentially American phenomenon. Its emergence and its rise to importance within the Negro community are closely tied up with economic and social changes in the American community. Its behavior as well as its mentality is a reflection of American modes of behavior and American values. What may appear as distortions of American patterns of behavior and thought are due to the fact that the Negro lives on the margin of American society. The very existence of a separate Negro community with its own institutions

within the heart of the American society is indicative of its quasi-patho-
logical character, especially since the persistence of this separate community has been due to racial discrimination and oppression.

As the result of this fact, the black bourgeoisie is unique in a number
of respects: First, it lacks a basis in the American economic system.
Among colonial peoples and among other racial minorities, the bourgeoisie usually comes into existence as the result of its role in the economic organization of these societies. But the black bourgeoisie in the
United States has subsisted off the crumbs of philanthropy, the salaries
of public servants, and what could be squeezed from the meager earn-
ings of Negro workers. Hence "Negro business," which has no significance in the American economy, has become a social myth embodying
the aspirations of this class. Then, because of the position of the Negro
in American life, it has been impossible for the black bourgeoisie to play
the traditional role of this class among minorities. The attempt on the
part of the Communist Party to assign to the black bourgeoisie the traditional role of this class, in what the Party defined as the struggle of
the "Negro people" for "national liberation," only tended to emphasize
the unreality of the position of the black bourgeoisie. Moreover, the
black bourgeoisie have shown no interest in the "liberation" of Negroes
except as it affected their own status or acceptance by the white community. They viewed with scorn the Garvey Movement with its nationalistic aims. They showed practically no interest in the Negro Renaissance.
They wanted to forget the Negro's past, and they have attempted to conform to the behavior and values of the white community in the most
minute details. Therefore they have often become, as has been observed,
"exaggerated" Americans.

Because of its struggle to gain acceptance by whites, the black bourgeoisie has failed to play the role of a responsible elite in the Negro
community. Many individuals among the first generation of educated Negroes, who were the products of missionary education, had a sense of
responsibility toward the Negro masses and identified themselves with
the struggles of the masses to overcome the handicaps of ignorance and
poverty. Their influence over the masses was limited, to be sure—not,
however, because of any lack of devotion on their part, but because of
the control exercised by the white community. Nevertheless, they occupied a dignified position within the Negro community and were respected. As teachers of Negroes, they generally exhibited the same sincere
interest in education and genuine culture as their missionary teachers.
Therefore they did not regard teaching merely as a source of income. On the other hand, today many Negro teachers refuse identification with the Negro masses and look upon teaching primarily as a source
of income. In many cases they have nothing but contempt for their Negro pupils. Moreover, they have no real interest in education and genuine culture and spend their leisure in frivolities and in activities designed to win a place in Negro "society."

When the opportunity has been present, the black bourgeoisie has exploited the Negro masses as ruthlessly as have whites. As the intellectual
leaders in the Negro community, they have never dared think beyond

a narrow, opportunistic philosophy that provided a rationalization for their own advantages. Although the black bourgeoisie exercise considerable influence on the values of Negroes, they do not occupy a dignified position in the Negro community. The masses regard the black bourgeoisie as simply those who have been "lucky in getting money" which enables them to engage in conspicuous consumption. When this class pretends to represent the best manners or morals of the Negro, the masses regard such claims as hypocrisy.

The single factor that has dominated the mental outlook of the black bourgeoisie has been its obsession with the struggle for status. The struggle for status has expressed itself mainly in the emphasis upon "social" life or "society." The concern of the Negro for "social" life and "society" has been partly responsible for the failure of educated Negroes to make important contributions within the fields of science or art. Educated Negroes have been constantly subjected to the pressures of the black bourgeoisie to conform to its values. Because of this pressure some gifted Negroes have abandoned altogether their artistic and scientific aspirations, while others have chosen to play the role of phony intellectuals and cater to the ignorance and vanities of the black bourgeoisie in order to secure "social" acceptance. Since middle-class Negroes have never been permitted to play a serious role in American life, "social" life has offered an area of competition in which the serious affairs of life were not involved. Middle-class Negroes who have made real contributions in science and art have had to escape from the influence of the "social" life of the black bourgeoisie. In fact, the spirit of play or lack of serious effort has permeated every aspect of the life of the Negro community. It has, therefore, tended to encourage immaturity and childishness on the part of middle-class Negroes, whose lives are generally devoted to trivialities.

The emphasis upon "social" life or "society" is one of the main props of the world of make-believe into which the black bourgeoisie has sought an escape from its inferiority and frustrations in American society. This world of make-believe, to be sure, is a reflection of the values of American society, but it lacks the economic basis that would give it roots in the world of reality. In escaping into a world of make-believe, middle-class Negroes have rejected both identification with the Negro and his traditional culture. Through delusions of wealth and power they have sought identification with the white America which continues to reject them. But these delusions leave them frustrated because they are unable to escape from the emptiness and futility of their existence. Gertrude Stein would have been nearer the truth if she had said of the black bourgeoisie what she said of Negroes in general, that they "were not suffering from persecution, they were suffering from nothingness," not because, as she explained, the African has "a very ancient but a very narrow culture." The black bourgeoisie suffers from "nothingness" because when Negroes attain middle-class status, their lives generally lose both content and significance.

LETTER FROM BIRMINGHAM JAIL

Martin Luther King, Jr.

[The "Negro Revolu tion" of the 1950's and early 1960's, which in the public mind probably had its beginning in the 1954 Supreme Court decision desegregating pub- lic schools, generally followed two paths: lawsuits pressed in state and federal courts, and the direct-action programs of such organizations as the NAACP, the Congress of Racial Equality (CORE), the Southern Christian Leadership Conference (SCLC), and the Student Nonviolent Coordinating Committee (SNCC). Although CORE had been founded in 1942, it had failed to attract much public attention or support among Negroes. After the Montgomery bus boycott in December, 1955, the pace of change became much more rapid. It was out of this encounter in Montgomery that the SCLC was formed in January, 1957, and the Rev- erend Martin Luther King, Jr., rose to prominence. As King battled the authorities in Montgomery, he also came to formulate a philosophy of nonviolence (King's affinity for the doctrines of Gandhi prompted him to make a trip to India in 1959) and, later, to develop the tactic of passive resistance, to combat attacks by whites. Negroes, he said, should meet "physical force with an even stronger force, namely, soul force." Initially, King and the SCLC were much concerned with voter registration in the South. After 1960 and the "sit-ins" in Greensboro, North Carolina, King adopted the direct action techniques of the students. Nonviolent demon- stration, in the hands of King, became a way to create tension, as he said, and, thus, to force negotiation on the issue of integration.

In 1963, one hundred years after emancipation, King and his followers chose Birmingham, Alabama, a bastion of "Jim Crow," as the target of their antisegregation drive. King explained the choice: "If Birmingham could be cracked, the direction of the entire nonviolent movement in the South could take a significant turn." While King's group was pressing a boycott that crippled business and forced Birmingham businessmen to negotiate a desegregation agreement, Attorney General Robert F. Kennedy acted to secure the registration of more than 2,000 Birmingham Negroes previously denied voting rights. Federal courts upheld the right of Negroes to nonviolent protest in Birmingham and elsewhere, but not before King had been arrested and jailed. Reprinted here is a letter, written from his cell on April 16, containing King's answer to charges by a group of eight Birmingham clergymen that he was in their city as an "outside agitator." More than a thousand besides King were arrested in Birmingham during a month of demonstrations in which Negroes were set upon by police dogs and sprayed with fire hoses. Most observers later conceded that Birmingham was a turning point in the civil rights struggle.

Standing behind the "revolution" and only tacitly supporting the active demonstrations and the boycotting techniques of the younger generation was the NAACP, which, since 1955, had been under the leadership of Roy Wilkins. Because of its position that the Negro's primary tactic should be litigation, the NAACP and its white liberal allies had entered a turbulent period since the 1954 victory in the courts in *Brown* v. *Board of Education*. After 1958, Wilkins came under constant criticism from the activists of the Left. He responded with internal reforms and by outlining new programs to meet the aspirations of the masses. In 1966, when the nonviolent techniques of King were repudiated by the Black Power advocates, Wilkins, Bayard Rustin, and others openly supported King, touching off a major debate within Negro leadership circles reminiscent of that between Booker T. Washington and W. E. B. Du Bois.

Nonviolent demonstration was not originated by King. Nor, for that matter, was the civil rights struggle and the notion that the philosophy of Gandhi might be useful to the American Negro. In 1941, A. Philip Randolph, who had been prominent in the labor movement ever since he organized the Brotherhood of Sleeping Car Porters in 1925, undertook a campaign to eliminate discrimination in employment by threatening a march on Washington by 100,000 blacks. The march was "postponed" after President Roosevelt issued Executive Order 8802 establishing a Fair Employment Commission. Randolph and others maintained their militant posture in 1942 and 1943 by keeping the possibility of a march on Washington alive. In 1942, Randolph launched a program of mass protest meetings and, the following year, announced a national civil disobedience movement and plans to train Negroes in the nonviolent techniques of Gandhi. The march on Washington was again postponed after the outbreak of rioting in Detroit in 1943.

Although it was not to become prominent for nearly twenty years, CORE was organized during this wartime crusade with the hope of sustaining the spirit of direct action. James Farmer, the organizer and first director of the organization, returned to CORE in 1961, after the "sit-in" movement, which began in earnest in February, 1960, had captured the imagination of students throughout the country. Unlike Montgomery, where Mrs. Rosa Parks's refusal to move to the rear of the bus was spontaneous, and Greensboro, where the students acted on their own initiative, the 1961 Freedom Rides were planned in advance by an organization that had nearly two decades of experience in direct action behind it. Farmer himself organized the rides, which resulted in an order by the Interstate Commerce Commission banning segregation in interstate terminal facilities that became effective on November 1, 1961.

Another aspect of the civil rights movement, which until 1966 was very much an interracial affair, centered around the activities of SNCC. Its members were volunteers, mostly students and ex-students, who left their schools and jobs to become full-time workers in the field. SNCC's first executive secretary was James Forman, a Chicago schoolteacher who agreed to take on the job in October, 1961. SNCC decided, after some internal debate, to begin its work by attempting to register Negro voters in areas of the South where Negroes lived in large numbers. The voter registration drives continued for several years and were later aided by the Voting Rights Act of 1965.

Many of those who were involved in the sit-ins in 1960–61, including the early leaders of SNCC, were imbued with the nonviolent philosophy of King. SNCC, in fact, developed out of King's effort to form a student component of the SCLC in 1960. The link between SNCC and those involved in sit-ins was not organizational but rather one of common commitment. SNCC supported the sit-ins and later the Freedom Rides, and many who were initiated through these activities became prominent in SNCC.

These three groups were the prime movers in the Civil Rights movement that culminated in the struggle in Birmingham and the March on Washington, both in 1963. The idea for the march had been brought forward again by A. Philip Randolph and endorsed by most Negro groups and many whites—30,000 of whom participated in the march. The total number at the march, which terminated at the Lincoln Memorial, exceeded 200,000. The activities were nationally televised, and, thus, many millions participated vicariously. The high point of the day was a speech delivered by Dr. King, whose closing words, taken from an old Negro spiritual, were inscribed on his tombstone: "Free at last! Free at last! Thank God Almighty, we are free at last!"]

My Dear Fellow Clergymen:

While confined here in the Birmingham city jail, I came across your recent statement calling my present activities "unwise and untimely." Seldom do I pause to answer criticism of my work and ideas. If I sought to answer all the criticisms that cross my desk, my secretaries would have little time for anything other than such correspondence in the course of the day, and I would have no time for constructive work. But since I feel that you are men of genuine good will and that your criticisms are sincerely set forth, I want to try to answer your statement in what I hope will be patient and reasonable terms.

I think I should indicate why I am here in Birmingham, since you have been influenced by the view which argues against "outsiders coming in." I have the honor of serving as president of the Southern Christian Leadership Conference, an organization operating in every southern state, with headquarters in Atlanta, Georgia. We have some eighty-five affiliated organizations across the South, and one of them is the Alabama Christian Movement for Human Rights. Frequently we share staff, educational and financial resources with our affiliates. Several months ago the affiliate here in Birmingham asked us to be on call to engage in a nonviolent direct-action program if such were deemed necessary. We readily consented, and when the hour came we lived up to our promise. So I, along with several members of my staff, am here because I was invited here. I am here because I have organizational ties here.

But more basically, I am in Birmingham because injustice is here. Just as the prophets of the eighth century B.C. left their villages and carried their "thus saith the Lord" far beyond the boundaries of their home towns, and just as the Apostle Paul left his village of Tarsus and carried the gospel of Jesus Christ to the far corners of the Greco-Roman world, so am I compelled to carry the gospel of freedom beyond my own home town. Like Paul, I must constantly respond to the Macedonian call for aid.

Moreover, I am cognizant of the interrelatedness of all communities and states. I cannot sit idly by in Atlanta and not be concerned about what happens in Birmingham. Injustice anywhere is a threat to justice everywhere. We are caught in an inescapable network of mutuality, tied in a single garment of destiny. Whatever affects one directly, affects all indirectly. Never again can we afford to live with the narrow, provincial "outside agitator" idea. Anyone who lives inside the United States can never be considered an outsider anywhere within its bounds.

You deplore the demonstrations taking place in Birmingham. But your statement, I am sorry to say, fails to express a similar concern for the conditions that brought about the demonstrations. I am sure that none of you would want to rest content with the superficial kind of social analysis that deals merely with effects and does not grapple with underlying causes. It is unfortunate that demonstrations are taking place in Birmingham, but it is even more unfortunate that the city's white power structure left the Negro community with no alternative.

In any nonviolent campaign there are four basic steps: collection of the facts to determine whether injustices exist; negotiation; self-purification; and direct action. We have gone through all these steps in Birmingham. There can be no gainsaying the fact that racial injustice engulfs this community. Birmingham is probably the most thoroughly segregated city in the United States. Its ugly record of brutality is widely known. Negroes have experienced grossly unjust treatment in the courts. There have been more unsolved bombings of Negro homes and churches in Birmingham than in any other city in the nation. These are the hard, brutal facts of the case. On the basis of these conditions, Negro leaders sought to negotiate with the city fathers. But the latter consistently re-fused to engage in good-faith negotiation.

Then, last September, came the opportunity to talk with leaders of Birmingham's economic community. In the course of the negotiations, certain promises were made by the merchants—for example, to remove the stores' humiliating racial signs. On the basis of these promises, the Reverend Fred Shuttlesworth and the leaders of the Alabama Christian Movement for Human Rights agreed to a moratorium on all demonstra-tions. As the weeks and months went by, we realized that we were the victims of a broken promise. A few signs, briefly removed, returned; the others remained.

As in so many past experiences, our hopes had been blasted, and the shadow of deep disappointment settled upon us. We had no alternative except to prepare for direct action, whereby we would present our very bodies as a means of laying our case before the conscience of the local and the national community. Mindful of the difficulties involved, we de-cided to undertake a process of self-purification. We began a series of workshops on nonviolence, and we repeatedly asked ourselves: "Are you able to accept blows without retaliating?" "Are you able to endure the ordeal of jail?" We decided to schedule our direct-action program for the Easter season, realizing that except for Christmas, this is the main shop-ping period of the year. Knowing that a strong economic-withdrawal pro-gram would be the by-product of direct action, we felt that this would be the best time to bring pressure to bear on the merchants for the needed change.

Then it occurred to us that Birmingham's mayoralty election was com-ing up in March, and we speedily decided to postpone action until after election day. When we discovered that the Commissioner of Public Safety, Eugene "Bull" Connor, had piled up enough votes to be in the run-off, we decided again to postpone action until the day after the run-off so that the demonstrations could not be used to cloud the issues. Like many others, we waited to see Mr. Connor defeated, and to this end we endured postponement after postponement. Having aided in this community need, we felt that our direct-action program could be de-layed no longer.

You may well ask: "Why direct action? Why sit-ins, marches and so forth? Isn't negotiation a better path?" You are quite right in calling for negotiation. Indeed, this is the very purpose of direct action. Nonviolent direct action seeks to create such a crisis and foster such a tension that a community which has constantly refused to negotiate is forced to con-front the issue. It seeks so to dramatize the issue that it can no longer be ignored. My citing the creation of tension as part of the work of the nonviolent-resister may sound rather shocking. But I must confess that I am not afraid of the word "tension." I have earnestly opposed violent tension, but there is a type of constructive, nonviolent tension which is necessary for growth. Just as Socrates felt that it was necessary to create a tension in the mind so that individuals could rise from the bondage of myths and half-truths to the unfettered realm of creative an-alysis and objective appraisal, so must we see the need for nonviolent gadflies to create the kind of tension in society that will help men rise from the dark depths of prejudice and racism to the majestic heights of understanding and brotherhood.

The purpose of our direct-action program is to create a situation so crisis-packed that it will inevitably open the door to negotiation. I therefore concur with you in your call for negotiation. Too long has our beloved Southland been bogged down in a tragic effort to live in monologue rather than dialogue.

One of the basic points in your statement is that the action that I and my associates have taken in Birmingham is untimely. Some have asked: "Why didn't you give the new city administration time to act?" The only answer that I can give to this query is that the new Birmingham administration must be prodded about as much as the outgoing one, before it will act. We are sadly mistaken if we feel that the election of Albert Boutwell as mayor will bring the millennium to Birmingham. While Mr. Boutwell is a much more gentle person than Mr. Connor, they are both segregationists, dedicated to maintenance of the status quo. I have hope that Mr. Boutwell will be reasonable enough to see the futility of massive resistance to desegregation. But he will not see this without pressure from devotees of civil rights. My friends, I must say to you that we have not made a single gain in civil rights without determined legal and nonviolent pressure. Lamentably, it is an historical fact that privileged groups seldom give up their privileges voluntarily. Individuals may see the moral light and voluntarily give up their unjust posture; but, as Reinhold Niebuhr has reminded us, groups tend to be more immoral than individuals.

We know through painful experience that freedom is never voluntarily given by the oppressor; it must be demanded by the oppressed. Frankly, I have yet to engage in a direct-action campaign that was "well timed" in the view of those who have not suffered unduly from the disease of segregation. For years now I have heard the word "Wait!" It rings in the ear of every Negro with piercing familiarity. This "Wait" has almost always meant "Never." We must come to see, with one of our distinguished jurists, that "justice too long delayed is justice denied."

We have waited for more than 340 years for our constitutional and God-given rights. The nations of Asia and Africa are moving with jet-like speed toward gaining political independence, but we still creep at horse-and-buggy pace toward gaining a cup of coffee at a lunch counter. Perhaps it is easy for those who have never felt the stinging darts of segregation to say, "Wait." But when you have seen vicious mobs lynch your mothers and fathers at will and drown your sisters and brothers at whim; when you have seen hate-filled policemen curse, kick and even kill your black brothers and sisters; when you see the vast majority of your twenty million Negro brothers smothering in an airtight cage of poverty in the midst of an affluent society; when you suddenly find your tongue twisted and your speech stammering as you seek to explain to your six-year-old daughter why she can't go to the public amusement park that has just been advertised on television, and see tears welling up in her eyes when she is told that Funtown is closed to colored children, and see ominous clouds of inferiority beginning to form in her little mental sky, and see her beginning to distort her personality by developing an unconscious bitterness toward white people; when you have to concoct an answer for a five-year-old son who is asking: "Daddy, why do white people treat colored people so mean?"; when you take a cross-country drive and find it necessary to sleep night after night in the uncomfortable corners of your automobile because no motel will accept you; when you are humiliated day in and day out by nagging signs reading "white" and "colored"; when your first name becomes "nigger," your middle name becomes "boy" (however old you are) and your last name becomes "John," and your wife and mother are never given the respected title "Mrs."; when you are harried by day and haunted by night by the fact that you are a Negro, living constantly at tiptoe stance, never quite knowing what to expect next, and are plagued with inner fears and outer resentments; when you are forever fighting a degenerating sense of "nobodiness"—then you will understand why we find it difficult to wait. There comes a time when the cup of endurance runs over, and men are no longer willing to be plunged into the abyss of despair. I hope, sirs, you can understand our legitimate and unavoidable impatience.

You express a great deal of anxiety over our willingness to break laws. This is certainly a legitimate concern. Since we so diligently urge people to obey the Supreme Court's decision of 1954 outlawing segregation in the public schools, at first glance it may seem rather paradoxical for us consciously to break laws. One may well ask: "How can you advocate breaking some laws and obeying others?" The answer lies in the fact that there are two types of laws: just and unjust. I would be the first to advocate obeying just laws. One has not only a legal but a moral responsibility to obey just laws. Conversely, one has a moral responsibility to disobey unjust laws. I would agree with St. Augustine that "an unjust law is no law at all."

Now, what is the difference between the two? How does one determine whether a law is just or unjust? A just law is a man-made code that squares with the moral law or the law of God. An unjust law is a code that is out of harmony with the moral law. To put it in the terms of St. Thomas Aquinas: An unjust law is a human law that is not rooted in eternal law and natural law. Any law that uplifts human personality is just. Any law that degrades human personality is unjust. All segregation statutes are unjust because segregation distorts the soul and damages the personality. It gives the segregator a false sense of superiority and the segregated a false sense of inferiority. Segregation, to use the terminology of the Jewish philosopher Martin Buber, substitutes an "I—it" relationship for an "I—thou" relationship and ends up relegating persons to the status of things. Hence segregation is not only politically, economically and sociologically unsound, it is morally wrong and sinful. Paul Tillich has said that sin is separation. Is not segregation an existential expression of man's tragic separation, his awful estrangement, his terrible sinfulness? Thus it is that I can urge men to obey the 1954 decision of the Supreme Court, for it is morally right; and I can urge them to disobey segregation ordinances, for they are morally wrong.

Let us consider a more concrete example of just and unjust laws. An unjust law is a code that a numerical or power majority group compels a minority group to obey but does not make binding on itself. This is *difference* made legal. By the same token, a just law is a code that a majority compels a minority to follow and that it is willing to follow itself. This is *sameness* made legal.

Let me give another explanation. A law is unjust if it is inflicted on a minority that, as a result of being denied the right to vote, had no part in enacting or devising the law. Who can say that the legislature of Alabama which set up that state's segregation laws was democratically elected? Throughout Alabama all sorts of devious methods are used to prevent Negroes from becoming registered voters, and there are some counties in which, even though Negroes constitute a majority of the population, not a single Negro is registered. Can any law enacted under such circumstances be considered democratically structured?

Sometimes a law is just on its face and unjust in its application. For instance, I have been arrested on a charge of parading without a permit. Now, there is nothing wrong in having an ordinance which requires a permit for a parade. But such an ordinance becomes unjust when it is used to maintain segregation and to deny citizens the First-Amendment privilege of peaceful assembly and protest.

I hope you are able to see the distinction I am trying to point out. In no sense do I advocate evading or defying the law, as would the rabid segregationist. That would lead to anarchy. One who breaks an unjust law must do so openly, lovingly, and with a willingness to accept the penalty. I submit that an individual who breaks a law that conscience tells him is unjust, and who willingly accepts the penalty of imprisonment in order to arouse the conscience of the community over its injustice, is in reality expressing the highest respect for law.

Of course, there is nothing new about this kind of civil disobedience. It was evidenced sublimely in the refusal of Shadrach, Meshach and Abednego to obey the laws of Nebuchadnezzar, on the ground that a higher moral law was at stake. It was practiced superbly by the early Christians, who were willing to face hungry lions and the excruciating pain of chopping blocks rather than submit to certain unjust laws of the Roman Empire. To a degree, academic freedom is a reality today because Socrates practiced civil disobedience. In our own nation, the Boston Tea Party represented a massive act of civil disobedience.

We should never forget that everything Adolf Hitler did in Germany was "legal" and everything the Hungarian freedom fighters did in Hungary was "illegal." It was "illegal" to aid and comfort a Jew in Hitler's Germany. Even so, I am sure that, had I lived in Germany at the time, I would have aided and comforted my Jewish brothers. If today I lived in a Communist country where certain principles dear to the Christian faith are suppressed, I would openly advocate disobeying that country's antireligious laws.

I must make two honest confessions to you, my Christian and Jewish brothers. First, I must confess that over the past few years I have been gravely disappointed with the white moderate. I have almost reached the regrettable conclusion that the Negro's great stumbling block in his stride toward freedom is not the White Citizen's Counciler or the Ku Klux Klanner, but the white moderate, who is more devoted to "order" than to justice; who prefers a negative peace which is the absence of tension to a positive peace which is the presence of justice; who constantly says: "I agree with you in the goal you seek, but I cannot agree with your methods of direct action"; who paternalistically believes he can set the timetable for another man's freedom; who lives by a mythical concept of time and who constantly advises the Negro to wait for a "more convenient season." Shallow understanding from people of good will is more frustrating than absolute misunderstanding from people of ill will. Lukewarm acceptance is much more bewildering than outright rejection.

I had hoped that the white moderate would understand that law and order exist for the purpose of establishing justice and that when they fail in this purpose they become the dangerously structured dams that block the flow of social progress. I had hoped that the white moderate would understand that the present tension in the South is a necessary phase of the transition from an obnoxious negative peace, in which the Negro passively accepted his unjust plight, to a substantive and positive peace, in which all men will respect the dignity and worth of human personality. Actually, we who engage in nonviolent direct action are not the creators of tension. We merely bring to the surface the hidden tension that is already alive. We bring it out in the open, where it can be seen and dealt with. Like a boil that can never be cured so long as it is covered up but must be opened with all its ugliness to the natural medicines of air and light, injustice must be exposed, with all the tension its exposure creates, to the light of human conscience and the air of national opinion before it can be cured.

In your statement you assert that our actions, even though peaceful, must be condemned because they precipitate violence. But is this a logical assertion? Isn't this like condemning a robbed man because his possession of money precipitated the evil act of robbery? Isn't this like condemning Socrates because his unswerving commitment to truth and his philosophical inquiries precipitated the act by the misguided populace in which they made him drink hemlock? Isn't this like condemning Jesus because his unique God-consciousness and never-ceasing devotion to God's will precipitated the evil act of crucifixion? We must come to see that, as the federal courts have consistently affirmed, it is wrong to urge an individual to cease his efforts to gain his basic constitutional rights because the quest may precipitate violence. Society must protect the robbed and punish the robber.

I had also hoped that the white moderate would reject the myth concerning time in relation to the struggle for freedom. I have just received a letter from a white brother in Texas. He writes: "All Christians know that the colored people will receive equal rights eventually, but it is possible that you are in too great a religious hurry. It has taken Christianity almost two thousand years to accomplish what it has. The teachings of Christ take time to come to earth." Such an attitude stems from a tragic misconception of time, from the strangely irrational notion that there is something in the very flow of time that will inevitably cure all ills. Actually, time itself is neutral; it can be used either destructively or constructively. More and more I feel that the people of ill will have used time much more effectively than have the people of good will. We will have to repent in this generation not merely for the hateful words and actions of the bad people but for the appalling silence of the good people. Human progress never rolls in on wheels of inevitability; it comes through the tireless efforts of men willing to be co-workers with God, and without this hard work, time itself becomes an ally of the forces of social stagnation. We must use time creatively, in the knowledge that the time is always ripe to do right. Now is the time to make real the promise of democracy and transform our pending national elegy into a creative psalm of brotherhood. Now is the time to lift our national policy from the quicksand of racial injustice to the solid rock of human dignity.

You speak of our activity in Birmingham as extreme. At first I was rather disappointed that fellow clergymen would see my nonviolent efforts as those of an extremist. I began thinking about the fact that I stand in the middle of two opposing forces in the Negro community. One is a force of complacency, made up in part of Negroes who, as a result of long years of oppression, are so drained of self-respect and a sense of "somebodiness" that they have adjusted to segregation; and in part of a few middle-class Negroes who, because of a degree of academic and economic security and because in some ways they profit by segregation, have become insensitive to the problems of the masses. The other force is one of bitterness and hatred, and it comes perilously close to advocating violence. It is expressed in the various black nationalist groups that are springing up across the nation, the largest and best-known being Elijah Muhammad's Muslim movement. Nourished by the Negro's frustration over the continued existence of racial discrimination, this movement is made up of people who have lost faith in America, who have absolutely repudiated Christianity, and who have concluded that the white man is an incorrigible "devil."

I have tried to stand between these two forces, saying that we need emulate neither the "do-nothingism" of the complacent nor the hatred and despair of the black nationalist. For there is the more excellent way of love and nonviolent protest. I am grateful to God that, through the influence of the Negro church, the way of nonviolence became an integral part of our struggle.

If this philosophy had not emerged, by now many streets of the South would, I am convinced, be flowing with blood. And I am further convinced that if our white brothers dismiss as "rabble-rousers" and "outside agitators" those of us who employ nonviolent direct action, and if they refuse to support our nonviolent efforts, millions of Negroes will, out of frustration and despair, seek solace and security in black-nationalist ideologies—a development that would inevitably lead to a frightening racial nightmare.

Oppressed people cannot remain oppressed forever. The yearning for freedom eventually manifests itself, and that is what has happened to the

American Negro. Something within has reminded him of his birthright of freedom, and something without has reminded him that it can be gained. Consciously or unconsciously, he has been caught up by the *Zeitgeist*, and with his black brothers of Africa and his brown and yellow brothers of Asia, South America and the Caribbean, the United States Negro is moving with a sense of great urgency toward the promised land of racial justice. If one recognizes this vital urge that has engulfed the Negro community, one should readily understand why public demonstrations are taking place. The Negro has many pent-up resentments and latent frustrations, and he must release them. So let him march; let him make prayer pilgrimages to the city hall; let him go on freedom rides—and try to understand why he must do so. If his repressed emotions are not released in nonviolent ways, they will seek expression through violence; this is not a threat but a fact of history. So I have not said to my people: "Get rid of your discontent." Rather, I have tried to say that this normal and healthy discontent can be channeled into the creative outlet of nonviolent direct action. And now this approach is being termed extremist.

But though I was initially disappointed at being categorized as an extremist, as I continued to think about the matter I gradually gained a measure of satisfaction from the label. Was not Jesus an extremist for love: "Love your enemies, bless them that curse you, do good to them that hate you, and pray for them which despitefully use you, and persecute you." Was not Amos an extremist for justice: "Let justice roll down like waters and righteousness like an ever-flowing stream." Was not Paul an extremist for the Christian gospel: "I bear in my body the marks of the Lord Jesus." Was not Martin Luther an extremist: "Here I stand; I cannot do otherwise, so help me God." And John Bunyan: "I will stay in jail to the end of my days before I make a butchery of my conscience." And Abraham Lincoln: "This nation cannot survive half slave and half free." And Thomas Jefferson: "We hold these truths to be self-evident, that all men are created equal . . ." So the question is not whether we will be extremists, but what kind of extremists we will be. Will we be extremists for hate or for love? Will we be extremists for the preservation of injustice or for the extension of justice? In that dramatic scene on Calvary's hill three men were crucified. We must never forget that all three were crucified for the same crime—the crime of extremism. Two were extremists for immorality, and thus fell below their environment. The other, Jesus Christ, was an extremist for love, truth and goodness, and thereby rose above his environment. Perhaps the South, the nation and the world are in dire need of creative extremists.

I had hoped that the white moderate would see this need. Perhaps I was too optimistic; perhaps I expected too much. I suppose I should have realized that few members of the oppressor race can understand the deep groans and passionate yearnings of the oppressed race, and still fewer have the vision to see that injustice must be rooted out by strong, persistent and determined action. I am thankful, however, that some of our white brothers in the South have grasped the meaning of this social revolution and committed themselves to it. They are still all too few in quantity, but they are big in quality. Some—such as Ralph McGill, Lillian

Smith, Harry Golden, James McBride Dabbs, Ann Braden and Sarah Patton Boyle—have written about our struggle in eloquent and prophetic terms. Others have marched with us down nameless streets of the South. They have languished in filthy, roach-infested jails, suffering the abuse and brutality of policemen who view them as "dirty nigger-lovers." Unlike so many of their moderate brothers and sisters, they have recognized the urgency of the moment and sensed the need for powerful "action" antidotes to combat the disease of segregation.

Let me take note of my other major disappointment. I have been so greatly disappointed with the white church and its leadership. Of course, there are some notable exceptions. I am not unmindful of the fact that each of you has taken some significant stands on this issue. I commend you, Reverend Stallings, for your Christian stand on this past Sunday, in welcoming Negroes to your worship service on a nonsegregated basis. I commend the Catholic leaders of this state for integrating Spring Hill College several years ago.

But despite these notable exceptions, I must honestly reiterate that I have been disappointed with the church. I do not say this as one of those negative critics who can always find something wrong with the church. I say this as a minister of the gospel, who loves the church; who was nurtured in its bosom; who has been sustained by its spiritual blessings and who will remain true to it as long as the cord of life shall lengthen.

When I was suddenly catapulted into the leadership of the bus protest in Montgomery, Alabama, a few years ago, I felt we would be supported by the white church. I felt that the white ministers, priests and rabbis of the South would be among our strongest allies. Instead, some have been outright opponents, refusing to understand the freedom movement and misrepresenting its leaders; all too many others have been more cautious than courageous and have remained silent behind the anesthetizing security of stained-glass windows.

In spite of my shattered dreams, I came to Birmingham with the hope that the white religious leadership of this community would see the justice of our cause and, with deep moral concern, would serve as the channel through which our just grievances could reach the power structure. I had hoped that each of you would understand. But again I have been disappointed.

I have heard numerous southern religious leaders admonish their worshipers to comply with a desegregation decision because it is the law, but I have longed to hear white ministers declare: "Follow this decree because integration is morally right and because the Negro is your brother." In the midst of blatant injustices inflicted upon the Negro, I have watched white churchmen stand on the sideline and mouth pious irrelevancies and sanctimonious trivialities. In the midst of a mighty struggle to rid our nation of racial and economic injustice, I have heard many ministers say: "Those are social issues, with which the gospel has no real concern." And I have watched many churches commit themselves to a completely other-worldly religion which makes a strange, un-Biblical distinction between body and soul, between the sacred and the secular.

I have traveled the length and breadth of Alabama, Mississippi and all the other southern states. On sweltering summer days and crisp autumn mornings I have looked at the South's beautiful churches with their lofty spires pointing heavenward. I have beheld the impressive outlines of her massive religious-education buildings. Over and over I have found myself asking: "What kind of people worship here? Who is their God? Where were their voices when the lips of Governor Barnett dripped with words of interposition and nullification? Where were they when Governor Wallace gave a clarion call for defiance and hatred? Where were their voices of support when bruised and weary Negro men and women decided to rise from the dark dungeons of complacency to the bright hills of creative protest?"

Yes, these questions are still in my mind. In deep disappointment I have wept over the laxity of the church. But be assured that my tears have been tears of love. There can be no deep disappointment where there is not deep love. Yes, I love the church. How could I do otherwise? I am in the rather unique position of being the son, the grandson and the great-grandson of preachers. Yes, I see the church as the body of Christ. But, oh! How we have blemished and scarred that body through social neglect and through fear of being nonconformists.

There was a time when the church was very powerful—in the time when the early Christians rejoiced at being deemed worthy to suffer for what they believed. In those days the church was not merely a thermometer that recorded the ideas and principles of popular opinion; it was a thermostat that transformed the mores of society. Whenever the early Christians entered a town, the people in power became disturbed and immediately sought to convict the Christians for being "disturbers of the peace" and "outside agitators." But the Christians pressed on, in the conviction that they were "a colony of heaven," called to obey God rather than man. Small in number, they were big in commitment. They were too God-intoxicated to be "astronomically intimidated." By their effort and example they brought an end to such ancient evils as infanticide and gladiatorial contests.

Things are different now. So often the contemporary church is a weak, ineffectual voice with an uncertain sound. So often it is an archdefender of the status quo. Far from being disturbed by the presence of the church, the power structure of the average community is consoled by the church's silent—and often even vocal—sanction of things as they are.

But the judgment of God is upon the church as never before. If today's church does not recapture the sacrificial spirit of the early church, it will lose its authenticity, forfeit the loyalty of millions, and be dismissed as an irrelevant social club with no meaning for the twentieth century. Every day I meet young people whose disappointment with the church has turned into outright disgust.

Perhaps I have once again been too optimistic. Is organized religion too inextricably bound to the status quo to save our nation and the world? Perhaps I must turn my faith to the inner spiritual church, the church within the church, as the true *ekklesia* and the hope of the world. But again I am thankful to God that some noble souls from the ranks of organized religion have broken loose from the paralyzing chains of conformity and joined us as active partners in the struggle for freedom. They have left their secure congregations and walked the streets of Albany, Georgia, with us. They have gone down the highways of the South on tortuous rides for freedom. Yes, they have gone to jail with us. Some have been dismissed from their churches, have lost the support of their bishops and fellow ministers. But they have acted in the faith that right defeated is stronger than evil triumphant. Their witness has been the spiritual salt that has preserved the true meaning of the gospel in these troubled times. They have carved a tunnel of hope through the dark mountain of disappointment.

I hope the church as a whole will meet the challenge of this decisive hour. But even if the church does not come to the aid of justice, I have no despair about the future. I have no fear about the outcome of our struggle in Birmingham, even if our motives are at present misunderstood. We will reach the goal of freedom in Birmingham and all over the nation, because the goal of America is freedom. Abused and scorned though we may be, our destiny is tied up with America's destiny. Before the pilgrims landed at Plymouth, we were here. Before the pen of Jefferson etched the majestic words of the Declaration of Independence across the pages of history, we were here. For more than two centuries our forebears labored in this country without wages; they made cotton king; they built the homes of their masters while suffering gross injustice and shameful humiliation—and yet out of a bottomless vitality they continued to thrive and develop. If the inexpressible cruelties of slavery could not stop us, the opposition we now face will surely fail. We will win our freedom because the sacred heritage of our nation and the eternal will of God are embodied in our echoing demands.

Before closing I feel impelled to mention one other point in your statement that has troubled me profoundly. You warmly commended the Birmingham police force for keeping "order" and "preventing violence." I doubt that you would have so warmly commended the police force if you had seen its dogs sinking their teeth into unarmed, nonviolent Negroes. I doubt that you would so quickly commend the policemen if you were to observe their ugly and inhumane treatment of Negroes here in the city jail; if you were to watch them push and curse old Negro women and young Negro girls; if you were to see them slap and kick old Negro men and young boys; if you were to observe them, as they did on two occasions, refuse to give us food because we wanted to sing our grace together. I cannot join you in your praise of the Birmingham police department.

It is true that the police have exercised a degree of discipline in handling the demonstrators. In this sense they have conducted themselves rather "nonviolently" in public. But for what purpose? To preserve the evil system of segregation. Over the past few years I have consistently preached that nonviolence demands that the means we use must be as pure as the ends we seek. I have tried to make clear that it is wrong to use immoral means to attain moral ends. But now I must affirm that it is just as wrong, or perhaps even more so, to use moral means to preserve immoral ends. Perhaps Mr. Connor and his policemen have been rather nonviolent in public, as was Chief Pritchett in Albany, Georgia, but they have used the moral means of nonviolence to maintain the immoral end of racial injustice. As T. S. Eliot has said: "The last temptation is the greatest treason: To do the right deed for the wrong reason."

I wish you had commended the Negro sit-inners and demonstrators of Birmingham for their sublime courage, their willingness to suffer and their amazing discipline in the midst of great provocation. One day the South will recognize its real heroes. They will be the James Merediths, with the noble sense of purpose that enables them to face jeering and hostile mobs, and with the agonizing loneliness that characterizes the life of the pioneer. They will be old, oppressed, battered Negro women, symbolized in a seventy-two-year-old woman in Montgomery, Alabama, who rose up with a sense of dignity and with her people decided not to ride segregated buses, and who responded with ungrammatical profundity to one who inquired about her weariness: "My feets is tired, but my soul is at rest." They will be the young high school and college students, the young ministers of the gospel and a host of their elders, courageously and nonviolently sitting in at lunch counters and willingly going to jail for conscience' sake. One day the South will know that when these disinherited children of God sat down at lunch counters, they were in reality standing up for what is best in the American dream and for the most sacred values in our Judaeo-Christian heritage, thereby bringing our nation back to those great wells of democracy which were dug deep by the founding fathers in their formulation of the Constitution and the Declaration of Independence.

Never before have I written so long a letter. I'm afraid it is much too long to take your precious time. I can assure you that it would have been much shorter if I had been writing from a comfortable desk, but what else can one do when he is alone in a narrow jail cell, other than write long letters, think long thoughts and pray long prayers?

If I have said anything in this letter that overstates the truth and indicates an unreasonable impatience, I beg you to forgive me. If I have said anything that understates the truth and indicates my having a patience that allows me to settle for anything less than brotherhood, I beg God to forgive me.

I hope this letter finds you strong in the faith. I also hope that circumstances will soon make it possible for me to meet each of you, not as an integrationist or a civil-rights leader but as a fellow clergyman and a Christian brother. Let us all hope that the dark clouds of racial prejudice will soon pass away and the deep fog of misunderstanding will be lifted from our fear-drenched communities, and in some not too distant tomorrow the radiant stars of love and brotherhood will shine over our great nation with all their scintillating beauty.

Yours for the cause of Peace and Brotherhood,
MARTIN LUTHER KING, JR.

MY DUNGEON SHOOK: LETTER TO MY NEPHEW ON THE ONE HUNDREDTH ANNIVERSARY OF THE EMANCIPATION

James Baldwin

[The 100th anniver-
sary of the Emancipation Proclamation was ambiguously observed in
the United States. Some Negroes and many whites marked the date—
January 1, 1963—as of vast importance in American history, and paid
homage to the men—mainly one man, Abraham Lincoln—who, a century
before, had been instrumental in freeing the slaves. Emancipation was,
as James Baldwin had pointed out in 1948, the "one major, devastating
gain" made by the Negro in America. "All that has followed from that,"
Baldwin continued, "brings to mind the rather unfortunate image of
bones thrown to a pack of dogs sufficiently hungry to be dangerous." On
the eve of the 100th anniversary, Baldwin summed up the feelings of a
large number of Americans, both white and black, in the remark: "You
know, and I know, that the country is celebrating one hundred years of
freedom one hundred years too soon." It was the penultimate remark in
a letter that Baldwin wrote to his nephew and published in December,
1962. A slightly revised version of the letter reprinted here appeared,
together with an eloquent sermon on the black man's burden, "Down

at the Cross: Letter From a Region in My Mind," as *The Fire Next Time* (1963).

Baldwin was born in Harlem in 1924. At age fourteen, he became a preacher, and, at twenty-four, he went to Paris, where he completed three books. *Go Tell It on the Mountain*, a novel, was published in 1953. *Notes of A Native Son*, a collection of essays (mostly biographical), appeared in 1955, and *Giovanni's Room*, another novel, was brought out the following year. After he returned to the United States in 1958, Baldwin was turned to as a literary spokesman for the Negro. With the success of *The Fire Next Time*, in 1963, it became a commonplace to praise his essays over his fiction (a third novel, *Another Country*, had come out in 1962).

One of Baldwin's recurrent themes is what he, along with others, calls the search for an identity. The black man, he feels, has achieved an identity as an American. It was achieved in the face of the white man's refusal to recognize the Negro as human and despite the "intolerable anxiety in the minds and lives of his masters" that the development of this identity produced. The problem was that the white man's identity was also based on the same refusal to see the Negro's humanity. This unholy symbiosis had left both blacks and whites with a view of Negro life as debased and impoverished; a view that was, perhaps, comfortable enough for white men, but utterly demoralizing for the black. What Baldwin stressed was that it was no less demoralizing for the white.

Baldwin's essays have always had a tone of moral urgency about them. His message is reminiscent of Woolman's: Oppression hurts the oppressor as much as it does the oppressed. The wages of sin are the destruction of the moral spirit. "At the root of the American Negro problem," Baldwin wrote in 1953, "is the necessity of the American white man to find a way of living with the Negro in order to be able to live with himself." The history of this problem is the history of a spectacle of oppression, "at once foolish and dreadful," in which both the oppressor and the oppressed were motivated by a need to protect his identity. It remained to be seen, Baldwin added, in 1963, whether love and recognition of the black man's presence by dedicated men would end the racial nightmare. "If we do not now dare everything," he concluded, "the fulfillment of that prophecy, recreated in a song by a slave, is upon us: *God gave Noah the rainbow sign, No more water, the fire next time!*"

The apocalyptic tone of *The Fire Next Time* had an indisputable impact on both the Negro and white communities. It came at a time when the Negro alliance with white liberals was being severely tested by the growing impatience that was evident in the black community. It was Baldwin, as much as any writer, who had put the white liberal on the spot since the war. He had pointed out that the liberal, despite his equalitarian dream, had never gotten rid of the notion that black was the color of evil, an accusation that could not be evaded by good works. Baldwin had made the liberal feel guilty whenever he paid the maid her wages. Without denying the progress of one hundred years, Baldwin pointed out that the condition of the Negro hadn't really changed much; but it seemed to him that it would now have to change.

The urgency of Baldwin's message was a true reflection of the mood of the black community. For five successive summers, violence, burning, and looting flared in the ghettoes of the North. For a time, his apocalyptic tone seemed justified. The enigmatic prophecy of the fire suggested the image of destructiveness and evil, which, in the national psyche, the Negro symbolized. But, as in the more famous biblical prophecy, there was also the suggestion that the fire of this second baptism would be a righteous one.]

Dear James:

I have begun this letter five times and torn it up five times. I keep seeing your face, which is also the face of your father and my brother. Like him, you are tough, dark, vulnerable, moody—with a very definite tendency to sound truculent because you want no one to think you are soft. You may be like your grandfather in this, I don't know, but certainly both you and your father resemble him very much physically. Well, he is dead, he never saw you, and he had a terrible life; he was defeated long before he died because, at the bottom of his heart, he really believed what white people said about him. This is one of the reasons that he became so holy. I am sure that your father has told you something about all that. Neither you nor your father exhibit any tendency towards holiness: you really *are* of another era, part of what happened when the Negro left the land and came into what the late E. Franklin Frazier called "the cities of destruction." You can only be destroyed by believing that you really are what the white world calls a *nigger*. I tell you this because I love you, and please don't you ever forget it.

I have known both of you all your lives, have carried your Daddy in my arms and on my shoulders, kissed and spanked him and watched him learn to walk. I don't know if you've known anybody from that far back; if you've loved anybody that long, first as an infant, then as a child, then as a man, you gain a strange perspective on time and human pain and effort. Other people cannot see what I see whenever I look into your father's face, for behind your father's face as it is today are all those other faces which were his. Let him laugh and I see a cellar your father does not remember and a house he does not remember and I hear in his present laughter his laughter as a child. Let him curse and I remember him falling down the cellar steps, and howling, and I remember, with pain, his tears, which my hand or your grandmother's so easily wiped away. But no one's hand can wipe away those tears he sheds invisibly today, which one hears in his laughter and in his speech and in his songs. I know what the world has done to my brother and how narrowly he has survived it. And I know, which is much worse, and this is the crime of which I accuse my country and my countrymen, and for which neither I nor time nor history will ever forgive them, that they have destroyed and are destroying hundreds of thousands of lives and do not know it and do not want to know it. One can be, indeed one must strive to become, tough and philosophical concerning destruction and death, for this is what most of mankind has been best at since we have heard of man. (But remember: *most* of mankind is not *all* of mankind.) But it is not permissible that the authors of devastation should also be innocent. It is the innocence which constitutes the crime.

Now, my dear namesake, these innocent and well-meaning people, your countrymen, have caused you to be born under conditions not very far removed from those described for us by Charles Dickens in the London of more than a hundred years ago. (I hear the chorus of the innocents screaming, "No! This is not true! How *bitter* you are!"—but I am writing this letter to *you*, to try to tell you something about how to handle *them*, for most of them do not yet really know that you exist. I *know* the conditions under which you were born, for I was there. Your countrymen were *not* there, and haven't made it yet. Your grandmother was also there, and no one has ever accused her of being bitter. I suggest that the innocents check with her. She isn't hard to find. Your countrymen don't know that *she* exists, either, though she has been working for them all their lives.)

Well, you were born, here you came, something like fourteen years ago; and though your father and mother and grandmother, looking about the streets through which they were carrying you, staring at the walls into which they brought you, had every reason to be heavyhearted, yet they were not. For here you were, Big James, named for me—you were a big baby, I was not—here you were: to be loved. To be loved, baby, hard, at once, and forever, to strengthen you against the loveless world. Remember that: I know how black it looks today, for you. It looked bad that day, too, yes, we were trembling. We have not stopped trembling yet, but if we had not loved each other none of us would have survived. And now you must survive because we love you, and for the sake of your children and your children's children.

This innocent country set you down in a ghetto in which, in fact, it intended that you should perish. Let me spell out precisely what I mean by that, for the heart of the matter is here, and the root of my dispute with my country. You were born where you were born and faced the future that you faced because you were black and *for no other reason*. The limits of your ambition were, thus, expected to be set forever. You were born into a society which spelled out with brutal clarity, and in as many ways as possible, that you were a worthless human being. You were not expected to aspire to excellence: you were expected to make peace with mediocrity. Wherever you have turned, James, in your short time on this earth, you have been told where you could go and what you could do (and *how* you could do it) and where you could live and whom you could marry. I know your countrymen do not agree with me about this, and I hear them saying, "You exaggerate." They do not know Harlem, and I do. So do you. Take no one's word for anything, including mine— but trust your experience. Know whence you came. If you know whence you came, there is really no limit to where you can go. The details and symbols of your life have been deliberately constructed to make you believe what white people say about you. Please try to remember that what they believe, as well as what they do and cause you to endure, does not testify to your inferiority but to their inhumanity and fear. Please try to be clear, dear James, through the storm which rages about your youthful head today, about the reality which lies behind the words *acceptance* and *integration*. There is no reason for you to try to become like white people and there is no basis whatever for their impertinent assumption that *they* must accept *you*. The really terrible thing, old buddy, is that *you* must accept *them*. And I mean that very seriously. You must accept them and accept them with love. For these innocent people have no other hope. They are, in effect, still trapped in a history which they do not understand; and until they understand it, they cannot be released from it. They have had to believe for many years, and for innumerable reasons, that black men are inferior to white men. Many of them, indeed, know better, but, as you will discover, people find it very difficult to act on what they know. To act is to be committed, and to be committed is to be in danger. In this case, the danger, in the minds of most white Americans, is the loss of their identity. Try to imagine how you would feel if you woke up one morning to find the sun shining and all the stars aflame. You would be frightened because it is out of the order of nature. Any upheaval in the universe is terrifying because it so profoundly attacks one's sense of one's own reality. Well, the black man has functioned in the white man's world as a fixed star, as an immovable pillar: and as he moves out of his place, heaven and earth are shaken to their foundations. You, don't be afraid. I said that it was intended that you should perish in the ghetto, perish by never being allowed to go behind the white man's definitions, by never being allowed to spell your proper name. You have, and many of us have, defeated this intention; and, by a terrible law, a terrible paradox, those innocents who believed that your imprisonment made them safe are losing their grasp of reality. But these men are your brothers—your lost, younger brothers. And if the word *integration* means anything, this is what it means: that we, with love, shall force our brothers to see themselves as they are, to cease fleeing from reality and begin to change it. For this is your home, my friend, do not be driven from it; great men have done great things here, and will again, and we can make America what America must become. It will be hard, James, but you come from sturdy, peasant stock, men who picked cotton and dammed rivers and built railroads, and, in the teeth of the most terrifying odds, achieved an unassailable and monumental dignity. You come from a long line of great poets, some of the greatest poets since Homer. One of them said, *The very time I thought I was lost, My dungeon shook and my chains fell off*.

You know, and I know, that the country is celebrating one hundred years of freedom one hundred years too soon. We cannot be free until they are free. God bless you, James, and Godspeed.

Your uncle,
JAMES

SPEECH AT THE HARVARD LAW SCHOOL FORUM OF DECEMBER 16, 1964

Malcolm X

["Throughout his-
tory," W. E. B. Du Bois wrote at the turn of the century, "the powers
of single black men flash like falling stars, and die sometimes before
the world has rightly gauged their brightness." It is a fair guess that these
words will apply to Malcolm X, whose career was cut short just before
his fortieth birthday.

Malcolm was born in Omaha, Nebraska, in 1925. He and his family
later moved to Lansing, Michigan. His father, Earl Little, who was killed
—Malcolm believed, by white racists—was a Baptist preacher and a
follower of Marcus Garvey. His mother, whose father was white and who
herself looked white, was born in the British West Indies. The family
did not survive the Depression intact. In 1937, Louise Little suffered a
breakdown and was assigned to the State Mental Hospital. Five of the
seven children, including Malcolm, were placed with foster parents.
Within a year, Malcolm was put in a reform school. He had completed the
eighth grade in public school, where he played basketball and, in the
seventh grade, had been elected class president. Malcolm, who had been
a good student, bitterly describes his ambition to become a lawyer. He
confided his hopes to his English teacher, a Mr. Ostrowski, who advised
him that it was an unrealistic goal for a "nigger." The rebuke, which
he reported to his autobiographer, Alex Haley, many years later, made
a lasting impression.

Upon completing the eighth grade in Michigan, Malcolm went to live with a half sister, Ella, in Roxbury, Massachusetts. He soon gravitated to the hustler society of Lower Roxbury and, after the war started, to New York's Harlem. Now known as "Detroit Red," his life revolved around several hustles, including narcotics, prostitution, and armed robbery. After four years of living by his wits and exploiting all available prey, Malcolm was forced to leave New York by the notorious West Indian Archie, the man who had initiated the green Malcolm into the hustler society and, in 1945, in characteristic hustler fashion, bullied him into a duel. Malcolm reports the affair as something of a standoff, with himself having a slight edge, but he nevertheless left for Boston, where he formed his own robbery gang. In 1946, he was convicted on several counts of robbery and sent to prison for seven years. It was in prison that he became a follower of Elijah Muhammad and, with the zeal characteristic of religious conversion, adopted the ascetic teachings of the Black Muslims. It was in prison, too, that he taught himself to read and got his first opportunity at public speaking.

Upon his release from prison in 1952, Malcolm returned to Detroit, abandoned his slave-name, Little, and, as a young Muslim minister, began preaching the separatist doctrine of Muhammad. Malcolm X's efforts at recruiting in the next decade coincided with a phenomenal rise in the Muslim membership, and his appointment as the sect's first "national minister," in 1963, gave him a prominence which rivaled that of the leader of the movement.

The Muslim insistence on black separatism and avoidance of active participation in the civil rights struggle gradually alienated Malcolm, and a growing tension between him and Muhammad led to his being suspended from his ministry and ordered to remain silent for ninety days late in 1963. (The ostensible reason for his being silenced by Elijah Muhammad was for a remark made after the assassination of President Kennedy and repeated, in the speech below, about "chickens coming home to roost.") Malcolm, who was now a public figure, broke publicly with Elijah Muhammad in March, 1964, and formed the Muslim Mosque, Incorporated. A month later, he journeyed to Mecca and Africa (a second African trip lasted from July to the end of November), and, in June, he launched still another group, the Organization of Afro-American Unity. Malcolm was psychologically unprepared for the split with Muhammad. For twelve years, he had given his unquestioning support to the man who had pulled him out of the gutter and made him a national figure. Muhammad's teachings had become so much his own that he likened the shock of separation to a cosmic upheaval. "I felt as though something in *nature* had failed, like the sun, or the stars. It was that incredible a phenomenon to me—something too stupendous to conceive."

But a sense of his own mission kept him going. El-Majj Malik El-Shabazz, formerly Malcolm X, formerly "Detroit Red," formerly Malcolm Little, was a man with a dark past who had developed a vision of his people delivered from bondage, and, like John Woolman 200 years earlier (but now with the aid of the mass media), he actively entered the struggle to lead them on this pilgrimage. He repudiated the doctrine of nonviolent resistance to American racism. With electrifying rhetoric, he urged an identification of the race struggle in the United States with the struggle for independence in Africa, and he began formulating plans to force the cause of American blacks before the international forum of the United Nations, a technique tried shortly after World War II by the NAACP. All of these themes are taken up in the speech, given after his second trip to Africa and a trip to England, which is reprinted here.

Malcolm was eulogized as a "black shining prince" after his death. He had captured the devotion of millions of black people and, in a curious way, gained the quiet approval of many whites. In retrospect, it is the white following that elicits some surprise. Most white liberals, despite a commitment to integration, still felt that the Negroes were a debased and inferior minority. Malcolm, because of what he was rather than what he said, absolved them of the necessity of feeling that. It was, of course, for much the same reason that he became a hero for blacks.

The white praise became manifest only after Malcolm's death. Speculation about how his ideas might have developed became rampant. It was claimed that his thought was still growing, that he was retreating (or advancing) from racism, and, some suggested, that he would eventually have worked out a *rapprochement* with Martin Luther King. All of these speculations were in the way of eulogies from various quarters. There were a few dissenters. It was suggested that, after his break with the Black Muslims and, alone for the first time in his public career, Malcolm was unable to formulate any consistent outlook or plan of his own and that his posture became more and more that of a boy chasing flies in an attempt to rid the jungle of beasts.

Malcolm was murdered in February, 1965, while delivering a speech to his followers at the Audubon Ballroom in Harlem. His death, along with the assassination of Martin Luther King, Jr., three years later, was generally conceded to mark the end of an era.]

I first want to thank the Harvard Law School Forum for the invitation to speak here this evening, more especially to speak on a very timely topic—*The African Revolution and Its Impact on the American Negro.* I probably won't use the word "American Negro," but substitute "Afro-American." And when I say Afro-American, I mean it in the same context in which you usually use the word Negro. Our people today are increasingly shying away from use of that word. They find that when you're identified as Negro, it tends to make you "catch a whole lot of hell" that people who don't use it don't catch.

In the present debate over the Congo, you are probably aware that a new tone and a new tempo, almost a new temper, are being reflected among African statesmen toward the United States. And I think we should be interested in and concerned with what impact this will have upon Afro-Americans and how it will affect America's international race relations. We know that it will have an effect at the international level.

It's already having such an effect. But I am primarily concerned with what effect it will have on the internal race relations of this country—that is to say, between the Afro-American and the white American.

When you let yourself be influenced by images created by others, you'll find that oftentimes the one who creates those images can use them to mislead you and misuse you. A good example: A couple of weeks ago I was on a plane with a couple of Americans, a male and a female sitting to my right. We were in the same row and had a nice conversation for amout thirty-five to forty minutes. Finally the lady looked at my briefcase and said, "I would like to ask you a personal question," and I knew what was coming. She said, "What kind of last name could you have that begins with X?" I said, "Malcolm." Ten minutes went by, and she turned to me and said, "You're not Malcolm X?" You see, we had a nice conversation going, just three human beings, but she was soon looking at the image created by the press. She said so: "I just wouldn't believe that you were that man," she said.

I had a similar experience last week at Oxford. The Oxford Union had arranged a debate. Before the debate I had dinner with four students. A girl student looked kind of cross-eyed, goggle-eyed and otherwise, and finally just told me she wanted to ask me a question. (I found out she was a conservative, by the way, whatever that is.) She said, "I just can't get over your not being as I had expected." I told her it was a case of the press carefully creating images.

Again I had a similar experience last night. At the United Nations a friend from Africa came in with a white woman who is involved with a philanthropic foundation over there. He and I were engaged in conversation for several minutes, and she was in and out of the conversation. Finally I heard her whisper to someone off to the side. She didn't think I was listening. She said—she actually said this—"He doesn't look so wild, you know." Now this is a full-grown, so-called "mature" woman. It shows the extent to which the press can create images. People looking for one thing actually miss the boat because they're looking for the wrong thing. They are looking for someone with horns, someone who is a rabble-rouser, an irrational, antisocial extremist. They expect to hear me say [that Negroes] should kill all the white people—as if you could kill all the white people! In fact, if I had believed what they said about the people in Britain, I never would have gone to Oxford. I would have let it slide. When I got there I didn't go by what I had read about them. I found out they were quite human and likable. Some weren't what I had expected.

Now I have taken time to discuss images because one of the sciences used and misused today is this science of [image making]. The power structure uses it at the local level, at the national level, at the international level. And oftentimes when you and I feel we've come to a conclusion on our own, the conclusion is something that someone has invented for us through the images he has created.

I'm a Muslim. Now if something is wrong with being Muslim, we can argue, we can "get with it." I'm a Muslim, which means that I believe in the religion of Islam. I believe in Allah, the same God that many of you would probably believe in if you knew more about Him. I believe in all of the prophets: Abraham, Moses, Jesus, Muhammad. Most of you are Jewish, and you believe in Moses; you might not pick Jesus. If you're Christians, you believe in Moses and Jesus. Well, I'm Muslim, and I believe in Moses, Jesus, and Muhammad. I believe in all of them. So I think I'm "way up on you."

In Islam we practice prayer, charity, fasting. These should be practiced in all religions. The Muslim religion also requires one to make the pilgrimage to the Holy City of Mecca. I was fortunate enough to make it in April, and I went back again in September. Insofar as being a Muslim is concerned, I have done what one is supposed to do to be a Muslim.

Despite being a Muslim, I can't overlook the fact that I'm an Afro-American in a country which practices racism against black people. There is no religion under the sun that would make me forget the suffering that Negro people have undergone in this country. Negroes have suffered for no reason other than that their skins happen to be black. So whether I'm Muslim, Christian, Buddhist, Hindu, atheist or agnostic, I would still be in the front lines with Negro people fighting against the racism, segregation, and discrimination practiced in this country at all levels in the North, South, East, and West.

I believe in the brotherhood of all men, but I don't believe in wasting brotherhood on anyone who doesn't want to practice it with me. Brotherhood is a two-way street. I don't think brotherhood should be practiced with a man just because his skin is white. Brotherhood should hinge upon the deeds and attitudes of a man. I couldn't practice brotherhood, for example, with some of those Eastlands or crackers in the South who are responsible for the condition of our people.

I don't think anyone would deny either that if you send chickens out of your barnyard in the morning, at nightfall those chickens will come home to roost in *your* barnyard. Chickens that you send out always come back home. It is a law of nature. I was an old farm boy myself, and I got in trouble saying this once [about President Kennedy's assassination], but it didn't stop me from being a farm boy. Other people's chickens don't come to roost in your doorstep, and yours don't go to roost on theirs. The chickens that this country is responsible for sending out, whether the country likes it or not (and if you're mature, you look at it "like it is"), someday, and someday soon, have got to come back home to roost.

Victims of racism are created in the image of racists. When the victims struggle vigorously to protect themselves from violence of others, they are made to appear in the image of criminals; as the criminal image is projected onto the victim. The recent situation in the Congo is one of the best examples of this. The headlines were used to mislead the public, [to create] wrong images. In the Congo, planes were bombing Congolese villages, yet Americans read that (How do they say it?) American-trained anti-Castro Cuban pilots were bombing rebel strongholds. These pilots were actually dropping bombs on villages with women and children. But because the "American-trained" and "anti-Castro Cubans" were applied, the bombing was legal. Anyone against

Castro is all right. The press gave them a "holier than thou" image. And you let them get away with it because of the labels. The victim is made the criminal. It is really mass murder—murder of women, children, and babies. And mass murder is disguised as a humanitarian project. They fool nobody but the people of America. They don't fool the people of the world, who see beyond the images.

Their man in the Congo is Tshombe, the murderer of the rightful Prime Minister of the Congo. No matter what kind of language you use, he's purely and simply a murderer. The real Prime Minister of the Congo was Patrice Lumumba. The American government—your and my government—took this murderer and hired him to run the Congo. He became their hired killer. And to show what a hired killer he is, his first act was to go to South Africa and to hire more killers, paying them with American dollars. But he is glorified because he is given the image of the only one who could bring stability to the Congo. Whether he can bring stability or not, he's still a murderer. The headlines spoke of white hostages, not simply hostages, but white hostages, and of white nuns and priests, not simply nuns and priests, but white nuns and priests. Why? To gain the sympathy of the white public of America. The press had to shake up your mind in order to get your sympathy and support for criminal actions. They tricked you. Americans consider forty white lives more valuable than four thousand black lives. Thousands of Congolese were losing their lives. Mercenaries were paid with American dollars. The American press made the murderers look like saints and the victims like criminals. They made criminals look like victims and indeed the devil look like an angel and angels like the devil.

A friend of mine from Africa, who is in a good position to know, said he believed the United States government is being advised by her worst enemy in the Congo, because an American citizen could not suggest such insane action—especially identifying with Tshombe, who is the worst African on earth. You cannot find an African on earth who is more hated than Tshombe. It's a justifiable hatred they have toward him. He has won no victory himself. His Congolese troops have never won a victory for him. Every victory has been won by white mercenaries, who are hired to kill for him. The African soldiers in the Congo are fighting for the Stanleyville government. Here Tshombe is a curse. He's an insult to anyone who means to do right, black or white. When Tshombe visited Cairo, he caused trouble. When he visited Rome last week, he caused trouble, and the same happened in Germany. Wherever Tshombe goes, trouble erupts. And if Tshombe comes to America, you'll see the worst rioting, bloodshed, and violence this country has ever seen. Nobody wants this kind of man in his country.

What effect does all this have on Afro-Americans? What effect will it have on race relations in this country? In the U.N. at this moment, Africans are using more uncompromising language and are heaping hot fire upon America as the racist and neo-colonial power par excellence. African statesmen have never used this language before. These statesmen are beginning to connect the criminal, racist acts practiced in the Congo with similar acts in Mississippi and Alabama. The Africans are pointing

out that the white American government—not all white people—has
shown just as much disregard for lives wrapped in black skin in the
Congo as it shows for lives wrapped in black skin in Mississippi and in
Alabama. When Africans, therefore, as well as we begin to think of Negro
problems as interrelated, what will be the effect of such thinking on
programs for improved race relations in this country? Many people will
tell you that the black man in this country doesn't identify with Africa.
Before 1959, many Negroes didn't. But before 1959, the image of Africa
was created by an enemy of Africa, because Africans weren't in a position to create and project their own images. The image was created by
the imperial powers of Europe.

Europeans created and popularized the image of Africa as a jungle, a
wild place where people were cannibals, naked and savage in a countryside overrun with dangerous animals. Such an image of the Africans was
so hateful to Afro-Americans that they refused to identify with Africa.
We did not realize that in hating Africa and the Africans we were hating ourselves. You cannot hate the roots of a tree and not hate the tree
itself. Negroes certainly cannot at the same time hate Africa and love
themselves. We Negroes hated the African features: the African nose,
the shape of our lips, the color of our skin, the texture of our hair. We
could only end up hating ourselves. Our skin became a trap, a prison;
we felt inferior, inadequate, helpless. It was not an image created by
Africans or by Afro-Americans, but by an enemy.

Since 1959 the image has changed. The African states have emerged
and achieved independence. Black people in this country are crying out
for their independence and show a desire to make a fighting stand for it.
The attitude of the Afro-American cannot be disconnected from the attitude of the African. The pulse beat, the voice, the very life-drive that is
reflected in the African is reflected today here among the Afro-Americans. The only way you can really understand the black man in America and the changes in his heart and mind is to fully understand the
heart and mind of the black man on the African continent; because it is
the same heart and the same mind, although separated by four hundred
years and by the Atlantic Ocean. There are those who wouldn't like us
to have the same heart and the same mind for fear that that heart and
mind might get together. Because when our people in this country received a new image of Africa, they automatically united through the new
image of themselves. Fear left them completely. There was fear, however, among the racist elements and the State Department. Their fear
was of our sympathy for Africa and for its hopes and aspirations and of
this sympathy developing into a form of alliance. It is only natural to
expect us today to turn and look in the direction of our homeland and
of our motherland and to wonder whether we can make any contact
with her.

I grew up in Lansing, Michigan, a typical American city. In those days,
a black man could have a job shining shoes or waiting tables. The best
job was waiting tables at the country club, as is still the case in most
cities. In those days, if a fellow worked at the State House shining shoes,
he was considered a big shot in the town. Only when Hitler went on the

rampage in 1939, and this country suffered a manpower shortage, did the black man get a shot at better jobs. He was permitted a step forward only when Uncle Sam had his back to the wall and needed him. In 1939, '40, and '41, a black man couldn't even join the Army or Navy, and when they began drafting, they weren't drafting black soldiers but only white. I think it was well agreed upon and understood: If you let the black man get in the Army, get hold of a gun, and learn to shoot it, you wouldn't have to tell him what the target was. It was not until the Negro leaders (and in this sense I use the word Negro purposely) began to cry out and complain—"If white boys are gonna die on the battle-fields, our black boys must die on the battlefields too!"—that they started drafting us. If it hadn't been for that type of leadership, we never would have been drafted. The Negro leaders just wanted to show that we were good enough to die too, although we hadn't been good enough to join the Army or Navy prior to that time.

During the time that Hitler and Tojo were on the rampage, the black man was needed in the plants, and for the first time in the history of America, we were given an opportunity on a large scale to get skills in areas that were closed previously to us. When we got these skills, we were put in a position to get more money. We made more money. We moved to a better neighborhood. When we moved to a better neighbor-hood, we were able to go to a better school and to get a better education, and this put us into a position to know what we hadn't been receiving up to that time. Then we began to cry a little louder than we had ever cried before. But this advancement never was out of Uncle Sam's good-will. We never made one step forward until world pressure put Uncle Sam on the spot. And it was when he was on the spot that he allowed us to take a couple of steps forward. It has never been out of any internal sense of morality or legality or humanism that we were allowed to ad-vance. *You have been as cold as an icicle whenever it came to the rights of the black man in this country.* (Excuse me for raising my voice, but I think it's time. As long as my voice is the only thing I raise, I don't think you should become upset!)

Because we began to cry a little louder, a new strategy was used to handle us. The strategy evolved with the Supreme Court desegregation de-cision, which was written in such tricky language that every crook in the country could sidestep it. The Supreme Court desegregation decision was handed down over ten years ago. It has been implemented less than ten percent in those ten years. It was a token advancement, even as we've been the recipients of "tokenism" in education, housing, employ-ment, everything. But nowhere in the country during the past ten years has the black man been treated as a human being in the same context as other human beings. He's always being patronized in a very paternalistic way, but never has he been given an opportunity to function as a human being. Actually, in one sense, it's our own fault, but I'll get to that later on. We have never gotten the real thing. (Heck, I'll get to it right now.) The reason we never received the real thing is that we have not displayed any tendency to do the same for ourselves which other human beings do: to protect our humanity and project our humanity.

I'll clarify what I mean. Not a single white person in America would sit idly by and let someone do to him what we black men have been letting others do to us. The white person would not remain passive, peaceful, and nonviolent. The day the black man in this country shows others that we are just as human as they in reaction to injustice, that we are willing to die just as quickly to protect our lives and property as whites have shown, only then will our people be recognized as human beings. It is inhuman, absolutely subhuman, for a man to let a dog bite him and not fight back. Let someone club him and let him not fight back, or let someone put water hoses on his women, his mother and daughter and babies and let him not fight back . . . then he's subhuman. The day he becomes a human being he will react as other human beings have reacted, and nobody [in humanity] will hold it against him.

In 1959, we saw the emergence of the Negro revolt and the collapse of European colonialism on the African continent. Our struggle, our initiative, and our militancy were in tune with the struggle and initiative and militancy of our brothers in Africa. When the colonial powers saw they couldn't remain in Africa, they behaved as somebody playing basketball. He gets the basketball and must pass it to a teammate in the clear. The colonial powers were boxed in on the African continent. They didn't intend to give up the ball. They just passed it to the one that was in the clear, and the one that was in the clear was the United States. The ball was passed to her, and she picked it up and has been running like mad ever since. Her presence on the African continent has replaced the imperialism and the colonialism of Europeans. But it's still imperialism and colonialism. Americans fooled many of the Africans into thinking that they weren't an imperialist power or colonial power until their intentions were revealed, until they hired Tshombe and put him back to kill in the Congo. Nothing America could have done would have ever awakened the Africans to her true intentions as did her dealings with this murderer named Tshombe.

America knew that Africa was waking in '59. Africa was developing a higher degree of intelligence than she reflected in the past. America, for her part, knew she had to use a more intelligent approach. She used the friendly approach: the Peace Corps, Crossroads. Such philanthropic acts disguised American imperialism and colonialism with dollar-ism. America was not honest with what she was doing. I don't mean that those in the Peace Corps weren't honest. But the Corps was being used more for political purposes than for moral purposes. I met many white Peace Corps workers while on the African continent. Many of them were properly motivated and were making a great contribution. But the Peace Corps will never work over there until the idea has been applied over here.

Of course the Civil Rights Bill was designed supposedly to solve our problem. As soon as it was passed, however, three civil rights workers were murdered. Nothing has been done about it, and I think nothing will be done about it until the people themselves do something about it. I, for one, think the best way to stop the Ku Klux Klan is to talk to the Ku Klux Klan in the only language it understands, for you can't talk

French to someone who speaks German and communicate. Find out what language a person speaks, speak their language, and you'll get your point across. Racists know only one language, and it is doing the black man in this country an injustice to expect him to talk the language of peace to people who don't know peaceful language. In order to get any kind of point across our people must speak whatever language the racist speaks. The government can't protect us. The government has not protected us. It is time for us to do whatever is necessary by any means necessary to protect ourselves. If the government doesn't want us running around here wild like that, then I say let the government get up off its . . . whatever it's on, and take care of it itself. After the passage of the Civil Rights Bill, they killed the Negro educator Pitt in Georgia. The killers were brought to court and then set free. This is the pattern in this country, and I think that white people (I use the word white people because it's cut short; it gets right to the point) are doing us an injustice. If you expect us to be nonviolent, you yourselves aren't. If someone came knocking on your door with a rifle, you'd walk out of the door with your rifle. Now the black man in this country is getting ready to do the same thing.

I say in conclusion that the Negro problem has ceased to be a Negro problem. It has ceased to be an American problem and has now become a world problem, a problem for all humanity. Negroes waste their time confining their struggle to civil rights. In that context the problem remains only within the jurisdiction of the United States. No allies can help Negroes without violating United States protocol. But today the black man in America has seen his mistake and is correcting it by lifting his struggle from the level of civil rights to the level of human rights. No longer does the United States government sit in an ivory tower where it can point at South Africa, point at the Portuguese, British, French, and other European colonial powers. No longer can the United States hold twenty million black people in second-class citizenship and think that the world will keep a silent mouth. No matter what the independent African states are doing in the United Nations, it is only a flicker, a glimpse, a ripple of what this country is in for in the future, unless a halt is brought to the illegal injustices which our people continue to suffer every day.

The Organization of Afro-American Unity (to which I belong) is a peaceful organization based on brotherhood. Oh yes, it is peaceful. But I believe you can't have peace until you're ready to protect it. As you will die protecting yours, I will die protecting mine. The OAAU is trying to get our problem before the United Nations. This is one of its immediate projects on the domestic front. We will work with all existing civil rights organizations. Since there has been talk of minimizing demonstrations and of becoming involved in political action, we want to see if civil rights organizations mean it. The OAAU will become involved in every move to secure maximum opportunity for black people to register peacefully as voters. We believe that along with voter registration, Afro-Americans need voter education. Our people should receive education in the science of politics so that the crooked politician cannot exploit us. We must put ourselves in a position to become active politically. We believe that the OAAU should provide defense units in every area of this country where workers are registering or are seeking voting rights, in every area where young students go out on the battlefront (which it actually is). Such self-defense units should have brothers who will not go out and initiate aggression, but brothers who are qualified, equipped to retaliate when anyone imposes brutally on us, whether it be in Mississippi, Massachusetts, California, or New York City. The OAAU doesn't believe it should permit civil rights workers to be murdered. When a government can't protect civil rights workers, we believe we should do it. Even in the Christian Bible it says that he who kills with the sword shall be killed by the sword, and I'm not against it. I'm for peace, yet I believe that any man facing death should be able to go to any length to assure that whoever is trying to kill him doesn't have a chance. The OAAU supports the plan of every civil rights group for political action, as long as it doesn't involve compromise. We don't believe Afro-Americans should be victims any longer. We believe we should let the world know, the Ku Klux Klan know, that bloodshed is a two-way street, that dying is a two-way street, that killing is a two-way street. Now I say all this in as peaceful a language as I know.

There was another man back in history whom I read about once, an old friend of mine whose name was Hamlet, who confronted, in a sense, the same thing our people are confronting here in America. Hamlet was debating whether "To be or not to be"—that was the question. He was trying to decide whether it was "nobler in the mind to suffer (peacefully) the slings and arrows of outrageous fortune," or whether it was nobler "to take up arms" and oppose them. I think his little soliloquy answers itself. As long as you sit around suffering the slings and arrows and are afraid to use some slings and arrows yourself, you'll continue to suffer. The OAAU has come to the conclusion that it is time to take up whatever means necessary to bring these sufferings to a halt.

THE LEGACY OF MALCOLM X, AND THE COMING OF AGE OF THE BLACK NATION

LeRoi Jones

[Black nationalism is usually identified with the radical Negro cause. The desire to form a separate state, which can be called nationalism in its extreme form, is born of a loss of hope among Negroes of ever achieving full participation in American democracy. It is not surprising that this sentiment has been most apparent whenever the burden of systematic exclusion from the benefits provided by an open community has seemed most unbearable.

The prophets of nationalism, notably, Martin Delany in the nineteenth century and Marcus Garvey and Malcolm X in the twentieth, have relied on what is by now a familiar rhetoric. Focusing on the common oppression of all "men of color," they have celebrated the African past and the achievement of blacks in an attempt to reinforce the Negro spirit. They have prophesied a new age of independence and, sometimes, even the evolution of a superior race. All of these men have pondered deeply the predicament of black men in their native land. "We love our country, dearly love her," Delany lamented in 1852, "but she does not love us—she despises us." If you are forever assigned to servant status in a country where everyone else can aspire to be something more, and if the combined weight of numbers and emotion is against you, it makes little sense even to acquire the franchise. You can, in the end, only vote for people who pass laws against you. From this point of view, the desire for a separate state is only a natural conclusion from the realization that some kind of state is necessary for the good life.

Territorial Black Nationalism, which seeks a separate state either in Africa or elsewhere, is not to be confused with nationalism in a broader sense. This broader cultural nationalism, at least among the masses of black people, is a twentieth-century phenomenon. It espouses many of the same doctrines as before; but it does not insist on a separate black state. Because of this similarity, the transition from one to the other is relatively easy. The career of Malcolm X, for example, embraced both forms of nationalism.

Nationalism in either form has always been accompanied by a heightened race awareness and a delicate sensitivity to the oppression, affronts, and disparagement that are the almost daily emotional fare of the masses of Negroes. Nationalist movements have been criticized by black and white for preaching a doctrine of hate, a kind of racism in reverse that emphasizes the potential hostility of the common enemy—the white man—in order to promote the unity of blacks. The hope of future triumphs, the critics argue, is only artificially stimulated by the memories of past suffering. Slavery is no longer a reality, they insist, and a doctrine of hate can only consume those who promote it. The nationalist has replied that the threat of violence is, indeed, real and that its source has always been in the white community. The question, he argues, has never been whether blacks will resort to violence, but, rather, what form the white man's violence will take next. Given the depth of the oppression that has been perpetrated by whites, most black Americans have had only one choice: between hating whites and hating themselves. This conclusion points to another enemy: the self-hatred of the black man (the monomaniacal whiteness within), which is also reinforced by white social practice. And the nationalist has known that this, too, is a source of unity: thus, the affirmation of black values *over* white. When the white culture is repudiated, then the slave becomes free and feels *national* soil underfoot for the first time. "We must act now," LeRoi Jones wrote in 1962, "in what I see as an extreme 'nationalism,' *i.e.,* in the best interests of our country, the name of which the rest of America has pounded into our heads for four hundred years, *Black.*"

Black nationalism, with its shift of emphasis from equality to sovereignty, has always foundered on the problem of its Zion. The land question is transformed, in Jones's thinking to one of culture. The national soil is here in America, for this is the true homeland of *Black.* Black is itself a country—where the last, Jones seems to be saying, shall be first.

Jones's writings are the best example of the cultural nationalism that has flourished among many younger writers and political activists of the 1960's. The essay reprinted here was dated 1965 and was one of the twenty-five that comprise *Home* (1966). In the introduction, Jones said that he thought the essays, which were arranged chronologically, revealed a movement toward his natural gift—his blackness. "By the time this book appears," he predicted, "I will be even blacker."]

1

The reason Malik was killed (the reasons) is because he was thought dangerous by enough people to allow and sanction it. Black People and white people.

Malcolm X was killed because he was dangerous to America. He had made too great a leap, in his sudden awareness of *direction* and the possibilities he had for influencing people, anywhere.

Malcolm was killed because he wanted to become official, as, say, a statesman. Malcolm wanted an effective form in which to enrage the white man, a practical form. And he had begun to find it.

For one thing, he'd learned that Black Conquest will be a *deal*. That is, it will be achieved through deals as well as violence. (He was beginning through his African statesmanship to make deals with other nations, as statesman from a *nation*. An oppressed Black Nation "laying" in the Western Hemisphere.)

This is one reason he could use the "universal" Islam—to be at peace with all dealers. The idea was to broaden, formalize, and elevate the will of the Black Nation so that it would be able to move a great many people and resources in a direction necessary to *spring* the Black Man.

"The Arabs must send us guns or we will accuse them of having sold us into slavery!" is international, and opens Black America's ports to all comers. When the ports are open, there is an instant *brotherhood of purpose* formed with most of the world.

Malcolm's legacy was his life. What he rose to be and through what channels, *e.g.*, Elijah Muhammad and the Nation of Islam, as separate experiences. Malcolm changed as a minister of Islam: under Elijah's tutelage, he was a different man—the difference being, between a man who is preaching Elijah Muhammad and a man who is preaching political engagement and, finally, national sovereignty. (Elijah Muhammad is now the second man, too.)

The point is that Malcolm had begun to call for Black National Consciousness. And moved this consciousness into the broadest possible arena, operating with it as of now. We do not want a Nation, we are a Nation. We must strengthen and formalize, and play the world's game with what we have, from where we are, as a *truly* separate people. America can give us nothing; all bargaining must be done by mutual agreement. But finally, terms must be given by Black Men *from their own shores*—which is where they live, where we all are, now. The land is literally ours. And we must begin to act like it.

The landscape should belong to the people who see it all the time.

We begin by being Nationalists. But a nation is land, and wars are fought over land. The sovereignty of nations, the sovereignty of culture, the sovereignty of race, the sovereignty of ideas and ways "into" the world.

The world in the twentieth century, and for some centuries before, is, literally, backward. The world can be understood through any idea. And the purely *social* condition of the world in this millennium, as, say, "compared" to other millennia, might show a far greater loss than gain, if this were not balanced by concepts and natural forces. That is, we think ourselves into the balance and ideas are necessarily "advanced" of what is simply here (*what's going on*, so to speak). And there are rockets and super cars. But, again, the loss? What might it have been if my people were turning the switches? I mean, these have been our White Ages, and all learning has suffered.

And so the Nationalist concept is the arrival of conceptual and environmental strength, or the realization of it in its totality by the Black Man in the West, *i.e.*, that he is not of the West, but even so, like the scattered Indians after movie cavalry attacks, must regroup, and return that force on a fat, ignorant, degenerate enemy.

We are a people. We are unconscious captives unless we realize this— that we have always been separate, except in our tranced desire to be the thing that oppressed us, after some generations of having been "programmed" (a word suggested to me by Jim Campbell and Norbert Wiener) into believing that our greatest destiny was to become white people!

2

Malcolm X's greatest contribution, other than to propose a path to internationalism and hence, the entrance of the American Black Man into a world-wide allegiance against the white man (in most recent times he proposed to do it using a certain kind of white liberal as a lever), was to preach Black Consciousness to the Black Man. As a minister for the Nation of Islam, Malcolm talked about a black consciousness that took its form from religion. In his last days he talked of another black consciousness that proposed politics as its moving energy.

But one very important aspect of Malcolm's earlier counsels was his explicit call for a National Consciousness among Black People. And this aspect of Malcolm's philosophy certainly did abide throughout his days. The feeling that somehow the Black Man was different, as being, as a being, and finally, in our own time, as judge. And Malcolm propounded these differences as life anecdote and religious (political) truth and made the consideration of Nationalist ideas significant and powerful in our day.

Another very important aspect of Malcolm's earlier (or the Honorable Elijah Muhammad's) philosophy was the whole concept of land and land-control as central to any talk of "freedom" or "independence." The Muslim tack of asking for land within the continental United States in which Black People could set up their own nation, was given a special appeal by Malcolm, even though the request was seen by most people outside the movement as "just talk" or the amusing howls of a gadfly.

But the whole importance of this insistence on land is just now beginning to be understood. Malcolm said many times that when you speak about revolution you're talking about land—changing the ownership or usership of some specific land which you think is yours. But any talk of Nationalism also must take this concept of land and its primary importance into consideration because, finally, any Nationalism which is not intent on restoring or securing autonomous space for a people, *i.e.*, a nation, is at the very least shortsighted.

Elijah Muhammad has said, "We want our people in America, whose parents or grandparents were descendants from slaves, to be allowed to establish a separate state or territory of their own—either on this continent or elsewhere. We believe that our former slavemasters are obligated to provide such land and that the area must be fertile and minerally rich." And the Black Muslims seem separate from most Black People because the Muslims have a national consciousness based on their aspirations for land. Most of the Nationalist movements in this country advocate that that land is in Africa, and Black People should return there, or they propose nothing about land at all. It is impossible to be a Nationalist without talking about land. Otherwise, your Nationalism is a misnamed kind of "difficult" opposition to what the white man has done, rather than the advocation of another people becoming the rulers of themselves, and sooner or later the rest of the world.

The Muslims moved from the Back-to-Africa concept of Marcus Garvey (the first large movement by Black People back to a National Consciousness, which was, finally, only viable when the Black Man focused on Africa as literally "back home") to the concept of a Black National Consciousness existing in this land the Black captives had begun to identify as home. (Even in Garvey's time, there was not a very large percentage of Black People who really wanted to leave. Certainly, the newly emerging Black bourgeoisie would have nothing to do with "returning" to Africa. They were already created in the image of white people, as they still are, and wanted nothing to do with Black.)

What the Muslims wanted was a profound change. The National Consciousness focused on actual (nonabstract) land, identifying a people, in a land where they lived. Garvey wanted to go back to Jordan. A real one. The Nation of Islam wanted Jordan closer. Before these two thrusts, the Black Man in America, as he was Christianized, believed Jordan was in the sky, like pie, and absolutely supernatural.

Malcolm, then, wanted to give the National Consciousness its political embodiment, and send it out to influence the newly forming third world, in which this consciousness was to be included. The concept of Blackness, the concept of the National Consciousness, the proposal of a political (and diplomatic) form for this aggregate of Black spirit, these are the things given to us by Garvey, through Elijah Muhammad and finally given motion into still another area of Black response by Malcolm X.

Malcolm's legacy to Black People is what he moved toward, as the accretion of his own spiritual learning and the movement of Black People in general, through the natural hope, a rise to social understanding within the new context of the white nation and its decline under hypocrisy and natural "oppositeness" which has pushed all of us toward "new" ideas. We are all the products of national spirit and worldview. We are drawn by the vibrations of the entire nation. If there were no bourgeois Negroes, none of us would be drawn to that image. They, bourgeois Negroes, were shaped through the purposive actions of a national attitude, and finally, by the demands of a particular culture.

At which point we must consider what cultural attitudes are, what culture is, and what National Consciousness has to do with these, *i.e.*, if we want to understand what Malcolm X was pointing toward, and why the Black Man now must move in that direction since the world will not let him move any other way. The Black Man is possessed by the energies of historic necessity and the bursting into flower of a National Black Cultural Consciousness, and with that, in a living future, the shouldering to power of Black culture and, finally, Black Men . . . and then, Black ideals, which are different descriptions of a God. A righteous sanctity, out of which worlds are built.

3

What the Black Man must do now is look down at the ground upon which he stands, and claim it as his own. It is not abstract. Look down! Pick up the earth, or jab your fingernails into the concrete. It is real and it is yours, if you want it.

But to want it, as our own, is the present direction. To want what we are and where we are, but rearranged by our own consciousness. That is why it was necessary first to recrystallize national aspirations behind a Garvey. The Africans who first came here were replaced by Americans, or people responding to Western stimuli and then Americans. In order for the Americans to find out that they had come from another place, were, hence, alien, the Garvey times had to come. Elijah said we must have a place, to be, ourselves. Malcolm made it contemporarily secular.

So that now we must find the flesh of our spiritual creation. We must be *conscious*. And to be conscious is to be *cultured*, processed in specific virtues and genius. We must respond to this National Consciousness with our souls, and use the correspondence to come into our own.

The Black Man will always be frustrated until he has land (A Land!) of his own. All the thought processes and emotional orientation of "national liberation movements"—from slave uprisings onward—have always given motion to a Black National (and Cultural) Consciousness. These movements proposed that judgments were being made by Black sensibility, and that these judgments were *necessarily* different from those of the white sensibility—different, and after all is said and done, inimical.

Men are what their culture predicts (enforces). Culture is, simply, the way men live. How they have come to live. What they are formed by. Their total experience, and its implications and theories. Its paths.

The Black Man's paths are alien to the white man. Black Culture is alien to the white man. Art and religion are the results and idealized supernumeraries of culture. Culture in this sense, as Sapir said, is "The National Genius," whether it be a way of fixing rice or killing a man.

I said in *Blues People*: "Culture is simply how one lives and is connected to history by habit." Here is a graphic structure of the relationships and total context of culture:

```
                          God
                           ↑
                  ↖  RELIGION  ↗
                      ↖  ↑  ↗
              ←————————  CULTURE  ————————→
                      ↙  ↓  ↘
                       ART
                  ↖  ↓  ↗
                 ↙ POLITICS ↘
                           ↑
                        NATION
                           ↓
                          Man
```

God is man idealized (humanist definition). Religion is the aspiration
of man toward an idealized existence. An existence in which the func-
tions of God and man are harmonious, even identical. Art is the movement forward, the understanding progress of man. It is feeling and
making. A nation (social order) is made the way people *feel* it should
be made. A face is too. Politics is man's aspiration toward an order.
Religion is too. Art is an ordering as well. And all these categories are
spiritual, but are also the result of the body, at one point, serving as
a container of feeling. The soul is no less sensitive.

Nations are races. (In America, white people have become a nation, an
identity, a race.) Political integration in America will not work because
the Black Man is played on by special forces. His life, from his organs,
i.e., the life of the body, what it needs, what it wants, to become, is
different—and for this reason racial is biological, finally. We are a different *species*. A species that is evolving to world power and philosophical
domination of the world. The world will move the way Black People
move!

If we take the teachings of Garvey, Elijah Muhammad and Malcolm X
(as well as Frazier, DuBois and Fanon), we know for certain that the
solution of the Black Man's problems will come only through Black
National Consciousness. We also know that the focus of change will be
racial. (If we *feel* differently, we have different *ideas*. Race is feeling.
Where the body, and the organs come in. Culture is the preservation of
these feelings in superrational to rational form. Art is one method of
expressing these feelings and identifying the form, as an emotional
phenomenon.) In order for the Black Man in the West to absolutely
know himself, it is necessary for him to see himself first as culturally
separate from the white man. That is, to be conscious of this separation
and use the strength it proposes.

Western Culture (the way white people live and think) is passing. If
the Black Man cannot identify himself as separate, and understand what
this means, he will perish along with Western Culture and the white man.

What a culture produces, is, and refers to, is an image—a picture of a process, since it is a form of a process: movement seen. The changing of images, of references, is the Black Man's way back to the racial integrity of the captured African, which is where we must take ourselves, in feeling, to be truly the warriors we propose to be. To form an absolutely rational attitude toward West man, and West thought. Which is what is needed. To see the white man as separate and as enemy. To make a fight according to the absolute realities of the world as it is.

Good–Bad, Beautiful–Ugly, are all formed as the result of image. The mores, customs, of a place are the result of experience, and a common reference for defining it—common images. The three white men in the film *Gunga Din* who kill off hundreds of Indians, Greek hero-style, are part of an image of white men. The various black porters, gigglers, ghostchumps and punkish Indians, etc., that inhabit the public image the white man has fashioned to characterize Black Men are references by Black Men to the identity of Black Men in the West, since that's what is run on them each day by white magic, *i.e.*, television, movies, radio, etc.—the Mass Media (the *Daily News* does it with flicks and adjectives).

The song title "A White Man's Heaven Is a Black Man's Hell" describes how complete an image reversal is necessary in the West. Because for many Black People, the white man has succeeded in making this hell seem like heaven. But Black youth are much better off in this regard than their parents. They are the ones who need the least image reversal.

The Black artist, in this context, is desperately needed to change the images his people identify with, by asserting Black feeling, Black mind, Black judgment. The Black intellectual, in this same context, is needed to change the interpretation of facts toward the Black Man's best interests, instead of merely tagging along reciting white judgments of the world.

Art, Religion, and Politics are impressive vectors of a culture. Art describes a culture. Black artists must have an image of what the Black sensibility is in this land. Religion elevates a culture. The Black Man must aspire to Blackness. God is man idealized. The Black Man must idealize himself as Black. And idealize and aspire to that. Politics gives a social order to the culture, *i.e.*, makes relationships within the culture definable for the functioning organism. The Black man must seek a Black politics, an ordering of the world that is beneficial to his culture, to his interiorization and judgment of the world. This is strength. And we are hordes.

4

Black People are a race, a culture, a Nation. The legacy of Malcolm X is that we know we can move from where we are. Our land is where we live. (Even the Muslims have made this statement about Harlem.) If we are a separate Nation, we must make that separateness where we are. There are Black cities all over this white nation. Nations within nations. In order for the Black Man to survive he must not only identify himself as a unique being, but take steps to insure that this being has, what the

Germans call *Lebensraum* ("living room") literally space in which to exist and develop.

The concepts of National Consciousness and the Black Nation, after the death of Malik, have moved to the point where now some Black People are demanding national sovereignty as well as National (and Cultural) Consciousness. In Harlem, for instance, as director of the Black Arts Repertory Theatre School, I have issued a call for a Black Nation. In Harlem, where 600,000 Black People reside.

The first act must be the nationalization of all properties and resources belonging to white people, within the boundaries of the Black Nation. (All the large concentrations of Black People in the West are already nations. All that is missing is the consciousness of this state of affairs. All that is missing is that the Black Man take control. As Margaret Walker said in her poem "For My People": *A race of men must rise, and take control.*)

Nationalization means that all properties and resources must be harnessed to the needs of the Nation. In the case of the coming Black Nation, all these materials must be harnessed to the needs of Black People. In Harlem, it is almost common knowledge that the Jews, etc., will go the next time there's a large "disturbance," like they say. But there must be machinery set up to transfer the power potential of these retail businesses, small industries, etc., so that they may benefit Black People.

Along with nationalization of foreign-owned businesses (which includes Italian underworld businesses, some of which, like the policy racket, can be transformed into a national lottery, with the monies staying with Black People, or as in the case of heroin-selling, completely abolished) must come the nationalization of all political voices setting up to function within the community/Nation.

No white politicians can be allowed to function within the Nation. Black politicians doing funny servant business for whites, must be eliminated. Black people must have absolute political and economic control. In other words they must have absolute control over their lives and destinies.

These moves are toward the working form of any autonomous nation. And it is this that the Black Man must have. An autonomous Nation. His own forms: treaties, agreements, laws.

These are moves that the conscious Black Man (artist, intellectual, Nationalist, religious thinker, dude with "common sense") must prepare the people for. And the people must be prepared for moves they themselves are already making. And moves they have already made must be explained and analyzed. They, the people, are the bodies. . . . Where are the heads?

And it is *the heads* that are needed for the next move Black People will make. The move to Nationhood. The exact method of transformation is simple logistics.

What we are speaking about again is sovereignty. Sovereignty and independence. And when we speak of these things, we can understand just how far Malik went. The point now is to take ourselves the rest of the way.

Only a united Black Consciousness can save Black People from annihilation at the white man's hands. And no other nation on earth is safe, unless the Black Man in America is safe. Not even the Chinese can be absolutely certain of their continued sovereignty as long as the white man is alive. And there is only one people on the planet who can slay the white man. The people who know him best. His ex-slaves.

SOURCES

BALDWIN, JAMES (1924–   ). "My Dungeon Shook: Letter to My Nephew on the One Hundredth Anniversary of the Emancipation," in *The Fire Next Time*. New York: Dell, 1964, pp. 13–22.

BANNEKER, BENJAMIN (1731–1806). *Copy of a Letter from Benjamin Banneker, to the Secretary of State, with his Answer*. Philadelphia, 1792. Reprinted from a copy in the New York Historical Society.

DELANY, MARTIN ROBINSON (1812–80?). *The Condition, Elevation, Emigration, And Destiny of the Colored People of the United States, Politically Considered*. Philadelphia, 1852, pp. 197–214. Reprinted in *American Negro: His History and Literature Series*. New York: Arno Press, 1968.

DOUGLASS, FREDERICK (1817–95). *Narrative of the Life of Frederick Douglass, an American Slave, Written by Himself*. Boston, 1845, chapters 1, 2, 6, and 7. Available in several modern editions.

DU BOIS, WILLIAM EDWARD BURGHARDT (1868–1963). "Of Mr. Booker T. Washington And Others," chapter 3 of *The Souls of Black Folk*. Chicago, 1903. 5th ed. Chicago, 1904, pp. 41–59. Available in several modern editions. "The Colored World Within," chapter 7 of *Dusk of Dawn: An Essay Toward the Autobiography of a Race Concept*. New York, 1940. New York: Schocken, 1968, pp. 173–220.

FORTEN, JAMES (1766–1842) [and RUSSELL PERROTT?]. "An Address to the Humane and Benevolent Inhabitants of the City and County of Philadelphia." *Minutes of the Proceedings of a Special Meeting of the Fifteenth American Convention . . .* , Vols. I–IV, pp. 69–72. Reprinted from Carter G. Woodson, *Negro Orators and Their Orations*. Washington, D.C., 1925, pp. 52–55.

FRAZIER, E. FRANKLIN (1894–1962). *Black Bourgeoisie*. New York: Collier, 1962, pp. 176–95.

GARVEY, MARCUS (1887–1940). *Philosophy and Opinions of Marcus Garvey*. Edited by Amy Jacques-Garvey. Vol. I of two volumes, separately published. New York, 1923, pp. 63–78. Reprinted in *American Negro: His History and Literature Series*. New York: Arno Press, 1968.

HUGHES, LANGSTON (1902–67). "The Negro Artist and the Racial Mountain." *Nation*, June 23, 1926, Vol. 122, No. 3181, pp. 692–94.

JEFFERSON, THOMAS (1743–1826). *Notes on the State of Virginia.* London, 1787. Reprinted from *The Writings of Thomas Jefferson: Being His Autobiography, Correspondence, Reports, Messages, Addresses and Other Writings, Official and Private.* Edited by H. A. Washington. In 9 volumes. Vol. VII, New York, 1861, pp. 379–87. See also Banneker.

JONES, LEROI (1934–   ). "The Legacy of Malcolm X, and the Coming of the Black Nation," in *Home: Social Essays.* New York: Morrow, 1966, pp. 238–50.

KING, MARTIN LUTHER, JR. (1929–68). "Letter from Birmingham Jail," in *Why We Can't Wait.* New York: Signet, 1964, pp. 76–95.

LOCKE, ALAIN LEROY (1886–1954). *The New Negro.* Edited by Alain Locke. New York, 1925. Atheneum, 1968, pp. 3–16.

"OTHELLO." "Essay on negro slavery." *American Museum,* November, 1788, pp. 414–17; December, 1788, pp. 509–12.

TURNER, NAT (1800–31). *The Confessions of Nat Turner, The Leader of the Late Insurrection in Southampton, Va., As fully and voluntarily made to Thomas R. Gray, In the prison where he was confined, and acknowledged by him to be such when read before the Court of Southampton; with the certificate, under seal of the Court, convened at Jerusalem, Nov. 5, 1831, for his trial. Also, An Authentic Account of the Whole Insurrection. With Lists Of The Whites Who Were Murdered. And Of The Negroes Brought Before The Court Of Southampton, And There Sentenced, etc.* Baltimore: Published by Thomas R. Gray, 1831. Reprinted from *Anglo-African Magazine,* December, 1859, pp. 386–96.

VASSA, GUSTAVUS (1745–1801?). *The Interesting Narrative of the Life of Olaudah Equiano, or Gustavus Vassa, The African.* London, 1789. Reprinted from *The Life of Olaudah Equiano or Gustavus Vassa, The African.* Boston, 1837, pp. 30–52.

WALKER, DAVID (1785–1830). *Appeal, in Four Articles, Together with a Preamble, to the Colored Citizens of the World, but in Particular, and very Expressly to Those of the United States of America.* 2d ed., Boston, 1830. Reprinted from *Walker's Appeal, With a Brief Sketch of His Life. . . .* Edited by Henry Highland Garnet. New York, 1848. Reprinted in *American Negro: His History and Literature Series.* New York: Arno Press, 1969.

WARREN, EARL (1891–   ). *Brown et al.* v. *Board of Education of Topeka et al.* 347 U.S. 483.

WASHINGTON, BOOKER TALIAFERRO (1856–1915). "Speech at the Atlanta Exposition," from *The Story of My Life and Work.* Rev. ed., Naperville, Ill., and Atlanta, Ga., 1900, pp. 165–71. / "What I Am Trying To Do." *World's Work,* November, 1913, pp. 101–7.

WOOLMAN, JOHN (1720–72). *Some Considerations on the Keeping of Negroes, Recommended to the Professors of Christianity of Every Denomination.* Philadelphia, 1754. Reprinted from *The Journal and Essays of John Woolman. . . .* Edited by Amelia Mott Gummere. New York, 1922, pp. 334–47.

WRIGHT, RICHARD (1908–60). "How 'Bigger' Was Born." (Pamphlet) New York: Harper, 1940. A shorter version of this lecture appeared in *Saturday Review,* June 1, 1940, pp. 17–20.

X, MALCOLM (1925–65). Speech at the Harvard Law School Forum of December 16, 1964. *The Speeches of Malcolm X at Harvard.* Edited by Archie Epps. New York: Apollo Editions, 1969, pp. 161–75.

INDEX